A HISTORY OF IRELAND

A
HISTORY
OF
IRELAND

Peter and Fiona Somerset Fry

BARNES
&NOBLE
BOOKS
NEW YORK

This edition published by Barnes & Noble, Inc.,
by arrangement with Routledge.

1993 Barnes & Noble Books

ISBN 1-56619-215-3

Printed and bound in the United States of America

M 9 8 7

CONTENTS

ILLUSTRATIONS

PREFACE

This is a short history of Ireland. It covers the story of Ireland from the arrival of the first prehistoric human beings – Middle Stone Age people – from mainland Britain some 8000 years ago, and it brings the story up to the 1970s. It follows our recent short *History of Scotland* (RKP, 1982), and it has much the same objective, that is, to summarize in one volume the history of a part of the British Isles, whose origins, development and aspirations have on the whole been different from those of the other parts. It aims, moreover, to help correct the imbalance in the availability and the spread of knowledge and understanding of Ireland among the populations of the mainland countries, especially England which for over seven centuries ruled Ireland, on the whole very badly.

Problems between Ireland and Britain are much in the forefront today but, as we hope to show in these pages, there have been difficulties ever since the Normans first went to Ireland in the 1160s–1170s to carve for themselves feudal domains and to impose an alien ruling class upon part of the indigenous population. The impact of the Normans, coupled with Tudor and Stuart plantations and the heavy imbalance of advantage with disadvantage obtained by the Irish as a result of the Act of Union of 1800, have left their mark upon Ireland, probably forever, and there may always be huge gaps in understanding how the Irish feel about British involvement in their country, even though the south obtained its independence over sixty-five years ago. We hope this book may be a small contribution towards enlarging that understanding.

We are very grateful to a number of institutions and individuals that have helped us during the research and writing of this book. Chief among these are Wolfson College, Cambridge, of which Peter Somerset Fry is a senior member, the University Library at Cambridge, and Mr Donal O Luanaigh and the staff of the National Library of Ireland. Special thanks are due to Dr Brian Walker, of Queen's University, Belfast, for many valuable comments on the later part of the text, to Dr Brendan Bradshaw, of Queen's College, Cambridge, who read the MS throughout and saved us from a number of errors, and to Dr Conor Gearty, of Emmanuel College, Cambridge, for some valuable help and comment. We are also very grateful to Mrs Eileen Griffiths, of Dublin, Dr Eilís Brady, of the Royal Irish Academy, and Mícheál Ó Cearúil, of Maynooth College, for their invaluable help with the Irish forms of names. Readers unfamiliar with the Irish forms will find the Anglicized forms in brackets in the Index.

In acknowledging our gratitude to those mentioned above, we wish to stress that none of them bears any responsibility whatsoever for anything that we have said or have not said. The opinions expressed are our own.

Fiona and Peter Somerset Fry

CHAPTER 1

MIGRATIONS
AND
MONUMENTS:

THE FIRST 6000 YEARS

Ireland was one country of Europe that had no Old Stone Age. The latest of the Palaeolithic people, known also as Advanced Hunting People, who flourished in parts of western Europe and created remarkable works of art like the animal portraiture at the Lascaux caves in France and the Altamira caves in Spain, moved across the seas into England and Wales, and also directly to Scotland, in search of game. They appear, however, to have baulked at crossing over to Ireland, then an uninhabited isle. Had they done so, among the game they would have been able to hunt in Ireland was the giant Irish deer, *megaceros*, whose antler span was about 10 feet across. They would also have found horses, ordinary-sized deer, some forms of cattle and pigs, and a variety of fish in the country's rivers and lakes. Still, they did not come, and when in the seventh or sixth millennium BC human beings did enter Ireland for the first time, they arrived in virgin countryside.

The first settlers were Mesolithic (Middle Stone Age) people, known also as Late Hunting People, and they have left numerous sites, particularly in the eastern coastal areas and in Ulster and Donegal. Some settlers came from southern Scotland and the Argyll islands into Antrim and from there into the rest of Ulster and elsewhere. Others may have come from more southerly parts of Britain, especially from Wales, and some more directly by sea from south-west Europe. Their history is shadowy and the details of their lives and their communities are sparse. But we know that they hunted and fished (particularly the latter, to judge from the contents of excavated rubbish mounds). And we have evidence of their domesticating animals like oxen, goats and sheep, and of making rough pottery. The period of these Mesolithic settlers lasted into the next period of intrusive settler migrations, the Neolithic (New Stone Age) era. These people first came to Ireland sometime in the fifth millennium BC and gradually, or maybe forcefully, absorbed some, if not all, of the Mesolithic communities with whom they collided.

The principal surviving monuments left by Neolithic people in Ireland over what is a very large time span (*c.* 4000–2000, BC) are their stone-built tombs. These vary considerably in size and shape, but they can be categorized. They were built for individual or communal burial. Roughly in order of time, the tombs are court tombs, gallery tombs, passage tombs, portal tombs and wedge tombs. In addition to these fully or partly exposed stone structures, there were a variety of earth-covered tombs (long barrows, round barrows), some containing stone cists, some having chambers of layered clay and stone pieces, some with wooden chambers (the wood has since disappeared but left traces). These earthen tombs are dealt with later. The earliest of the stone tombs so far found may possibly be of Mesolithic origin, particularly one or two of the early court tombs. But on the whole the several hundred stone tombs of Ireland are Neolithic. Some of them may have been raised very early in that period.

The Neolithic settlers in Ireland were the first people to till its soil. Some came from Britain, others made much longer sea journeys from Europe, as is suggested by the siting of many stone monuments on the coasts. They made a significant impact upon the Irish countryside, not only with their tombs and barrows, but also by their forest clearance, cereal growing, development of peat, house construction (Lough Gur, for example), their pottery craft and manufacture, and of course their making of stone tools and weaponry, especially their axe factories such as those in Co. Antrim which were sufficiently busy to export to mainland Britain. It is reasonable to assume that such people, well advanced upon their predecessors of the Mesolithic Age, must have used some form of language, structured or otherwise, had highly developed local societies, enjoyed dancing, flute playing, possibly even sang and told stories. Certainly, they produced some of the finest examples of megalithic art, among

2

which are the decorations at the passage tomb at Newgrange (see p. 341).

Up to the 1960s it was widely held that Neolithic communities in Europe and Britain derived their building technology – and many other techniques, too – from the earliest civilizations of the world in the Near East, like Sumer (Mesopotamia) and Egypt. This theory of diffusion of knowledge and skills from the Near East outwards into the Mediterranean, central and western Europe and the British Isles has recently come in for serious reappraisal, largely through the application of more modern techniques of dating to surviving monuments and artefacts. One pioneer, Professor Colin Renfrew, has gone as far to say that much of European prehistory needs to be rewritten, and that seems unchallengeable. The reappraisal has compelled specialists

1.   Passage grave at Newgrange, Co. Meath (*c.* 3200 BC)

to redate some of the more interesting and dramatic monuments in Spain, Brittany, Denmark, and the British Isles (especially Scotland and Ireland), and among the best known in the last named countries that have been confidently redated are the Maes Howe chambered tomb on Orkney mainland, now put at c. 3400 BC–3200 BC, and the passage grave at Newgrange, Co. Meath, now dated to c. 3200 BC, or perhaps earlier. Those familiar with the accredited dates of the earliest Egyptian pyramids of stone (for example, the Step Pyramid of Zozer, c. 2700 BC) will see that Newgrange now antedates the Pyramid Age by at least half a millennium. Clearly, Neolithic stone technologists working in Co. Meath in the fourth millennium were not receivers of instruction from Egypt – or from anywhere else in the Near East, for that matter.

That Newgrange, or any other contemporary monuments, were indigenous fourth millennium architecture – and architecture it most certainly is – establishes that the history of Ireland goes back further than many authorities used to allow. It gives us the chance to show a continuous story of more than 5000 years of an inhabited Ireland, beginning in the fourth millennium. The history of the country from the early fourth millennium down to the late third millennium when the Irish Bronze Age began to replace the Neolithic Age is not recountable in narrative form, but we can put down some markers along the time chart by looking briefly at a consecutive series of types of stone monument erected throughout the period. In doing so, we may remember that the human story in Ireland begins further back in the seventh millennium BC, getting on for 9000 years ago.

Court tombs may have been invented by Mesolithic builders in Ireland; they were certainly built in some quantity by early Neolithic settlers. A court tomb has an unroofed court surrounded by a wall of large standing stones (orthostats) or by dry-stone walling. The orthostats were in some cases set at intervals with stone wall infilling. The burial gallery opens into the court at one end, as at Creevykeel, Co. Sligo, or there are two galleries, one at each end as at Ballyglass, Co. Mayo and at Deerpark, Co. Sligo. The galleries in both types, and in several other types, are divided into chambers (or segments) by upright slabs. Some court tombs are arranged differently, the centre being an elongated gallery segmented inside – a gallery tomb – with an open-end horseshoe court at one end, like Browndod, Co. Antrim, or at each end, like Cohaw, Co. Cavan. Courts are circular or oval in plan. Most court tombs have a frontal façade of stone wall, which in some cases joins the walls of the court or courts to the outer tomb kerb. Flanking the entrance from the court into the gallery or galleries are a pair of jamb stones. Jamb stones are also used to form part of the separating walls between chambers, which means that you can step through from one chamber into another, but in other examples, the chambers are shut off from each other by larger slabs placed between jambs.

Court tombs were erected over a long period in Ireland, probably from the mid-fourth millennium to the end of the Neolithic Age, about 2000 BC, but they were not the only kind of burial structure of the period. Contemporary with them for many centuries were passage tombs or graves. The passage tomb may have been an innovation of Mesolithic communities in western Europe, a suggestion advanced in the light of recent dating of several passage tombs in Brittany to the fifth millennium BC. If it was, the Neolithic immigrants who moved into Mesolithic areas certainly adopted it as a burial structure, along with the court tomb and the gallery tomb, and probably some of the earthen barrow types as well. If this happened in Brittany, it could also have happened in Ireland.

The passage tomb consists of a central chamber of stone, sited in a round or oval tumulus. The tomb is approached through a narrow passage lined by stone slabs, in some cases a long one as at Newgrange where it is almost 21 yards (19m). The linings are huge upright slabs along each side, roofed by equally large lintels, occasionally domed by means of corbelling, rather than flat. Many passages have stone sills dividing them into segments. At the inner end of the passage is a central stone-lined chamber which rises taller than the passage, in some cases more than twice as high (Newgrange). Off the central chamber are two, or in some cases two pairs, or even three pairs, of smaller lower-ceilinged chambers where the burials took place. There is also a chamber at the rear. Some passage tomb plans are akin to a Latin Cross, which is of course coincidence. The central chamber, which may be round, rectangular, trapezoid or polygonal, is sometimes vaulted using a dry-stone technique of laying large stones flat and sloping slightly upwards and inwards, each over-

5

hanging the one underneath, until the space at the top can be covered completely and centrally by a single horizontal capstone. The proportion of the stone tomb to the size of the earth mound covering it varies; at Newgrange, the mound is nearly 87 yards (80m) across, while the passage-plus-chambers extend to less than 27 yards (25m). At Harristown, Co. Waterford, on the other hand, the passage is well over half the diameter of the mound (6m: 9m). Sizes of passage tombs also vary widely. Most are smaller than about 87 yards (80m) across (including the mound), the stone chambers being as little as 4¼ yards (4m) in some instances. Some are small enough to have the capstone of the central chamber resting directly upon a single ring of upright stones (a number of these are at Carrowmore, Co. Sligo).

Passage tombs were erected mainly on rising ground, hill-tops and mountainsides. They are often grouped, as in the Boyne Valley (Brú na Bóinne) complex which include Newgrange, Knowth, Dowth, as at Carrowmore, west of Sligo town, at Sliabh na Caillighe (Loughcrew), Co. Meath, and Carrowkell, Co. Sligo. Some tombs are scattered on the Dublin Wicklow mountains, notably the many-chambered tomb at Seefin. There are about 300 passage tombs in Ireland, but they are not all of the early Neolithic period. Some, like a few of those in Waterford, could be of the transition period from Late Neolithic to Early Bronze Age (i.e. end of the third millennium).

Before leaving passsage tombs, we should take a look at the sort of domestic finds discovered at or near some of the monuments. Grave goods in Irish passage tombs are not of the variety or extravagant quality of the glories discovered in the tomb of Pharaoh Tutankhamun of fourteenth-century BC Egypt. Generally, excavators have isolated a simple variety of objects, chiefly personal ornaments like bone pins, stone balls (like marbles), beads of coloured stone, and pendants. Finds have also included sherds of very early pottery, mainly hemispherical bowls of coarse texture and rough decoration. Some pieces have loop and/ or lozenge designs. What is interesting is that more practical things like tools and weapons have not been found with the corpse burials, though such things as serrated flint scrapers (for leatherwork?), axe and chisel heads of stone, and so on, have been identified in the earth nearby.

Passage tombs were erected in many parts of western Europe

during the long Neolithic Age, notably in Spain, Portugal, France, Denmark, Britain and Ireland. By common agreement the passage tomb at Newgrange is among the very finest of all those that have survived anywhere in the world. And as a bonus to those who are keen to see a complete surviving passage tomb, Newgrange has the virtue of having been marvellously and most skilfully restored with evident relish by the Irish National Parks and Monuments Commission. Newgrange is one of the major attractions among all Irish ancient monuments.[1]

The next type of burial tomb, in order of time, was the portal tomb. This type is as a rule single-chambered (though dual chambers are known, as at Ballyrennan, Co. Tyrone). Generally, the entrance is flanked by substantial orthostats, and in some cases a third slab is placed between to close off the entrance. On the top of the tomb is placed a very substantial capstone, horizontally or sloping upwards towards the entrance with a slight overhang. The capstone at Browne's Hill, Co. Carlow, at about 100 tons weight, is massive, indeed overwhelming, as is that at Proleek, Co. Louth. They may have been lifted by means of ramps and wooden levers. Occasionally, there is a secondary roofing stone underneath part of the capstone, as at Ballynagearagh, Co. Waterford. The height of the portal tomb varies between about 2m and 3m at the entrance end, but the area of the tomb is usually very small, 5 to 7m by 4 to 5m. Many portal tombs are set in at one end of a long barrow of earth: occasionally, there is a portal at each end. Portal tombs are regarded as derivatives of the earlier court tombs and are reckoned to date from several centuries later than the previous two types, that is, starting about 2500 BC, and ending perhaps about 2200 to 2100 BC, as the Irish metal ages begin.

Overlapping the last period of the portal tombs was the age of the wedge tombs, and this coincided with the transition from Stone Age to Bronze Age in Ireland, and by the appearance in Ireland of the Beaker people. This interesting period was characterized by a gradual change from the custom of collective burial to one of individual burial, one of the features of the Beaker people. Beaker people came from Europe, directly by sea to Ireland. They were sophisticated farmers and stockbreeders, who had begun to use copper, and later bronze, as well as stone, and so put down their settlements in areas in which copper ores were available, in Ireland in the western part, especially Munster. They buried their dead in the crouched position (which we call crouched burial) in smallish chambers under cairns and they filled the chamber with an assortment of weapons and possessions, among which was a variety of decorated drinking beakers – hence the name for these particular immigrants, who had already been metalworking in western Europe for some centuries. The drinking vessels were usually very finely decorated. The tombs in Ireland are known as wedge tombs, and some were covered with earth, others left exposed. They were smaller and less complex than court or passage tombs. More than 400 have so far been identified in Ireland, mainly in the west. Their principal features are long, narrow, single or in-line chambers, the dual chambers separated by septal slab, wider at the entrance and tapering towards the rear (cf. a good example at Culdaly, Co. Sligo.) The roof slabs usually rest upon the chamber walls which are as a rule orthostats. We are talking about small structures, seldom over 10m overall, many as little as 2m, the smaller ones having capstones hewn out of one piece of stone. Many such wedge tombs have yielded Beaker pottery, as well as metal fragments.

On the eastern side of Ireland, at much the same time as the immigration of the Beaker people in the west, there were intrusions of a contemporary people known as the Food Vessel folk, who came from Europe via Britain. They are so called from the fact that their burials were marked by placing food vessels with the corpses in the tombs. The food vessels were of two distinct types, bowls and vases. Generally, bowls were placed with crouched burials, vases with incinerated remains. Food Vessel folk used metals like the Beaker people and may have moved forward to bronze before them. Food Vessel folk interred their dead in stone cists under earth, or used earlier passage tombs long since giving up by Neolithic people for communal burial. One passage tomb used by the Food Vessel folk was the Mound of the Hostages tomb at Tara (see p. 16).

After the Food Vessel folk came the Cinerary Urn people, bronze-using and in some areas mixing with later Food Vessel folk. The Cinerary Urn people are differentiated from the latter by their practice of cremating their dead and burying the ashes in inverted urns, individually not collectively, in tombs. It is

2. The Mound of the Hostages, Hill of Tara (courtesy of the Irish Tourist Board)

difficult to disentangle the other differences between the two, except that the Urn people seem to have discontinued the use of stone cists for tombs. These people appear to have become absorbed in time by successors in the late second millennium and there is an unsatisfactory space in the record to follow, which cannot be usefully filled on present knowledge.

The Irish Bronze Age lasted probably from about 2200 BC right through to *c.* 600 BC. This may seem a very long time, but it was nearly as long for Scotland (*c.* 2200–*c.* 700). Interestingly, it was late Beaker folk from Ireland who took over to Scotland the art of annealing copper, thereby hardening it to make it more effective for tools, and later on, the skill of alloying copper with arsenical ores and later still with tin, to make bronze, thus leading Scotland into its Bronze Age. The term Bronze Age is generally taken to cover the preliminary period when copper was used on its own as material for axe and dagger blades, and some more domestic articles, too, before metalworkers discovered how to alloy copper with arsenical ores (and later, tin) and how to cast the tougher, more useful product, bronze. During the Irish

9

Bronze Age, metalworkers also worked with gold for personal ornaments, such as torcs (neck-rings) and lunulae (crescent necklets), both of which were exported to Britain in exchange, perhaps, for articles of faience (glazed frit for beads, usually of blue colours achieved by using copper ores) and amber that probably originated from the Baltic. A necklace of beads of bronze, faience and amber was found in the lower part of the tomb of the Mound of the Hostages at Tara (p. 9).

Although there are few remains of tombs of Bronze Age origin compared with the earlier ages – some of the Bronze Age people reused earlier megalith structures – other aspects of Bronze Age civilization have been left behind. High on the list are stone circles, some erected to surround important burial mounds, more put up for religious ceremonies or secular gatherings. Well over 100 good circles have been identified from this period, many dating from about 2100 BC to the mid-second millennium. Stone circles varied widely in size: many were very small, only 3 to 10m across, and having only a few stones in the ring. More than 90 circles are identifiable in south-west Ireland (Cork and Kerry) alone. Another concentration is in west Ulster, especially Co. Tyrone. Two good examples of smaller circles are at Dromleg, Co. Cork and Lissyviggeen, Killarney, Co. Kerry. The largest circle is that at Grange, Co. Limerick.

Among rich relics of the Irish Bronze Age are numerous artefacts like cauldrons, trumpet horns, sheet-bronze buckets, the first swords in Ireland (c. 1300 BC, short, heavy swords, good for cutting and slashing), shields, spears and daggers. Much of the surviving material displays evidence of high skill and craftsmanhip. Goldware was also executed to very high standards (cf. gold disc, Tedavnet, Co. Monaghan, mid-second millennium; gold spiral ornament, Donnybrook, Co. Dublin, c. 1000 BC; gold torc, Tara, c. 1000 BC; gold lunula, Ross, Co. Westmeath, c. mid-second millennium).

The evidence for the dwelling places of Neolithic and Bronze Age Ireland is scant, as it is in other European countries. Among the earliest identifiable remains are those at Ballyglass, Co. Mayo. These are trenches and postholes indicating a rectangular wooden long house, probably thatched in its time, about 13m by 6m, which has been dated to the mid-third millennium BC. An even earlier find is at Ballynagilly, Co. Tyrone, also rectangular, of about 3000 BC and also with contemporary pottery finds. This one may be linked with a nearby court tomb of early Neolithic date. Probably the most interesting group of remains are those at Lough Gur, Co. Limerick. A collection of houses on Knockadoon, at Lough Gur, date to earlier Neolithic times. There has been a series of brilliant excavations and reconstructions of Neolithic buildings here, pioneered by the late Professor Ó Riordáin. The houses were substantial framed structures, some round, some rectangular, with turf walls and with timber or in some cases stone footings, and thatched roofs, the thatch probably taken from rushes from the nearby lough. Artefact remains showed that the occupants used locally made round-based decorated pots for storage and flatter-bottomed pots for cooking. There was evidence of extensive tree-felling and ground cultivation, from axe blades and antler picks. Also found were a variety of domestic tools of bone, like needles and awls, and flint knifeblades. And there were many items of personal ornament and of house decoration. Interestingly, some of the axe blades appear to have been imported from the great axe factories of Co. Antrim, over 100 miles away, especially from those at Tievebulliagh and of Rathlin Island which, as has been noted earlier (p. 2) were exported to southern Scotland and southern Britain. At Knockadoon, meanwhile, there are some signs of cultivated terraces edged by large stones of the period. At Slieve Breagh, Co. Meath, traces of two 5m-diameter post-built round houses of Neolithic date were discovered.

One of the best known of Irish prehistoric dwelling types is the *crannóg*, a timber house, or small group of huts, on an island artificially built in a lake or on its edge. The island was usually surrounded by a palisade wall. The *crannóg* emerged as a building type towards the middle of the first millennium BC (say, *c.* 600), perhaps earlier, and was a late Bronze Age feature. That is not to say that Neolithic people did not build *crannógs* – they may have. Among the earliest *crannóg* remains so far uncovered have been those attributed to what is called the Dowris phase of the late Bronze Age, demonstrated in the Dowris district of Co. Offaly. The name *crannóg* stems from the Gaelic *crann* = tree. *Crannógs* were erected on piles driven into a lake or marshland, or on log foundation, or on piles of stones. The determining feature is that the dwelling and its enclosure are on an artificial island. One of the first to be excavated was at Lagore, Co. Meath, originally examined in 1838–9, and re-examined in the 1930s. Today some *crannógs* do not appear to be so obviously lake dwellings because the surroundings have altered over the centuries. There was a splendid exposure of piling and palisading at the *crannóg* at Ballinderry (No. 2), Co. Offaly, which was examined in the 1930s. This type of dwelling which began so long ago continued to be constructed and used right into the Christian era (mid-fifth century AD) onwards. In some cases there is evidence of a second and even a third consecutive building or set of buildings erected upon the remains of a previous and identical structure. Other *crannógs* include those at Rathtinaun, Co. Sligo, Lough Faughan, Co. Down (which has a stone kerb), and Rathjordan, Co. Limerick, where the island has a stone surface on top of a base of peat and timber (this site is extremely early, having yielded a sherd of Beaker pottery). More than 200 *crannógs* have been identified in Ireland, some of them of early Christian date. They are of particular interest to the archaeologist and the historian because, as Ó Ríordáin commented, the natural moisture prevailing at a *crannóg* site has helped to preserve objects that would have decayed under drier conditions. The finds often include articles of wood, leather and textiles, and they 'demonstrate that carpentry of good quality was practised in ancient times'. *Crannógs*, it seems, were built and occupied by Bronze Age people, Iron Age people, early Christians – and possibly by some of the last of the Neolithic peoples, too. It is a long tradition.

In European countries, as in the Near and the Far East, the Bronze Age gradually gave way to the Iron Age. The introduction of this superior metal, iron, to Europe followed the collapse of the Hittite Empire in Asia Minor in the twelfth century BC. Iron technology had been a virtual monopoly of the Hittites, who kept its manufacture processes secret for centuries. By about 1000 BC iron was in wide use in Dorian Greece and by about 900 in Italy and in most other parts of central Europe. At about this time there emerged the collection of peoples known as the Celts – (from the Greek word, *Keltoi* = barbarians). They were a mass of loosely associated peoples who arrived in central Europe some time towards the end of the second millennium BC. They appear to have been descendants of a variety of European Bronze Age folk mingled with wanderers from central Asia. They spoke two branches of the indo-European family of languages, known as P-Celtic and Q-Celtic, and speakers of one probably understood speakers of the other. The Celts knew how to breed and manage horses, skills learned from their Asiatic forebears. They also understood iron technology and were to develop it extensively.

The earliest Celts in Europe are often called Hallstatters, from one of their settlements found at Hallstatt in Austria in the 1860s. The Hallstatters buried their dead in timber chambers under earthmounds. Hallstatt was one settlement in a scattering of many throughout central Europe of this period, which are all characterized by their use of iron, their weapons, and their spoke-wheeled vehicles. The Hallstatt era gave way in time to another and in some respects more advanced age, the La Tène era, named after the Swiss village of La Tène on the Thiele, by Lake Neuchatel. Here, also in the 1860s, another Celtic settlement was found, the remnants of a substantial village with a variety of important objects. Many were of metal but in a distinctly different style from Hallstatt. Here, too, a vehicle was found, a two-wheeled chariot which had been drawn by a pair of horses yoked to a centre pole. The wheels were spoked and the rims fitted with an iron band like a tyre. There were several weapons including an iron version of the older slashing sword of bronze. The two types of Celtic civilization were blending, with the La Tène perhaps more dominant in most areas because it was more vigorous, and as they advanced the people began to spread to other parts of Europe and then to the British Isles. At the same time, or perhaps earlier, the older Hallstatt culture spilled over into southern France and into the Iberian peninsula.

The movements of the La Tène Celts and the Hallstatt Celts in the British Isles have not been easy to trace – indeed, still are not – but it is clear that one major Celtic trait, intertribal fighting, affected many parts of both Britain and Ireland, and this is indicated in their fortifications. Yet it was not the Celts who started to build fortifications in Ireland but rather Late Bronze Age people, those who built *crannógs* for domestic residences.

Contemporary with *crannógs* were the earliest hill-forts of Ireland, and among the first were Rathgall, Co. Wicklow, where there are remains of a hillfort surrounded by a series of ditches and banks, and at Mooghaun, Co. Clare, which has three rings of stone wall, both sites being dated to late Bronze Age. Hill-forts were also built by early Iron Age people, and some fifty from Bronze Age and Iron Age periods have been identified, most of them of considerable size (up to about 18 acres in area) though there are some quite small, like Freestone Hill, Co. Kilkenny, which is 4 acres. The hill-forts in the north and east are usually of single bank (or stone wall) and ditch (i.e. univallate), while those in the south and west are generally two or more banks (or stone walls) and more than one ditch (i.e. multivallate). The hill-fort at Tara, Co. Meath, was for a time to become the royal seat of the chief Uí Néill kings (see below) and the univallate hill-fort at Dun Ailinne (Allen), Co. Kildare, the seat of the kings of Leinster (see p. 28).

The other – and more numerous – kind of residential building was the ring-fort, much smaller, usually sited on top of a hill (whereas a hill-fort *is* the hill-top with the banks (or walls) following the contours on the slopes). The dwelling in a ring-fort is surrounded by a circular bank and ditch. Although a kind of ring-fort was known in the late Bronze Age, ring-forts are really a feature of the Irish Iron Age. We shall return to them below.

When the Iron Age began to replace the Bronze Age in Ireland we are not certain whether this was in the first days of the Celts, or before their arrival. Certainly, the first Celts to arrive in Ireland were well versed in iron technology, and they were Hallstatters, or descendants of Hallstatters. They came in the mid-first millennium BC, and settled chiefly in the west and the south, suggesting that they came by the direct sea route from southwest Europe, predominantly Spain and Portugal. They spoke Q-Celtic, the ancestral language of Irish, and on the whole they favoured the multivallate hill-fort. They also built smaller ring-forts.

Perhaps about a century later, La Tène Celts began to reach northern and parts of eastern Ireland (some ventured west as well), as is shown by the Turoe Stone in Co. Galway, carved in La Tène style). They had come from Scotland and what is now northern England. They have left many artefacts of considerable artistic skill and beauty, including familiar Celtic gold torcs like the superb collar found at Broighter, Co. Derry, jewellery like the lovely bronze brooch at Navan Fort, Co. Armagh (first

14

3. The Broighter collar (courtesy of the National Museum of Ireland)

century BC), war trumpets of bronze like the first-century BC specimen at Loughnashade, Co. Armagh, ornamental sword scabbards, and so forth. And they produced carved stones, some of high skill and artistry. One interesting and vigorous example of La Tène sculptured stone is the two-headed figure on Boa Island, Co. Fermanagh, of the first century BC. La Tène people spoke P-Celtic, the ancestral tongue of Welsh and Breton, and so perhaps would have understood the conversation of their kinsmen in Wales. In some parts of Wales, there are megalithic and other stone monuments clearly showing cultural links with contemporary phases in Ireland, like the Trefignath burial chamber in Anglesey, which has a segmented gallery akin to the third millennium BC types in Ireland, and the Barclodiad y Gawres passage tomb on cruciform plan in Anglesey, with stone carving, perhaps contemporary with Carrowkeel, Co. Sligo or with the tombs of the Boyne Valley (see above, p. 6).

15

There was another immigration, or series of immigrations, of P-Celtic speaking people from North Wales across to Meath and Leinster. People from this immigration or their descendants occupied the royal site of Tara, Co. Meath, which had begun as a Neolithic passage tomb site (the tomb is under the Mound of the Hostages), then become a Bronze Age Food Vessel folk site, then a Cinerary Urn Folk site (they despoiled the passage tomb but left behind a remarkable collection of artefacts of bronze and pottery of their own culture). The mound is some 70 feet across and a little over 9 feet tall. It incorporates a stone cairn beneath a clay skin, grafted on to the earlier passage tomb. Inside the cairn were found several stone cists. At some stage of Celtic occupation, a hill-fort was raised on the hill (now called Ráith na Ríogh). This is an oval of about 980 feet by 780 feet (300m by 240m), on the hill where the latter is nearly 500 ft above sea-level and has the most commanding views of the countryside. The hill-fort enclosed the Mound of the Hostages in its northern arc. The hill of Tara was also to become the site of an Iron Age ring-fort complex, known as the Rath of the Synods, just outside the ditch and rampart of the hill-fort, to the north. It is called the Rath of the Synods by virtue of associations with St Patrick and other early Christian leaders in Ireland. The ring-fort was excavated in the 1950s and it became clear that the site had been occupied from the first to third centuries AD (the chief evidence being from a succession of defences and timber buildings and rebuildings).

For some time after their respective arrivals, the different Celtic immigrations lived in Ireland separately, cooperating here, squabbling and contending there, but forming an ascendancy that bent the earlier inhabitants into a state of slavery or serfdom. The La Tène people of Ulster, P-Celtic speaking, builders of a 15-acre hill-fort at Emain Macha (Navan Fort), Co. Armagh (on a site previously occupied by both Neolithic and Bronze Age people), which was to go through several developments including a ring-fort inside, and later to become the capital and royal seat of the Uí Néill of Ulster, were probably the ancestors of the people who figure in the Ulster epic, *Táin Bó Cúailnge*. Most notable among these are the great heroes Conchobar and Cú Chulaind, under whom the Ulster people dominated for a while the north of Ireland down to the river Boyne, and perhaps

16

exerted power over the people of Meath too. If Conchobar and Cú Chulaind were legendary, the power of Ulster was not, and these heroes probably represented real leaders of the time. Certainly, some later Irish kings modelled themselves on these legendary heroes. Their capital is known as Isamnion on Ptolemy's second-century AD map of the British Isles. Archaeology has shown it to have been a hill-fort in the fourth and third centuries BC and to have seen a series of rebuildings of structures (including a huge timber ritual building) on the site over the centuries. Other La Tène Celts settled in Connacht, and in time a series of earthworks, including ring-forts, arose at Cruachain, Co. Roscommon, in particular a large round mound, 85m across and 6m tall, at Rathcruachan. This series represented the royal seat of the kingdom of Connacht that prevailed for a time over the western part of the Ulster kingdom, where it founded the dominion of Ailech, with a multivallate hill-fort at Ailech, Co. Donegal, as its capital. Connacht also captured the royal seat at Tara. We do not have dates for these movements, but it is suggested that the struggle between Ulster and Connacht of the early AD period is a factual interpretation of the *Taín Bó Cúailnge*. Certainly, Ulster was later to be overcome by Connacht in the mid-fifth century, just after the foundation of Armagh, the principal church of the new religion, Christianity.

Among the earlier peoples over whom the Celts imposed their ascendancy were those who later became known to the Romans as the *Picti*, or painted men, a race of Irish inhabitants some of whom crossed into Scotland probably in the last centuries BC. Since northern Ireland was so close geographically to south-west Scotland we need not be surprised at evidence of a long history of cross-traffic between the two. The *Picti* (Picts) were known to P-Celtic people in Ulster as the *Prydyn*, and to the Q-Celtic people further down as the *Cruithi*.

Whatever the successes of the La Tène Celts in Ireland in the last centuries BC and the first centuries AD, it is clear that ultimately the Gaelic Celts (of Hallstatt descent) succeeded in imposing their form of the Celtic language on the whole country. This predominance of the Gaels is reflected in their construction of many thousands of ring-forts throughout the country, some of earth and timber (raths) and some of stone (cashels) – alternatively known in some quarters as lios and cahers. This is the ring-fort tradition, as it is called, associated with Iron Age Gaelic Celts in Ireland. The ring-forts, though in some cases defensive in appearance, were essentially residential only and they accommodated settlements of people in or near areas suitable for farming, mining, fishing or some other economic activity. The settlements had individual characteristics resulting from a variety of influences, but they also had some things in common: language, laws, religious rituals, burial customs (albeit with local differences), social and political structure (the *fine*, or joint family, and the *tuath*, or petty kingdom, see pp. 29-31 below), art and design, and probably other things of which we do not have enough evidence. We shall look at these features again in the next chapter, for the social and political structure of Ireland stayed much the same in the centuries immediately before the arrival of Christianity, as it did in the first few centuries that followed.

Ring-forts were the principal artefact of Iron Age Ireland, and they were built over many centuries, right into our present millennium (as at Beal Boru, Co. Clare, which dates from the eleventh century). The number of ring-forts is put at tens of thousands, perhaps as many as 50,000. Since we are talking about a class of building that was a standard community residence over a period of 1500 or more years, the number is not really excessive, especially when one takes into account the practice of abandoning one ring-fort after a period and erecting another nearby, somewhat later. The population of Ireland in the early part of the first millennium AD has been put at about 500,000. Demographic estimates are notoriously unreliable, yet in a land without cities or towns or even villages, half a million inhabitants at those times doesn't seem unreal. Most ring-forts housed farmsteads, protected livestock and offered accommodation for branches of the family, guests and workforce, and must have been occupied by an average of at least twenty. If half the ring-forts were all occupied by a family with dependents of this number, we arrive at a total population of half a million.

The ring-fort is generally round in plan, though ovals, squares, D-ends, rectangles and nondescript shapes are known. It seems nobody worried about the exact shape. Sometimes, two round forts are joined to form a figure of eight, as at Tara (in that case, one may have been erected beside the other at a later date), and occasionally more than two are joined, as at Cush, Co. Limerick, where there were six. This is fairly taken to indicate expansion of the community there. A ring-fort was protected by bank and ditch, the earth from the ditch providing the material for the bank. Sometimes the bank was of stone blocks, or stone rubble chipped out of local stone deposits, and in most of these instances there is no ditch. Good examples of rath are at Grange, Co. Limerick, Ardsoren, Co. Sligo, Cush, Co. Limerick, and of course the raths of Tara. Interesting remains of cashels are at Moneygashel, Co. Cavan, Carraig Aille, Co. Limerick and Staigue, Co. Kerry. Sizes vary hugely. The space enclosed is anything from 11 yards (10m) across to more than 65 yards (60m) (a few, even larger), while the defences also vary, from a simple narrow ditch and bank of overall width as little as 6 or 7 yards to a triple bank and ditch complex of overall width as much as 87 yards (80m). But a triple bank and ditch arrangement round an enclosure is not necessarily evidence of fortification against military assault. It could equally be reliable protection for inhabitants against non-military danger such as wild animals, cattle rustling, sheep stealing. It is likely, also, that in some instances two or more rings of bank and ditch indicated special status of the occupant. Layouts of enclosures vary widely and excavations suggest a range of uses, singly or in combination, simultaneously or in succession, such as metalworks, glassworks, farming, livestock accommodating, pottery, and of course headquarters for tribal chiefs.

Not surprisingly one finds a variety in the modifications and extensions to ring-forts; chambers in the banks for look-out men, as at Leacanbuaile, Co. Kerry, underground passages and chambers (souterrains), additional buildings of later date for different uses. The structures inside ring-forts were of timber or stone, or both, and they were rectangular, round, or oval. Square-plan houses have been reconstructed inside the ring-fort at Leacanbuaile, providing fine examples of ring-fort contents. There is a reconstructed oval house inside the ring-fort at Carrigillihy, Co. Cork (of very early date) and the ring-fort at Staigue has interesting features like flights of steps along the inside of the stone surrounding wall. At charred outline of a round house was found at Grange, Co. Limerick. At Dubh Cathair, Aran Islands, there are remains of several stone-built huts inside the ring-fort; these were not excavated but have been visible for a long time. At Tara, there is a flattened earth mound enclosed in two concentric banks and ditches, which has the outline of a rectangular house inside, known as the Forad (Royal Seat), and this is one of the pair of ring-forts that are in the figure of eight we have mentioned above.

Souterrains abound in Ireland, and most are found inside ring-forts. Some are found outside, and some are found quite unconnected with ring-forts. They are like those in Scotland, where they are alternatively called weems, or earth-houses, of which far fewer were erected than in Ireland. Technically, a souterrain consists of an underground passage, either with the roof at ground level or sunk a little below. They sometimes lead to chambers with stone floors, walls and ceilings. They were cut in rock or clay, were often roofed with horizontal slabs, but also with timber beams, as at Ballycatteen, Co. Cork. Many were long, some extending to 80 feet or so. They were often sited underneath residential buildings inside the ring-fort. Some had an opening in the ring-fort's wall, others opened just outside the wall, as at Dunbeg, Co. Kerry. Souterrains were employed as places where to hide in time of danger (particularly to conceal women and small children, and no doubt valuable livestock, too.) They were also used for storing valuable possessions. There is some evidence that souterrains served for more than just a few hours waiting for a raid come to an end: charcoal remains and signs of chimney flues here and there indicate fires for cooking and heating over long periods, so perhaps they had residential uses. Certainly, too, souterrains were much in use for grain storage. They are not easy to date: the discovery of Bronze Age artefacts in them is not evidence of Bronze Age origin. Currently it is thought that they are contemporary with Iron Age ring-forts, early and late, and, as in Scotland, they were being built well into the Christian era.

In 55 BC, and again in 54, Julius Caesar invaded Britain and exacted tribute from Celtic chiefs in the Thames Region whom he had vanquished in battle. His principal opponents were the Belgae, Belgic Celts originating from nothern France who had themselves invaded and settled in southern Britain c. 150–100 BC and imposed their dominion upon earlier peoples already there. They are often known as Iron Age C People, and the history of first century BC Britain is marked by the intense rivalry between the Belgae and the non-Belgic tribes. Some of the Belgae crossed into Ireland, probably before the first century AD, and they might have been those invaders whom ancient Irish legend refers to as Firbolg. Caesar himself was aware of the Irish (*Gallic War*, Book V, Ch. 13., 'in which direction lies Ireland, smaller by one half than Britain). This reference in the commentaries he sent to Rome brought Ireland for the first time into the mainstream of European history. It is an appropriate place to end one chapter and to begin another in Ireland's story.

CHAPTER 2

CELTS
AND
CHRISTIANS

The history of Ireland's Celtic Iron Age and of the first four and a half centuries AD was not written down at the time, because the Celts did not write, indeed they did not see the need to write. They committed things to memory and passed them on orally. This is what is called the oral tradition. Probably the *áes dána*, that is, the intellectual class (see p. 32) knew how to write but deliberately did not commit their knowledge to script so as to concentrate the power of memory and to ensure the purity of the knowledge as it was passed down orally. There was also an element of keeping the secret in order to maintain superiority over others. When Celts did begin to commit anything to permanence in the form of writing, their first script was a cumbrous and unimaginative usage of short horizontal or diagonal lines on stone slabs, known as Ogham or Ogam script, and limited to the recording of names and genealogies. It emerged in the early centuries AD and was a crude system that served to represent Greek or Latin letters. Generally thought to have been Irish in origin, Ogham inscriptions have also been found in other Celtic parts, such as Wales, the Isle of Man and Scotland. As a script for recording historical events, listing laws, or defining religious procedures, for example, it can be seen from the photograph of an Ogham stone (p. 23) that it would have been well-nigh useless.

The age of writing probably began in Ireland in the fourth century. Such history of that era as has been written down was

22

4. An Ogham stone (courtesy of the National Parks and Monuments)

composed after, and in many cases long after, the events its records. In some cases it was the written down version of the oral traditions.

It is easy to think that the absence of literacy is an indication of backwardness, but in the case of the Celts that is to underrate the degree to which they trained their memories and the heights of eloquence to which their oral techniques rose, not only among the professional classes but also among others. In those skills the Irish Celts were every bit as advanced as their kinsmen in Britain and in Gaul, whose oral proficiency was commented on with some wonder by such Roman authors as Cato the Elder, Poseidonios, Diodorus Siculus, Lucian and the great Julius Caesar himself.

The development of the memory and of oral technique was indispensable to the Celts as their only means of communicating with each other down the generations. Many techniques were clothed in artificial forms. The prestige of their leaders was heightened by continuous boasting about their past deeds and the deeds they were going to perform in the future, through the use of poetic oratory employing allusion and exaggeration, the panegyrics being recited by bards who learned them by heart and developed their oratorical skills to give new meanings and add fresh hyperbole on each rendering. This propaganda on their leaders' behalf was much enhanced by continual comparison with the deeds of earlier heroes and heroines, real and imaginary, in structured canons of verse or prose in which facts and legends were mixed, to the delight of the leaders and those around them, but to the despair of later historians! The Celtic love of display, of fine clothes, of handsome weaponry, of beautifully executed jewellery, was exploited to the full to decorate the overall public relations image.

These exercises in propaganda were carried into the whole field of education of the young in Irish society. Tribes and tribal histories and genealogies were more easily committed to memory by being rendered in metrical forms which the Celts recognized very early on as an effective memory stimulator, as well as an essential tool in saving the material to be learned from dissipation and eventual disintegration. In addition to history and genealogy, other subjects were taught and committed to memory, such as astronomy, geography, religion, mythology, law and science.

Among the most complete of the earliest written records of oral traditions of Irish history is the *Táin Bó Cúailnge* (*The Cattle Raid of Cooley*), already mentioned (p. 16). Regarded in some quarters as the greatest of the Irish sagas, it points to an Ireland of four kingdoms, or peoples, in a period that is at the start of the Christian era. Curiously, the story is mainly about the efforts of Queen Medb of Connacht to capture the finest bull in Ireland, which belonged to Conchobar, king of Ulster, but it is a vehicle for much useful material about later Iron Age Ireland, social, domestic, economic, that can be verified through archaeology and through comparison with known matter relating to other Celtic societies of the same period. Meanwhile, in an otherwise extremely grey area of legend-cum-history of the early centuries AD we can identify a little about Irish political and military activity of the time.

Although the government at Rome had been aware of the existence of Ireland, certainly from the time of Caesar and probably even earlier, no attempt was made to invade the island right through to the collapse of the Empire at the end of the fifth century. The only recorded occasion upon which a Roman general even considered it was during the fifth year of the governorship of the province of Britain of Cn. Julius Agricola, namely, 78–85 AD. Agricola's son-in-law, P. Cornelius Tacitus (c. 55–120 AD), the great Latin historian, tells us (in Ch.XX1V of his short biography of Agricola) that his father-in-law believed the conquest of Ireland would be relatively easy: '. . . he had welcomed an exiled Irish chief, and kept him in his entourage until an occasion arose when he might use him. . . . I often heard him say that he could conquer Ireland and hold it down with as little as one legion (about 6000 men) plus a few auxiliaries . . . and that it would be worthwhile doing so to keep the Britons frightened by a Roman military presence on all sides of them.'[1] There were, of course, trading links between Romans (whether European or Romano-British) and the Irish, and doubtless further excavations in Ireland will in time give a better understanding of the extent of these commercial activities.[2]

But if no Roman army ever attacked Ireland from Britain, Irish raiders in groups or in larger contingents certainly attacked Britain in Roman times. As one authority put it: 'The Irish were a threat in Wales by the late third century, and a positive menace by the fourth.'[3] This is clear from structural alterations to forts in west Britain, notably Caernarfon (Segontium) and (later) erection of new forts at Caer Gybi (Holyhead, Anglesey) and on or near sites of earlier forts, as at Cardiff and Lancaster. The activities of the Irish against Britain during those times began as a series of sea raids up and down the western side, especially in Wales, the north-west (Cumbria) and southern Scotland (Galloway), starting in the mid-third century and increasing in intensity. In the fourth century some raiders began to settle in parts along the coast, others ventured further inland. There is evidence of an Irish assault upon the Romano-British civitas capital at Wroxeter (Uriconium) in Shropshire. By the end of the fourth century things had got very bad. The Irish took advantage of the withdrawal of Roman forces from Caernarfon and the recall of Legio XX from Chester (Deva) in the 380s to settle in large numbers, some making homes in the Lleyn peninsula (which included the Caernarfon site). Lleyn gets its name from the Laigin, the men of Leinster.

At the beginning of the fifth century, history begins to become disentangled from legend in Ireland, and it is possible, by using a variety of sources – such as the *Táin*, other sagas, inscriptions and so on – to start building up a patchwork of key names and occasional rough dates. One of the first historical rulers in Ireland was Niall Noígiallach (Niall of the Nine Hostages), who appears to have been a king from about 400 for thirty years or so.

For some if not all the time he ruled from Tara, possibly as an under-king of the then ruling house of Connacht, of which he was a relative. In or about 405 he led an expedition against Britain, landing either along the coast of southern Wales or, as is also considered, higher up in Cumbria. If the latter, he may have captured a young Romano-British boy, aged about 16, named Patricius, son of Calpurnius, a decurion (local magistrate) perhaps from Carlisle (Luguvallum). This was the future St Patrick. It was not the first royal raid on Britain, but it does seem that thereafter expeditions increased in frequency, many of them not so much for gathering booty as for permanent settlement in Britain. Such emigration continued throughout the century, to an extent that has provoked the comment by Charles Thomas that Irish settlers in West Britain in the fifth century may have been as numerous as the germanic (i.e. Jute, Angle, Saxon) peoples in the south and east of Britain.[4]

Niall won fame by this and perhaps other expeditions and, with his brothers and later some of his sons, succeeded in holding sway over the northern half of Ireland, overcoming in the process the kingdom of the Ulaid people (Ulidia), the original ruling aristocracy of Ulster (one of whose prominent members had been embodied in the mythical Conchobar). The Ulidian capital had been Emain Macha (Navan Fort). These events marked the emergence of a dynasty, the Uí Néill, which was to dominate Irish political history for centuries, and as Ó Néill to remain a force to be reckoned with right down to the seventeenth century. Three of Niall's sons founded kingdoms in the Ulster period, and their descendants were known as the northern Uí Néill. Others founded kingdoms in the Irish midlands, and these rulers were the southern Uí Néill. As the northern Ui Neill enlarged their hold upon the north, they drove the Ulaid to the extreme north-east, now Co. Antrim, where the latter settled to form a small kingdom that came to be called Dal Riata. Some time during the fifth century, some Dal Riata people crossed the sea and settled along the coasts of Argyll and its islands in south and west Scotland. We shall meet these people again.

Emain Macha became the capital of some people of shadowy origin called the Airgialla, which means 'givers of hostages' and which suggests a kingdom in subservience to the northern Uí Néill. They may help to explain Niall's second name Noígiallach (of the Nine Hostages). One of Niall's sons, Laoghaire (Leary), succeeded at Tara towards the end of the third decade of the fifth century, and it was he that welcomed St Patrick at his court in 432, although it was not to be at Tara that Patrick set up his church but further north at Armagh, only a mile or so from Emain Macha (then the Airgialla capital).

In the southern half of Ireland, meanwhile, the fifth century saw the rise of the two groupings, Munster and Leinster. Munster in the fifth and sixth centuries was a collection of southern kingdoms with fluid boundaries, and the same sort of rivalries as Connacht and Ulster; most of the Munster kingdoms were ruled by members of the Eóganacht dynasty, descended from Eógan (of whom nothing historical is known). Some of Eógan's descendants are said to have emigrated to Britain (probably to Scotland) and to have returned at about the beginning of the fifth century to impose themselves upon the countryside. One of the leading members of the dynasty was Conall Corc who founded the kingdom of Cashel in Co. Tipperary, which was to become the dominant kingdom among several that emerged in Munster, whose histories are very vague indeed. Kings of Cashel claimed to be overlords of all the others. Corc's grandson may have been Óengus, who ruled Cashel from the mid-fifth century to his death in c. 490. He is noted for having been defeated in thirty battles in a vain attempt to enlarge his territory at the expense of neighbours. Among the Munster kingdoms were groups of vassal people known as the Déisi, and they are interesting as having been semi-independent allies of the Eóganacht rulers and having assisted them in border wars with Connacht. Some of the Déisi were given lands taken from the southern end of Connacht, approximately what is now Co. Clare, and these folk later came to be called the Dál Cais people and their kingdom Dál Cais (pp. 53–4).

As for the Leinster region, this was dominated in the fifth and sixth centuries by two groups of the Laigin people. The northern Laigin were often at war with the Uí Néill in the midlands, but there seem to have been relatively peaceful relations between Leinster and Munster, so much so that Eoin McNeill, in his *Phases of Irish History*,[5] describes that part of Ireland as having probably enjoyed greater tranquillity than any other realm in Western Europe. The histories of the various kingdoms, even the chief figures and the dates, are problematic to summarize, and no attempt will be made to do so here. Readers should turn to the excellent and detailed work *Ireland before the Vikings*, by Gearóid Mac Niocaill.[6]

It was into this confusing geographical and political structure of Ireland that Christianity began to make its appearance, not actually with St Patrick but here and there in isolated places some time before him, through individual believers who came from Britain or Europe, or both, probably more in search of trade than converts. But before tracing this we should look briefly at the structure of Celtic society in those early times. Because of the lack of written records of Celtic history in Ireland before the mid-fifth century, we cannot be at all precise over the chronology of the development of laws and political arrangement, the growth of society institutions, or the expansion of arts, crafts, trades, industries, agriculture or economics. But there is a measure of agreement about a general picture.

By the end of the first millennium BC the Celts in Ireland had overcome and pressed into servitude the indigenous population, governing them as a warrior aristocracy. Because there was no interference from outside, not even in the first centuries AD from Rome, they were able to develop as they wanted. In Europe, Celts had for long remained nomadic before settling in those parts now revealed as a result of excavation, such as Hallstatt, La Téne, Vix, and several others, and surely many others which we have so far not discovered. In Ireland, they stopped being nomadic early on and settled in suitable locations, some in areas that were already the long-established homelands of the peoples they overcame and perhaps absorbed. The Celts did not, however, see Ireland as a part of the world where they might construct an united nation, and for centuries they clung steadfastly to their traditional tribalism. The society that developed was in many of its aspects common to all the Celts, but each tribe retained its integrity and individuality.

It has often been said that all free Celts were equal, but from the beginning there were distinct class divisions. Celtic society, like so many others in early civilized history, was hierarchical. Under the kings were nobles, warriors, the *áes dána* (the intelligentsia), and the freemen (small farmers, craftsmen, etc). At the bottom, and with no rights, were slaves. These divisions were enumerated in what is called the brehon law, a law that was, at least until the sixth century AD, an oral one, transmitted with great accuracy through the judgments and interpretations of skilled professional jurists known as brehons (from the Irish *brithem* or judge). Brehon law held in some parts of Ireland right down to the sixth century AD. It was a remarkably enlightened law in some respects, and almost entirely free from the brutal killing and mutilation so characteristic of medieval European law.

Ireland was divided into numerous very small kingdoms, which during the first centuries AD (and possibly before) loosely belonged to one or other of the five larger provincial kingdoms of, to use their more familiar names, Connacht, Leinster, Meath, Munster and Ulster. Probably there were more than 100 smaller kingdoms in the earlier period, and as many as 150 or so by the seventh century. These were known as *tuatha (tuath*=tribe, or people, or clan) and each was ruled by a *rí*, or king, who might if his *tuath* was very small be an under king to a greater *rí*, or *rí ruirech* (and this *rí ruirech* might be an under king to a provincial king). This vassalage would generally be marked by the giving of a hostage, or hostages, to the higher king, and was often quite voluntary, for it afforded protection for the smaller tuath.

Kingship of a *tuath* was both elective and hereditary, though it seems that in the earlier centuries it was elective only. The successor under the dual system was chosen from the ruling family but not necessarily a son, nephew or even grandson – and certainly there was no primogeniture. The choice had, however, to be male, for women did not normally count (though we must not overlook the legendary Medb who represented a real-life queen of considerable power). Quite often, the successor would be selected before the incumbent king died; if there was disagreement about the heir after the king's death, it led sometimes to warfare. The chosen man had also to be a strong and effective leader of a society that was rural and pastoral, with limited crop agriculture. There were no towns or villages, and the largest communal settlement was the rath (or the cashel), or at most a small cluster of these (or, after the arrival of Christianity, a monastery, which in early Christian Ireland was a group of wooded huts round a small church). Raths or cashels of kings were generally identified by their being surrounded by two complexes of banks and ditches, as stipulated in brehon law. The king's responsibilities included command in war, ritual observances and duties, presiding over the *tuath* assembly, the *oenach*, and accommodation and protection of any hostages held. In Irish society the *tuath* king was not the final judge in legal disputes of criminal cases.

The rights and duties of those under the kings were also prescribed by the brehons, and accepted because the members of the *tuath* had a deep-seated respect for the law and for the brehons who made the judgments. Wrongs were righted not by execution or imprisonment but by restitution or redress. For example, murder might be atoned for by blood-money. Wrongs were regarded as offences against honour, or 'face', and each free man had what is called his honour-price, assessable in terms of currency which in Irish society of those times was cattle, or in some instances female slaves *(cumal)*. One surviving law tract indicates a *cumal* as being equal in value to six young heifers. Personal possessions could also be impounded to satisfy honour-price, particularly weapons, which were among the most prized possessions. If an offence was committed, it was not simply the duty of the miscreant to pay the honour-price, or some part of it, to the wronged person, it was the responsibility of the whole kin of the miscreant to see that restitution was made.

The *tuath* was the political unit of early Irish society. The other unit was the social one, the *fine*, or family group (kin group), and the one was not necessarily connected with the other. The *fine* was more than just a family of parents and their children, it was an extended family of all males with a great grandfather in common up to and including second cousins (and of course the female members as well). This class of *fine* appears to have been the standard, and known as the *derbfine*, or sure kin. There were enlarged versions, such as the *iar-fine*, (five generations) and the *indfine* (six). In these groupings we are considering some pretty large units, made possible by the prevailing loose approach to matrimony. Bigamy, for example, was neither illegal nor uncommon; concubinage was regular and the offspring were not necessarily excluded. It was this kind of approach that produced the clans of Scotland.

The custom that the *fine* was responsible for the actions of its individual members helped to create and maintain a remarkably stable society, and possibly the job of governing the *tuath* and keeping the peace was simpler than we might think. The individual counted for little in the community. He did not as a rule own land exclusively, only jointly with other members. So, members tended to watch over each other, and the *fine* acted as its own corporate police force, in the absence of any central organization governing the country or administering law. Sometimes, to achieve greater protection and stability, the practice of fostering children was used to strengthen links between the *tuatha*. Young children, often sons of higher class, were put under the care of a foster father and mother among their own *fine*, or among a neighbouring *fine* or even, perhaps, fostered by a king. The children were fostered from age seven to seventeen (boys) and seven to fourteen (girls), and of course grew up to feel strong loyalty to their adopted family,

The foregoing has been but a brief summary of kingship and Irish social structure, and it has to be remembered that there were differences in the various regions and over the many centuries. The very fragmented character of Irish society militated against anything being standard or uniform over the whole country.

Probably the most important element of early Irish society was the *áes dána*, loosely, the men of art. This interesting elite – for it was an elite – was accorded a status similar to that of the nobility and yet allowed membership from any class. Birth was not a necessary qualification. A skilled craftsman from the ordinary freeman class was as eligible as a brehon. The term 'art' in the definition covers a far greater scope than artist, and embraces druids, brehons, poets and bards (there is a difference), historians, doctors, craftsmen. This class was a national and not a tribal one, and its members moved freely round Ireland, across tribal boundaries, from kingdom to kingdom. Among the *áes dána* were the *filid*, or intellectual poets. They were much more than mere versifiers. They were thinkers, and in some instances juridical thinkers, and they crystallized into poetic form a wide range of important matters for oral transmission, like genealogical tables of chiefs of *tuatha*, stories about leading men and women, past and present, mythological and real, language grammar and vocabulary, traditions, customs, aspects of brehon law and so forth. As has been said, they were the voice of authority. But their poetic compositions were delivered not so much by themselves as through another sector of the *áes dána*, the bards, who were the mouthpieces of the *filid*. Bards were orators and reciters who went through long training in bardic schools, which had intensive courses on memorizing.

Members of the *filid* were responsible for the production of one of the first native Irish histories of Ireland, the *Lebor Gabála*, during the early Christian period. This book, the title of which means *The Book of the Takings*, tells how Ireland was first peopled, and records a series of invasions over the centuries. Invasions really meant migrations in most cases. The book is a mix of fact and legend but it marks the beginning in literary form of the Irish historical tradition, and it was compiled in the Irish tongue using letters of the Latin alphabet, probably early in the sixth century. It is one of the earliest works of any kind in this form. It emerged at a time when scholars in Ireland were beginning to write things down, a landmark in communication in which the *filid* played the leading role and which was to have a lasting influence. Indeed, it has been said that the *filid* did more than any other agency to sustain the survival of the Gaelic language and tradition right down to the seventeeth century.

During the first quarter of the fifth century there were enough practising Christians in Ireland to attract the attention of head-quarters at Rome. The number is not known, the Christians were under no sort of organization and there were no leaders, unless some initiatives were taken by one or two druids who found the faith intellectually interesting but left no record. Pope Celestine I (422–32) and his advisers considered the time had come to construct a church organization in Ireland, and in *c.* 431 sent Palladius as a missionary and first bishop. We do not know what Palladius achieved, indeed if he ever reached Ireland, for he died in 432. So, Rome sent a second missionary and bishop, St Patrick. It was not his first visit. As a boy aged about sixteen and brought up as a Christian in Cumbria (see p. 26), Patrick had been captured on one of the raids of Niall Noígiallach and was enslaved for about six years in Co. Antrim. Then he escaped and found his way to Gaul where he went to study at the monastery at Tours, moving on a few years later to the monastery at Auxerre, headed by St Germanus.

Patrick was made bishop in 432. Possibly because of his knowl-edge of the Irish, he was chosen to take over from Palladius. There is no reason to disbelieve the claim Patrick later made, that he had long nursed the ambition to bring Ireland into the Chris-tian fold. Sometime in 432, he landed in Ulster and proceeded to the district where he had once been enslaved, where legend has it that he converted his old master, who was now a chief. The story of St Patrick, and that of his mission, was written by himself, and he was also the subject of biographies by writers in the earliest literary tradition in Ireland.[7] Yet there is much of his story that is argued still: even the dates of his mission are disputed, but here they are taken as *c.* 432 – 61. It is now argued by some scholars that his work was confined to the north-east, which reached into Meath and Connacht. We need not doubt that he had some sort of meeting with King Laoghaire (Leary), son of Niall of the Nine Hostages, whose seat was at Tara, or if not with the king at least with a representative. At the time, Laoghaire was only one of several Irish kings, possibly not even an important one. It may even be that Patrick was obliged to pass through Laoghaire's territory while on his mission and was simply making a courtesy call. What is significant is that Patrick was not molested. Laoghaire himself remained unconverted to Christianity, but one of his sons was later to become a bishop.

Patrick's career can only be summarized here. During it he faced all manner of dangers, is said to have been arrested and imprisoned many times (sometimes actually manacled in irons) by druids who led the opposition to the new faith he was attempting to organize. But on the whole his mission was popular with most, even if the ruling strata saw Christianity as a threat to their order. The measure of his success is well shown by the fact that the establishment of his church was not accompanied by martyrdom. Many druids clung fast to their traditional beliefs long after Patrick's death, but seem to have tried to resist the spread of Christianity by argument rather than persecution. It was not so in other parts of Europe.

Patrick spent several years establishing his mission and setting up an organization in Ulster on the Roman model. He appointed many bishops and priests (some authorities say as many as 350 bishops). He baptized thousands of people, travelled extensively through a land that had no roads like those that networked the Roman Empire, and built perhaps more than fifty churches of timber. Some of these were given to the charge of women priests, who were an accepted part of the early Irish church. During his mission he is said to have founded the church that was to become his episcopal seat, at Armagh, close to Emain Macha. One of his great achievements was the introduction of monasticism into Ireland and the founding of monasteries for both sexes. He planned that the new Irish church should develop along episcopal lines but in fact it was to become monastic after his death. He also introduced the Irish to the Latin language, a key factor in the start of the Irish native literary tradition.

St Patrick died in about 461 at Saul, and may have been buried at Armagh. He was to become and still is perhaps the most famous person in Irish history. Among the legends about him is the story that he once plucked a handful of shamrock stalks from the grass to demonstrate to some potential converts the meaning of the Trinity – and thus the shamrock became the Irish national emblem. There is also the suggestion that he rid the island of its population of snakes.

Naturally, he could not have carried out his work alone, and we have the names of several other missionaries who may have been part of his team, or just been working separately at much the same time. Among them were Secundinus who worked in Meath, Auxillius in north Leinster, and Benignus who succeeded Patrick at Armagh.

Christianity was slow to advance in Ireland. There was no 'instant evangelization',[8] and when by the mid-sixth century the church had taken root and was winning over druid opposition, what had emerged was not as St Patrick dreamed of, a Roman organization headed by archbishop and bishops, with dioceses of parishes, but a monastic Christianity in which monasteries were the religious centres, headed by abbots (in some instances abbots and bishops worked alongside, with the abbots in charge). To some extent St Patrick contributed to the non-realization of his dream because he had introduced monasticism, and even founded monasteries himself.

The early Irish monasteries were not like those we think of in medieval Britain and Ireland: rather they were little towns of streets of wooden huts and halls clustered round a church. Among the buildings were schools for teaching religion as well as many other things. The monastic domination of Irish Christianity was to last right into the twelfth century. For the most part the monastic orders and their houses remained native in structure and organization, unaffected by changes and improvements in the continental orders, but this did not relieve them of the need for reform or reinvigoration from time to time.

It is easy to see why the Irish church began and developed in such an individual manner. The lack of towns and urban communities, of road networks, the geographical remoteness, the political divisions, the ease with which Irish culture was able to absorb and become fused with Latin cultural elements without allowing the latter to predominate, even the personalities of the first leaders in the church, all conspired to produce an establishment that functioned as a series of monastic community centres, autonomous yet linked, operating in some respects like the *tuatha* themselves. Some abbots nominated their successors from their own families, others were elected from the family. Abbacies became hereditary. This strengthened the role of the abbots, and for a long time they were collectively the head of the church; even popes had to address themselves to them all and not to any one archbishop or other single head, because there was no such individual.

The monastery – and by this we mean the whole community, not the buildings – maintained the best relations it could with neighbouring *tuatha*. Ancient law texts mention some *tuatha* headed by abbots or bishops. Kings often gave lands to new monastic creations or to existing communities, though only by consent of the whole *tuath*, for land belonged to the *tuath* not the ruler. It was a kind of partnership gradually accepted even by druids once they saw the Christians were not out to destroy them and their organization by violence but rather to try to convert them peacefully by persuasion and compromise – an example that later Christian 'missions' in other parts of the world would have done well to follow.

From the earliest days, the monastery became involved in every activity in the locality, sometimes being the principal moving force but trying to work within a framework of cooperation, particulary between the upholders of the older pagan traditions and the new evangelists. This compromise was a happy blending of old and new and it reached out even into the arts and learning. There were monks and laymen, and together they worked in the fields, they taught in the schools, they ran markets and workshops, they provided libraries and further education, they studied, read, discussed, they took up craft skills and produced wonderful artefacts, they prayed, sang, fasted, all like any other monastic community but more openly and alongside secular members of *tuatha*. Some of the community of monks married and had children: some broke the law and paid the penalty like anyone else. Indeed, the monastery was the nearest thing to a city or regional capital that Ireland had.

Some of the early Irish Christians chose not to be part of such community-spirited monasteries, preferring the ascetic existence of the hermit. They were often exiles who imposed exile upon themselves as a sacrifice, who retired to the remotest corners of Ireland, by or near the sea, and built themselves tiny establishments like Sceilg Mhichíl (Skellig Micheal), an island off Kerry, or Devenish in Lough Erne, or Kildreelig off Bolus Head. For many this meant cutting themselves off from their families, their *tuatha*, from the countryside they loved, but the motivation was powerful and they accepted the isolation. For some, this kind of withdrawal was imposed upon them by a monastic community for the commission of an offence or series of offences. One of the most celebrated examples of self-imposed exile was that chosen by Colum Cille (St Columba) who, in 563 abandoned his native Ulster to set up a monastery on the island of Iona off Argyll in Western Scotland, from which he introduced Christianity to the Dal Riata people that had emigrated to the mainland from Co. Antrim a century or so earlier.

Monastic Christianity was gradually accepted by the *áes dána* who wanted to be part of the new learning that went with it, a learning that was greatly helped along by the introduction of Latin and by the concomitant development of the written word. Of course there were some who clung to the older oral tradition for as long as they could, but the evidence is that on the whole the intellectuals took to writing with enthusiasm, fascinated perhaps by the adapting of Latin letters to the Gaelic language. They seem to have relished the visual permanence of their language, thoughts, laws, history and other things in manuscript form, and soon they were enjoying the advantages of Latin, to them a new, structured, lucid language in which they could read all sorts of works hitherto unknown to them. We may not be far out in thinking that this intellectual ferment produced the same sort of excitement as that created in Europe by the introduction of printing in the fifteenth century. Among the *áes dána* there arose a demand for Latin books, old texts and new works alike. They in turn began to produce manuscripts in their own tongue and in Latin, which found a ready following in Europe (increasingly so during the Golden Age, pp. 42–3).

We do not know which was the first monastery to be set up in Ireland, but among the earliest was Armagh, founded upon the episcopal church of St Patrick. Two others, contemporary or maybe even earlier, were Dunshaughlin, founded by Secundinus in Patrick's time, and Killashee, set up by Auxilius near Naas in Kildare, also in the fifth century. Not very much later were several foundations by scholar-monks from St Ninian's monastic establishment, Candida Casa (The White House), at Whithorn in Kirkcudbrightshire, Southern Scotland, including St Enda's monastery on the largest of the Aran Islands off Galway, Tigernach's monastery at Clones, and St Finnian's at Moville (which benefitted from a complete set of the Gospels brought by the saint from Rome). In this period (end of the fifth to the mid-sixth century), the Aran community produced two great scholars, St Finnian of Clonard (*c.* 500–50), 'the teacher of the saints of Ireland', who founded Clonard (which became a centre for Latin studies) and who in his time taught thousands of people, and St Ciaran (*d.* 549), founder of Clonmacnoise (described by an early authority as famous for its 'tuneful choirs'). Another great scholar was Brendan (*c.* 484–577) who spent years as a navigator and is believed to have crossed the Atlantic before settling down to the scholastic life and founding Clonfert. Finnian and Brendan are thought to have studied with St Dafydd of Menevia, patron saint of Wales, and teacher of numerous Irish saints and scholars. Another early Irish ascetic was Brigid (*c.* 453–523), daughter of an Ulster royal family, who founded several monasteries, among them one at Kildare which became a double house for men and women and was headed jointly by an abbot and an abbess. Probably the most famous of all the scholar-monks of the age was Colum Cille.

Colum Cille was born in about 520, a connection of the Uí Néill family which provided kings for parts of Ulster. He studied under St Finnian of Moville and founded his first monastery at Derry, in 546. Colum Cille had a brilliant mind, was by nature gentle but occasionally could be quarrelsome. He spent some time at a bardic school and began to write poetry in Latin (and perhaps in his native tongue, too), some of which is considered among the best of his time. Poetry was to remain important to him for the rest of his life; when he was at Iona, visiting poets were said always to have received a special welcome as his guests. Colum Cille was also a skilled scribe in an age when most Irish scholars were fascinated by the new art of illuminated writing. In the Royal Irish Academy there is a sixth century MS fragment known as the Cathach, which is the remains of a psalter said to have been copied out by him perhaps when he was at Moville (see p. 40). It is probably the oldest surviving manuscript from Western Europe.

In 553, Colum Cille founded the monastery at Durrow, Co. Meath, by which time he had evolved his own house rule, the Columban rule, of which we have some details from his biographer Adamnán (writing at Iona in the seventh century). Other monasteries are attributed to him, provable and otherwise, but

5. The Cathach manuscript. The oldest surviving Irish manuscript in Latin and traditionally held to have been copied by Colum Cille from a book belonging to St Finnian, about 560 AD. (Courtesy of the Royal Irish Academy)

there is no doubt about his main foundation, at Iona in 563. Sometime in the 560s Colum Cille felt moved to go into exile, following a major upheaval between factions in the church (some say he was actually banished), and he took with him twelve teacher colleagues to the small island of Iona, off the larger island of Mull, Argyllshire. It had been allotted to him by the king of Dal Riata, and there he set up a monastery that was to become the most renowned seat of learning in the Celtic world for the next three centuries. Here, Colum Cille set out on a mission to convert the pagan inhabitants of west and north Scotland to Christianity, among whom were the northern Picts under their chief, Brude, who though not himself known to have accepted the faith, did not prevent his subjects from so doing. Soon, daughter houses of Iona began to be established on the mainland, and by the time of Colum Cille's death in 597, Christianity had taken root in many parts of Scotland. Coincidentally, in that year, an Italian missionary, Augustine, landed in Kent, southern England, and set up a monastery at Canterbury, preparatory to launching the conversion of the Anglo-Saxons of Kent.

The coincidence is of particular interest. Up to the arrival of St Patrick in Ireland, the Irish had been quite unaffected by the Romanization of western Europe and southern Britain, and had developed a culture that was a typical north European culture, foreign to Mediterranean concepts and to Latin order and discipline. Likewise, Ireland was ignored by the waves of invasion of Britain by Jutes, Angles and Saxons in the fifth century, which effectively crushed the roots of Christianity in southern Britain (though not in Wales). These troubles isolated Ireland from western Europe, thus letting its civilization continue to develop in its own special way and to absorb Christianity as it wanted. This enriched the national culture and stimulated enthusiasm for learning, and it may even have tamed the more warlike *tuath* chiefs. Much of the activity of the early Christians was directed to the development of monasticism, as we have seen, and this together with the isolation enabled the Irish to guard their interpretations of Christianity and preserve the scholarship that went with them, and thus to hand down what would otherwise have been lost. By the end of the sixth century Irish Christianity had already begun to be exported: it had gone to Scotland with Colum Cille and to parts of Europe with some of his contemporaries, notably with Columbanus (543–615) who taught first at Bangor in northern Ireland and then went to France to found monasteries at Luxeuil and at Fontaine, in the 580s. Columbanus evolved his own monastic rule. His last and greatest foundation was at Bobbio in northern Italy, in 613. In the interval he had made a remarkable series of tours of Europe to found, or get others to found, monasteries. His influence was wide-ranging, and some of his foundations, particularly Luxeuil and Bobbio, were to become rallying points for later missions from Ireland.

Among those that followed Columbanus, or worked contemporaneously, were St Gall (founder of St Gallen, Switzerland), St Killian (Wurtzburg) and Fursa (Peronne). The exodus of Irish scholar-saints does not, however, mean that there were no other centres of Christianity in western Europe; there were many, particularly in Italy. Ireland's great contribution was the evangelization of north-west Europe. And we must not forget the work of Irish scholars in England, after more than a century of almost total lack of contact between Ireland and the pagan southern British mainland. Aidan, fetched from the Iona community by King Oswald of Northumbria (who had accepted baptism during a period of exile which he is thought to have spent in Iona), set up a church on the island of Lindisfarne in 653 and sent missions into mainland Northumbria and Mercia, sometimes against strong opposition from Penda, king of Mercia. Lindisfarne was to become what one authority has called 'as much a fragment of Ireland abroad as Iona itself'.[9] Pagan England was converted almost to the line of the Chiltern hills inside the thirty years between Aidan's arrival and the summoning of the Synod of Whitby in 664. The conversion was to be challenged less by recalcitrant pagan kings than by ideas coming into southern England after the mission of Augustine to Kent. At Canterbury, he had begun to convert the Kentish people and introduced them to a version of Christianity directly emanating from Rome, and it was different from the Irish version.

One of the differences was over the method of fixing the date of Easter. Another was about the part of a priest's head which should be shaved for the tonsure. The Irish Church did not have episcopal dioceses like elsewhere in the Latin Church, and the role of their bishops was far less important, often limited to sacrament supervision or providing advice to leaders of *tuatha*.

Some of the differences were eventually resolved at the Synod of Whitby, where the Anglo-Saxon bishop of York, Wilfred, prevailed over the Irish delegation led by St Colman from Iona (then also bishop of Lindisfarne), and thereafter Roman customs began gradually to be accepted in the areas originally brought to the faith by the Irish, that is, northern England and Scotland, and eventually in Ireland itself.

This was to have a demoralizing effect upon the Irish Church, however, and one result was a renewal of the missionary activity of the Church abroad. There was a fresh exodus of Irish scholar-saints to Europe, particularly to the north and west, a movement accompanied by the export of the Golden Age of Irish civilization and art. This was not totally an outgoing of native Irish missionaries, but included the coming to Irish monasteries of European students and others anxious to learn and to develop ideas and skills which they could then take back again to Europe.

The Golden Age was a period of high artistic and literary creativity fostered by the blending of Latin with Irish cultures, associated with and emanating from religion, pagan and Christian alike. This creativity was manifested in epic and contemplative poetry, in manuscript illumination, in metalwork (especially gold, silver and iron), in jewellery and enamelling, in stone carving, in woodwork and leatherwork, perhaps even painting of a kind, although there are no surviving examples beyond the illuminations of manuscripts. The *Book of Kells* and the *Book of Durrow* are but two examples of the unique skills we have come to admire in the Irish illuminated manuscripts of the age. The Ardagh Chalice (mid-eighth century) is a glorious example of Irish gold filigree and coloured enamelwork craftsmanship, the Tara Brooch (early eighth century) of silver-gilt with gold filigree panels and decorations of coloured glass and amber is typical no doubt of jewellery worn by high class women of the day. Numerous stone crosses were hewn and carved, and then erected at sites all over Ireland, well illustrated by those at Ahenny, Co. Tipperary (eighth century), Muiredach at Monasterboice (early ninth century), and the slab at Tullyhase, Co. Cork (eighth century). By the ninth century Irish learning and art had won for themselves the widest repute and the highest admiration throughout Europe.

The spread of Irish evangelism and culture went on into the

ninth century, right into the courts of kings and dukes, among them the heirs of Charlemagne. Charles the Bald, king of France (840–77), appointed the Irish scholar and theologian, Johannes Scotus (Eriugena, 813–77) as head of the court school (or chief professor). Fergil (or Vergil), bishop of Salzburg, the Irish born and educated scholar-mathematician, taught that the world was round. Other scholars worked in monasteries and similar centres in France and Germany, building up libraries in Latin. Greek, Irish and other tongues, organizing churches, teaching in schools, and writing, endlessly writing.

The story of Ireland over the four centuries *c*. 400 to *c*. 800 is widely described as having been a happy one, with only few important political or military upheavals. (Of how many other medieval states can that be said?) But the country was not in any sense united. Although the idea of a high king, or *ard rí*, was a dream for some men – and a nightmare for others – in practical terms no one ruler was able in that period to enforce sovereignty over the dozens of other royal family heads. At best, as Curtis has said, the *ard rí* was but the president of a loose union of states. Towards the end of the period this had come to mean little more than Connacht, Leinster, Ulster and Munster, each having several kingdoms with incessantly changing boundaries within. If anything held the Irish together at all, it was Christianity and culture: the abbots, bishops, priests, scholars and artists were not confined by being members of one *tuath* or another from crossing borders and wandering freely about the whole country. Monasteries flourished in all parts, and in many instances played the composite roles of town, hostel, penitentiary, school, university, religious centre and sanctuary. Possibly, Ireland might have developed institutions such as were emerging in England (such as local government, shire courts, fyrds and so forth) and thus moved towards political unity, but the opportunities were drastically curtailed by the beginning of the long period of Viking raids, and when eventually the Vikings and the native Irish did settle down to some kind of coexistence, a different Ireland had emerged.

CHAPTER 3

THE VIKING CONTRIBUTION

Much has been written about the Vikings, not only by themselves through their sagas and by their descendants in the Scandinavian countries, but also by historians from those lands where they made the most impact, particularly England, Wales, Scotland and Ireland. In recent times, the Vikings have rightly been revealed as much more than hordes of savage, illiterate seaborne warriors bent on looting and burning monastic buildings, towns, villages, homes and the farming countryside. Large areas of Europe, coastal and inland (notably, inland north Russia) can safely credit the Vikings with an influential role upon their mainstream development. In some places, for example York in England, recent discoveries of Viking activities and settlement have compelled a rethink of the history of the period there. In Ireland, in some respects it would be difficult to exaggerate the effects of the Viking invasions that began at the end of the eighth century, or the contribution of the Viking settlers to the development of the country.

The Vikings were a group of peoples in Scandinavia (Norway, Denmark, Sweden and parts of Finland) who first entered the stage of European history in the later eighth century. They had of course been in Scandinavia for centuries. The nature of their countryside, mountains, fjords, islands, thick forestation, restricted the space available for farming and it also compelled them to rely upon ships and boats for getting about. They became skilled in a variety of crafts, perhaps most famously as ship-builders. Their early ships were small craft for crossing fjords, hugging coastlines and island hopping, and were shallow and flat-bottomed. In the seventh century they invented the keel and they devised other improvements like the square sail and the side oar blade rudder (mounted on the starboard side near the stern and guided by a straight horizontal tiller). By the eighth century they were building sea-going long ships of high speed and manoeuvrability, powered by sail and by oars (see figure 6).

This technology enabled the Vikings to venture further out to sea, far away from their home coastlines, and its evolution coincided with what seems to have been a major but not yet fully explained population explosion in Scandinavia, one that was shared with most European countries at the time. This explosion led inevitably to a major expansion in trading activity everywhere, and the growing demand for farming land compelled the Vikings to begin searching for new places in which to live, farm

6. The Gokstad ship (courtesy of the University Museum of National Antiquities, Oslo)

and trade. In the eighth century, Norwegian Vikings began to descend as raiders and as colonizers upon Shetland and Orkney, Iceland, Greenland and probably the Hebrides too. Swedes began to open up the Baltic and colonize north Russia, developing direct landward and river trade routes to the heart of the Byzantine Empire, at Constantinople itself, and Danes crossed to England and Wales in search of booty, trade and land. At the very end of the eighth century some of the Norwegian Vikings from Orkney and Shetland, and perhaps the Hebrides and the Isle of Man, started to descend upon Ireland. There were several motives: some were interested in trade, some were looking for new places to settle and farm, and some were bent only on adventure and quick material gain with hit-and-run raids like those being made by their Danish kinsmen upon the English coasts from about 787. For the adventurers the richest pickings were to be found in the monasteries and churches of Ireland.

The first recorded raid on Ireland was a descent upon Lambay Island off Dublin in 795, when the church there was looted and burned: in the same year there were raids on monasteries at Inismurray and Inisbofin on the west coast. And before the year was over, other Norwegian Vikings had carried out the first of several disastrous raids upon St Columba's monastic foundation and community on Iona, off the west of Scotland, and carried of jewelled sacred vessels and ornaments of precious metal, and set fire to buildings. These are the earliest known examples of Viking violence (but they are not the first instances of violence against monasteries in Ireland, for the Irish themselves were guilty of it on numerous occasions in the centuries before 795, see pp. 49–50). Meanwhile, it is very likely that before 795 more peaceful Norwegians had ventured to Ireland in search of land on which to settle.

Settlement in Ireland was not a major problem in the eighth century. There were considerable areas that were uninhabited. Those coming in peace would be likely to have received a welcome from Irish neighbours. The Viking way of life was not very different from that of the Irish, but one key difference was that the Irish were Christian while the Vikings still worshipped a pantheon of pagan gods. The Vikings had much to bring to Ireland in ideas and practical skills. By about 800, several earthwork-defended towns had been founded and were rising fast among the Viking peoples in their own Scandinavian home-lands, notably Birka in Sweden, Hedeby in Denmark and Skiringssal (Kaupang) in Norway, all of which have been exca-vated in some detail. No doubt the Norwegian Vikings who came to Ireland in the last years of the eighth century knew about some of these towns that had been built as commercial centres to handle the rapidly expanding wealth arising from increased trading – and from piracy and looting. In due course, Vikings were to build towns in Ireland, the first towns of any kind to be raised in the island (see pp. 48, 51), and in so doing were to provide the Irish with a whole new conception of the possibilities of international trade, with its obvious benefits. Among the spin-offs were the first home-minted coinage in Ireland, the develop-ment of merchant shipping and innovations in building. They also showed the Irish the advantages of municipal government, for Ireland had no local government resembling the experiments of the Anglo-Saxons in England of the same period.

In the first years of the ninth century there were more raids on the Irish mainland by Viking adventurers. In mentioning them it is fair to state that most of the records of such assaults come from monastic annals, and in the absence of alternative and perhaps less prejudiced sources it is easy to see the accounts as corroboration of the reputation for violence enjoyed by the Vikings, to the exclusion of more constructive activities. Yet the raids did result in the large-scale theft of valuable treasures, for many examples of Irish artefacts have been found in excavations of Viking pirate graves back in the Scandinavian homelands (such as an Irish bronze mount found in a ship grave at Myklebosted in Norway). Some of the raids took place along the north-east coast of Ulster, others along the west coast, edging downwards towards Munster. Iona, meanwhile, was attacked again, in 801, 806 and 807 and in the last year the abbot Cellach decided to take the survivors of the community (nearly seventy monks lost their lives in the 806 raid) back to Ireland, carrying with them the remains of the monastery's treasures. At Kells, in Co. Meath, Cellach established a new monastery with the depleted community and this was consecrated in 814. One of the treasures said to have been carried from Iona to Kells was a splendidly illuminated manuscript of the Gospels, unfinished, and which was continued in the new establishment. It has become world-renowned as the *Book of Kells*.

In the second decade of the ninth century, Vikings raided Umall and Connemara, neither of them containing treasure-filled monasteries, which suggests the raids had different objectives; and in 812 there is a record that the Vikings were seen off by the people of Umall. Others descended upon places in Co. Kerry. We may be talking here about Vikings anxious to settle rather than dash in and loot. Later in the decade Vikings were appearing along the east coast, reaching as far south as Wexford, and Ó Corráin[1] suggests that the Vikings had circled the whole Irish coastline by the 820s. One of the monasteries to receive attention was the island community of Sceilg Mhichíl, a few miles off the Kerry Coast.

From the 830s the character of the raids began to change: the hit-and-run by single ship or small group of ships which, we now know, never penetrated more than a few miles inland, gave way to larger fleet assaults with the intention of settling and establishing communities, though not without the penetration of violence and destruction along the way, in many instances. Sixty Viking ships appeared in the mouth of the river Boyne in 837, and about the same number arrived in the mouth of the Liffey, and the areas beside both rivers were ravaged far and wide. Meanwhile, over on the west in Connacht there was wide-scale devastation, some of it along the banks of the Shannon. In 839 a fleet made its way into Lough Neagh and from there a raiding party ransacked Armagh and other places. This marked the beginning of the deep penetration of the Irish countryside, which was to go on for years. Some of the monasteries, already famous in Europe, fell victim to attack, including Clonfert, Lorrha, Terryglass and the great Clonmacnoise.

The Vikings now began to build military bases and make fortified harbours (longphorts) to protect their ships, and beside which eventually to construct their first permanent settlements. The fortifications were earth walls with wooden palisades and the occasional wooden watch-tower. One early settlement was at Annagassan (Linn Duachaill) on the Louth coast. Another was Dublin (*Dubhlinn*, or Black Pool) whose origins are interestingly documented from a range of artefacts discovered in excavations of ninth-century Viking cemeteries there. Dublin was started in the 840s as a longphort near an Irish monastic establishment, and soon grew into an important town.

How did the Irish respond to the raids? Although the country was divided into halves, the northern nominally under the rule of the Uí Néill at Tara and the southern under the Eóganachta at Cashel in Munster, the response was localized, because the country was still made up of many kingdoms, none owing – or at least giving – allegiance to another. There was no national army and no national leader under whom to rally. Nor was there, to begin with, an organized navy to repel the invaders while still at sea. Worse, the Irish kings had for a long time been fighting one another, and had not been averse to raiding and plundering monasteries themselves in the process. Indeed, it is likely these raids did more damage overall than the whole of the Viking onslaught. They had been doing so at least since the beginning of the seventh century and were still at it at the end of the eighth, when the Vikings began to raid. Ó Corráin says that in the first quarter of the ninth century some 26 plunderings can be attributed to Vikings: in the same period there were 87 acts of violence by the Irish against the Irish. Burning of churches was a common feature of warfare in Irish society. Fedelmid mac Crimthainn, king and bishop of Cashel (820–47), earned the reputation for burning more churches than the Vikings of his time.

As if this were not enough, the monastic communities themselves had often resorted to warfare to resolve differences. In 760, for example, the monastery at Clonmacnoise fought the community of Durrow which sustained some 200 killed and wounded. In 807, communities at Cork fought with those at Clonfert. There were cases where monasteries went to the aid of kings in their dynastic or territorial squabbles with other kings, which demonstrates not only the wealth of the monasteries but also their political influence. By this time it was customary for the office of abbot or bishop to be hereditary, which produced an extra dimension to the struggle for power. Allowances have to be made for the possibility that monastic annalists blamed the Vikings for raids and robberies carried out by Irish kings or even rival monasteries. This is not an attempt to whitewash the Vikings: their own records betray their devotion to fighting without trying to excuse it. But it highlights the fact that Ireland degenerated into anarchy in the eighth and ninth centuries. In the mid-ninth century there are instances of Irish kings and Irish abbots and bishops forming alliances with Viking leaders in the latters' quarrels with other Vikings. At sea, meanwhile, Vikings were fighting another.

The Irish had begun to rally effectively sometime in the 830s and 40s, to try to meet the Viking danger. They were helped by the altered character of the raids. Once the Vikings constructed their longphorts, these in turn became the target for Irish attack. The Irish also began to build fleets of ships to challenge the enemy at sea. The monastic communities also took defensive measures and even went over to the attack. They rebuilt churches and other damaged wooden buildings using stone, and many sites were equipped with a new stone bell-house, or round tower, to act as a watch-tower and place of refuge during a raid. These round towers had their entrance at first-floor level, accessible by ladder which could be pulled up in time of danger. Remains of about 100 have been traced, though only a few are standing to any great height, among them Nendrum, Co. Down, Devenish, Co. Fermanagh (a fine example) and St Kevin's at Glendalough, Co. Wicklow.

Among the more successful military counter-attacks was a rout of the Vikings at Skreen in 848 by Máel Sechnaill I, king of Tara, who slew 700 Vikings and then went on to devastate the new Viking settlement at Dublin. This king, one of the few to be described in the annals as king of Ireland, spent much of his time fighting with a succession of other Irish kings, particularly the Eóganacht rulers of Munster. He died in 862, leaving the Uí Néill kingdom of Tara in a strong position.

The warfare between the Irish and the Vikings and the inter-tribal squabbling continued in tandem to the end of the ninth century and beyond, but they went hand in hand with a rapid blending between the two peoples, through intermarriage at many levels and through the acceptance by most Vikings of Christianity. Members of the families of Irish kings and dynastic abbots and bishops married into Viking families (Olaf, one of the Norse kings of Dublin, married the daughter of the king of the northern Uí Néill, Áed Findliath). The Viking settlements found themselves drawn into the disputes between the various Irish kingdoms. There was cultural mingling, and the Vikings began to adopt the Celtic Irish language as theirs, with a liberal

7. The Round Tower, Glendalough (courtesy of the Irish Tourist Board)

sprinkling of Scandinavian words absorbed in it, which are still in use today. In the last years of the ninth century and in the early tenth century, more Viking towns emerged, including Waterford, Wexford, Wicklow, Limerick, Cork and Carlingford.

51

Early in the tenth century there was a renewal of large-scale Viking raids on Ireland. This time the raiders came not from Scandinavia but from Scotland and northern England, made up of warriors from families long established in those parts. Many areas of Ireland were attacked, and the worst affected area appears to have been Munster, which was penetrated deeply in several sectors. some Irish kings came to the aid of other Irish kings. Niall Glúndub of Tara had some success against the Vikings but in 919, he was slain along with other Irish kings helping him in a skirmish with the Vikings of Dublin who were by then a powerful Norse kingdom, with lands from Drogheda down to Wicklow, and who also had interests in the kingdom of York in England. For several years the Dublin Vikings had things their own way, for they had built up considerable military strength which they made available to other Vikings in difficulties elsewhere. But gradually the power of the Dublin Vikings was worn down, as native kings like Donnchad of Tara, Niall's successor, and Muirchertach mac Néill of the northern Uí Néill combined to attack them in Dublin and managed to set fire to the town and the ships more than once. In 944 another Tara king joined with a Leinster king and attacked Dublin. Two other main centres of Viking power with which the Irish had to contend were Limerick and Waterford. The whole period is a confused picture of violent raids, shifting alliances, sea battles and endless anarchy. Yet ordinary life went on. In the Viking areas better farming techniques were developed, and the new towns were becoming centres of great trading and commercial activity, creating international markets for a variety of commodities such as textiles, wine, wool, leather products, greatly influencing the economy of Ireland as a whole. Their superior river and sea craft made trade movement between Ireland and Scandinavia and the western countries of Europe much easier. When the Viking city of Limerick was sacked by Mathghamain, king of the Dál Cais (see p. 53) in 968, they [the raiders] carried off their jewels and their best property, and their saddles beautiful and foreign, their gold and their silver; their beautifully woven cloth of all colours and of all kinds. The fort and the good town they reduced to a cloud of smoke and to red fire afterwards, as is required in an Ó Briain text of the twelfth century. This gives an inkling of the wealth and property in a Viking city of the time. It was in the trading and commercial world that many Viking words came to be adopted into the Irish language, like *margad* for market. At this time coinage began to appear, initially as English pennies, but before the end of the century as local coinage minted in Dublin. Some examples have survived, such as those of the last decade of the tenth century (now in the British Museum).

One of the biggest single factors in the success of the Vikings in Ireland must be the state of disorder and confusion they found in the Irish monarchy. There was practically no cooperation, no understanding of alliance, between the four main kingdoms (Ulster, Connacht, Leinster, Munster), or between the many sub-kingdoms nominally owing allegiance to one or other of the four. Indeed, few Irishmen grasped the concept of national unity. The high kingship, which in theory carried the right to call out a national army in time of danger, was seldom recognized in any one person by everyone else. The role was not an hereditary one, even though the Uí Néills who, from Tara, ruled much of the north and some of the east, had some claim and did from time to time assert it. Máel Sechnaill (*c*. 840–62) of Tara was recognized for part of his reign, and after his death his successors continued to claim similar recognition. That they did so seems in part due to success in overawing the Eóganacht kings of Munster over a long period. The Eóganacht power had in any case been in decline through the spreading of Viking settlements in Munster and the failure of the Eóganacht king stands out in this period, Cellachán, who ruled from Cashel from *c*. 936 to 954, but even he spent some time as a captive of the Uí Néill.

In the second half of the tenth century, a new power emerged in Ireland, one which was eventually to do more to contain and reduce Viking power and influence than any hitherto, and that was Dál Cais in west Munster. This was a small kingdom situated astride the river Shannon in Co. Clare, once part of the over-kingdom of Connacht and later one of the Munster kingdoms. In about 953 Mathghamain succeeded his brother as king of Dál Cais and seems to have made his mark very quickly with an alliance with Cellachán of Cashel. Ten years later, he marched against the Eóganacht capital and took it. In 967 Mathghamhain defeated the Vikings of Limerick at Sulchóid, and captured their city (it is this capture that is described in the extract above, p. 52). He won more successes but in 976 was murdered as the result of some treachery on the part of seemingly friendly neighbouring rulers, and the Dál Cais kingship passed to his brother Brian, who was destined to become the greatest name in all Irish history.

The years 976 to 1014 are among the most dramatic in the earlier history of Ireland. They saw a steady rise upward in the fortunes of Brian himself, of Dál Cais, of Munster and finally of Ireland. He seems to have had just the sort of characteristics of a national leader that Ireland so badly needed yet had neither found nor even sought before. What we know of him beyond isolated details of his achievements is extremely sketchy and often unreliable. We do not know what he looked like, we are not even sure about his date of birth, which had been given variously as mid-920s (which would make him almost ninety at the battle of Clontarf in 1014) or the early is more probable. He has loomed larger and larger since his death, which itself was dramatic, his reputation encrusted with a mix of legend and myth, as may be expected when a national leader significantly changes the course of the history of the nation. Brian's story, as far as we can trace it, is a stirring one, that we may only summarize here.

Dál Cais had already begun to have ambitions to dominate Munster in Mathghamhain's time. When he succeeded Mathghamhain, Brian had a larger aim, no less than to secure the high kingship of all Ireland. He wanted not the empty title held on and off by the Uí Néill ruling (or not ruling, as the case may be) from Tara, but an undisputed role with which to make real the concept of national unity and put the Viking presence in Ireland under national control. He began by defeating Ivar, Viking ruler of Limerick, dealt with those kings who had killed his brother, and proceeded to set himself up as king of all Munster at Cashel, displacing the last of the Eóganacht kings. Meanwhile, in 980, the Uí Néill high king, Máel Sechnaill II, ruling at Tara, won a major victory against the Viking Dubliners, and then, viewing with some alarm the rising strength of Brian, attacked the latter's homeland of Dál Cais. Brian retaliated with a series of attacks upon Uí Néill territories in Connacht, both by land and by means of ships up the Shannon. He captured the king of Osraige, and later invaded the kingdom of Meath. Then in 988 he again took ships up the Shannon, ravaging Connacht and Meath, and in 991 made his first assault on Leinster.

Over the next years, the struggle between Brian and Máel Sechnaill continued, with varying fortunes, until in 997 the two met to agree to divide Ireland between them. A year later, the agreement was holding firmly enough for the two to combine against a new threat from the Dublin Vikings, complicated by a revolt by the king of Leinster. This was the earliest sign of the kingdom of Leinster's tendency to refuse to accept any over-lordship, from whatever quarter it was presented, a tendency to be repeated several times right through to the twelfth century. The revolt this time was sternly crushed by Brian at the battle of Glenn Máma in 999, and Dublin was attacked. Its king, Sitric, was driven out and only allowed to return after agreeing to pay tribute and swear allegiance.

By the year 1000 Brian had decided to make a bid for the sole high kingship, and in 1002, after various manoeuvres he persuaded Máel Sechnaill to yield the title, symbolically at Tara, and he did so without resort to arms. It was to take Brian another four years to establish the claim and to enforce authority over the whole country, and even then there were one or two king-doms that swore but did not honour allegiance, and these had to be coerced. Yet by 1005 Brian had done more than any previous king to make good a claim to the high kingship.

In 1005 Brian made a progress round much of the north and on the way visited Armagh. There he distributed gold to the church and formally signalled his endorsement of Armagh's arch-bishop as head of the Irish Church. While there, too, he caused to be added to the ninth century *Book of Armagh* a colophon describing him as Imperator Scottorum (Emperor of the Irish). Clearly he saw himself in that role and had proved it by his ability to force many kings to pay him tribute (his surname, Bóroime (Boru), means Taker of Tributes). Yet it is one thing to call yourself Emperor of Ireland and quite another to make your writ run supreme throughout the land. Much of the remainder of his reign was absorbed with consolidating his position, exacting further tribute, suppressing revolt, accommodating or containing the Vikings. But it left time also for a number of more peaceful and constructive tasks which can be properly ascribed to his initiative or sponsorship.

His panegyrists likened him unto Charlemagne, even to the great Caesar himself. We may not wish to go all the way along that road, but the events of his career do provide some proof of a long-cherished ambition to bring order and continuity of government to Ireland on something like a national scale. Certainly, poets and historians of the eleventh and twelfth centuries believed it and it cannot be solely because they wanted to but had no evidence. There are indications of the beginnings of an artistic and literary renaissance in his long reign, for which he is entitled to some responsibility. He has been credited, probably fairly, with a hand in rebuilding, or helping the cause of, monasteries and schools, and in improving communications in the country. There seems to have been a reduction in Viking activity and this must be a positive factor. In the ecclesiastical field he presided over a recovery in the fortunes of the church and its role in society, especially in Munster, doing so partly through the agency of relatives appointed as abbots and bishops. One brother became abbot of Killaloe, a cousin succeeded that brother there, and a nephew became abbot of Terryglass.

By 1012, when Brian was over seventy (or over eighty five if we take the earlier birth date), the precarious unity he had been constructing was beginning to show signs of strain. A number of upsets between kings in the north and a resurgence of trouble with the Dublin Vikings destabilized the situation, and there was much marching and counter-marching for several months. Máel Sechnaill appealed to Brian to assist in quelling the Dubliners who had formed an alliance with Máel Mórda, king of Leinster. Late in 1013, Brian and Máel Sechnaill gathered their forces near Dublin ready to blockade the town and force a surrender, but the city held and Brian altered the strategy. The Dubliners, under their king Sitric, now decided, perhaps as a last desperate throw, to appeal for help from kinsmen abroad, such as Sigurd, earl of Orkney, and Brodar and Ospak, chiefs in the Isle of Man. They responded, and some time in April 1014 the Vikings and the Leinstermen were ready for confrontation.

For some reason we do not know, at this critical stage Brian and Máel Sechnaill fell out, and the latter withdrew his army and returned north. Brian was thus deprived of a significant part of his military strength. He must also have been concerned that once again Leinster chose to support the Vikings. Nonetheless, he felt he had enough forces with which to face his enemies. Towards the end of the month the opposing armies drew up at

Clontarf, close to the sea in Dublin Bay, and on 23rd which was Good Friday, the battle began, 'a bloody struggle of men who fought on foot.' Although Brian was too old to take active command on the day (this fell to his son Murchad), he watched from a guarded enclosure on the sidelines. The struggle, probably the greatest so far fought on Irish soil, lasted all day and in it many leaders on both side fell, including Murchad, and on the enemy side Máel Mórda, Sigurd and Brodar. But the greatest casualty of all was old Brian himself, struck down with an axe by a fleeing Viking who caught sight of him in the enclosure, his guards apparently not at the time protecting him. Another of Brian's sons, Donnchad, led his men in hot pursuit of the enemy who had broken and fled from the field, some towards the ships in Dublin Bay, others to find refuge wheresoever they could find it.

The Irish royal forces had won a resounding victory, but the sweetness of it was expunged in every breast by the death of the king. Sadly his body was borne in state to Armagh where it was buried 'with great ceremony'.

The victory at Clontarf has come down through the centuries as the final and lasting national triumph of the forces of Ireland over the power of the Vikings, achieved because for once the kingdoms of Ireland combined to bring it about. But it was not quite like that. Brian's army was composed chiefly of loyal Munstermen. Many other regional forces remained neutral. Máel Sechnaill was sulking in the north. The men of north Leinster were on the enemy side, and it was they more than any other who were defeated that day, losing their king, Máel Mórda. The Dublin Vikings and their erstwhile allies from across the sea were no match for the forces of Munster, and it was really a victory of Munstermen. Yet the victory did stop once and for all any attempt by the Vikings to conquer Ireland. And if the victory was not all that legend cracks it up to be, we cannot ignore that the sagas of the Vikings themselves recorded it as a victory for Ireland: as the writer of one of them put it, 'Brian fell, but won at last'.

CHAPTER 4

THE COMING

OF THE

NORMANS

Clontarf was a sad victory. Not only Brian himself, but his son Murchad, who had led Brian's army, was killed, and many Irish nobles alongside him. Yet Viking ambition was stopped from that day, the Vikings contenting themselves thereafter with developing the towns they had founded at Dublin, Cork, Wexford, Waterford and Limerick, and the ports of the eastern seaboard. The Vikings set up the shops and trading posts which the Irish were not interested in providing for themselves and served Ireland peacefully as merchants, seamen and farmers. The Viking towns became independent, self-sufficient republics, cut off from each other by land and communicating only by sea. They made alliances with local kings but gave no allegiance except, occasionally, to the high king.

Brian had united almost the whole of Ireland in his fight against the Vikings. After Clontarf, this political unity fell apart. Neither of Brian's two surviving sons, Tadg and Donnchad, proved strong enough to take over the high kingship and it reverted to that Máel Sechnaill whom Brian had ousted. After Máel Sechnaill's death in 1022, it became little more than an honorary position, the real power belonging to the seven provincial kings. Brian had usurped the high kingship for the best of reasons, but he had set a bad example, and during the next 150 years the high kingship went to whoever could take it. Between 1070 and 1130, Brian's Munster produced two high kings, Leinster two and Connacht one. A new term, 'king with opposition', became current, to describe those high kings who could get a majority among the provincial kings but not the support, or submission, of all of them.

Nevertheless there were islands of peace in 'swordland' – those lands which had been won by the sword. The Viking wars had disrupted the artistic and spiritual life of the monasteries, and Irish craftsmanship had, for a time, fallen behind that of Europe, but in the eleventh and twelfth centuries Irish civilization enjoyed a renaissance. Beautiful illuminated manuscripts were inscribed once more, new poetry was written and the kings became patrons of the arts, suggesting new works and making gifts to the centres where they were made. The great processional Cross of Cong was made in Co. Mayo between 1123 and 1136 to enshrine a relic of the true cross; in 1134 the finest of Ireland's Romanesque churches, Cormac's chapel on the Rock of Cashel, was dedicated; it forms part of a complex of buildings crowning the summit of a rocky outcrop. Another beautiful Romanesque building, the Nun's church at Clonmacnoise, was handsomely endowed in the 1150s.

But the monasteries had changed. The rigours of the old monastic rules of Colum Cille and St Brénaind were forgotten. Many of the monks kept concubines and lived with their families in the countryside around their monasteries, treating them as colleges, or centres of culture and devotion, which they might visit from time to time. In an age when other countries were founding universities – the universities of Bologna, Oxford and Paris were established in the eleventh and twelfth centuries – the Irish, who had had an international reputation for scholarship, felt no urge to follow suit. They already had centres of learning in their monasteries.

The Irish Church was unhappy about the laxity of the monks. In 1139 Máel Sechnaill (better known as St Malachy), the bishop of Armagh, stayed with one of the greatest of European churchmen, St Bernard, abbot of Clairvaux, and poured out his complaints. The Irish Church was too often subordinated to lay princes, who quartered their troops on religious houses; monasteries were in the hands of lay abbots, called coarbs, appointed from priestly families on the same hereditary principle as poets and brehons – they took precedence over those in holy orders, even the bishops themselves; church services were seldom held, and when they were, there was little preaching and no singing

or chanting; and the laity, who paid no tithes, were quite unin-
structed in the Christian faith. Ireland, St Malachy told St
Bernard, was Christian in name but in reality heathen.

The abbey of Clairvaux belonged to the Cistercian order, which
followed an austere and simple rule. St Malachy was much
impressed by it; Cistercians established their monasteries in wild
and lonely places, which reminded him of the white martyrdom,
or self-imposed exile, of early Irish monks, and they tilled the
fields themselves, as Colum Cille had urged his followers to do.
St Malachy felt that Cistercian monks might lead Irish monasticism back to its true and ancient path, and he left four of his
party behind at Clairvaux to learn the Cistercian rule. St Bernard,
for his part, sent a group of Cistercian monks to Ireland. In
1142 they started building a Cistercian abbey at Mellifont, near
Drogheda, which, before long, had five daughter houses.

At the same time St Malachy speeded up the reforms which
had already been begun. He organized bishoprics and parishes.
He had stone churches built and introduced singing into church
services. The holy offices were conducted regularly and the laity
began to be instructed. Although St Malachy died in 1148, worn
out at fifty-four, his work came to fruition in 1152, when the
Synod of Kells was convened at Mellifont. It was the greatest
gathering ever held of the Irish Church, and the pope sent a
cardinal to it, John Paparo, as papal legate. Bishops, clergy and
many lay princes watched while the cardinal invested the
primate, the archbishop of Armagh, and three other archbishops,
of Cashel, Tuam and Dublin, with the *pallium*, a lamb's wool
collar emblematic of their office; the Irish Church was at last
linked directly with Rome. It only needed a period of peace,
stability and good government to consolidate the progress made.

But the country fell into violence and disorder. Alliances
shifted, hostages were given and seized, fierce rivalries broke
out, churches and homesteads were burned, and men from the
different kingdoms fought and raided one another. Kings
adopted the cruel Viking custom of blinding their hostages and
rivals. As a blind chieftain could not rule, a king could eliminate
a rival by blinding instead of killing him, and so avoid putting
murder on his conscience. Toirrdelbach Ua Conchobair, who
became high king in 1119, had been the only ruler after Brian
Bóroime to impose some semblance of unity upon Ireland. But

he had not brought peace. He had been simply the most ferocious of the kings of the time – the strongest swimmer in the tides of war. Then in 1151, in the midst of all the turmoil, an event of apparent insignificance took place. Diarmait Mac Murchada, the king of Leinster, carried off Derbforgaill, the wife of Tigernán Ua Ruairk, the king of Bréifne (where Cavan and Leitrim are now). The next year Derbforgaill was back under her husband's roof; a trivial escapade seemed to be over; but as a result of it, everything was to change.

Tigernán could not forgive the insult he had suffered. He conceived an implacable hatred of the younger Diarmait and years later, in 1166, he saw his chance for revenge. Diarmait had allied himself with Muirchertach Mac Lochlainn, who had succeeded Toirrdelbach as high king, and Muirchertach had earned the revulsion of the Irish kings and chieftains by treacherously blinding the king of Ulidia, although he had already submitted to Muirchertach and had his submission guaranteed by other princes. In the furore that followed, Toirrdelbach's son Ruadrí Ua Conchobair won the high kingship, Diarmait Mac Murchada lost his patron, Tigernán attacked him, the Ostmen[1] of Dublin and various Leinster chieftains, who normally supported him, joined in the attack and Diarmait was, in effect, driven out of his kingdom. On 1st August 1166 he took the step which has blackened his name for ever. Taking his marriageable daughter Aífe with him, he sailed to the port of Bristol, which was already familiar to him, to seek the aid, in the form of an army, of Henry II of England.

One hundred years earlier, England had been conquered by the Normans, aggressive cousins of those Vikings who had made such inroads into Ireland. The Normans had been Northmen, that is, Scandinavians, mainly from Norway, whose hunger for new lands and opportunities had led them, in the ninth and tenth centuries, to northern France, where they had wrested a duchy from the native aristocracy and then adopted the French language, manners and customs. They had advanced upon England because they had many ties of blood and culture with the Danish settlements already there, but the possession of England had not satisfied them. Within five years of the

Conquest, they had sent military expeditions southwards to the Mediterranean, to capture ports in southern Italy, establish a Norman kingdom in Sicily and even reach the Balkans.

Yet the Irish do not seem to have feared the restless energy of the Normans. Irishmen travelled abroad constantly as churchmen, missionaries and scholars. They visited Rome and the courts in France and Germany, where they must have heard tales of Norman ambition and military prowess. They visited Canterbury, too, and watched the Norman takeover in neighbouring England. When they returned to Ireland, they probably talked of what they had seen and heard to their kings and chieftains, who did not travel abroad themselves. Perhaps Irish churchmen kept aloof from politics when they travelled; perhaps they were too unworldly to recognize political dangers. Or perhaps the Irish kings, deeply embroiled in constant internal warfare, ignored such warnings as they were given; they may have felt the danger, to which their neighbour had succumbed, would pass them by, just as the Romans had so many centuries before. Or perhaps the Irish, both churchmen and kings, had so little sense of nationhood they did not think an invasion would matter.

Diarmait spent about a fortnight in Bristol, staying with a rich and influential merchant there who knew Henry well. Then he set off to find him. Henry was not only king of England; he ruled more of France, including Normandy, than the French king himself, and it was early in 1167 when Diarmait came up with him in Aquitaine. Henry greeted Diarmait with his usual bluff amiability, made him gifts and, in return for Diarmait's allegiance, gave him permission to recruit help from among his barons. Henry could not lose by the arrangement. He had not promised to help Diarmait personally, but if Diarmait found enough support among Henry's vassals to win his kingdom of Leinster back, Henry, as his overlord, would have a foothold in Ireland. He gave Diarmait an open letter, addressed to 'all his liegemen, English, Normans, Welsh and Scots', which read: 'know you that we have taken Diarmait, prince of the men of Leinster, into the bosom of our grace and goodwill. Wherefore, too, whosoever within the bounds of our dominions shall be willing to lend him aid, as being our vassal and liegeman, in the recovery of his own, let him know that he has our favour and permission to that end.' Then, the possible annexation of Ireland so handily accomplished, Henry let the matter of Diarmait and Diarmait's kingdom slip from his mind.

Diarmait went back to Bristol and looked for help. He had Henry's letter read out in public several times, and made liberal offers of land and bounty. For a while, there was no response. Then Richard Fitzgilbert de Clare, the Norman earl of Pembroke, generally known as Strongbow, came forward. He was out of favour at court, restless, discontented, and eager for an adventure like the Irish one. He obtained Henry's written consent to it, Diarmait offered him the hand of his daughter Aífe in marriage and the deal was done. Next, Diarmait went into South Wales to recruit the help of Strongbow's kinsmen, the sons and grandsons of Nesta, a Welsh princess, whose descendants are known collectively as the Geraldines. Two of them, Maurice Fitzgerald

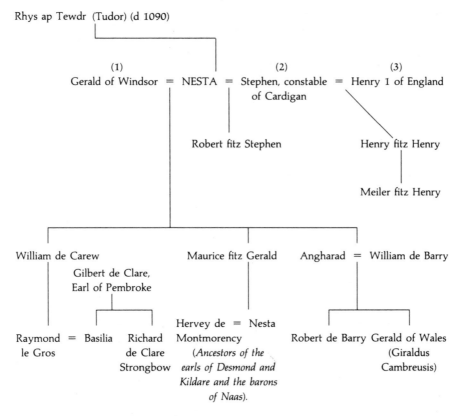

8. Family tree of the Geraldines

and Robert Fitzstephen, agreed to bring their forces to Ireland the following spring in return for the Viking town of Wexford, which Diarmait considered owed him allegiance, and some land outside it.

Diarmait did not wait for his Norman supporters. Taking a handful of mercenaries with him, he sailed for Ireland in the autumn of 1167 and lay low in a monastery at his capital, Ferns, for the winter, when he was not being attacked by the high king, Ruadrí Ua Conchobair, or Tigernán Ua Ruairc, until on May 1, 1169, Fitzstephen arrived at Bannow, near Wexford, with 40 knights and about 400 archers, some of them mounted. Maurice de Prendergast, one of a colony of Flemish mercenaries settled in Wales by Henry I, arrived the following day with 200 more men. Diarmait joined them outside Wexford with 500 Irishmen, and together they assaulted the walls. The next day the city fell and Diarmait gave it to Fitzstephen, as he had promised. The chastened Ostmen supplied a contingent to Diarmait's army, many of the Leinster clans returned to their allegiance and Diarmait made several more or less successful forays against those who still held out. He made his peace with the high king and gave him one of his sons as a hostage; he is supposed also to have agreed in secret not to bring any more foreigners into Ireland and to send Fitzstephen and Prendergast away again. But then Maurice Fitzgerald arrived, eager for action. Diarmait ravaged the country around Dublin with him and sent Fitzstephen off to Limerick, to help his son-in-law bring down the high king.

Diarmait, restored as king of Leinster, aspired towards the high kingship himself. He was still owed help by his daughter's betrothed, Strongbow. He wrote to the Welsh–Norman earl, reminding him of his two-year-old promise, and in May, 1170, Strongbow sent Raymond Le Gros, one of the Geraldines, ahead of him with about ninety men. They landed at a rocky headland called Baginbun on the south coast of Wexford, and encamped behind a huge double rampart, some 700 feet long and 40 feet wide, which cut them off from the hostile mainland. Before long an army of Ostmen from Waterford and Irish from Munster, perhaps two thousand of them,[2] advanced upon the small Norman force. But the Normans were quick, disciplined and ingenious; they stampeded a herd of cattle, kept as a food supply behind the ramparts, towards their attackers, whose foremost

9. The double rampart at Baginbun (courtesy of the Commissioners of Public Works in Ireland)

ranks were routed, and then fell upon them, killing several hundred and taking seventy prisoners. But seventy prisoners was too many; the tiny band of Normans could not hold them. With ruthless cruelty they broke their limbs and threw them over the cliffs and into the sea.

At the last moment, when Strongbow was about to embark, messengers came from Henry forbidding the expedition. Too late – Strongbow had made his plans, collected his men and set his sights on Ireland. Two hundred knights and a thousand archers took ship with him at Milford Haven and landed near Waterford on 23rd August, an event described prophetically in the Irish *Annals of Ulster* as 'the beginning of the woes of Ireland'. Two days later, aided by Raymond, he took Waterford by assault. Diarmait brought Aífa to him and their marriage was solemnized in Waterford cathedral. The immigrant Normans were developing family ties with an Irish princely house. They had come to stay.

Leaving a garrison to hold Waterford, Diarmait and Strongbow marched on Dublin. The high king, Ruaidrí Ua Conchobair, and Tigernán Ua Ruairc were encamped at Clondalkin, less than ten miles from the city, and the usual approaches from the south had been plashed: the branches of trees had been bent and tied across the paths through the thick forest that surrounded the city, and ambushes laid. But Diarmait led Strongbow and his army over the mountains from Glendalough and they reached Dublin unopposed. While the Ostmen were negotiating with them about a surrender, Raymond Le Gros and another Geraldine, Miles de Cogan, rushed the walls and captured the city. The high king thought the Ostmen had deserted him, and left Dublin to its fate. The most important town in the country, the gateway to Ireland for any army from Wales or England, was in foreign hands. Strongbow consolidated his position, while Diarmait took the opportunity of raiding Bréifne. Then in May 1171 Diarmait died, aged sixty-one, at Ferns.

When Diarmait betrothed his daughter Aífa to Strongbow, he may, or may not, have promised Strongbow that he could inherit the kingdom of Leinster after his death. Under the feudal law of the Normans, such an inheritance would have been perfectly possible, and Strongbow assumed the kingship. But a king could not name his successor under Irish law. When a king died, his successor had to be elected from amongst eligible members of the royal family, 'a stranger in sovereignty' was unacceptable and the succession could never pass through a woman. Diarmait had no eligible sons left; one had been blinded in 1168 and another, given as a hostage, killed. But he had a nephew, Muirchertach, and the people of Leinster rallied to him.

Not only Muirchertach and the men of Leinster but people from all over Ireland were by now seriously alarmed by the presence of the Normans, as were the Viking cousins of the Dublin Ostmen, who had settled in the Isle of Man and the Western Isles of Scotland. During the summer of 1171 Dublin was besieged by land and sea; Viking ships lay in Dublin harbour and a small force of Vikings and Ostmen camped outside the city and attacked the Normans. The high king brought men from his own kingdom of Connacht and also summoned the kings of Ulaid, Airgialla and Midhe with their hostings. Tigernán Ua Ruairc came from Bréifne and Muirchertach from Leinster. Altogether, Ruaidrí had an army of perhaps 30,000 to bring against the Normans.

The Irish were brave but indolent soldiers, still armed, as they had been at Clontarf, with spears, throwing darts and battleaxes, the short bow and age-old slings and stones. They still wore no armour and fought as a horde, in disarray. Their leaders did not know how to assault the thick stone walls of a town, so they simply placed their men around Dublin and prepared to sit it out, starving the Normans into submission. But the Normans had the most advanced military techniques in Europe. Strongbow had no more than 200 knights, 400 other mounted men and 1,500 archers and foot soldiers in Dublin, but they were highly trained, equipped with the latest weapons and effectively armoured with helmets and chain-mail. And they disliked being cooped up behind city walls. When two months had passed and they were running seriously short of food, some 600 of them slipped quietly out of the beleaguered city in three divisions, spread out and attacked the flank of the Irish army. The Irish were taken completely by surprise; the high king and some hundreds of his followers were caught bathing in the river. And the great besieging army was totally routed.

Henry II watched these events with some anxiety. Strongbow and the Geraldines were too successful: suppose Strongbow were to conquer Ireland, become high king and abandon his allegiance? Henry certainly did not want a strong and separate Norman-led kingdom off the Welsh coast; his whole empire would be threatened by that. Earlier in the year, before Diarmait's death, he had ordered all his subjects in Ireland to return home before Easter on pain of forfeiture and perpetual banishment. In response he had received a letter from Strongbow, carried by Raymond Le Gros, protesting that all he had acquired in Ireland was through the royal favour. But Henry was not satisfied. He assembled an impressive force, with 500 knights and about 3,000 archers, portable wooden towers for sieges and castle building, and vast quantities of provisions, and then summoned Strongbow to him. Strongbow obeyed the summons and renewed his oath of fealty to Henry; he was always prudent enough to maintain his allegiance. Henry took the best of Strongbow's conquest for himself – Dublin, the eastern coastal strip and all the coastal towns and fortresses – and confirmed Strongbow in possession of Leinster. Then he set out for Ireland with his

10. Strongbow's tomb in Christchurch Cathedral, Dublin (courtesy of the Irish Tourist Board)

army to claim the homage of all the kings and chieftains of Ireland.

By what right did Henry, a foreign monarch, claim the homage of Irish kings?

The story is a long one. Centuries earlier, in 601, the pope of the time had given St Augustine, who was archbishop of Canterbury and a primate of England, authority over all the Celtic Churches in Britain, which included the Church in Ireland. The Irish Church had, nevertheless, developed independently, although the Vikings, as they became converted to Christianity, had sent their bishops to Canterbury for consecration. Since 1140, however, the Vikings had been looking increasingly to the Irish Church to consecrate their bishops and in 1152, when Ireland obtained her own primate at the Synod of Kells, the Viking republics had decided they need send their bishops to Canterbury no longer.

The invasion of Ireland was suggested to Henry a year later, in 1155, when he held a council at Winchester. It was probably the archbishop of Canterbury, Theobald, who brought the subject up; his power was being curtailed by the rise in status of the Irish Church. 'But,' wrote the chronicler, Robert de Torigny, 'since (Henry's) mother the empress Matilda opposed it, the expedition was for the time being set aside.' Henry had only succeeded to his throne in 1154, England had been misgoverned for years by his predecessor, Stephen, and he had Normandy and other lands to rule as well. His hands were full. He may have found the empress Matilda's objection a handy excuse – he may even have put her up to it.

However it was, sometime during the next ten months, that is between November 1155 and July 1156, archbishop Theobald's secretary, John of Salisbury, spent three months with the pope in southern Italy. The pope was Adrian 1V, the only Englishman ever to become pope, and John of Salisbury had known him for many years. They were very good friends. 'Adrian confessed in public and in private that he loved me above all mortals,' John of Salisbury wrote later. 'He would have me drink out of his cup and eat out of his dish.' Pope Adrian may already have sent Henry a Papal bull, or official letter, called by historians the bull *Laudabiliter*,[3] inviting him to 'go into the island of Ireland for the purpose of subjecting that people to the laws and to root out the weeds of vice'. John of Salisbury asked him to grant Henry hereditary rights over Ireland. 'At my solicitation,' John of Salisbury wrote, 'he gave and granted Ireland to Henry II, the illustrious king of England, to hold by hereditary right.' Then he explained how the grant was to be made. 'He sent also by me a ring of gold, with the best of emeralds set therein, wherewith the investiture might be made.' In medieval times, when so many people were illiterate, it was common to offer a ring, a banner, or a sword as a token of contract. If the ring, or whatever it might be, was accepted, so was the land, or right, or status, or contract it betokened.[4] 'That same ring was ordered to be, and is still, in the public treasury,' John of Salisbury went on. Henry had accepted the hereditary grant of Ireland, which is generally known as Adrian's Donation, whether he meant to do anything about it or not.

But how could the pope grant Ireland, the land of a free people, to Henry II, king of England?

The answer lies in a highly dubious document, entitled the *Donation of Constantine*, which was fabricated either by a priest in the Curia, or a Frankish monk, in the eighth century or there-abouts for the convenience of the papacy. The Constantine referred to in the title was Constantine the Great, who ruled the Roman empire from 306 to 337 and moved the seat of empire from Rome to Byzantium, which was re-named Constantinople in his honour.

Constantine was the first Roman emperor to become a Christian, and the *Donation* describes how he gave his palace in Rome, the Lateran, to the papacy, 'together with the city of Rome and all the provinces, districts and cities of Italy and of the Western Region.' As Ireland had never been part of the Roman empire, Constantine had not been able to give Ireland away. But, the *Donation* went on, Constantine had also bestowed upon the Church 'our bounty. . . in India, Greece, Asia, Thrace, Africa, Italy and divers islands.' The list went far beyond the bounds of the Roman empire; it covered the whole of the known world.

Churchmen did not quite believe in the *Donation of Constantine* – John of Salisbury referred to islands which were 'said to belong' to the Church – but from the tenth century onwards popes made increasing use of it to bolster their authority and pope Adrian made a direct reference to it in the bull *Laudabiliter*. 'For, as your excellency acknowledges,' he wrote to Henry, 'there is no doubt that Ireland and all the islands upon which Christ, the sun of righteousness, has shone and which have accepted the lessons of the Christian faith, are subject to the law of St Peter and of the holy Roman church.' And that statement, even now, rings true; popes did have spiritual authority over the whole of western Christendom. In the eleventh and twelfth centuries, they established the superiority of spiritual over temporal power and regarded kings, even the greatest, as their vassals. Popes encouraged (though they could not command) Christian kings to do their bidding, and kings commonly sought the approval of the Vatican for their aggressive actions. Kings often disguised aggressive war, or war made for personal aggrandisement, as holy wars, or crusades, to bring the heathen or wrongdoers to Christ. William the Conqueror sought a licence from the pope for the invasion of England and received it in the form of a consecrated banner and a ring, not 'set with the best of emeralds' but, better still, with a hair of St Peter in it, and a letter urging him to 'reform the spiritual state of the misguided islanders'[5].

Henry II was following precedent. He wanted land; though his empire was vast, he had four troublesome sons who would all require kingdoms, and he could not let an opportunity for licensed conquest, in the name of the Lord, slip through his fingers.

St Malachy's descriptions, given in deep distress, of the unChristian laity of Ireland had been carried to the Vatican and, even though many reforms had been accomplished, the reputation of the Irish Church was still low; four archbishops had indeed received the prestigious *pallium*, but episcopal and parochial organization remained weak. The monasticism which St Malachy and all early Irish churchmen had loved and promoted was out of favour in the Vatican, and many of the Church's leaders felt that St Malachy's reforms, including, as they did, the establishment of so many Cistercian monasteries, were on the wrong lines. Irish bishops felt their role was merely to bless and ratify, whereas the Vatican wished them to instruct, guide and rule. The Church's teaching on marriage in particular was widely rejected in Ireland; the Irish still had a pre-Christian concept of marriage as a civil contract, easily made and easily broken, and when the Church not only required marriage to be for life, but forbade marriages between third cousins, or the third cousin of a deceased husband or wife, it became almost impossible for people living in small rural communities, amidst a most complex web of family relationships, to make a Christian marriage. So, while respect for religion was universal, many Irish people probably kept away from churches.

In 1171, Henry had reason to forget pope Adrian's invitation in *Laudabiliter* no longer. On New Year's Day he received news that Theobald's successor as archbishop of Canterbury, Thomas à Becket, had been murdered – by Henry's own knights and seemingly at Henry's order. Becket, who was twelve or fourteen years Henry's senior, had been a close friend of Henry in his younger days, and in 1162 Henry had given him his position of archbishop of Canterbury. Then Becket had changed; he considered himself greater than the king, came into open conflict with him and had to flee the country. In 1170 pope Alexander III forced Henry and Becket into a reconciliation. But it was a hollow truce: when Becket came back to England he virtually declared war on Henry and that, naturally, aroused in Henry the

strongest feelings of resentment. 'Who will rid me of this turbu-
lent priest?' he is said to have cried out in anger, and four
knights of his household, thinking they were doing his bidding,
straightway left his court in Normandy to ride for the coast
and Canterbury, where they struck Becket down within his own
cathedral. Henry had not authorized the murder – and, overcome
with grief and remorse, he shut himself up and would speak to
no-one for three days when he had news of it. Nevertheless the
whole of Christendom blamed him. He was prohibited from
entering a church until his guilt had been discharged, and in the
autumn of 1171 legates left Rome to see if he was truly penitent.
Henry escaped them, however; pope Adrian's injunction in the
bull *Laudabiliter* having tied in with his own interest in curbing
the power of Strongbow, he left France for England and then
Wales. On October 16 he embarked his considerable army in 400
ships lying at Milford Haven and set sail for Ireland.

Henry did not intend to fight in Ireland unless he had to. His
army, the most formidable ever seen in the country, was, he
hoped, largely for show; he wanted the Irish and the errant
Normans to be aware that he was the greatest king in western
Europe and submit to him accordingly. And so they did. His
force landed at Crook, near Waterford, and the next day he
entered the city. Strongbow formally surrendered it to him and
did homage for Leinster. Then Mac Carthaigh of Desmond, the
king of Cork, came in to Henry of his own free will, submitted
to him and gave hostages. Henry marched westwards, pausing
briefly at Lismore to meet the bishop there, an old man who had
been a monk at Clairvaux and was now appointed papal legate,
and then carried on to Cashel, where Domnal Ua Briain, the king
of Thomond, came in to him as well as other kings and chieftains.
Henry returned to Waterford and then set out for Dublin by way
of Ossory, receiving submissions, in what turned out to be a
triumphal progress, from the principal chieftains of Leinster and
the aged Tigernán Ua Ruairc. The high king, Ruaidrí Ua
Conchobair, came from his kingdom of Connacht to the banks
of the river Shannon to meet Henry's envoys, though he probably
did not come in to Henry as the other kings had. The princes of
Ulidia gave pledges, but the other Ulster princes, from the tribes

west of Lough Neagh, felt themselves to be so remote they need not trouble about the foreign king.

In Dublin Henry had a palace built, a marvellous structure of clay and wattles in the Irish style, and held a splendid Christmas court, which lasted from November to February, most affably entertaining the Irish princes and chieftains with food cooked in the English manner, sumptuously served on gold and silver dishes, set on tables covered with fine cloth. The Irish were suitably impressed and Henry was lighthearted, for his troubles with the papacy seemed to be over. Letters were arriving from pope Alexander III, Adrian's successor, sent to the bishops, the Irish princes and to Henry himself, commending the invasion 'so praiseworthily begun' and describing Henry, in words which must have been music to his ears, as 'the most beloved son in Christ'. And meanwhile the bishop of Lismore was arranging a synod at Cashel, which began on 2nd February and was attended by three archbishops and all the bishops of Ireland. The primate, a saintly octogenarian who lived entirely on milk, was too frail to make the long journey from Armagh, but gave Henry his wholehearted support. The synod condemned the marriage customs prevalent in Ireland, demanded the payment of tithes on a parochial basis and required that divine offices should be celebrated regularly everywhere. The bishops saw Henry as the agent of the pope, a powerful king capable of giving Ireland the peace and strong government the country so desperately needed.

Then in March Henry received disquieting news from England. His eldest son, Henry, was about to embark on a rebellion against him and, worse, the papal legates he had evaded in France were threatening an interdict, which would bar him from the sacraments, unless he returned to do public penance for the outburst of irritation by which he had unwittingly consigned Becket to death. He appointed Hugh de Lacy, another Norman baron from Wales, who had come over in his train, to be his justiciar, or chief officer, in Ireland, to counterbalance the power of Strongbow, whom he still did not trust, waited for a favourable wind and then, on 17th April 1172, took ship at Wexford and sailed away.

CHAPTER 5

TWO
NATIONS

Henry II had left Ireland, never to return. If this masterful, energetic and supremely gifted king had spent longer in the country
– if he had imposed his will throughout it, as the pope had
commissioned him to do – the history of Ireland over the next
seven centuries might have been a happier one.

To most modern people, of whatever nationality, it is reprehen-
sible that Henry and the Normans went into Ireland at all. The
state of the Irish nation was not their business and the Irish,
according to modern thinking, should have been left to work out
their own destiny. But in the twelfth century people did not
think like that. National boundaries were still fluid and national
identity was not a concept anyone considered. Henry, though
king of England, was a Frenchman who spent most of his time
in France and spoke French in England and in Ireland. The
Church, with its vast organization of bishops and archbishops
answerable only to Rome, was international and the Normans,
those practical, ruthless knights who so often carried out the
Church's commissions, fighting and adventuring in every
country in Europe from Scotland to the Balkans, never stayed
anywhere long enough to acquire a local patriotism. The de
Clares, de Barrys, de Montmorencys and the rest had been in
Wales less than a hundred years when they sent their sons, the
Geraldines, on into Ireland.

It was the duty of an upper class, which the Normans were,
to conquer – for conquest, which could mean no more than
acquisition, a bloodless takeover, was often a prelude to peace,

progress and the spread of new and advanced ideas. Henry failed in Ireland because he attempted too little there; he did not even try to give Ireland the peace, unity and strong central administration the Irish so greatly needed. William the Conqueror, by contrast, had stayed in England; he had imposed the Norman system, for better or for worse, throughout the country. Some people in England feel that Norman civilization was inferior to the Anglo-Saxon culture it superseded, and they may be right. But, ever since William landed at Pevensey, in Sussex, there has been nothing anyone in England could do but accept the gifts the Normans brought, in the way of increased order, an efficient administration and an advanced judicial system, and assimilate them.

There was never a Norman conquest of Ireland. When Henry sailed from Wexford in 1172, he left a partially conquered country, as divided as it had ever been. Most of what had once belonged to the Ostmen, that is, Dublin and its hinterland, Wexford, Waterford and other stretches of the south and east coasts, were now Crown lands. Strongbow had Leinster and the justiciar, Hugh de Lacy, the rich plains of the old kingdom of Meath, which he studded with castles and manors. The rest of Ireland remained under the uncertain control of the high king, Ruaidrí Ua Conchobair.

This division suited Henry. There was no danger of a Norman-led kingdom on his flank so long as the Irish, under their kings and high kings, could maintain their separateness. In October 1175, he concluded a treaty with Ruaidrí Ua Conchobair, made at Windsor, which protected his position as high king in return for a tribute of one hide for every ten animals slain, which Rory was to collect from the provincial kings under him. But the Treaty of Windsor soon broke down. Ruaidrí could barely control his own provincial kingdom of Connacht, and was quite incapable of collecting tribute from his neighbours. And Henry, as the absentee lord of Ireland, a kind of superior high king, could not shore up such weakness. In 1177 he decided to let the Treaty of Windsor go. The Normans were establishing their own order at the point of a sword, and Henry began to support them; they were more likely to bring peace and good order to Ireland than the native kings. Henry was an oath-breaker, faithless: even his friends were agreed upon that. He took the Irish towns of Cork and Limerick into his own hand, and granted away large tracts of land, belonging to native kings whose allegiance he had accepted five years earlier, to the Norman barons. The kingdom of Cork went to Robert Fitzstephen and Miles de Cogan with the proviso 'if you can win it' – an open invitation to warfare – and the kingdom of Limerick, which embraced the modern counties of Clare, Limerick and Tipperary, as well as north Kerry, to Philip de Braose. Other Normans carved out kingdoms for themselves without waiting for Henry's permission. Early in 1177 John de Courcy, the younger son of a Somerset knight, conquered Ulaid in a daring and brilliant campaign; with 22 knights and about 300 discontented foot soldiers, some of them archers, from the Dublin garrison, he made a four-day march northwards, surprised and took Downpatrick, the capital of Ulaid, and then defeated Ulster armies, many thousands strong, in two major battles.

Ireland needed more time and attention than Henry could give. For some years he had been toying with the idea of dividing his empire among his four surviving sons and ruling it on federal lines. His eldest son, Henry, had already been crowned to ensure his succession, not an unusual practice when the right of primogeniture could still be questioned, and was known as king Henry the Younger; his lands were England, Normandy and Anjou. Henry's second son, Richard, became duke of Aquitaine and the third, Geoffrey, duke of Brittany. Obviously Ireland, too, would benefit from the strong rule of a prince who was permanently in the country and in 1177, at a council of barons in Oxford, Henry gave the lordship of Ireland to his youngest and favourite son, John.

But John was only nine at the time and it was not until 1185, when he was seventeen, that Henry sent him to Ireland to receive the homage of the kings and nobility there, both Irish and Norman. But even then Henry, the fond parent, had over-estimated John. The young prince landed at Waterford, bringing with him a court of youths as frivolous and inexperienced as he was himself, and proceeded to insult the Irish. 'There met him at Waterford a great many of the Irish of the better class in those parts,' wrote Giraldus Cambrensis, who was present throughout John's visit. 'Our newcomers and Normans not only treated them with contempt and derision, but even rudely pulled them by their beards, which the Irishmen wore full long, according to the custom of their country.' When the outraged Irishmen made their escape and spread the story of John's insolent and childish behaviour, other Irish chieftains would have nothing to do with him and the kings of Connacht, Thomond and Desmond went so far as to form a defensive league against him. John offended the Norman settlers too, those who might be called old Ireland hands, when, disregarding their advice, he gave away the lands of loyal Irishmen to his own youthful followers; the kingdom of Limerick, which Philip de Braose had never managed to conquer, was re-granted to Theobald Walter, while Philip of Worcester and William de Burgh were both given lands in Tipperary. Then he put the care of the coastal castles and towns into his courtiers' hands. 'Keeping themselves carefully within the town walls,' wrote Giraldus, 'they spent their time and all that they had in drunkenness and surfeiting.' After eight months, Henry realized John's unfitness and recalled him.

John's rudeness and immaturity have gone down in history. Nevertheless, even on his first disastrous visit to Ireland, he had made a beginning at what was to be valuable work. His grants of land were not capricious, but linked up the lands already settled by the Normans. He made Hugh de Lacy the scapegoat for his failure with the Irish; de Lacy had been justiciar almost up to the time of John's arrival but, like Strongbow, had rendered his loyalty suspect by marrying an Irish princess. After John returned to England, John de Courcy was appointed justiciar as a counter-balance to de Lacy, just as de Lacy had originally been installed to balance Strongbow. De Lacy's days were numbered in any case; in July 1186, he was murdered by an Irishman who objected to his quarrying stones for castle-building from the ruins of an abbey founded by Colum Cille – or, less colourfully, was in the service of a rival Irish lord. When de Lacy stooped, in the course of supervising the work, the Irishman swung his axe and cut his head off.

John de Courcy was a good and fair administrator but made the mistake of supporting the new king, Richard I, against John, when the two brothers quarrelled after Henry's death in 1189, and in 1192 de Courcy was replaced as justiciar by two more Norman adventurers, Peter Pipard and William le Pettit. Then in 1205 John, now king himself in succession to Richard, saw his chance to bring de Courcy down. He summoned de Courcy repeatedly to come to him but, tough and independent, de Courcy stayed away, so John granted the de Courcy land to the rival de Lacy family with the usual proviso 'if you can win it'. The de Lacys went after de Courcy and, through the treachery of his servants, caught up with him at his devotions in the monastery at Downpatrick. Before they captured him, he is reputed to have seized a wooden cross from a grave and killed thirteen of his attackers![1] The kingdom of Leinster, too, passed into different hands. In 1189, just before Henry's death, William the Marshal, one of the great noblemen of England, had married Strongbow's daughter and heiress, and during the years 1207–13, he spent much time on his Irish estates, developing them along Norman lines.

When John succeeded Richard I in 1199, the lordship of Ireland was merged with the Crown of England and Henry's idea of a resident English prince in Ireland was lost. But John did not forget Ireland in his wider responsibilities. After his dismal beginning there, he became an effective ruler of the country and completed much of Henry's work. He had a genuine interest in law and administration, which he used to curb the Norman magnates who had, hitherto, been subject to no law or government whatever. He began work on Dublin castle, which was to be the centre of government, and introduced the English judicial system, with sheriffs' courts, assize courts, travelling judges and trial by jury. Some counties were demarcated too, and in 1207 a coinage was struck incorporating, for the first time, the Irish harp. Sea trading was encouraged, and ships carrying wines and luxury goods to England and Scotland from Gascony, Spain and Portugal developed the habit of provisioning in Irish ports. In 1210 John made his second visit to Ireland, fought an energetic and successful military campaign against a Norman baron, William de Braose, and went out of his way to court the Irish princes, several of whom paid him homage in Dublin.

Thirty years after their arrival, the Normans controlled the whole of Ireland east and south of a line from Limerick past Lough Derg and the river Shannon to Lough Neagh and Coleraine. A mere handful of Norman adventurers, never more than 2,500 in number, had imposed themselves upon the Irish princes, either pushing them down to an inferior position or out of Norman Ireland altogether, into the west and the north. The Irish had been left behind by Europe in the race for military technology and training, and however courageously they might fight as individuals, and even as guerrilla bands, they could not withstand the showers of arrows loosed from Norman, or Welsh, crossbows, which the Normans used like modern artillery, to soften up the enemy before the main attack. Nor could they resist the weight of the Norman cavalry. The Irish sometimes rode to the battlefield, sitting on their horses without saddle or stirrups and often guiding them, not with reins and a bridle, but a stick. But they always dismounted to fight. The Normans, on the other hand, rode into battle on warhorses brought over from England. Their charging knights were the medieval equivalent of the modern tank: foot soldiers were swept away when the heavily armoured Norman cavalry bore down upon them in closed ranks, with nine- and ten-foot lances couched for the thrust. Then, when the Normans had gained the submission of the Irish, or driven them away, they would throw up castles, from which groups of archers could survey the surrounding countryside and hold off Irish attacks.

Before 1200 Norman castles were simple wooden structures, a steep-sided mound of earth being thrown up from a ditch, with a wooden tower on top. At ground level there was a bailey, or courtyard, where cattle and horses could be kept and soldiers quartered, surrounded by another ditch and a rampart with a pallisade on top. A wooden motte-and-bailey could, however, easily be set on fire, and after 1200 the Normans built their castles more permanently of stone. John de Courcy ringed his territory in Ulster with impregnable stone castles and the de Lacys did the same in Meath; throughout Norman Ireland, wherever there was a threat from a disgruntled Irish chieftain, or a thrusting Norman neighbour, castles were built on hills, in the bends of rivers and on coastal promontories. They were garrisoned by knights and archers, and became home for the local lord.

Most of Ireland was lost to the native princes, but still the Normans were not content. Richard de Burgo, who held Limerick and Tipperary, coveted the kingdom of Connacht as well and, because he had powerful connections in England, obtained a

11. Trim castle (courtesy of the Irish Tourist Board)

grant of most of it. The Ó Conchobhairs, the royal family of Connacht, were loyal tributaries of the English king. But the Normans wanted – and the Normans took. In 1235 de Burgo, accompanied by the justiciar, Maurice Fitzgerald, led a spectacular array of knights, men-at-arms and archers across the river Shannon at Athlone, and parcelled out the lowlands of Connacht to de Lacys, Geraldines and others, keeping the plain east of Lough Corrib for himself. Soon only Leitrim and Roscommon, from the whole of western Ireland, remained in Irish hands.

Wherever the Normans established themselves, the face of the countryside changed. In the east and the south there were increasing areas of neatness and order. Villages appeared; the castle, of wood or stone, was joined by a manor, a mill, workshops, clusters of thatched wooden houses, a church, and often a monastery or a friary. Towns grew up; at the heads of valleys, where rivers were bridged or could be forded, or roads intersected, there would be more substantial merchants' houses, a church or a stone cathedral, perhaps in the new Romanesque style and, most important of all, a market-place. Towns were given the right to hold markets and, very often, an annual eight-day fair.

Norman lands were organized along feudal lines. The tenant-in-chief – Strongbow, Hugh de Lacy, or whoever he might be – held his lands of the king and, in return, guaranteed to give the king, firstly, his advice and, secondly, the service of a specified number of knights, armed, trained and mounted, whenever called upon. The advisory function was important because it led to the development of parliament, and the rent paid in knight service provided the king with the basis of an army; the rent for Meath was 50 knights and for Leinster 100. When king John died in 1216, the rent for the whole of Norman Ireland was 427 knights. Feudalism was a way of using newly conquered land to support a ready-made professional army, which would not only garrison and hold down the conquered territory, but fight abroad for the king.

A tenant-in-chief raised the required number of knights by dividing his land into fiefs and letting it out to suitable tenants in return for knight service. A fief had to be large enough to provide a knight with a living. But a knight was a gentleman; he and his retainers had no thought of working the land themselves. They were far too busy practising their skills as horsemen and doing weapons training. So they encouraged the Irish peasantry, the betaghs, or food producers, to remain. 'And if the Irish who have fled wish to return to the land of the barons of the king of England they may do so in peace,' the Treaty of Windsor declared in 1175, 'doing for the English the services they were wont to do for their lands.' These services only amounted to 30 days a year, comparing very favourably with the 100 days' service English peasants usually gave their lords, and most of the betaghs settled down under the new order happily enough. The Normans put a stern end to the cattle-raiding, hostings and never-ending local conflicts which had caused the small man much misery under the Irish kings and, although there were still many minor raids and disturbances, especially in the marcher areas, Norman Ireland merited the title it was soon given of the land of peace.

Although the Irish were still pastoralists, discouraged by the endless conflict in the Irish areas from becoming settled farmers – cattle and sheep could be driven away from danger, whereas crops were too easily stolen or burnt – the betaghs took readily to cultivation and the open field system, which their Norman overlords introduced. The arable land of each lord's manor was divided into several very large fields, often well over 100 acres, which were worked according to a three-year rotation. Winter crops, such as wheat and rye, were planted one year and a spring crop, barley for brewing, peas or oats the next. During the third year the land was left fallow, for farm animals to graze upon and manure. As in England, these large fields were divided into strips, belonging to the betaghs and such English tenants as the manor might contain.

Surplus meat, grain and dairy products were sold in the towns. Horses and farm animals were brought to market, as well as sacks of wool, honey, hides and leather, and fresh and salt fish, particularly salmon and herrings. The native Irish still preferred life in the countryside – 'they have little use for the moneymaking of the towns,' Giraldus commented – and the new trading centres were inhabited by Normans, Ostmen, Flemings, Welshmen, and sometimes the English. While the language of the countryside, even in Norman areas, was Irish, in the towns it was Norman–French.

Since John's time, Norman Ireland had developed a considerable export trade with England and the continent. English iron, beer, fine linen cloth and salt came into Irish ports, while Irish smoked and salt salmon went to England, as well as the bulk of the corn grown in the Norman areas, which fed the king's armies. Irish horses, too, found a ready export market; they were notably small, light and fast. The coarse weatherproof wool used for weaving Irish mantles and great quantities of Irish hides went to Italy, drawing the attention of Italian bankers to the country's potential wealth. They visited Ireland, invested heavily in Irish trade and set up a banking system.

But outside the towns, the foreign population remained thin on the ground. Only Munster, Leinster and eastern Ulster were thoroughly feudalized; the whole province of Connacht yielded no more than ten knights to the Crown. Some twenty or thirty years after the invasion, the first wave of Norman adventurers – John de Courcy, Hugh de Lacy and some of the Geraldines – had died, leaving infant heirs, or none at all. Their lands reverted temporarily to the Crown and were looked after by less energetic agents.

The first Normans had believed that other adventurers would follow them from England, Wales and Scotland. In England particularly there was a shortage of land, and the lure of a large, fertile country where land was going cheap would seem to be great, but the English regarded Ireland as hostile and dangerous. They were fully occupied with wars against France and Scotland, and John's son, Henry III, gave them no encouragement to make the trip. He was indifferent to his other island and, during the fifty-six years of his reign, never once visited it. The more capable English officials preferred to stay at home, where advancement lay, and while the Norman baronage weakened, the standard of central government from Dublin also declined. And the tide turned.

The Irish had never been conquered. When the Normans took over Irish land, the Irish princes moved away, while the lesser chieftains simply drove their cattle into the woods and hills. The Normans and Irish lived side by side, the Normans cultivating the lower ground and the Irish keeping the land more than 600 feet above sea level. Especially in the rough, high country of the west, the Irish lived as they had always done, driving their cattle into the mountains for their summer pastures, setting up their simple summer camps, or booleys, and living in the open air. Irish kings still dined out of doors, sitting at trestle tables with their servants – a lack of class distinction which horrified the Normans! – while poets and harpists reminded them of the glories of the old provincial dynasties, the five bloods.

In the struggle with the Normans, the Irish lack of unity turned from a weakness into a strength. There were so many Irish kings, fluidly combining and recombining, that they were impossible to defeat. As soon as one Irish king, or combination of kings, went down, others appeared. To attempt to catch them was like bobbing for apples at Halloween. Irish princely families were in no danger of dying out, as the leading Norman families were; due to the laxity of Irish marriage customs, chieftains often had enormous families. Pilib Mág Uidhir, the lord of Fir Manach, had twenty sons by eight different mothers and at least fifty grandsons, and Toirrdhelbach Ua Domnaill, the lord of Tír Conaill, had eighteen sons by ten different mothers and fifty-nine grandsons!

And the Irish kings were winning victories. In 1257 Gofraid

Ua Domnaill invaded Sligo and defeated a Norman force at Credan, and in 1258 his brother Domnall Óc mac Domnaill returned to Ireland from Scotland, where he had been fostered, and put a stop to the Norman advance westwards from Lough Neagh. The Mac Carthaighs, who had been hemmed into the extreme south-west by the Fitzthomas branch of the Geraldines, broke out; in 1261 they won a fierce battle at Callann, in the mountains near Kenmare, against the Norman forces of Munster and an army commanded by the justiciar, William de Dene. Fitzthomas, his son and many of his followers were killed. Then in 1270 Aedh Ua Conchobair, the king of Connacht, met Ralph d'Ufford, the next justiciar, Walter de Burgo, the son of that Richard de Burgo who had led the Norman array across the Shannon in 1235, and 'all the foreigners of Erin with them' at the ford of Athankip, near Carrick-on-Shannon, and the Norman army was routed; they left arms and suits of mail scattered all over the battlefield as they fled.

When Domnal Óc mac Domnaill returned from Scotland, he had brought an army of Scottish mercenaries with him, who soon became famous as the gallowglasses, a corruption of the Irish

12. Gallowglasses from Roscommon Abbey (courtesy of the Commissioners of Public Works in Ireland)

term for foreign soldiers. They were men from the Western Isles, partly Norse and partly Gaelic, who fought as foot soldiers protected, like the Normans, with helmets and long coats of mail. They were armed with a dagger and a heavy, long-handled battleaxe which, powerfully swung, could inflict terrible injuries and even shear through plate armour. Each gallowglass had an assistant, rather like the squire who accompanied a Norman knight, whose job was to carry his coat of mail, and a boy who did the cooking.

With the coming of the gallowglasses, the military inferiority of the Irish was over. But if they were to consolidate their victories, they knew they must have a leader, a high king with real power. In 1258 Aedh Ua Conchobair went with Tadhg Ua Briain, king of Thomond, to Brian Ua Néill of Cenél Eógain and acclaimed him as high king. Brian was killed in battle soon afterwards, but a need had been acknowledged, a principle established, and in 1263 Haakon, the king of Norway, was invited to be high king; for the first time, the Irish were looking abroad for help against the Normans. But Haakon, too, died soon after the offer was made.

In 1254 Henry III gave the lordship of Ireland to his eldest son Edward, a boy of fourteen. Edward, however, had even less interest in Ireland that his father, and all plans for him to visit his lordship came to nothing. Under his rule, justiciars came and went so rapidly that central government only operated spasmodically, and the administration became increasingly inefficient and corrupt. Henry III had been careful not to take too much from the Norman colony, for fear it would not be able to defend itself against the Irish, but when Edward succeeded him in 1272, all such restraint was thrown to the winds. Edward I was a handsome, vigorous man who fought in the Crusades and in France, held down Wales with huge stone castles and tried to conquer Scotland. His wars and the magnificent style of his court cost huge sums of money; he remembered the prosperity of Norman Ireland and decided to milk the country for all it was worth. In 1295 he sent Sir John Wogan to Ireland as his justiciar with instructions to raise both men and money from Ireland, and Wogan bled the Irish government white. Almost 3,200 men were sent from Ireland to the Scottish wars in 1296 and a further 2,500 in 1301, all paid and provisioned out of the Irish privy purse.

Edward II, who succeeded his father in 1307, has gone down in history as a poor sort of a king, weak and frivolous. But he was less damaging to Ireland than his majestic father had been. In 1312 he told his Irish treasurer that, in the past, Irish revenues had been put to the wrong use. 'The funds left in Ireland have not been sufficient to preserve the peace there,' he wrote. 'The Irish burn, kill, rob and commit other transgressions against the peace in an intolerable manner. Henceforth all Irish revenue is to be spent in Ireland to preserve the peace there and to carry out other arduous duties of government.' But it was too late. The Irish government could no longer curb the excesses of the magnates, who behaved as if they were above and beyond the law – or at any rate the justiciar! And the Irish kings, knowing that the government had thousands of men away, fighting in foreign wars, once again invited a foreign prince to oust the English and become high king.

The English war with Scotland had culminated in defeat for Edward II at the battle of Bannockburn in 1314, when the English knights, bogged down in soggy watermeadows, had fallen easy victims to Scottish longbowmen fighting for Robert the Bruce, crowned king of Scotland in defiance of the English eight years earlier. Robert had a brother, Edward, who had made several visits to Ireland, and when the Irish heard of the Scottish success, Domnall Ó Néill, the king of Ulster, put the Irish proposition to him. The Scots and the Irish shared a common Gaelic ancestry, there had always been Scottish settlers in Ulster, which was only separated from Scotland by the North Channel, thirteen miles wide at its narrowest point, and Scottish gallowglasses had turned the tables for the Irish. A Scot seemed an obvious choice for the high kingship. There would be advantages for the Scots as well. If Ireland rose in rebellion, the stream of fighting men from Ireland which swelled the English armies opposing the Scots would dry up; the two Gaelic peoples might even make common cause against the English.

Edward accepted the Irish invitation with his brother Robert's blessing. On 25 May 1315 he landed near Larne with 200 ships and perhaps 6,000 experienced soldiers, soon supplemented by local Irishmen and gallowglasses. The Ulster chieftains immediately repudiated Richard de Burgo, known as the Red earl of Ulster, who had been their suzerain, and before long Fedlimid

Ua Conchobhair, the king of Connacht, did the same. Nevertheless the Red earl refused to co-operate with the justiciar to resist the invasion, regarding it as a matter for him alone, and very soon became, in the words of an Irish annalist, 'a wanderer up and down Ireland, with no power of lordship'. By the end of June Edward had taken and burned Dundalk, and in September the Red earl was finally knocked out of the contest at Connor.

There seemed no stopping the Scots and their Irish allies. Edward went into Meath, defeated Roger Mortimer, the lord of Trim, and early in 1316 marched into Leinster. The Irish government could do nothing, and the various Norman magnates were too suspicious of each other to co-operate; most of them wanted, above all else, to keep their neighbours' armies off their lands because of the damage they could do, and they let Bruce through, more or less by default. The Irish of Munster were so encouraged when they saw it that they rose in rebellion.

Bruce, however, turned back to the north, and early in the summer he was crowned in Ulster at Faughart, north of Dundalk. When Carrickfergus fell to him in September he set up his court there, dispensed justice, hanged lawbreakers and prepared to win the whole of Ireland. Within Ulster he had massive support, Norman as well as Irish, but elsewhere people were half-hearted. He made a brief trip back to Scotland and persuaded Robert to come to Ireland, which he did early in 1317. Then, with his brother beside him, he sought to strengthen his position by making a grand circuit of Ireland, like one of the old high kings 'with opposition', forcing submissions, taking hostages and exacting tribute. Unfortunately this display of strength coincided with a famine which, in 1317, afflicted much of Europe, and when the Scottish army had helped themselves from the depleted countryside, as well as burning crops and driving off cattle in a show of authority, they left such a trail of ruined manors, destruction, misery and starvation behind them that the Irish, thoroughly alienated, decided 'Scottish foreigners are less noble than our own foreigners' and did not rise for them. Early in May, the Scots returned to Ulster and Robert went back to Scotland.

The justiciar, Edmund Butler, a Norman magnate from Munster, had led what forces he could muster against the Scots when they landed, and the Bruce army had been successfully kept out of Dublin. But after the depredations of Edward I,

Norman Ireland was no longer taxable and the Irish government could not pay adequate forces. The English government, realizing Ireland was almost gone, at last provided funds – and Ireland turned from a financial asset to a liability for the English Crown. In April Roger Mortimer, who was a great English noble besides the lord of Trim, returned from England as the king's lieutenant, superseding Butler, and reasserted government authority in Meath, Leinster and Munster. In the autumn of 1318 Edward Bruce, who had lain low in Ulster for eighteen months, came to battle once more, meeting a superior force under the Norman, John de Bermingham, at Faughart, where he had so recently been crowned king of Ireland. The Scots were defeated and Edward killed. The Irish annalists universally condemned him. 'In this Bruce's time,' one of them wrote, 'for three years and a half, falsehood and famine and homicide filled the country, and undoubtedly men ate each other in Ireland'.

The invasion had ripped Ireland savagely apart: exposing the weakness of the central government, the arrogant disloyalty of the Anglo-Norman lords and the pettiness of the Irish princes, who were still unable to take the larger and less insular view. If the Irish had risen wholeheartedly for Edward Bruce – not a mere handful of them, but the great majority – the government in Dublin would have been toppled and the power of the Normans broken; even the effects of the famine would have been less severe for, with willing support from the Irish, the Scots army would not have needed to wreak the havoc it did. The federation of Celtic states, which Robert the Bruce had dreamed of, might even have brought England to defeat – and the history of every country in the British Isles taken a very different turn.

There was virtually no rule in Ireland after the Bruce invasion. The government was too weak to collect its revenues; the income from escheats, lands whose owners had died without heirs, which had been over £7,000 in the late thirteenth century, dwindled to a ludicrous £30 by 1340. Customs duties, including the valuable impost of wines, fell from some £3,000 to almost nothing. Government officials, finding their salaries were only partially paid, doubled up on their jobs and took bribes in order to make a living. All honour and efficiency were lost.

Pardons were handed out to great noblemen far too freely – even to those guilty of treachery. The Red earl had arrogantly refused to co-operate with the justiciar during the invasion, and so well convinced the people of Dublin of his treachery that they flung him into prison, yet afterwards he was given his lands back. The de Lacys had sided openly with Bruce and Mortimer had had to chase them out of Meath, but they, too, had their lands restored. The debts of the great were readily forgiven too. In 1329 the Red earl was forgiven the rent he owed for Connacht. A debt of nearly £3,500 owed by the earl of Desmond was cancelled, and in 1335 the earl of Ormond, of the rising Butler family, was let off heavy fines. In the same year the city of Limerick was allowed to escape with a payment of only £6 on a debt of more than £1,000! In the past, pardons had been granted in return for a service to the Crown, such as participation in a foreign war, but after the Bruce invasion repayment was waived to save the government's face; it was better for the government to seem to forgive a debt than impotently fail to collect it.

Not surprisingly, the great lords despised and flouted the government; successive justiciars struggled gamely to assert themselves against a crowd of nobles head and shoulders more powerful than they. Increasingly they found themselves, and the king they represented, ignored. Ireland was breaking up into a number of independent states, each with its own ruling house, private army and enthusiasm for public quarrels. Maurice Fitzthomas, created earl of Desmond, had a body of fighting men, known as Mac Thomas's Rout, which terrorized the south-west, burning villages and churches, robbing and killing – a quarrel between the earl and the Powers family of Waterford, which began because one of the Powers had called Desmond a rhymer (a wandering Irish bard), caused enormous damage and loss of life; in Cork and Waterford alone the damage was assessed at the huge sum for those days of £100,000. Elsewhere the major tenants of the feudal nobles, those who might be called the second rank amongst the English of Ireland, rose against their overlords; they resented their position as feudal vassals and wanted to be recognized as captains of their nations, or lords of their countries, as the Irish of similar status were. In 1329 John de Bermingham, created earl of Louth after the Bruce invasion, several of his relatives and 160 others in his household were massacred in a tenants' rebellion, and in 1333 the Brown earl of Ulster, the 21-year-old grandson of the Red earl, was murdered, again by his tenants, at the Ford of Carrickfergus; his widow fled to England with their only child, Elizabeth, and the de Burgos in Ulster died out.

In 1342 Elizabeth married Lionel, duke of Clarence, the third son of the English king, Edward III, who succeeded his father, Edward II, in 1327, and the earl of Ulster, being a royal duke, inevitably became an absentee. Other great lords in Ireland, such as Roger Mortimer, were absentees as well. They had lands in England which required their attention and a duty to attend upon the king. Those who were not absentees were, in the civil service jargon of the time, hibernicized: becoming, in a famous phrase, more Irish than the Irish themselves. Since the days of Strongbow, leading Norman and Irish families had intermarried, and after a generation or two most Norman magnates had Irish mothers and spoke Irish as their first language. They were fostered with Irish princely families, and when they grew up aristocratic Irish children were fostered with them and their – probably Irish – wives. In Irish society the ties of affection between children and their foster parents were usually stronger than with their real parents, and this custom of fostering gradually knit the two races together. The Normans kept poets and harpists as the Irish did; the Red earl was so well known as a patron of the Irish arts that, when he died in 1326, his elegy was composed in Irish, and when the earl of Louth was murdered, his poet Ó Cerbhaill, one of the best in Ireland, fell with him. The third earl of Desmond, who held his title from 1359 to 1398, was himself a Gaelic poet, known as Gerald the Rhymer.

The native Irish were flooding back: fighting hundreds of petty battles with Norman and English men-at-arms, driving their cattle down from the mountains and pushing the settlers back to the towns and the south-eastern coasts. In Ulster several new native states were set up, the Ó Néill dynasty ruling once more in Tyrone, and the absentee earl left no more than the coastal strip of Antrim and Down. In 1327 Leinster, which had been a Norman earldom since the days of Strongbow, began electing its own kings once more; and Domhnall Mac Murchadha, the first of the new line, soon recovered his ancestor Diarmait's palace at Ferns. The Ó Broins and Ó Tuathails began pressing into the

English areas of Leinster from the east, the Ó Conchobhairs of Offaly and the Ó Mordhas of Leix from the west. Everywhere the English withdrew to the river valleys – and then the river valleys were threatened and the settlements isolated. Before the Bruce invasion, English settlements had been sheltered by a broad marcher area, which stretched right across the country, fortified with castles and always ready for war. By the end of the century, English officials living outside Dublin, especially those in the town of Carlow, where the English Exchequer had been unwisely moved around 1360, were demanding danger money.

When the Normans came to Ireland, they had no thought of racial discrimination. Gradually, however, it had come about. As the Normans never conquered the whole country, for many years the Irish and Norman cultures remained distinct and the Normans, as conquerors always do, felt theirs was superior. The first act of discrimination came in 1216, when king John directed that Englishmen should be preferred to Irishmen as incumbents of cathedral churches, a direction promptly denounced by the pope as 'an unheard of audacity . . . a bold and wicked abuse'. But the main discrimination was not so much in the religious as the legal sphere. English law could only be applied where there were English courts, that is, in the Norman colony. Irishmen living under Irish chiefs were excluded from the royal and sheriffs' courts, unless they were descended from one of the ancient royal families, and Irishmen living within the Norman system were so depressed in status that they were unlikely to take legal action on their own behalf. The Latin legal term *hibernicus*[2] had come to mean an unfree man, a slave, whose property, and even life, were deemed to belong to his lord.

In 1318, when Edward Bruce was lying passive in Ulster, the pope received a letter, called the *Remonstrance*, from Domhnall Ua Néill, Bruce's foremost supporter, giving the grounds the Irish had for throwing off their allegiance to the English lord of Ireland. Besides charging the kings of England with making speculative grants of Irish land to their followers, quite contrary to the missionary spirit of Adrian's *Donation*, he complained bitterly of the lack of protection and rights accorded Irishmen under the English legal system. 'No Irishman may sue an Englishman,' the *Remonstrance* asserted. 'No man of this race is

91

punished for the murder of an Irishman, even the most eminent; an Irishwoman, no matter how noble, who marries an Englishman is deprived at his death of her dowry; on the death of an Irishman the English seize his property, thus reducing to bondage the blood which flowed in freedom from of old.' Referring to an incident when an Anglo-Irish cleric, Friar Simon, the brother of the bishop of Connor, had declared that, if he killed an Irishman, he would nonetheless celebrate mass immediately afterwards, the *Remonstrance* summed up: 'The English say it is no more sin to kill an Irishman than it is to kill a dog.' It was an impassioned, emotive appeal, in part propaganda and in part the genuine expression of an Irish sense of wrong. The pope had sent it on to Edward II and some grievances were ameliorated.

But as the English position in Ireland disintegrated, so discrimination increased. It became urgent for the goverment to bolster the loyalty of the English in Ireland. After having several justiciars of low rank who commanded little respect, in 1361 Edward III sent the duke of Clarence to Ireland as viceroy, to regain his own lands in Ulster, if he could, and to stem the Irish advance. Clarence campaigned in Leinster and Munster, as well as in Ulster, but the Anglo-Irish supported him very reluctantly against their Irish neighbours, he was unable to win any permanent victories, and after five years he had had enough. There was more glory to be won in England and France.

Ever since 1264[3] the king's representative in Ireland had summoned a parliament when he wanted to place an act on the statute roll, test opinion, seek advice, or impress a government policy upon the Anglo-Norman colony. The earliest parliaments had consisted only of an upper House of Lords and bishops, developed from the old barons' council, which had a duty to proffer advice, but, as the fourteenth century advanced, a House of Commons, with knights representing the countryside and burgesses from the towns, was generally summoned as well. In 1366, as a last throw before his departure, Clarence summoned a parliament to Kilkenny, which passed thirty-five enactments designed to keep the two nations apart, which became famous as the Statutes of Kilkenny. In the following year he left the country.

Like other acts of colonial apartheid, those in South Africa for instance, the Statutes of Kilkenny were intended not so much as an attack on the native race as an attempt to preserve the cultural identity (and the loyalty) of their conquerors: to prevent them being assimilated, swamped even, by a far more numerous native people. The English in Ireland, according to the preamble to the Statutes, had in the past used the English language and been governed according to English law, with the Irish in subjection to them; but now many English were forsaking English fashions and customs to adopt the manners, fashions and language of the Irish, as well as making marriage and many other alliances with the Irish; they were forgetting the English language, their allegiance to the English king and their subjection to the English law. Henceforth they were forbidden to foster their children amongst the Irish, to marry Irish men or women and to sponsor Irish children at baptism. Their disputes were to be resolved according to English and not brehon law or 'the law of the marches', which was a combination of the two.

The English were not to keep Irish minstrels, poets or story-tellers, who had been known to spy out the lie of the land for Irish insurgents. Nor were they to sell horses or armour to the Irish; in time of war, they were not to sell them food either. Englishmen were to retain their surnames of colour, trade or place, and Irishmen living amongst them must adopt English surnames if they were to have English status. Englishmen were to practise archery, so as to be ready for war, and to ride in the English manner, with a heavy saddle, stirrups and a bridle. Above all, Englishmen must speak English. 'If they use the Irish speech', read a statute, 'they shall forfeit their lands to their lords until they undertake to use English.' A very famous statute forbade 'the games which men call hurling', which was probably not the modern Irish game of hurling but an Anglo-Irish equivalent of it.

Although the Statutes were not specifically directed against the Irish, the official attitude of hatred and contempt for them, and for all things Irish, was made abundantly clear. They were consistently referred to as 'the Irish enemies' and the English, or Anglo-Irish, who had taken up Irish ways as 'the degenerate[4] English'. These English were, in the current Irish phrase, 'the middle nation', English born in Ireland of English, or perhaps Anglo-Irish, parents, and the object of much government suspicion, being variously described as 'the king's Irish rebels' and 'the rebellious English'. They, for their part, were chagrined not to be given high office, which was reserved for a third more trusted category, the English-born.

The Statutes of Kilkenny could not be enforced; there was never the administrative machinery to compel the large mixed populations of the English areas to comply with them. They were little more than a dead letter in the government's vain attempt to stem the flood of Irishness. For many years the Anglo-Irish forbore to marry Irish women because their children and heirs would be illegitimate, but they still sent their children to be fostered with the Irish, and they still stood godfather to Irish children. They kept their poets and harpists, they wore the thick Irish mantle and tight Irish trews and grew their hair in long Irish glibes. And Irish was the tongue spoken everywhere, not only in the hills and forests, but the towns and villages of the colonial east, and even the cities of Dublin and Waterford. But the legal position of the two nations remained distinct. However rebellious an Anglo-Irishman might be, however 'degenerate', if he could show himself to be of English origin, or, better still, descended from one of the 'families of the first conquest', he stood fair to be pardoned. But an Irishman, unless he spoke and dressed like an Englishman, rode his horse in the English manner and had taken an English name, was considered to be in servitude to the English and without rights to marry, foster, own property or trade among the English. So long as the English lord of Ireland could uphold the rights of the minority, the two nations were never to become one.

The minor English, the craftsmen, labourers and small tenant farmers, felt deeply threatened by the Irish revival. In 1367, just after Clarence' departure, the Irish Council complained to Edward III that the 'Irish enemies', and probably 'the king's Irish rebels' as well, 'rode in hostile array' through every part of the land, 'committing homicides, robberies and arsons, pillaging, spoiling and destroying monasteries, churches, castles, towns and fortresses.' They were probably exaggerating to make their point, but the conclusion they reached was accurate enough. 'The land is at point to be lost', they said, 'if remedy and help are not immediately supplied.'

Edward was prepared to spend handsomely on Ireland in the short term, in order to defend his subjects and restore profitability to the country, but not to pump out money indefinitely. He sent into Ireland a vigorous and forceful deputy, William of Windsor, with a contract to provide men-at-arms and archers in return for £10,000 in the first year, £8,000 in the second and £6,000 in the third; after that, he was to find the resources he needed from the Anglo-Irish themselves. Windsor screwed the necessary money out of the Anglo-Irish at parliament after parliament, by fair means and foul; one parliament was summoned to the middle of nowhere, where its members had neither food nor lodging, and starved into submission, and the recalcitrant members of another were thrown into prison. But he failed; the Anglo-Irish would not be coerced. Then in 1380 the English parliament, in an attempt to help, passed a draconian Statute of Absentees for Ireland, which decreed that all absentees with lands, benefices, or offices in Ireland should return to them. If they did not, two-thirds of the profits from them, the rents and other emoluments, should be forfeited to the justiciar and spent on their defence. But this, too, failed; the more important absentees sold their estates to the Anglo-Irish, some of them to the 'king's Irish rebels', and pulled out of Ireland altogether.

The truth was that England had neither the men nor the money to defend the 'obedient English'. The Black Death had struck for the first time in 1348, when the population of England was about four million; by the end of the century, after further outbreaks of plague, it had fallen to two-and-a-half million. And there were many calls on English manpower. The Hundred Years' War between England and France had broken out in 1337, and there were constant threats from the Scots and the Welsh. In Ireland, the Black Death ravaged the densely populated towns and villages of the English colony, killing almost 40 per cent of the people there, but the far more numerous Irish, still leading their wandering life, were scarcely touched by it. In the second half of the fourteenth century, with 'the king's Irish rebels' included, the population of Gaelic Ireland propably equalled some 60 per cent of the population of England, or one-and-a-half million. With all her other commitments, England could not cope with that.

In 1377 Edward III died and was succeeded by his 10-year-old grandson, Richard II. Lacking the interest in France of his predecessors, Richard turned his mind to Ireland and in 1394, when he was 27, decided to pay his lordship a visit. Tall and fair, with a foppish appearance – he is said to have been the first person to use handkerchiefs – he had great courage and a flair for diplomacy; he could see the other side. In writing to his uncle, the duke of York, he described the Irish princes as 'rebels only because of grievances and wrongs done to them on one side and lack of remedy on the other. If they are not widely trusted and put in good hope of grace, they will probably join our enemies.' Before he left England, he wrote to Ó Néill promising 'to do justice to every man'. And justice the Irish certainly expected of him. When he landed in Waterford, accompanied by such great absentees as his heir the earl of Ulster, another Roger Mortimer, and a splendid array of some six or seven thousand men, the Irish welcomed him. 'I know I have transgressed against your excellency before these times,' wrote Muiris Ó Conchobhair of Offaly, 'mainly because I found no-one to do justice between the English and me.' Irish chieftains had always wanted to deal with the lord of Ireland himself, and not with a low-born justiciar.

Richard spent the great medieval feast of Christmas at Dublin castle. Eighty Irish princes and chiefs submitted to him and promised obedience in return for a renewed title to all lands they had held at the beginning of the century. The lands they had 'usurped', or retaken, since were to be given up and a new English colony created east of a line from Dundalk to the river Boyne and down the river Barrow to Waterford, an area which came to be known as the English Pale.[5]

Richard was delighted with himself – it had all been much easier than he had expected. But he neglected to summon a parliament which might ratify the new arrangements and the Irish chieftains, while acquiring legal ownership under the king of their old lands, did not give up any of their new 'usurped' lands, and no-one later on could make them do it. When Richard sailed away in May 1395, like Henry II and John before him he left his task unfinished.

Hardly had Richard's successor, Henry IV, assumed the crown in 1399 than he received another of those distressful cries for help from 'the obedient English', which the Irish Council had so often passed on before. Art Mac Murchadha, king of Leinster, and the earl of Desmond were at war with the loyal earl of Ormond; O'Neill, too, was threatening war – he had given

96

13. Art Mac Murchadha Caomhánach riding out to parley with Richard II's envoy, the earl of Gloucester (courtesy of the National Library of Ireland)

hostages to Richard and not had them back. 'The land is in danger of final destruction if it be not quickly relieved and succoured,' the Irish Council wrote. 'The Irish enemies are strong and arrogant and of great power, and there is neither rule nor power to resist them.' But England was running out of money; Henry could not afford to send yet another expensive military expedition. In the summer of 1401 he sent his son Thomas, a boy of thirteen, to rule in Ireland, with the promise of £8,000. But the money could not be raised and within a year Thomas was out of funds. A year after that he was deeply in debt; his notes of hand were not honoured and his government in disrepute.

Ireland was almost without formal government. The land was so troubled that it was no longer possible to hold parliaments, or courts of justice, outside Dublin, and the Pale had shrunk from the colony envisaged by Richard II to no more than the modern counties of Louth, Meath, Dublin and Kildare.

Beyond the Pale, the Irish and the Anglo-Irish were left to their own devices. The aristocracies of both sides continued to carve out lordships for themselves, which they ruled as they pleased, and warfare was constant. The Anglo-Irish, like the Irish, preyed on their neighbours' cattle after the ancient pattern and there were endless feuds and faction fights. Every lord kept his private army of several hundred men, quartered on his tenants according to the old custom of coign and livery, whereby tenants were obliged to feed and house them, look after their horses, and sometimes provide them with money, for a stipulated period each year.

Yet the 'king's Irish rebels' and the 'Irish enemies' were slowly finding a new equilibrium. They lived in much the same way and, despite the Statutes of Kilkenny, became linked ever more closely in a network of aristocratic marriages, fostering and the exchange of hostages. And a new stability, a kind of peace, was being born. It did little for the common Irish. 'The wretched and filthy people', wrote a French poet, Jean Creton, 'some in rags, others girt with a rope, had the one a hole, the other a hut for their dwelling.' They cooked their curds and oatcake on an open fire and ate it sitting on the ground. But early in the fifteenth century the great Anglo-Irish lords began building handsome and easily defensible tower houses, part castle and also part palace, and encouraging the arts of peace. The poets sang a sweetly as ever on the new theme of courtly love, which the Normans had introduced from France. The scribes were illuminating anthologies of verse, and noblemen were building up libraries where books written in French, English, Latin and Irish stood side by side.

Art Mac Murchadha ruled in Leinster until his death in 1418, when he was succeeded by his son Donnchadh. The Ó Néills of Tyrone ruled from Dundalk to the north coast, from Coleraine to Derry, and the earldom of Ulster shrank until it reached no farther than Ballymena and the river Braid in the north, and Lisburn and Newry in the west. Anglo-Irish earls controlled the south and the east; the estates of the Butlers, headed by the earls of Ormond, stretched from Kilkenny and Waterford westwards to Cork, while the two Geraldine earls, of Desmond and Kildare, had palatine powers, Desmond over much of Munster and Kildare from the Wicklow hills to the borders of Meath.

Since the disastrous governorship of Thomas, the boy prince, deputy after deputy had left Ireland heavily in debt. Henry IV, Henry V and his son Henry VI were ruining England with their insistence on fighting endless wars against France, and the money allowed to government servants was increasingly being given in the form of tallies, that is, IOUs, which might, or might not, be redeemed later on. Not surprisingly, the Crown was finding it increasingly difficult to find anyone who was both competent, willing and rich enough to take on the role of deputy in Ireland. Sir Thomas Stanley, deputy from 1431 to 1434, was owed well over £3,000 three years later and Lord Welles, who was deputy from 1438 to 1441, was still owed £2,000 in 1442. Deputies often recouped themselves one way or another; they could generally claim a percentage of the taxes they collected. But the reputation of the government was lowered, and the good, solid minor English, those who gave the Crown most loyalty, suffered; artisans and traders went unpaid for the equipment and uniforms they supplied, small farmers had the deputy's army quartered on them (even though the exactions of coign and livery were supposed to be illegal) and the soldiery themselves were unpaid. And the Pale went on shrinking. Each deputy made forays into the lands beyond it, brought in such chieftains as he could catch, negotiated the release of prisoners and return of stolen cattle, fostered alliances and obtained temporary submissions. The black rents, or protection money, which the 'obedient English' in the marcher areas paid the Irish would be suspended – until the deputy and his men engaged themselves elsewhere.

Then in July 1447 Ireland received what she was always demanding, a deputy from the English royal house. He was Richard, duke of York, and his appointment was for ten years. England, while losing the war with France, was already preparing for a civil war between the Lancastrians, who supported the weak but saintly Henry VI, and the Yorkists, of whom the duke was, naturally, the most prominent. Henry hoped that, by sending York to Ireland, he would be removing him from the scene. But York saw the appointment as an opportunity to gain Ireland for the Yorkist cause, an aim in which he succeeded admirably. Descended from the great names of Norman Ireland, de Burgo, de Lacy and Mortimer, and from Brian Bóroime as well, he 'got him such love and favour' from almost every section of the people of Ireland that 'their sincere and lovely affection could never be separated from him and his lineage', according to an English chronicler. He left Ireland in 1450 but came fleeing back again in 1459 after a Yorkist defeat in England, and summoned a parliament to Drogheda, about fifteen miles north of Dublin, where he was given almost sovereign powers.

In 1460 the same parliament described its own constitutional position in relation to the English parliament. 'The land of Ireland is, and at all times hath been,' the parliament stated, 'corporate of itself by the ancient law and customs used in the same, freed from the burden of any special law of the realm of England, save only such laws as by the lords spiritual and temporal and the commons of the said land had been in great council or parliament there admitted, accepted, affirmed and proclaimed.' It was a fundamental statement of the determination of the Anglo-Irish magnates who dominated the Irish parliament to preserve Irish independence under the king.

York returned to England, only to be killed in battle on the last day of the year. Nevertheless fortune was with the Yorkists and his son was crowned Edward IV in March, 1461. He was a strong, forceful king, determined to be felt, and in November the English parliament passed an act of attainder against the Butlers and other Lancastrian sympathizers depriving them of their lands and rights in the parliament's jurisdiction, and in 1462 the Irish parliament followed suit. Waterford and Kilkenny declared for Ormond, but Thomas, seventh earl of Desmond, led 20,000 men against the Butler faction, wasted the Butler lands and defeated the Butler armies. The Butlers faded temporarily from the scene.

In 1463 Desmond, as the most powerful nobleman in Ireland, was made deputy for four years and then, in 1467, succeeded by the English earl of Worcester. Edward was determined to show the Anglo-Irish, and the Geraldines in particular, who was master, and in February 1468 Worcester summoned a parliament to Drogheda, where the Geraldines were very unpopular. Desmond was warned not to attend, but ignored the warning and arrived to find himself and the earl of Kildare the object of a government attack. They were accused of 'horrible treasons and felonies as well as in alliance, fosterage and alterage[6] with the Irish enemies of the king as in giving to them horses, harness and arms' contrary to the Statutes of Kilkenny. It was a trumped-up charge; no nobleman in Ireland could survive without breaking some of the Statutes of Kilkenny; but Desmond was beheaded on 14th February. The whole country was shocked and inflamed. The executed earl's son James rose up in arms, receiving a great deal of support, ravaged the king's lands in Meath, and swore that none of his house would ever again attend parliament or the Irish Council, or enter any walled town belonging to the king except at their own pleasure. From that day onwards the Geraldines of Desmond declared themselves to be Irish.

With Ormond a Lancastrian and Desmond driven with brutal clumsiness into the Irish camp, power moved inevitably to the house of Kildare. The seventh earl, charged with treason at Drogheda alongside Desmond, managed to escape capture, had his attainder reversed later in the year, and was made justiciar and then deputy in 1470, inaugurating a dynastic rule which was to last for the next sixty years.

When Kildare died in 1477, he was succeeded as deputy, as well as in the earldom, by his 21-year-old son Gearóid, who came to be known to both Irish and English as Gearóid Mór, and sometimes the Great Earl. 'A mighty man of stature,' according to the English historian Stanyhurst, 'full of honour and courage', he was quick to anger and equally quick to forgive, generous, commanding and respectful of religion. He lived in considerable splendour at his castle of Maynooth, a short ride away from Dublin, and hawked and hunted on the plain of the Curragh. He spoke English, Irish and some Norman-French, and probably read several languages, including Latin, but, like other nobles, left writing to his secretaries. He had all the qualities people expected in a great nobleman.

In 1478 Edward deprived Kildare of his office and sent Lord Grey from London to replace him as deputy. A trial of strength followed. In no time the young earl had called a parliament, which confirmed him in his office, and Lord Grey, the king's appointment, had to withdraw. Edward, who had defeated Desmond, could not defeat Kildare; the Great Earl was confirmed in a power – the power of an all-but king – which was never again seriously challenged.

It was a power based on a network of family alliances built up over several generations. The Great Earl's mother was a Geraldine of Desmond, he had been fostered with Ó Domhnaill in Donegal and his sister Eleanor was married to Conn Ó Néill of Tyrone, who ruled in Ulster.[7] His first wife was Alison Fitzeustace, daughter of the treasurer of Ireland, and his second wife, whom he married in 1496, an Englishwoman with royal connections, Elizabeth St John.

And it was a power supported by immense riches. The Kildare estates were vast, comprising the counties of Kildare, Wicklow, Leix and Offaly and, later on, a large part of Carlow. Beyond that family wealth there was the right of the deputy to raise taxes, collect tribute and receive the forfeited rents of absentees – to gather into his own hands all the revenues of Ireland. He had to pay government officials and arm his kerns and gallowglasses (whom his tenants maintained), but could keep the considerable surplus for himself.

Edward IV died in 1483, leaving two young princes, and was succeeded by his twelve-year-old son, Edward V. But the young king's uncle, Richard, duke of Gloucester, appointed Lord Protector, had Edward and his brother sent to the Tower of London. Some say Gloucester had them murdered there; others that he has been gravely maligned. Either way, the princes were never seen again and a few weeks later Gloucester was crowned king of England as Richard III. Two years later, however, he was killed in the last battle of the civil war and the victorious Lancastrian leader, of the Welsh Tudor family, ascended the throne as Henry VII.

Kildare prudently married his daughter to a leading member of the Lancastrian Butlers. But when in 1487 a Yorkist pretender to the English throne, a ten-year-old boy named Lambert Simnel, was brought to Dublin by an Oxford priest, he was, in an extraordinary incident, crowned in Christ Church cathedral before the deputy and almost everyone else of importance in Ireland! However he was made prisoner soon enough when he landed in England, and set to work to work by a lenient Henry in the royal kitchens!

Henry could do no more than rebuke Kildare. A new king, still shaky on his throne, he had neither the power nor the means to administer punishment, and in 1488 the Great Earl was pardoned for his flagrant disloyalty. But when the king's envoy,

Sir Richard Edgecombe, was sent to Ireland to receive the deputy's submission, Kildare treated him with obvious disdain. Instead of going to Edgecombe, as protocol demanded, he most arrogantly kept Edgecombe waiting for a month before receiving him, with almost regal state, at his lodgings in Dublin. Then in 1491, when a second Yorkist pretender, Perkin Warbeck, landed in Cork, Kildare invited the king of Scots to send support for the so-called prince.

Henry decided to clip the Great Earl's wings. In 1494 he sent Sir Edward Poynings to replace him as deputy. Inevitably the two fell out, and with his small army of a thousand well-trained men, a determined Poynings arrested Kildare and sent him to England.

Then in December Poynings called a parliament and brought Anglo-Ireland firmly to heel. There were to be no more appointments made for life, Irish accounts were to be audited by the English Exchequer and the laws of England were to prevail in Ireland: so much for the declaration of the 1460 parliament that 'the land of Ireland is corporate of itself'. Then, in an enactment which has gone down in history as Poynings' law, bills had to be approved by the king and his council, or parliament, in England before they could be put to an Irish parliament.

Kildare was soon reinstated. 'He is meet to rule all Ireland,' Henry is reputed to have said, 'seeing all Ireland cannot rule him.' But Kildare, when all's said and done, never did rule Ireland; the ultimate responsibility was never his. He enjoyed the perquisites of greatness and, because so many of the reins were in his hands, Ireland acquired a sort of peace. But even the responsibility for local law and order was not his, but the king's. And Kildare was content with that. He was not a patriot; he never seriously tried to wrest the government of Ireland away from England. The Irish loved him as a home-grown grandee; they appreciated his splendour and the humiliation of such English officials as Edgecombe. But the fruits of his arrogance and disloyalty were Poynings' parliament, the end of all notions of Anglo-Irish Home Rule and, ultimately, the conquest of Ireland.

CHAPTER 6

TUDOR COLONISTS

In England, Henry VII arranged a marriage for his eldest son, Arthur, with Catherine of Aragon, a princess of Spain. In 1501 the couple were married, both aged fifteen. Then tragedy struck: four and a half months after the wedding, Arthur died. Henry was a thrifty man. He had spent much time and effort promoting the alliance with Spain and he did not want them wasted. Nor did he want to return Catherine's dowry. So he betrothed the young widow to his second son, who was to become Henry VIII.

The Church, however, forbade the marriage of a widow and her deceased husband's brother. Catherine remained in England, living in the retirement suited to her widowhood, until the necessary dispensation had come from the pope. Then, a few months after Henry's accession to the throne in 1509, he and Catherine were married.

For a time they lived together happily enough. Catherine was pretty and artistic, while Henry was handsome and intelligent. But the Tudor dynasty was still young, and Henry was anxious for an heir. Catherine's first child, a son, died in infancy, the second, born in 1516, was a daughter, and others were stillborn. Henry, deeply disappointed, appealed to the pope for a declaration of annulment of his marriage, so that he could replace the ageing Catherine with a younger, and probably more fruitful, wife. Such annulments were quite often granted, but the pope had political reasons for refusing this one, and for six years Henry's application was held up. But he pushed ahead with his plea, and asked the pope to annul the marriage on the grounds that the original papal dispensation allowing it had been illegal. No pope, Henry argued, had the right to grant a dispensation contrary to the teachings of the Bible – and the Bible said no man could marry his brother's widow.

Henry had become desperate. His new love, Ann Boleyn, was pregnant; he needed to marry her quickly in order to legitimize the child. Without such pressure, Henry would have been very unlikely to take a line which attacked the authority of the pope and savoured of a new and powerful heresy – Protestantism.

About two centuries earlier, John Wycliffe, a professor of divinity at the university of Oxford, had started a protest movement for the reform of abuses and corruption within the Church. Similar movements were begun by Jan Hus in Bohemia and, a century later, by Martin Luther in Germany; Luther posted his famous 95 theses on the church door at Wittenberg in 1517. Protestants wanted a return to the teachings of the Bible, which had become far more widely available since the invention of printing in the fifteenth century, and less interference by priests between man and God. The Church had reacted by declaring that Protestants were heretics and the civil authorities had them burned at the stake. Protestants realized that their only hope was to win Europe's rulers over to their side against the Church, and they formulated a doctrine that kings – usually called 'princes' – were set up by God to control the religious as well as the secular aspects of their subjects' lives. They taught that it was the duty of the Protestant Christian to obey his prince in everything – except, of course, becoming a Catholic.

Henry was supremely autocratic. He did not depend for his power on the support of great nobles, as earlier kings had done, nor, as his successors would do, on parliament. The officials who served him were wholly dependent on his favour. When he read a treatise entitled *The Obedience of a Christian Man* by the English Protestant William Tyndale, he commented: 'This book is for me and all kings to read.' Almost against his will, he was leading his country into Protestantism. In 1533 he appointed Thomas Cranmer, a mildly Protestant Cambridge don who favoured the annulment of his marriage to Catherine, as archbishop of Canterbury. Cranmer pushed the annulment through and then crowned Ann, whom Henry had secretly married, queen of England. Ann's child, too, turned out to be a girl – the future queen Elizabeth I – but there was no going back. In December, three months after the birth, Henry repudiated papal supremacy over the English Church. By act of parliament, he became 'under Christ the Supreme Head of the Church of England.' The Reformation in England still had a long way to go, but the break with Rome had been made.

No whiff of Protestantism reached Ireland, so far away in the Atlantic. The Irish Church had decayed over the last two centuries, like the Church elsewhere, but it still held the loyalty and affection of the Irish people.

Irish bishops, priests and monks were still likely to be 'married', not according to the rites of the Church, but the ancient Gaelic custom which allowed them concubines. Their children were illegitimate in the eyes of the Church, and barred from entering the priesthood unless they could acquire special dispensations – but in the fourteenth century the popes, who were very short of funds, began trading eagerly in such dispensations. The Irish Church slipped back into the old system of a hereditary priesthood, dominated by major ecclesiastical families. The coarbs, who were the 'heirs and successors' of early saints, were once more reserving certain benefices for themselves and claiming the revenues of abbeys and bishoprics as their own family property. A fourteenth century archbishop of Cashel was the father of an archbishop of Tuam, who was the father of a bishop of Elphin. The bishop's son, a coarb, was the father of two priests and the grandfather of an archdeacon. And so it went on, with a 'married' priesthood begetting more priests, well into the seventeeth century.

The diocesan and parochial structure had been undermined by poverty and continual war. Some bishops were permanently absent because their diocese' could not support them. Others had no proper cathedrals. Clonmacnoise and Ardagh were both cathedral cities, but in 1517 there were only twelve wretched cabins at Clonmacnoise and fourteen at Ardagh. Both cathedrals were in ruins, and at Ardagh even the altar was in the open air! Prayers were seldom said nor mass celebrated in such places. The lower clergy received scant respect; they were miserably poor, some without rectories, and eked out their tiny incomes by charging exhorbitantly for baptisms, weddings and funerals.

Pastoral care had always come from the monasteries – the great

Cistercian foundations and the older-style colleges of 'married' monks and laymen. They were centres of religious devotion, education and learning, as well as refuges for the poor, the sick and travellers, who stayed overnight in monasteries where there were no inns. But by the fifteenth century the Cistercian monasteries had almost dwindled away, and their pastoral role been largely taken over by a great number of small friaries, from each of which a dozen or so friars would go out among the people. The Irish Church, whatever its difficulties, had no wish whatsoever to follow the English Church out of the papal fold. But Henry was determined, and he took steps to strengthen his position in Ireland.

From 1515 onwards for the next twenty years, the Irish Council sent Henry eloquent and colourful reports on conditions within the Pale, which was, by this time, a stockaded enclosure with a few border crossings. English settlers were depicted as an exploited, half-starved people, almost indistinguishable from the Irish, trebly burdened by the payment of black rents to the chiefs along the border, having the deputy's army quartered on them, and the exactions of the lords of the Pale, which included coign and livery, the maintenance of horses and hounds, and payments towards Christmas and Easter festivities. In return they should have been given protection against the so-called 'wild' Irish, but only too often the marcher lords found it less trouble to let the Irish through their lands to make their preys of cattle unhindered. Irish chiefs near the border all employed a professional cow-stealer, known ironically as 'the caterer' and boasted that they 'eat their beef from the English Pale'.

The reports were fundamentally true, though exaggerated; the situation within the Pale had been declining for the best part of a century. But the object of the Irish Council in sending them to Henry was not so much to help the 'obedient English' as to discredit the Anglo-Irish deputy, the ninth earl of Kildare.

The Great Earl, Gearóid Mór, had died in 1513 and been succeeded by his son, Gearóid Óg, who was equally able and popular; he, too, had become the deputy, as he was the only man in Ireland with the wealth and family connections to do the job. But his power was too great. Cardinal Wolsey, who had become Henry's chancellor of England in 1515, called him scornfully 'the king of Kildare' and Henry began to see him as one of those 'overmighty subjects' whom a powerful monarch must needs curb. When Kildare's rival, the earl of Ormond, persuaded the Irish Council to ask for an English deputy, Henry sent the earl of Surrey, an appointment which flattered the Anglo-Irish as Surrey had royal blood.

English monarchs could never decide whether to try for a total conquest of Ireland or to divide and rule, by playing off one magnate against another. Henry was cruel – the cruellest monarch England ever had – but he was not warlike, and he sent Surrey to Ireland in 1520 with instructions to bring the Irish into submission and obedience 'by sober ways, politic drifts and aimiable persuasions', that is, to negotiate: but to negotiate from strength. Surrey had an army of 1,100 as well as an ample budget, and he had considerable success; a large number of Irish chiefs, bowing before the wind, came in to him – so many that he began to study the possibilities of a total conquest and wrote a memorandum to Henry recommending that it could be undertaken with 5,000 men, not an unreasonable number as the Irish could raise 22,000, paid, equipped and provisioned by England. As the conquest progressed, castles and towns would have to be built and English settlers brought in.

Such a scheme was far too expensive for Henry. When he came to the throne, he had been one of the richest kings in Europe, but he kept a lavish and splendid court. When Surrey asked to be recalled after eighteen months in Ireland, Henry replaced him with Ormond. But he had an inadequate Irish following and two years later Gearóid Óg was deputy once more.

He soon found his position precarious. Ann Boleyn's father, Sir Thomas Boleyn, was connected with the Butlers and Henry gave him the earldom of Ormond, pushing out the current earl. It meant that the Butlers, so long enemies of the Geraldines, had Henry's ear. And some strange tales reached that ear. Kildare's friends and kinsmen in the west, the earl of Desmond and the chiefs of the O'Briens, were intriguing with the Hapsburg emperor, Charles V, in favour of a Yorkist pretender to the English throne. Kildare turned a blind eye to the intrigues, not considering them worth bothering about, but Wolsey seized the opportunity they gave him. He summoned Kildare to London and, after a stormy interview, sent him briefly to the Tower.

But the imperious cardinal's days were numbered. When he

failed to get Henry the annulment he wanted, Wolsey was replaced in 1530 by Thomas Cromwell, a ruthlessly efficient servant of the state who believed as fervently as Henry in a strong monarchy. Cromwell would not tolerate a rival power in Ireland. For a while he held his hand – and then, in 1533, the Irish Council charged the deputy with appropriating heavy guns belonging to the Crown and moving them to his castle at Maynooth. Once again Kildare was summoned to London and put in the Tower. He was not in good shape; the year before he had been wounded in battle and 'never after', according to the Tudor historian Stanihurst, 'enjoyed his limbs, nor delivered his words in good plight'.

Before he left, Kildare had his eldest son, Lord Offaly, made deputy in his stead. Nicknamed Silken Thomas because of the silk garments he and his bodyguard wore, Offaly was a handsome, rash and inexperienced young man of twenty-one. Kildare advised him to defer to the Irish Council, 'for albeit in authority you rule them, yet in counsel they must rule you,' but not to trust them. He spoke with prescience: for, early in 1534, the English faction sent a rumour flying round Ireland that he had been beheaded, and a letter telling of his death was planted on a servant, who took it to Silken Thomas. The distraught young man went to one of his cousins, who urged him to avenge his father's death.

Other advisers urged prudence, but Silken Thomas would have none of it. Impetuously he looked for allies. Then on 11th June he rode through Dublin with 140 armed retainers to a meeting of the Irish Council, where he declared himself no longer Henry's man and called on all who hated cruelty to join him in rebellion. In vain the archbishop of Armagh begged him, with tears in his eyes, not to resort to such an extreme; a harpist in his entourage broke into a long praise-poem and exhorted him to vengeance. Silken Thomas flung down his sword of office and left.

For the next six weeks, Silken Thomas and his followers harried the people of the Pale and threatened Dublin. Then the city's archbishop, John Alen, who led the anti-Geraldine faction, decided to flee from Dublin castle, where he had taken refuge, and sail for England. He did not get very far; his boat went aground at Clontarf and he took shelter in a gentleman's house nearby. Next morning Silken Thomas caught up with him. His men hauled the archbishop out of bed and Silken Thomas, so the story goes, ordered them in Irish to 'take the churl away'. They mistook his meaning and dashed the archbishop's brains out.

What greater crime than to murder an archbishop? When the news reached the pope, he excommunicated Silken Thomas, and the Church cursed him in dreadful terms: wishing him leprosy and madness, hunger and thirst in this life and eternal damnation in the next. No house was to shelter him, no Christian to give him succour. This curse, which would have been taken quite literally in those days, was unkindly shown to the old earl, still languishing in the Tower, and in December he died, seemingly of despair.

Silken Thomas, now earl of Kildare himself, cast about him for help, sending gifts of hawks and Irish palfreys to Charles V, negotiating with the king of Scots and trying to stir up the O'Briens and O'Kellys. Sir William Skeffington, the new deputy, arrived in Ireland with a large army. He was an experienced soldier, who knew the country well, but old and delicate. For some time he remained in Dublin, ill. Then in March 1535 he led his army to Maynooth and took the castle there.

Silken Thomas was in Connacht. When he came hurrying back he met Skeffington, and his followers melted away; he was left without hope, friends, or even a good cause and had no choice but to surrender. He was sent to London and lodged in the Tower, like his father. Surrey, now the duke of Norfolk, advised with callous calculation that he should be kept in the Tower for a while as a hostage for the good behaviour of others and then, when there was no further 'commodity' in his survival, put to death. He stayed in the Tower for sixteen months, half-starved and half-naked, 'barefoot and barelegged divers times (when it was not very warm)', as he wrote to a servant. Then he was taken to Tyburn and hanged, drawn and quartered.

Five other Geraldines, Silken Thomas' uncles, were hanged with him as accessories to the rebellion. They had surrendered on terms – and were dishonourably killed. Noblemen from Ireland had no right of protection against the king, as English peers had through their House of Lords. Once in England, they fell easy victims to the monarch's wrath.

In Ireland there were fears for the safety of Silken Thomas' successor, his younger brother Gerald, who had been nine at the time of Thomas' arrest. He lived with his tutor, Thomas Leverous, within the Pale, until his uncles were arrested; then Leverous put the boy, who was suffering from smallpox, in a basket and carried him, even though he was gravely ill, to the castle of his sister, Lady Mary O'Conor, the wife of the chief of Offaly. But Offaly was close to the Pale, and as soon as Gerald was well enough he was taken westwards to Thomond and the chief of the O'Briens. After a few months he was passed on to the earl of Desmond and then to his aunt, Lady Eleanor MacCarthy.

Lady Eleanor was an energetic, strong-minded woman and a leading proponent of the Geraldine League, a combination of Irish and Anglo-Irish families (excluding the Butlers) determined to save the young earl. For the sake of her nephew, Lady Eleanor agreed to marry the Ó Domhnaill chief and set out with Gearóid for the wild moorlands, untouched by the Englishry, of Donegal. Yet even there she had her misgivings; she did not trust her new husband. So she arranged Gearóid's flight by sea. Wearing only the saffron shirt of a peasant and accompanied by the faithful Leverous, in 1539 the hope of the Geraldines took ship for France.

The story, with its cast of a rash, impetuous youth nobly inspired by love of his father, wicked enemies, a faithful servant, a fairy godmother and a boy carried to safety in a basket, has the quality of fairytale. The reality was less romantic. Blind loyalty to the monarch had never served the Kildare interest. Gearóid Óg was more likely to be released from the Tower and restored to his position as deputy if Ireland became ungovernable in his absence, and he may well have discussed rebellion, or some kind of disorder, before he left for England. He had no more desire to oust the English than his father had had, but he certainly wanted to remain the most powerful man in Ireland, head of a semi-autonomous house in a semi-autonomous land. But Silken Thomas was, as the fairy tale depicted, too young and inexperienced to play such a game, and Henry, the tyrant, scooped the board.

With the breaking of the Kildares, the road lay open for major royal encroachments in Ireland. As early as 1536, even before Silken Thomas' execution, a parliament which came to be known as the Reformation parliament was summoned. It began, predictably enough, by attainting Silken Thomas and forfeiting the Kildare lands. Then a bill was presented to it for the dissolution of the monasteries, which had just taken place in England. The Butlers, who had early declared for Henry against the pope, saw the opportunity dissolution offered of acquiring well cultivated church lands, with cottages, mills and orchards on them, and ensured, through a compound of threats and bribery, that the knights and burgesses in the Commons would not 'stick in the king's causes'. Only the lower clergy who, since 1370, had been represented in the Commons, held out against the bill, and were expelled for their pains.

Then parliament considered the bill of supremacy itself, which declared the king of England to be supreme head of the Church in Ireland, as he already was of the Church in England, displacing the pope. Almost every churchman sitting in parliament, from the archbishop of Armagh downwards, was opposed to the bill, but once again the Butlers came to the king's rescue, and when the archbishops of Cashel and Tuam, and eight bishops, had been persuaded to take the oath acknowledging Henry's supremacy, the opposition collapsed. Then in 1540 Sir Anthony St Leger, a new deputy, advised Henry that the Act of Supremacy would be more real in Ireland if the title lord of Ireland, which Henry II had had of the pope, were to be replaced with that of king. Ireland would no longer be Adrian's Donation, derived from the pope's superior authority, but Henry's kingdom, a possession of the English Crown by right of conquest and inheritance. Various monasteries within the Pale had already been dissolved, and the local nobility and gentry 'sweetened' by the acquisition of monastic lands at cheap rates. When St Leger summoned another parliament in 1541, its members welcomed the change in Henry's status. In Dublin, where the English officials mostly lived, it was greeted with joy.

Henry saw himself as the apex of a pyramid, with all rights and titles to land and offices devolving from him. He was the feudal overlord, the lawgiver and the ultimate judge. To bring the Irish princes and chieftains, who held their land according to Gaelic law and custom, into line with this feudal concept, he looked back to the days of Henry II and reintroduced the practice of Surrender and Re-grant. Chieftains were invited to surrender all their tribal lands to him, and receive them back immediately with a new title, valid under English law, and a promise of protection against their enemies. It did not sound a bad bargain, and in a couple of years some forty Irish chieftains had come in to St Leger, made their obeisance to Henry and opened negotiations to have their lands granted back to them, accompanied, for the first time in Irish history, by titles of nobility after the English manner. Ulick Burke, of the 'degenerate English' in Connacht, became earl of Clanricarde. Conn Bacach Ó Néill, of Ulster, promised to attend parliament and was made earl of Tyrone; his eldest son, Matthew, who, according to the laws of primogeniture, would succeed him, became baron of Dungannon. The reigning Ó Domnaill agreed to accept the title of earl of Tír Conaill, though it was not actually given to the Ó Domnaills until 1603, and the chief of the Ó Briains became earl of Thomond and baron Inchiquin; his son was baron Ibrackin.

The titles did not raise their possessors in Irish esteem; rather, they diminished them. As a later Ó Néill[1] was to put it so proudly: 'I care not to be made an earl unless I may be better and higher than an earl, for I am in blood and power better than the best of them . . . . My ancestors were kings of Ulster and Ulster is mine and shall be mine.' Conn Bacach accepted his earldom of Tyrone and swore allegiance to Henry with cynicism; the same year he was promising the pope he would defend the Catholic religion in Ireland.

Irish chiefs thought Surrender and Re-grant was no more than a whim of the English. They did not realize their re-granted lands, vested in the Crown, could be forfeited by the Crown. They were used to changing sides frequently; now they were on the king's side, and now the vagaries of their feuds and alliances blew them the other way. But under the new system they could find themselves accused of treason and their lands taken from them. There were to be no more easy pardons and no more deals, as there had been when the English king was merely lord of Ireland; now they were subjects who could be totally dispossessed.

Henry had rejected the policy of a conquest of Ireland because of the expense. He seldom interfered with the way the Irish princes ran their territories, or 'countries', for much the same reason; as Ireland brought him almost no revenue, the manner of its administration seemed to him hardly worth bothering about. He let Ireland be. But, in the ten years between 1537 and his death in 1547, the Geraldine League collapsed, leading to confiscations which brought an enormous acreage in Louth and Westmeath, into his hand. And the second of the policies put forward in Surrey's memorandum on the conquest of Ireland was taken up in the reign of Henry's son, the boy king Edward VI. The policy was plantation.

The original English colonists, the artisans, craftsmen and retainers who had followed their Anglo-Norman lords to Ireland in the Middle Ages, had either emigrated back to England because of the insecurity of the Pale, moved to a major town, such as Waterford, Cork, or Galway, or joined the Irish. English governments had always wished to build up a numerous, loyal and stable English population; with Crown lands so extensive, the opportunity to bring in new English families had obviously come.

The first plantation was to be in central Ireland, where bogs and woods had always sheltered the 'wild Irish' who attacked the Pale. Brian Ua Conchobhair, the chief of Offaly, had been outlawed for his support of the Geraldines, and with the attainting of Silken Thomas, the English lordship of Offaly had fallen in too. By 1556 elaborate plans had been made for the plantation of Offaly and the neighbouring land of Leix.

Only the western third of the area was to be left to the Irish. The rest was to be granted to about 160 settlers, Englishmen born either in England or Ireland, who were to build stout, defensible stone houses and, as an equivalent of knight service, provide the deputy with stated numbers of English men-at-arms. Planters were not to employ Irishmen born outside Leix or Offaly, nor Irishmen experienced in arms; they were not to marry among the Irish, nor have any dealings with Irishmen living outside the Pale, and their estates were to be passed on by primogeniture.

In the event, eighty separate grants of land were made to three classes of settler: gentlemen of the Pale, officers and soldiers of the English army and the 'loyal' Irish. The earl of Ormond, as a gentleman of the Pale, received 820 acres, officers and soldiers who had fought against the Geraldine League were generously rewarded, and Owen MacHugh O'Dempsey, who had killed Brian Ua Conchobhair's successor on the English behalf, was given 3,302 acres. But other Irish were deprived; and they rose in arms against the injustice of the confiscation and began a prolonged war against the government.

The plantation was, and was meant to be, a military occupation by a conquering foreign people, who were intended to impose their own culture on the natives. Naturally it aroused fierce resentment among the Irish; they came out of their fastnesses to burn the planters' farms, drive off their cattle and cut the throats of any Englishmen they came upon. For two generations, the planters struggled with them, winning in pitched battles and losing against guerrillas. The young earl of Kildare, who had been educated in Italy, returned, but he never became a power in the land, able to effect a reconciliation, and the planters, like the English of the medieval Pale, began to melt away. By the end of the century, most of the planted lands had reverted to the Irish.[2]

Edward VI was a delicate boy and in 1553, when he was sixteen, he died. His sister Mary succeeded him. She was the daughter of Henry VIII's first wife, the discarded Catherine of Aragon, and a fervent Catholic, eager to restore the pope as head of the Church in England and Ireland. The Irish bishops and clergy adopted her stance, with the wholehearted support of the laity, who had never lost their attachment to the pope. Then in 1558 Mary died and her sister Elizabeth came to the throne.

Elizabeth I was the daughter of Henry's marriage with Ann Boleyn, for which he had led England away from Rome, and her sympathies were Protestant. But she had a keen sense of political reality, and she saw the damage that constant changes of religion were doing to her people. She took on the leadership of the Church, which her father had bequeathed her, and used it to initiate a policy of toleration and compromise. In England the policy worked; a Protestant Church, secular in character, with no mass and a married clergy, gave the people a respite from extremes and was, by and large, accepted. In Ireland the new arrangements became the source of endless conflict. A brief parliament summoned in 1560 passed two Reformation acts[3] to impose Protestantism on Anglo-Ireland; the use of Cranmer's second book of common prayer, written in English, was made compulsory and the people directed to attend these Protestant services in English, although they did not understand them, on pain of a recusancy fine if they stayed away. The remaining two-thirds of the country was left to the pope.

All over Catholic Europe, as well as in Ireland, Elizabeth was regarded as illegitimate, and unlikely to remain for long on the throne she had wrongfully ascended. Catholics were convinced that, when the time was ripe, Philip II of Spain, or some other powerful Catholic sovereign, would unseat her on the pope's behalf. With her position so weak, she saw a disobedient Ireland as a constant menace to her security. Irish noblemen readily swore allegiance to her, and just as readily conspired with Spain or any other foreign power which would help them against their English, or even their Irish, enemies. Elizabeth could not allow Ireland to become a base for hostile fleets and armies. She always preferred negotiation to battle; England spent very little time openly at war during the forty-five years of her reign. Yet Ireland, she eventually decided, must be the object of a total conquest.

The first challenge to Elizabeth's rule came from Ulster, that land beyond the lakes and mountains that the English seldom penetrated. Conn Bacach Ó Néill, the first earl of Tyrone, named as his heir Matthew, baron of Dungannon. But Matthew was illegitimate, the child of one Alison Kelly, the wife of a blacksmith in Dundalk, and not recognized by Conn as his eldest son until he was sixteen. Until then, Conn's most likely heir had been his eldest legitimate son, Shane. Not surprisingly, the two claimants were soon at loggerheads and in 1558 Matthew was killed. The following year Conn Bacach died and Shane had himself elected, in the Irish manner, as the Ó Néill. The young Elizabeth might well have recognized Shane's claim to lead Ulster had not the deputy, the earl of Sussex, advised her that Shane was too powerful; if the English were to hold the balance of power in Ireland, she should support weaker chieftains.

In 1561 Elizabeth invited Shane to London. His flamboyant reputation went ahead of him: the English heard of his absolute power in Ulster, his immense riches, vast herds of cattle, tremendous drinking bouts and innumerable bastards. And when he appeared at court, proud, handsome, and ironically humorous, London's curiosity turned to admiration. A colourful figure with long black hair and yellow robes, he was followed everywhere, even into the queen's presence chamber, by two hundred

116

14. Irish warriors, drawn by Albrecht Dürer (courtesy of the National Gallery of Ireland)

gallowglasses, wearing wolfskins and armed with long-handled battleaxes. When he made his submission to Elizabeth, he prostrated himself before her, gave a huge Gaelic howl and spoke his piece in Irish, so neither she nor her courtiers knew what he was really saying! In subsequent negotiations he made it clear that his autonomy must be respected equally with the queen's, and, to make his point, he took himself very publicly to hear mass in the Spanish embassy.

Elizabeth detained Shane in England from January 1562, until May. By then his tanist,[4] Toirrdhealbhach Luineach mac Néill Chonnalaigh, had had Matthew's eldest son Brian, the new baron of Dungannon, killed and had tried to oust Shane. When Shane was able to return, he defeated Toirrdhealbhach and was soon, in the words of the deputy, the only strong man of Ireland. He made politic submissions now and then, but refused to allow English law or English officials into Ulster and kept up a continual correspondence with the queen's enemies in France, Spain and Scotland.

Like most Gaelic chiefs, Shane was constantly at war with his neighbours. They were the Scots of Antrim, originally mercenaries from the Hebrides, and the Ó Domhnaills of Donegal. In 1565 he defeated the Scots at Glenshesk, near Ballycastle, and the following year defeated and captured the chief of the Ó Domhnaills. The government, true to its policy of supporting the weak against the strong, was backing the Ó Domhnaills, and in 1567 they routed Shane's army in a surprise attack. Shane unwisely threw himself on the mercy of the Scots he had fought for so long, and they knifed him to death in a drunken brawl. His severed head was sent to Dublin, where it was still to be seen stuck on a pole outside the castle four years later.

In 1569 Sir Henry Sidney, one of the most upright and able of Elizabeth's deputies, called a parliament. Its first task was to attaint the name of Shane Ó Néill and confiscate his lands. The consequences of disobedience must be made clear. Then the parliament was persuaded to agree a subsidy to cover the next ten years, so that the queen's army in Ireland could pay its way, instead of being supported by coign and livery; tenants were to pay money rents instead of giving services. The old aristocratic system was to be cleared away in favour of middle-class English bureaucracy; Ireland was to be just like England.

But the Gaelic system of land tenure was not at all like the English one. When the same parliament passed an act depriving the Irish chieftains of their chieftaincies, both the Irish princes and the Anglo-Irish nobility became exceedingly nervous, and organized an opposition party. Sidney wanted to suspend Poynings' law – that law of the late fifteenth century which said that all legislation for Ireland must be framed in England. But the new opposition saw that Poynings' law could be of service to them by delaying legislation they did not like. Sidney got the suspension he wanted, but with very limiting conditions.

The leader of the opposition party was Sir Edmund Butler, the brother of the pro-English earl of Ormond. Sir Edmund had recently become the victim of a very worrying trend; Elizabethan adventurers, like their Norman predecessors, were seeing Ireland as a wild, unconquered land where they could get rich quick by carving out estates for themselves, and the province most open to this kind of colonization, being fertile, accessible by sea and predominantly Irish, was Munster, where the Butler lands lay. In December 1568 a fortune hunter from Devon, Sir Peter Carew, had brought a case in an English court for possession of the barony of Idrone, in Co. Carlow, which had once belonged to an earlier line of Carews, and won it from the Mac Murchadha Caomhánachs, an almost royal Irish house, on the grounds that few of their marriages had been made in church and their heirs had been, in English law, illegitimate. That an ancient and powerful Gaelic family, which had held its land for 400 years, should be so deprived was frightening enough, but part of the barony had belonged to Sir Edmund Butler and that, too, had gone to Sir Peter. If a Butler lost his land, who could feel safe?

In Munster, Gaelic traditions lived on. Every lord and gentleman had his poets and brehons, and the peasants gave coign and livery to bands of fighting men. The influence of France and Spain was as likely to be felt as that of England. Spanish ships anchored in the harbours of Cork and Youghal, bringing wine and sometimes arms, and taking in return fish, beef, hides and tallow. The earl of Ormond, cousin to the queen, ruled in the east, and the Gaelic Mac Carthaighs, whose chief was now the earl of Clancarthy, in the west. Between them were the lands of the southern Geraldines, headed by the earl of Desmond.

Ever since the execution of the seventh earl in 1468 the Desmonds had turned their backs on the English and ruled in the Gaelic manner. When the thirteenth earl died in 1558, the Desmond palatinate was stable and contented. But the fourteenth earl, Gearóid Fitzgerald, could not maintain that stability. He was weak, fearful and crippled – so crippled that he had to be helped on and off his horse. He had not been educated properly. His father could have sent him to the English court, with the sons of other Irish noblemen, to learn the ways of the world and, in particular, of the Tudor monarchy. But the old earl would not entrust his heir to the English, and Gearóid's only ties beyond the Geraldine group were uneasy ones with the Butlers; his wife, who was many years older than he, had been countess of Ormond.

Desmond and Ormond had a long-standing dispute over some land near Clonmel. While she lived, Lady Desmond contrived to keep the peace between them, but after her death in 1565 the two earls met in a skirmish at Affane, close to Clonmel. Elizabeth would not tolerate private armies and both of them, with Desmond's brother Sir John of Desmond as well, were summoned to London.

Ormond was soon pardoned, but Elizabeth was not impressed by the devious and sickly Desmond. Within a few weeks, both he and his brother found themselves in the Tower. Back in Munster, Desmond's cousin, Sir James Fitzmaurice, called out the Geraldines. They sacked villages and plundered homesteads, aided by Mac Carthaigh Mór and, for a while, Sir Edmund Butler. When Sir Henry Sidney came into Munster with his troops to put the rising down, he found the whole country burned and devastated, the crops lost and the people dying in the fields.

Fitzmaurice had the hot blood and thirst for action that his cousin Desmond lacked. And he was fervently religious; he wanted to lead a Catholic crusade to drive the Protestant English out of Munster. When, in 1570, the pope excommunicated Elizabeth and released her subjects from the duty of obeying her, Fitzmaurice, like many others of the Irish nobility, felt that the time for action had come.

He had spent many years on the continent, visiting the courts of France and Spain, as well as the Vatican, to raise support for Catholic Ireland. In 1571 he asked Philip II of Spain to send a Spanish prince to rule in Ireland, and another Geraldine, Maurice Fitzgibbon, archbishop of Cashel, urged Philip to take military action. But Philip remembered that forty years earlier his father, the emperor Charles V, had investigated the Irish situation and decided that the Desmonds could not be maintained against a Tudor monarchy. Philip doubted if much had changed. England would not give up her Atlantic possession without a struggle and Ireland was too poor to yield Spain any worthwhile revenue. He decided Ireland was not worth troubling about.

Sir John Perrott, a zealous and experienced soldier, was given the immediate task of restoring order in Munster. The Irish army of kerns and gallowglasses was larger than his, but he had heavy guns and the Irish had not. With Ormond's help, he embarked on a ruthless campaign of bombarding and mining castles, slaughtering their garrisons when they surrendered. In 1573 he took Kilmallock castle in Limerick, which Fitzmaurice had captured with scaling ladders and partially burned some four years earlier. Fitzmaurice came out of the woods and submitted to him; the rebellion seemed to be over. English justice was introduced into Munster, coign and livery stamped out, money rents introduced and the idlemen, who filled the private armies in times of war, set to work.

During the same year of 1573 Desmond and his brother were allowed to return. Neither Sidney nor Perrott thought much of the earl's qualities; when Perrott met him in Dublin, where he was kept in lodgings under 'easy restraint', he described him as fitter to rule Bedlam than Munster and urged the queen to recall him to England. But Desmond forestalled any such move by escaping from Dublin with his second wife, another Butler connection, who had shared his confinement in London, and travelling to Munster, where he was warmly welcomed. Brehon law and coign and livery were reinstated, idlemen flocked to his banner, and Fitzmaurice sent messages to Spain. A new deputy, Sir William Fitzwilliam, had neither men nor money to do anything about it.

For once Desmond seemed to be resolute. He prepared to defend some of his castles, destroy others and wait for foreign help to arrive. Then Fitzwilliam received reinforcements and the inevitable campaign to break the house of Desmond began. One of the Desmond castles was mined and the garrison killed when it tried to escape. Desmond realized too late that he could put up no defence and made a humble submission to the deputy, at the same time craftily putting his lands and property into a family trust, so they could not be forfeited.

Early in 1575 Fitzmaurice fled to France. Either from jealousy of his dashing cousin, or because he did not want to be seen to reward rebellion, Desmond had refused to give him the house and lands he felt he was entitled to. While Desmond sat on the fence in Munster, gathering his own army of 1,000 men on the one hand and seeking to make his peace with the deputy on the other, Fitzmaurice looked for European aid. In 1578 he found it – 2,000 men from the pope and another thousand from elsewhere. Then it vanished; foolishly he had given the command of this considerably army to a well-known English con-man called Sir Thomas Stukeley, and Stukeley lent them to the Portuguese for the battle of Alcazar. When Fitzmaurice returned to Ireland in 1579, he had only 300 men left.

Desmond wrote to tell the queen about Fitzmaurice's landing

and then awaited events. The English felt let down by Desmond's inactivity, but he was in a cleft stick; the spirited Fitzmaurice had appealed to Irish Catholicism and Desmond would have been without a following if he preferred the Protestant English. But if he backed Fitzmaurice and the rebellion succeeded, he might be deposed in his cousin's favour, a Gaelic election supplanting the law of primogeniture which had given him his earldom. The cautious and unattractive Desmond might find himself replaced by the fiery and charismatic Fitzmaurice.

Desmond was still hesitating when, a month after landing at Dingle, Fitzmaurice was killed in a skirmish. One reason for Desmond's continued loyalty to the English had gone. The gentry in Munster and even the Pale were rising – but still Desmond held aloof. Then, a year after Fitzmaurice's landing, a force of 700 Spaniards and Italians landed near Dingle and took over a castle called Dún an Óir, or fort of gold. After desperate pleas from the deputy to the queen, Perrott was sent, as an admiral, with four ships and 2,000 men. Rebel castles were, once again, stormed, including Dún an Óir. When the Spaniards and Italians surrendered and came out, their officers were taken prisoner, to earn the English ransom money, and the rest, some 600 men, mercilessly put to the sword.

Indecisive as ever, Desmond met Ormond and was given terms. He was to surrender certain castles and – far more difficult – his rebellious brothers, Sir John and Sir James, who had recently murdered two prominent and well-liked English officials. Desmond could not do it – his brothers would certainly have been hanged, and what kind of a following would he have had after that? Miserably he gave his son, Lord Garrett, as a hostage and earnest of his good intent. It was not enough. The English proclaimed him a traitor.

Then, at last, he became one. He accepted the role the English and Ormond had prepared for him. With his men he fell upon the port of Youghal, sacked it and desecrated the queen's coat of arms there. He had hoped to defend his castles, but one after another they were besieged and taken, and the garrisons slain. Ormond, who had gladly accepted the task of finishing off his rival, blocked his escape by sea, and gradually Desmond's small force dwindled. He became so sick and weak he had to be carried and then, with only five followers left, a priest, two horsemen, a kern and a boy, he hid in the wood of Glenageenty, which was near Tralee. In November 1583 he was tracked down by an angry peasant, whose cattle had been stolen and womenfolk outraged by members of his band. When at daybreak the peasant and his companions broke into the cabin where Desmond lay, the earl pleaded for his life. 'You have killed yourself long ago,' the peasant is said to have replied. Nevertheless Desmond's captors did not kill him straight away; not until, sick and helpless, they found him too much of an encumbrance to keep alive. Then they cut off his head and took it to Ormond.

Years later the English poet, Edmund Spenser, published a description of the people of Munster, stricken with famine, after the suppression of the rebellion in 1580–1. 'Out of every corner of the woods and glens,' he wrote. 'they came creeping forth upon their hands, for their legs would not bear them. They looked anatomies of death; they spake like ghosts crying out from their graves. They did eat of the dead carrions, happy where they could find them; yea and one another soon after, insomuch as the very carcasses they spared not to scrape out of their graves.' The armies of both sides had been feeding off the land, slaughtering the livestock and despoiling the crops, until every group of soldiers had been followed by a straggling band of starving peasants, from whom everything had been stolen. They ate any horse that died, entrails and all, without waiting to cook it, and bought dead horses off the soldiers, when they could not get them without payment. And to crown it all, in the final stage of the war the English had deliberately wasted five counties, so that any rebels left would be starved into submission. The country Spenser had seen eighteen months earlier, full of corn and cattle, had become a burned and depopulated waste-land. Due to the war, famine, sickness and the judicial severity of the English – Perrott had hanged sixty supposed rebels at one assize – Munster had lost most of its men. A greater number of women were left, but not enough to cultivate more than a tiny proportion of the once abundant land.

The province was ripe for plantation. The Desmond lands of some 500,000 acres were confiscated and surveyed, and in 1586 plans passed for settlement. About twenty large estates of some 2,000 acres each were to go to English 'undertakers', who would 'undertake' to build eighty-six houses on each estate and fill them with English families. With five or six people including children, to a family, that meant an influx of some 8,000 people, not necessarily Protestant but certainly English. The confiscated lands were, however, divided for the purposes of plantation into profitable and unprofitable categories; each 2,000-acre lot was to be of profitable land, but as much unprofitable land as the undertaker wanted could be added to it without cost. And there the greed of the Elizabethan speculators found its opportunity. Who was to say where the boundary between profitable and unprofitable land lay? The decision was taken by newly established English courts advised by English lawyers. Much undoubtedly profitable land was deemed unprofitable and included in the undertakers' estates, which were enlarged to four, six, eight, or even twelve thousand acres and upwards. Sir Walter Raleigh, soldier, sailor, explorer and royal favourite, ended up with 40,000 acres around Youghal.

Many of those granted land in the Munster plantation, including Raleigh, had fought as soldiers against the Munster rebels. Others were fortune-hunters, Englishmen on the make who saw Munster as a freebooter's paradise: a practice-ground for colonization and a first staging post on the way to America.

Yet the English did not settle in anything like the numbers the government had envisaged. Of some thirty who became undertakers, no more than thirteen were actually living on their estates in 1592, and only 245 English families, about 1,300 people, had been brought over and planted. They were too few to impose an English culture on their surroundings, or even to provide an effective garrison, and within a few years they, like so many generations of English in Ireland before them, had become indistinguisable from the Irish.

Connacht accepted English government with relative ease. The newly created earl of Clanricarde, of the Norman family of Burke, was steadfastly loyal, although his sons Ulick and John led a spasmodic resistance to the imposition of English law and the abolition of coign and livery for the best part of ten years. The Irish nobility, which combined an inordinate pride in its blood and lineage with an oppressive and overbearing attitude to its inferiors, had conceived an intense hatred of the middle-class

English officials who were making, it was said, the churl as good as the gentleman. Nevertheless, when Clanricarde died in 1582, Ulick took on his father's loyalty with his title.

In 1585 the nobility accepted the Composition of Connacht, whereby the old Irish chieftaincies were abolished in favour of English peerages, and the chieftain's domain became private family property with succession by primogeniture.

Only Ulster remained unconquered.

When Shane Ó Néill's name was attainted in 1567, his cousin, tanist and sometime rival Toirdhealbhach Luineach was, to all intents and purposes, his successor as Ó Néill, and the title of earl of Tyrone, which Shane had never taken, remained in abeyance. Hugh, the second son of the murdered Matthew, baron of Dungannon, a short, red-haired boy of nine, had been taken to England in 1559 by Sir Henry Sidney to be educated at his own highly cultured home in Kent. When Hugh's elder brother Brian was murdered in 1562, he became the third baron of Dungannon. He went back to Ireland in 1572 but kept up his powerful English connections and in March 1587 was recognized as earl of Tyrone.

He had been loyal to the English government of Ireland for fifteen years; he had sat in parliament and dutifully shared the rule of Ulster with Toirdhealbhach and the English marshal, Sir Henry Bagenal. He had helped the English put down Irish rebels, and taken the English side during the war in Munster. Elizabeth gave him permission to raise a force of 600 men for use in her service, and paid for them herself. She did not know that Tyrone changed this force every year, so that he had an ever-increasing number of trained soldiers in Ulster; nor did she know that, little by little, he was accustoming his peasants to the use of guns.

Tyrone, destined to be one of the greatest of all Irishmen, was cautious, secretive and slippery as an eel. As an Irish youth in England, and as an English-trained chieftain in Ireland, he had learned to play a double game. He was friendly, charming and apparently emotional, being given to bouts of weeping; doggedly brave, yet prudent. He took decisions slowly, and when he had made them, waited.

Elizabeth had already encouraged adventurers to enter Ulster. In 1572 she had backed Sir Thomas Smith, a classical scholar well versed in Roman accounts of colonization, when he tried to establish a settlement of English gentry and Irish peasants on the Ards peninsula, near Belfast, and in the following year she had granted the whole of Antrim to the earl of Essex in return for a share of the profits: an arrangement Sidney found shocking. Then in 1589 the chieftaincy of Monaghan, which thrust northwards into Ulster, was abruptly brought to an end; Hugh MacMahon, the chief, had driven off some cattle as a way of collecting his dues from his tenants and, at the same time, rescued some prisoners from the English sherriff. He was tried and executed – against all the tenets of Irish custom – and his lands, which he held on Surrender and Re-grant terms, forfeited to the Crown. The paramount chieftaincy was ended; in 1591 Monaghan was divided among seven MacMahons and a Mackenna, and subdivided among a number of freeholders who paid money rents.

Tyrone, like all the chiefs of Ulster, was frightened. Tudor bureaucracy was modern, efficient, egalitarian and sensible; it might in the long run bring the common Irish greater prosperity and peace. But Tyrone derived his power from the ancient, aristocratic system of the Gaels. He lived the Gaelic life, holding his councils on the hillsides rather than in his tall stone castle at Dungannon, banqueting in the open, as Irish chiefs had always done, with his poets and harpists, at a trestle table set up on the grass. His meat was stewed in animal skins, slung on sticks over a camp fire, his vegetables were watercress (the original shamrock) mushrooms and herbs from the woods. His drink was

15. An Irish banquet (Derrick, *Image of Ireland*, 1581)

ale, foreign wines, or the native whiskey, to which the English gave unstinted praise!

Gaelic society was still nomadic and pastoral. Vast herds of cattle were still driven from pasture to pasture; dwellings were still the simplest of huts in the summer, and in the winter low cabins built of mud, or clay, and wattle, roofed with turves, straw, or heather. An Elizabethan traveller, Fynes Morison, described the Irish at night. 'They sleep on the ground,' he wrote, 'without straw or other thing under them, lying all in a circle about the fire with their feet towards it. And their bodies being naked, they cover their heads and upper parts with their mantles.' Other writers were shocked by the nudity they some-times glimpsed under the rough, heavy Irish mantles; as colonists often do, the Elizabethans admired the physique of the 'savages' they had fallen among and envied their sexual freedom, while prudishly drawing their own skirts around them.

With Monaghan under English control, Fermanagh, the next county to Ulster, lay undefended. The chief, Hugh Maguire, paid the English 300 cows not to put in a sherriff; they took the cows and put in a sherriff just the same. Maguire rebelled and Tyrone, still apparently on the English side, was asked to put the rebellion down. He implored, lamented and protested his loyalty, in an agony of indecision.

He did not want war, but for years he had known he might not be able to avoid it. In 1586 his forces had numbered 1,160 horse and 5,780 foot. In 1592 he had 2,398 horse and 15,130 foot; enormous numbers for those days. He could claim help from thousands of Scots in Antrim and yet more from the Scottish mainland, and he had a ready supply of weapons and ammu-nition from Glasgow. He was in touch with Philip II of Spain; Ulster had been the only province to welcome and assist refugees from the Spanish Armada when its ships were wrecked on the Irish coast in 1588. In 1593 the aged Toirdhealbhach Luineach retired as Ó Néill and Tyrone[5] took the ancient title, which meant so much more in Ulster than any the English could bestow. From that day onwards he claimed the loyalty of all Ó Néills, Toirdhealbhach's people as well as his own.

In the west, Tyrone had powerful allies in the Ó Domhnaills. Their leader was Red Hugh, a fiery young man who had an implacable hatred of the English – with good reason. When he was fourteen or fifteen, Red Hugh and some other lads had been lured onto a ship carrying a cargo of wine and encouraged to sample it. They drank too much and found themselves locked into their cabin and the ship underway; they were being taken as hostages to Dublin. Red Hugh spent the next three years half-starved and in chains, a prisoner in Dublin castle with about thirty other teenagers and children, some as young as ten. On Christmas Eve 1591 he escaped with a companion by creeping through a garderobe chute and down a rope into the moat. The weather was freezing and the boys were caught in deep snow in the Wicklow hills; Red Hugh's companion died there, but he himself struggled to a rendezvous and from thence back to Ulster.

Red Hugh was not at all loath to help Maguire in Fermanagh. His Scottish mother had brought several thousand gallowglasses to Tír Conaill, and the Ó Domhnaill forces were formidable. Tyrone's brother, Cormac MacBaron, joined them and in August 1594 they defeated a small English force at the Ford of the Biscuits, near Enniskillen. Then Tyrone learnt from his spies that early in 1595 the government was to bring in reinforcements of 2,000 seasoned troops. Before they could arrive, Tyrone sent another brother, Art, to take Portmore Fort, an English strong-

16.   Hugh O'Néill, earl of Tyrone (courtesy of the National Library of Ireland)

hold on the river Blackwater, and destroy the bridge there. The clans rose, burning and ravaging as far south as Drogheda, and driving the colonists into the towns.

Tyrone used the same scorched-earth policy as the English in Munster, burning crops and driving away livestock, so that the English armies, which lived off the countryside, would starve, fall sick, and begin to melt away. He made his men plash the woods, so the English, who had to make long marches between one garrison and another, could not get through. The Irish dug pits and hid them with wickerwork and turves, so the English cavalry fell into them, and they laid ambushes, drawing the English into bogs and narrow places, where they were easily attacked. The Irish never came into the open, never gave battle, and Tyrone earned the nickname of the Running Beast.

Bagenal and his men were ambushed in the bogs at Clontibret, near Fort Monaghan, and attacked on both sides. They were showered with arrows before Tyrone's men burst out of the bushes and raced alongside them, seizing their bridles and stirrup leathers, hacking and stabbing with darts and javelins, and then whirling away again, out of sight. The English closed ranks and pressed on, hoping the attack would be short, as Irish attacks often were. But this time the kerns kept it up for six hours and won: they discovered that guerrilla tactics could defeat a disciplined English army. Soon after Red Hugh led a raid deep into Connacht and destroyed English homesteads there, driving the settlers into the castles and fortified towns. The west rose and within a month Connacht, which had seemed so stable, was throwing off English rule.

And then – Tyrone asked for a pardon! He had stripped the country bare almost to Dublin, so there was hardly a cow or a packhorse left for the English army; the people of the Pale were crying out to the government for protection, and the Irish had tasted victory. But Tyrone wanted to win the war, not battles, and his military technique was to waste the enemy – its energy, its money and its time. And the time the enemy wasted, he would use to train and unite his people. He strung the English along with hypocritical demands for peace and had the truce prolonged from October 1595 to February and then May 1596, while he smuggled in vast quantities of arms from Spain and Danzig, Glasgow, Liverpool and Chester. In June he was offered his pardon but refused to collect it in Dundalk. In July the English prepared for war, and in August Tyrone asked again for his pardon. Feebly the English agreed to take it to him; he accepted it with expressions of joy and had a volley fired in exuberant delight.

Elizabeth was still haggling with her commanders over money and supplies, and another year passed before the English had built up, armed and provisioned a sizeable force. Then they made a three-pronged attack on Ulster. The deputy, Lord Brough, led his men from Newry up the river Blackwater but found the woods impassable, they had been so thoroughly plashed, and failed to make his rendezvous with Sir Conyers Clifford at Bally-shannon. Clifford made a brilliant retreat into Connacht, success-fully fighting off Red Hugh's men for hour after hour. The third English force was ambushed and cut to pieces in Westmeath.

Tyrone made no change in his tactics. He dragged out the pause that followed the English defeat in parley after parley, while he waited for help from Spain. When he met Ormond and parleyed with him across a brook, he poured out his resentments: he should have been given his earldom sooner; Sidney, who had taken him to England, should never have supported Toirdheal-bhach. Then he gave his terms for peace. The Irish must have freedom of conscience, that is, the right to worship as they pleased, he himself must have a full pardon, all his followers' lands must be restored, English officials and garrisons must be removed and Ulster made a county palatine, which he would rule almost as a king.

In August 1598 the parleys came to an end. Bagenal moved north to penetrate Ulster with a long, straggling column of 4,000 foot and 300 horse. About two miles beyond Armagh, at a place called the Yellow Ford, Tyrone attacked the front of the column and Red Hugh the rear. Bagenal and three-quarters of his men were killed. The rest fled back to Armagh and locked themselves into the cathedral, where the Irish besieged them. The Irish Council wrote abjectly to Tyrone from Dublin, begging him to let the English army go – and Tyrone, though he had just won the greatest victory of the war, agreed, and went back to his tactic of wearing the English out. In return, the Irish Council allowed him Armagh and the castle at Portmore.

At the same time, Tyrone sent two of his guerrilla leaders

southwards, and the Irish rose: in Connacht, Leinster, where the earl of Kildare's loyalty became suspect, and the Pale. In Munster, where the people had been suppressed and terrified for sixteen years, the hated English planters were attacked and their homesteads burned, until they fled into the towns, and even to England, for protection. The Geraldines rejected as earl of Desmond the sad Protestant youth who had been born to the fourteenth earl in London and still lived there in captivity; instead they wanted his cousin James Fitzthomas and in January 1600 in Tipperary, he received the title at Tyrone's hands. With a record of victory and 30,000 men at his back, Tyrone was indeed a king in Ireland.

At last Elizabeth opened her purse. She raised the largest English army ever to have been sent to Ireland, consisting of 16,000 foot and 1,500 horse, and gave the command to the new deputy, Robert Devereux, earl of Essex, the stepson of that Essex who, with her help, had tried to set up a plantation amongst the Antrim Scots in 1573.

Essex was handsome, charming and popular. He was considered, largely without reason, to be a good soldier, but the real basis of his position was Elizabeth's favour; he had been the elderly queen's favourite, on and off, ever since he first came to court in 1587, aged 21. Recently, though, the queen had been cool towards him, and he set out for Ireland with the deepest forebodings. He knew that armies far smaller than his had failed to find food there, so the men had fallen sick and deserted. How could his huge force fare any better?

His fears were justified. He found all the countryside round Dublin wasted as a result of Tyrone's scorched-earth policies. There was no provender for his horses, and no bread or meat for his men. He was sent three months' supplies from England but, such was the corruption and inefficiency of English armies, most of the supplies vanished between the ports and the store-master. Following the usual pattern, his men began to fall sick and, whenever they had the chance, headed for home.

The Irish Council asked him to pacify Leinster and Munster, where most of its members had their lands and the English colonists were. So he turned south – and as soon as he had gone, Tyrone raided the Pale, destroying what food supplies there were, driving off cattle and stealing horses. For five months, Essex moved from castle to castle, town to town, in a gay and splendid cavalcade, leaving garrisons of a hundred men here, two hundred men there – who, once their food ran out, surrendered to the Irish waiting in the hills. Two-thirds of the huge English army was spent that way. There was a minor skirmish, which Essex lost, at the Pass of the Plumes, so named after the bright feathers in the Elizabethans' hats, Cahir castle was won by English cannon, and in the Curlew mountains of Connacht Red Hugh avenged his failure of 1597 by routing a force under Sir Conyers Clifford.

Then the queen ordered Essex north. The Irish Council still advised against an attack on Tyrone, but Essex wrote saying he was even then 'putting his foot in the stirrup' for the march, although his army was, by now, reduced to 4,000 men. Early in September he made contact with Tyrone. For three days his men pursued retreating kerns through the woods near Dundalk. Then Tyrone sent a messenger to Essex asking for a parley. Essex dismissed the messenger haughtily, but a couple of days later Tyrone sent him again: he wanted the queen's mercy and a parley. This time Essex agreed, and Tyrone engaged with him in another of those parleys across a brook, sitting on his horse in mid-stream, most respectfully bareheaded, while Essex stood on the bank. They were alone – no-one else was within earshot – and we shall never know what soft blandishments the wily, experienced Irishman offered the crass English earl. But a truce was agreed.

Essex hurried back to Dublin, where there were furious letters from the queen urging him to get on with the fighting, and he abandoned what was left of his good sense. Though Elizabeth had expressly forbidden him to leave Ireland without her permission, he felt he must explain his action to her in person, and raced to London. He galloped up to her court early one morning and, all filthy from his journey, burst unannounced into her bedchamber. She was surprised and delighted to see him – at first. Then the questioning began. She suspected him not only of disobedience but treachery. She put him under house arrest and while he languished, ill and in despair, considered what to do. After nine months he was brought before the court of Star Chamber, reprimanded and freed. But years earlier, in the days of his favour, Elizabeth had given him the patent, or monopoly, in sweet wines, and it had made him a rich man. It came up for renewal early in 1601 and she took it from him; he was not only disgraced, but impoverished as well. Hoping he was still popular, he tried to raise the citizens of London in his support; and he might have done so, had not the queen's agents gone among the people first. He was proclaimed a traitor, sent to the Tower and then tried for treason, condemned and beheaded.

Tyrone had never been more powerful than after Essex' collapse. He had won a bloodless victory – and a truce which, whether Elizabeth liked it or not, he could prolong for month after month, while his power grew. Once more he used Ormond to carry his terms for peace.

He had gone into rebellion because of a threat to his lands and position. His motives had been personal and selfish. But since then Irishmen from Munster, Connacht and even Leinster had risen to join him and he had come to see Ireland as one, an island where all the people everywhere had common characteristics and interests. He became a patriot: Ireland's first nationalist.

His terms for peace included all the Irish patriot demands to be made in the centuries to come. He demanded that the Catholic religion should be restored throughout Ireland and all religious houses turned over to Catholic churchmen. There should be a Catholic university; Trinity College, Dublin, which had been founded by Elizabeth in 1592, was Protestant and only served the Pale. All officers of state and judges should be Irishmen and all laws barring Irishmen from office repealed. On the other hand, no Irishman should be pressed into Crown service against his will. The plantations should be undone and the land returned; Irish chiefs should hold their land as they had done two hundred years earlier. Finally, Irishmen should be free to travel and trade in England on equal terms with Englishmen.

There was no way Elizabeth could accede to such demands. She could not risk a Catholic, pro-Spanish stronghold in the west, and the planters had to be protected. Tyrone enjoyed the fruits of victory for the winter, travelling south with 2,000 men, harrying everyone not on his side, and then, early in 1600, Elizabeth appointed Lord Mountjoy as Essex' successor.

Mountjoy was elegant, courtly, bookish and a gourmet. The

task in Ireland was by no means agreeable to him, but he accepted it because he was a friend of Essex, he had been in Ireland during Essex' futile campaign and he needed to redeem himself. He dropped his dainty ways in favour of austere military good sense and pursued his goal of defeating Tyrone with complete singlemindedness.

For years the English had been toying with the idea of placing strong garrisons in the north. Mountjoy did it; in May 1600 he created a diversion in the south to draw off Tyrone while Sir Henry Docwra sailed into Lough Foyle with sixty-nine ships and some 3,000 men, built forts at Ellogh and Cullmore, garrisoned them and went on to Derry. One of Toirrdhealbhach Luineach's sons came in to him, as well as a rival of Red Hugh Ó Domhnaill; Ulster was more or less encircled.

With Docwra on Lough Foyle, Mountjoy pressing up from the south and a third English army, under Sir Arthur Chichester, pushing in from the west, Tyrone hardly knew where to turn. He raided the Pale, so the people there might call to Mountjoy for help; but Mountjoy left them to their fate. He was lured here, harried there, and his forces split by the English. Mountjoy never let up, but campaigned right through the winter, which generals seldom did in those days. And he used the weapon of famine. He drove off livestock, fired the harvest and prevented the spring sowing. The people of the north began to suffer from the same dreadful hunger as Spenser had described in Munster.

Tyrone's support began to fall away, but he was not despondent; he was waiting and listening for news from Spain. Mountjoy was listening too – and when he heard the Spanish were sending an army to the Low Countries, he guessed from the renewed arrogance of the Irish that 'Low Countries' was a code word for Ireland. The question was: where would the Spaniards land? In the north, where Tyrone and Ó Domhnaill could join them immediately, or in Connacht, where they had so many allies? Mountjoy had started moving his troops from Munster to Connacht when, late in September 1601, the Spanish army landed far to the south at Kinsale, which Tyrone and his allies could only reach by a forced march of 300 miles through bog and dense woodland.

Mountjoy, who was at Kilkenny, hurried to Kinsale with all the men he could muster. His forces in the south were small, but he had to prevent a wholesale rising by a show of strength, even at the risk of attack by overwhelming Spanish forces. He settled his men on the hills outside Kinsale and called frantically for reinforcements. By the end of November he had 12,000 foot and 800 horse, mostly drawn from England and the northern garrisons. Tyrone, as usual, played a waiting game. He knew the Spaniards in Kinsale were comfortable, well provisioned and far less likely to fall sick than the besiegers, exposed on the cold, wet hillsides.

The Spanish ships had sailed away after disembarking their passengers and the river mouth filled with English men o'war. The Spaniards were heavily bombarded from sea and land, and early in November the Spanish commander sent a message to Tyrone asking for his help. Tyrone did not hurry; it was another week before he sent Red Hugh southwards and then set off himself. The combined Irish force was about 12,000, which he considered quite enough to cope with Mountjoy's ailing army.

Mountjoy appealed for yet another regiment from Dublin and then, on December 8, came upon Tyrone's horse only two miles away! He found the dense woods were filling up with Irishmen; the besiegers were becoming the besieged. Spanish ships arrived at Castlehaven, a few miles westward near Skibbereen, and Red Hugh's men joined up with them. Mountjoy's supplies were cut off by land, and ships sailing from England had the wind against them and could not reach him. By the end of December he had only a few days' rations left. His soldiers were sick and hungry; many died and many more deserted until he had only 1,500 fit men left.

Tyrone could have played his usual cool, waiting game and kept his men quietly in the woods, doing no more than harry the English while their numbers dwindled away. He could have maintained his tactic of fighting a guerrilla war and avoiding pitched battles. But Red Hugh was with him, longing, as always, for vengeance, and the Spaniards were beginning to complain of lack of food. Very early on Christmas morning, 1601, while darkness still shrouded the woods and hills, the Irish attacked. Mountjoy sent his horse against their rear – and they broke. They fled. The battle of Kinsale, one of the most important battles in the history of the wars between the Irish and the English, lasted less than three hours. The Spaniards, for whom Tyrone had waited so long and so hopefully, never joined in at all.

Red Hugh took ship for Spain, leaving his brother Ruaidrí as Ó Domhnaill in his place. Within a year he was dead, probably poisoned by an English assassin. Tyrone led the remains of his army back to Ulster, where his friends and allies fell away from him and the people cursed him for the famine, caused by the war, and the wasting of the land.

Mountjoy had the coronation stone of the Ó Néills at Tullahoge broken into pieces. There would be no more Ó Néills; the Gaelic order had gone. Tyrone tried to bargain for terms, but Elizabeth refused to accept any terms. He lived as a bandit in the woods, virtually an outlaw, until the king of France persuaded the queen, now dying, to accept his total submission. Mountjoy received it on 23rd March 1603, the day before she died. The two men met formally on 30th March and Tyrone spent an hour on his knees, weeping. He did not know, and Mountjoy forebore to tell him, that Elizabeth was dead and James of Scotland, a monarch far more friendly to him, had succeeded to the English throne.

Tyrone and Ruaidrí Ó Domhnaill went to London with Mountjoy. Tyrone received the major part of his lands back and his title of earl, and Ruaidrí became earl of Tír Conaill, the title promised the Ó Domhnaills some sixty years earlier. The North was to be shired, the English judicial system introduced and the people freed of their obedience to Ó Domhnaill and Ó Néill; the two earls were Gaelic princes no longer, but private noblemen.

The treatment of Tyrone was generous – so generous it earned him considerable hostility from English officials. When he was commanded to come to London in 1607, his friends feared for his liberty and even his life. His son Henry, who was serving in the Austrian army, arranged for a ship to sail from the Low Countries into Lough Swilly and Tyrone, with the new earl of Tír Conaill, prepared for an episode known to history as the Flight of the Earls. They collected together their families, friends and chief adherents – more than ninety of the leading people of the north – and on 14 September 1607, sailed away from Ireland. After landing in France, they travelled via the courts of Europe, which gave them little help, to Rome, where they spent the rest of their days in exile. Tyrone died, aged sixty-five, in 1616.

CHAPTER 7

THE IRISH DISPOSSESSED

The Flight of the Earls was a disaster for Ireland. As Tyrone and Tír Conaill had sailed away in secret, they were deemed traitors and their lands forfeit. They left a vacuum behind them, and Sir Arthur Chichester, who had succeeded Mountjoy as deputy in 1601, saw immediately the opportunity for extensive plantation that had fallen into the government's lap. He had been toying with the idea of a minor plantation in Cavan, to be effected without, he believed, any injustice to the native Irish; now the same moderate plans, which provided for sizeable pockets of English and Scottish settlement in areas still left predominantly Irish, could be extended over the greater part of Ulster. He wrote immediately to the English Council to put his enlarged plan before them. Then in 1608 a minor chieftain, Sir Cahir O'Doherty of Inishowen, on the north coast, broke into sudden rebellion and burned the garrison town of Derry. The revolt was soon over – within four months O'Doherty was dead and his followers scattered – but the government in England had taken fright. Chichester's moderate schemes were pushed aside and in 1609 Articles of Plantation published which removed most of the Irish to specially designated areas (rather as the American Indians were to be moved to reservations in the nineteeth century) leaving 500,000 acres of good, cultivable land, about a quarter of the whole, to be taken for plantation.

Following along the lines of the Munster plantation, cultivable land was designated as profitable, and bog and woodland as unprofitable; the basic grants were to be of profitable land, with as much unprofitable land added as the grantee wanted. English or Scottish undertakers, the senior grantees, were to receive 2,000 acres each and to build a castle with a bawn, or fortified enclosure; servitors, those who had served the government and deserved well of it, usually army officers (many of them Scots), were to receive 1,500 acres each and to build a brick or stone house with a bawn. A third category, the 'deserving' Irish, were to have 1,000 acres each.

Undertakers and servitors had to take the Oath of Supremacy and were, therefore, Protestant. They were to raise armed men on behalf of the government, if required, and formed, in effect, a garrison. They were not to take Irish tenants, but to clear the unwanted Irish off their lands and bring in planters, preferably Scots, who would build towns and villages to form islands of 'civility'. But the old story repeated itself; neither English nor Scottish families showed any great eagerness to settle amongst the wild and dangerous Irish, so prone to rebellion, and the undertakers found it far more profitable to ignore the Articles of Plantation and take Irish tenants. The Irish were industrious, used to sparse living and so desperate to remain in their homes they would pay almost any rent, however extortionate. So they stayed – and such British settlers as did venture into Ulster found themselves thinly scattered among a population still predominantly Gaelic and Catholic.

One of the most famous plantations was made by the City of London in the county of Coleraine, later renamed Londonderry. The county's chief town, Derry, had been fortified and garrisoned by Sir John Docwra in 1600 and then in 1604, after Tyrone's defeat, incorporated as a city with Docwra as provost for life. Soon, however, he tired of the new city and it began to deteriorate. In 1609 James I persuaded the City of London to form a joint-stock company to plant Derry, the town of Coleraine and the country in between. In return for an investment of £20,000, the Londoners were to have the rich fisheries of the rivers Bann and Foyle, a long lease of customs duties and the opportunity to build a thriving export trade in timber, salmon, hides, iron ore and other commodities.

The plantation began vigorously and then flagged. Like so many city councils and corporations today, the Londoners seemed to pay more for less than anybody else would; they poured money into Derry and Coleraine, far beyond the stipulated £20,000, most of which turned into fat profits for contractors and middle men. Their first agent was sacked for corruption after three years, but ten years later Derry and Coleraine were still only half-built, lacking houses, strong fortifications and inhabitants.

Outside the two towns, the position was no better. The county of Londonderry had been divided into twelve parts, one for each of the City livery companies, but once again the castles and fortifications were poorly built and the houses too few. Those colonists, mostly English, who were persuaded to settle, so lacked confidence in their situation that they neither stocked nor worked their land, but preferred to let it for high rents to the Irish. Some planters had several landholdings which they farmed out, some were absentees and some, even, children, whose names were being used by their adult relatives. Altogether, the colonists were far too thin on the ground to withstand any concerted attack, or even hold off the Irish wood-kerne, who harried and plundered them incessantly.

The ranks of these wood-kerns, or forest bandits, were being continually swelled. There was no class of Irish planter in Londonderry; all those Irish still on their lands were under-tenants of the English, paying such high rents that they were gradually becoming impoverished; an Irishman with a hundred cows in 1614, say, was likely to have only twenty left a dozen years later. Not long after that he would give up and, filled with hatred for his former masters, take to the woods.

By far the most successful colonists were the Scots. They were tough, dour, hardworking and well prepared to invest their time, money and energy in cultivating the land, building villages and setting up small industries. A large colony of Scots settled in North Donegal and there was a thin smattering of them all over the Ulster plantation. But the biggest Scottish settlements were outside the government scheme, in Antrim and Down.

The Scottish presence there was not new. Scots had settled in Antrim, only separated from Scotland by the thirteen-mile-wide North Channel, as far back as the thirteenth century, when the first Scottish gallowglasses came to Ireland and turned the tables against the Normans. Most were from the West Highlands or the Hebrides and when, in 1499, James IV of Scotland ended the independent lordship of the Isles, the Mac Domhnaills, who had been princes there, established themselves in the Glens of Antrim and seized the Route, those lands which lay between Coleraine and Ballycastle, ejecting the Irish MacQuillans.

James, being a Scot himself, was sympathetic to the Scots in Ireland. On his accession he confirmed the McDonnells in their possessions in Antrim and later, in 1620, made their leader, Sir Randal McDonnell, earl of Antrim. Sir Randal was a Catholic, which James did not normally approve of, and had ties with the Scottish Highlands, which James did not approve of either: the Highlanders had revolted against him in 1599 and again in 1607. But, although the second rebellion was led by his uncle Angus, Sir Randal had welcomed the refugees from the Scottish Lowlands who had fled to Antrim. They were just the kind of settlers James wanted in Ulster; Protestant and Lowland Scots, and Sir Randal had set them up with farms.

James also gave his support to two Scottish adventurers, Hugh Montgomery and Sir James Hamilton, who were busily engaged in private colonization schemes in south Antrim, north Down and the Ards. The country around Belfast was almost uninhabited when they took over; in the campaigns of 1602 and 1603 Chichester had, on his own admission, killed all the Irish he came across, irrespective of sex or rank. There was no-one left to remove; and when the two Scots acquired the greater part of the O'Neill estates at Clandeboy, in Down, they were able to offer leaseholds of untrammelled wilderness to their Lowland Scottish countrymen, whom they brought over in large numbers. Both Hamilton and Montgomery were capable, energetic and on the spot; brilliant organizers who rebuilt old towns, founded new ones, established markets, built mills and harbours and set up industries. Within a generation, Scottish settlers had transformed Antrim and Down with their prosperous, peaceful and God-fearing settlements.

But the Scots worshipped God in a different way from the English. While their worship was Protestant, it was organized along independent lines. They gave unstinted support to king James, the first monarch to unite the crowns of England, Scotland and Ireland, but would not accept royally appointed bishops. Their Church was run by ministers and elders, chosen by themselves. For years they were left alone and hardly noticed: later they became known as Ireland's Presbyterians.

Meanwhile, positions were hardening on both sides of the main religious divide. 'Toleration is a grievous sin,' said the Protestant archbishop of Dublin in 1627, and twelve bishops supported him. Protestants were moving towards a nationalistic, rabidly anti-Catholic Puritanism; they wanted their church to be based even more firmly on the Bible, with simpler church services, plainer vestments and better sermons, preached by a well-educated and disciplined clergy. They wanted a stricter morality, too, in both private and public life, and less frivolity: changes which manifested themselves in a fashion for plain black clothing.

Little of this touched the Irish. The Protestant Church of Ireland established in Elizabeth's day was a weak and ineffective institution, manned by Englishmen, with bishops chosen for their politics rather than their spirituality, and a clergy so ill-trained and lazy they had no prospects in their own country. Very few of them spoke Irish. The services they took were in English, or, if their congregations failed to understand that, in Latin! Spenser, a Protestant himself, was highly critical of these English clergy, writing that 'they will neither for any love of God nor zeal of religion, be drawn forth of their warm nests and their sweet love's side to look into God's harvest, which is ever ready for the sickle, and all fields yellow long ago.' No wonder that the sickle, when it came, was a Catholic one.

Ever since the Reformation, when both England and Scotland had turned to Protestantism, the Vatican had made every effort to preserve Ireland for the Catholic faith. Missionaries had arrived in the country, and young Irishmen had been sent over to Catholic seminaries in France and Spain, later returning to live hard, poverty-stricken and celibate lives, teaching the neglected Irish people. For years the English authorities had let them alone. But after the pope had declared it lawful for a Catholic to assassinate a Protestant ruler – such as Elizabeth – Catholics had come to be feared. In 1581 recusancy fines and the penalties for celebrating or attending mass were sharply increased, and in 1585 all Catholic priests were ordered to leave the country or be regarded as traitors. The priests went into hiding and moved about the country disguised as labourers or herdsmen, and worked alongside their flocks. And the martyrdoms began. In the early years, there had been only two martyrs, both of them suspected of aiding Spain,[1] but in the last twenty years of Elizabeth's reign nearly a hundred Catholic clergy were imprisoned for long periods or done to death, many without trial. The Irish people rewarded these priests, who risked so much for them, with a total devotion.

By the seventeenth century, despite the laws and the lynchings, Catholic priests were everywhere – in the towns, in the castles, the villages, the peasants' cabins and the houses of the gentry of the Pale. The Old English, those English who were neither government officials nor newly arrived planters, sheltered them as readily as the Irish did. And gradually the habits of the people changed. While funerals remained the most popular of church rites – many an heir was brought near ruin by the lavishness of an Irish funeral feast – church marriages gradually came to be accepted as well.

After the Flight of the Earls, James needed to hold a parliament in Ireland. Elizabeth had ruled almost without parliaments; the government of Ireland had been a military one, and Irish parliaments had only represented the Anglo-Irish and the Pale. But James needed to pass acts of attainder against the earls of Tyrone and Tír Conaill, to ratify the confiscation and plantation of their lands, and to give credence to the establishment of the English judicial system throughout the country. His ministers also hoped to put the English penal code against Catholics, which was particularly severe, onto the Irish statute book.

Catholics were not barred from attending parliament in Ireland as they were in England; there would have been no real representation of any section of Irish society if they had been. But, first of all, the government wished to fix things so that Protestant members would be in a majority. The House of Lords did not present a problem; though all but four of the temporal lords were Catholic, the lords spiritual, the bishops, could out-vote them. In the Commons, however, the Protestants from the northern plantations were far outnumbered by the Old English gentry and burgesses, all Catholics, from Munster and Leinster. There were now 33 counties in Ireland, each entitled to return two members, and 41 boroughs returning one member each.

The government decided it must increase the number of members returned to the Commons. The only way to do it was by creating new boroughs, and between December 1612 and May 1613 charters were issued to 40 new boroughs, 18 of them in

Ulster. In each borough the corporation, or council,was to elect the parliamentary representative, and as people had to take the Oath of Supremacy in order to serve on a council, or corporation, their representatives were more or less bound to be Protestant. When parliament assembled on 18th May 1613, the Protestant majority was 24 to 12 in the Lords and 132 to 100 in the Commons.

But the Catholics would not have it. They complained to Chichester, the deputy, that many of the new boroughs were no more than 'miserable villages' not fit to be represented in the Commons, and then opposed the government-sponsored speaker and put up their own nominee, a former judge who had retired rather than take the Oath of Supremacy. When, inevitably, they were over-ruled, they left in a body, declaring that 'those within the house are no house'. And the Lords followed their example. The Protestants were left in possession of the field, but the Catholics had won a moral victory and parliament was prorogued four days after it had met.

It did not meet again until October 1614, by which time 11 of the 40 new boroughs had been deprived of representation and in two the results of their elections reversed. The Commons was left with 108 Protestants and 102 Catholics. The bills attainting the two earls were passed and that medieval attempt at apartheid, the Statutes of Kilkenny, declared obsolete – as, indeed, it was, religious differences having replaced cultural ones. The penal code against Catholics was not even introduced.

The government decided that, once again, Protestants must be brought into Ireland as settlers. The Ulster plantation still had a long way to go before it could be called a success, but the Anglo-Scottish population taking root in the north was the only sizeable group of Protestants in the country. Other plantation schemes had been mooted – for Longford, Wexford, Westmeath, Leitrim and Wicklow – and then dropped; now they were revived and put into execution. But land could no longer be acquired by confiscation; its owners had been far too cowed since Tyrone's defeat to rebel. So Crown lawyers started looking for loopholes in Irish and Old English land titles and reviving half-forgotten royal claims. Longford had once belonged to the earls of Shewsbury, but as they had been absentees in 1537 it had come into the queen's hand. Elizabeth had confirmed the Irish O'Farrells in possession, but James' lawyers found the O'Farrell title wanting. A similar Crown claim was made to Wexford, which had been in royal hands in the fourteenth century, and also to Leitrim.

James was a plain, downright, experienced Scot, learned, humorous and not immoral. Yet he believed he was right in what he was doing. Even the philosopher Francis Bacon wrote of the 'nobleness of the work' of plantation. James had no intention of totally dispossessing the current landowners; he wanted to carry out an operation rather like the old Surrender and Re-grant – with a sinister modification. A landowner whose title was found defective would receive a replacement title from the Crown, but only to three-quarters of his property; the remaining quarter would be kept for plantation. The Irish and Old English nobility and gentry were, naturally, jittery – as jittery as the gentry of Munster had been when Sir Peter Carew had dispossessed the Butlers in 1568. They already had a habit of sending one son abroad to train as a priest; now they began sending another to the Inns of Court in London to study English law.

Despite James' hopes, few of the undertakers on the new plantations did anything to spread either 'civility' or Protestantism. Like their predecessors elsewhere, they preferred Irish tenants and the high rents they paid to the trouble of bringing in English or Scottish planters and protecting them from the brigandage of the dispossessed Irish. Some were absentee landlords from the start, staying comfortably at home while the rents rolled in. Far more were New English officials, lawyers, or middlemen, who, from the deputy downwards, saw their work in Ireland as an opportunity to acquire cheap land and enrich themselves. In the Tudor era Englishmen had come to Ireland as adventurers, establishing the first outpost of an empire; in the seventeeth century they were businessmen. For the first time, the forests, fisheries and pastures of Ireland were seen as a vast, untapped source of wealth. Forests could be cleared and the timber exported; salmon, hides and flax sent abroad too. And if the Irish could be taught modern farming methods, so they would abandon such primitive practices as ploughing by the tail, wool plucking and corn burning[2] – what marketable crops the land would produce!

Some of these New English brought about the aims of plantation simply by the energy and dedication with which they pursued their business interests. During the 1620s Munster became a Protestant province second only to Ulster, due to the enterprise and ability of Richard Boyle, who became earl of Cork in 1620. He had arrived in 1588 as a penniless adventurer, bought up Sir Walter Raleigh's huge estates round Youghal in 1604, paying a mere £1,500 for them, and went on to build towns, found industries such as smelting and weaving, bring in English settlers and become immensely rich. He married his children into some of the best families in Ireland and England, and commanded eight votes in the Irish House of Commons. In 1628, at the culmination of his power, he was appointed one of the two lords justices who ruled Ireland when the deputy was away.

When James died in 1625, he bequeathed his son, Charles I, a war with Spain, which the English parliament had enthusiastically voted for. It had been less enthusiastic, however, about paying for the war, and after a mismanaged expedition to Cadiz, when an English fleet of ninety ships was badly defeated, Charles decided to raise a subsidy from Ireland. The Spaniards might well follow up their advantage with an invasion of Ireland, he argued, and it was reasonable that the Old English should prove their loyalty, always suspect because of their Catholicism, with a huge subsidy, amounting to £120,000, spread over three years. By a kind of gentleman's agreement, they were to have in return certain 'matters of grace and bounty', such as an abandonment of recusancy fines, complete security, even from royal claims, in any title to land going back sixty years, and a relaxation in the Oath of Supremacy for heirs wishing to inherit estates and lawyers practising at the Irish bar.

Protestants were still only a tiny minority, but they were the undertakers, the major planters, judges and officials; they could make themselves heard. Such magnates as the earl of Cork saw recusancy fines as an excellent means of raising revenue from Catholics without touching Protestants, and opposed what came to be known as the Graces, especially the sixty-year clause, which inhibited New English land-grabbing. The Old English had been led to believe that the Graces would be made law, but Charles was always ready to double-cross his subjects, and when the deputy, Lord Falkland, called a parliament, it was found invalid and Falkland recalled.

Falkland's successor was the most famous, efficient and hated of all the deputies who governed Ireland. He was Thomas, Viscount Wentworth, later earl of Strafford, a man of towering strength, courage and self-confidence, but insensitive and over-bearing. In 1628 he had been foremost among the English MPs who forced Charles to accept the Petition of Right, which protected the subject against the king. Yet his views were essentially royalist, and when Charles angrily dissolved the English parliament in 1629, Wentworth joined the Court party. With such a background in parliamentary management, he seemed the ideal person to handle the delicate matter of the Graces, and to raise revenue.

First, he had to find a balance between the Protestants and the Old English. 'We must there bow and govern the native by the planter and the planter by the native,' he had written while still in England; he would follow the old maxim of Divide and Rule. On his arrival in 1632, he flattered the earl of Cork just sufficiently to gain his goodwill and frighten the Old English, without committing himself to either party. And everyone remembered that, even before his arrival in Ireland, he had had Protestant planters in Fermanagh clapped into jail for opposing him; the iron hand had already dispensed with the velvet glove.

Before he set out for Ireland, Wentworth had declared his intention of building up the countryside, economic life and revenue. He found Dublin, with its muddy streets and boggy countryside, depressing in the extreme; he described in a letter how he looked out of his window in Dublin castle, a damp and dilapidated building, at a miserable old horse, fetlock-deep in ooze, cropping woefully at the filthy grass . . . Ireland seemed ripe for his practical and businesslike, even materialistic, attentions.

He was well aware of Ireland's possibilites as an island, ringed with ports, set in the sea trade of the Atlantic; Irish cattle, timber, hides, iron ore, meat and salt fish were exported and Continental wines, brandy and luxury goods, English beer, cloth and coal brought in. Limerick, Wentworth felt, could become a first-class harbour and Kinsale a naval dockyard for English ships and a revictualling port for the Spanish navy. The tax he favoured as a source of revenue was customs duty.

Wentworth was not disinterested. In those days the collection of the customs was farmed out, those who organized the collection keeping a proportion of what they brought in for their trouble, and Wentworth was the chief farmer of the Irish customs. The deputy and all officials made money quite legitimately from such opportunities. Nor was Wentworth primarily concerned with the welfare of the Irish. Although he hoped greater prosperity would turn them into a 'civil, rich and contented people', Ireland was very much the second of two kingdoms. Her economy was not permitted to interfere or compete with the English economy and she must remain dependent on England for some, at least, of her necessities. Nevertheless Wentworth was a strong enough deputy to defend Irish interests successfully when he felt they were being needlessly damaged. He kept down the export duty on Irish cattle and sheep destined for England and ensured that English horses could be imported without duty as the Irish breed needed improvement.[3] But the burgeoning of the economy was still in the future. In 1634 he called the parliament that might put the Graces on the statute book.

Wentworth knew very well that the Petition of Right had been pushed through the English parliament because Charles had neglected to 'pack' the parliament with his own supporters, and he was determined not to make Charles' mistake in Ireland. James had openly sold Irish peerages and Charles had created some too, so there were forty more members of the House of Lords, nearly all of them Protestant, than there had been in the last valid parliament in 1613. About half were absentees and Wentworth had the right to name their proxies; the House of Lords would be no problem. To win support in the Commons, he wrote personally to 100 boroughs and shires, asking them to elect candidates of his choice. Then, when he drew up the parliamentary programme, he made money matters – the size of the subsidy – the business of the first session, and legislation, such as the confirmation of the Graces, that of the second. The inference was clear: a generous subsidy would be rewarded with the legislation the members wanted.

The members voted unanimously for the subsidy Wentworth

required, the Old English and the Irish in the hope that he would ratify the principal Graces in the next session, and the Protestants in the equally fervent hope that he would not. The Protestants, outnumbering Catholics in the packed parliament, whatever their position in the country at large, had their way; Wentworth confirmed only ten of the fifty-one Graces, the rest being allowed only at the government's discretion. The two 'darling articles', as Wentworth described them, of the Old English, the sixty-year clause, which safeguarded their land titles, and another which specifically confirmed titles in Connacht, were refused. The Old English and Irish realized at last that Charles and his government were faithless and there was nothing they could do about it.

Wentworth held the common English view that only Protestant plantation could bring peace and 'civility' to Ireland. The confirmation of land titles in Connacht was withheld because that beautiful but infertile province, with its rocky coastline and thin inland soils, had never yet been planted. Crown lawyers were instructed to search for a royal claim to the lands of the earl of Clanricarde, who owned almost the whole province, and found that Edward VI had inherited the Burke lands through the marriage of Elizabeth de Burgo to Lionel, duke of Clarence, in 1342 (see page 90). Juries in Roscommon, Mayo and Sligo were threatened with a loss of property unless they did the government's bidding and allowed the claim, but when Wentworth pressed on to Galway, where the earl had his seat, the jurors, ten of whom were Clanricarde's kindred, threw it out. But Wentworth was not to be stopped; the sherriff who had empanelled the jury and the jurors themselves were all fined and imprisoned. Troops were moved into the city of Galway and a new jury summoned. Seeing the hopelessness of resistance, this jury did as it was asked and found for the king. Nevertheless, Wentworth decided to punish Galway by taking half the county for plantation instead of a quarter, as elsewhere. Soon after he heard of it Clanricarde, who was seventy-one, died – of a broken heart, his family said.

Wentworth had carried into Ireland the policy of Thorough, which Charles and his ministers would have used in England if they could. 'And so, Thorough let us go and spare not', Wentworth had written to his friend the English archbishop Laud. In the administrative sphere, Thorough was the minute and methodical attention to detail which had, in Wentworth's hands, made the Irish government efficient and the country rich as it had never been before. In other fields it was a policy of force: a ruthless determination to push through government aims whatever the opposition or consequences. It demonstrated Wentworth's strength and exposed his weakness, his blunderbuss tendency to go much too far. It earned him his nickname of Black Tom Tyrant.

Tyrant or no, Wentworth seems to have had a genuine concern for the little man and the poor. He put acts through the 1634 parliament which protected them from usurers and blackmailers, helped them obtain justice in a land where intimidation was rife, and supported small planters against the undertakers. But he alienated every other group. The Old English had been let down over the Graces, the Protestants had unpopular high church rituals thrust upon them, and in 1639 the Scottish Presbyterians in Ulster were made to swear an oath of allegiance, called the Black Oath; Charles' autocratic rule had aroused such resentment in Scotland that a Presbyterian group, the Covenanters, had raised an army against him, and Wentworth was determined the Scottish disaffection should not spread to Ireland.

Leading individuals were alienated too. When Wentworth examined the finances of the Established Church, which were in a poor state, he found much of the land set aside for it in each plantation had been filched away again. One of the chief offenders had been the earl of Cork. Through over-confidence, or perhaps through righteous zeal, Wentworth liked to tackle the mighty, and he forced Cork to surrender much of the church property he had acquired and pay a fine of £15,000. Cork squirmed and wriggled and went to the king, but eventually had to disgorge about £40,000.

Others were attacked and demolished too. Lord Mountnorris was making a good thing out of being vice treasurer, besides being one of those who, like Wentworth himself, farmed the customs. Wentworth had occasion to deliver a sharp reprimand to Mountnorris' brother, an army officer, and Mountnorris declared loudly at a dinner party that his brother should stick a knife into the deputy. Wentworth ignored the remark for months – and then arraigned Mountnorris before a court martial, which condemned him to death! There was no likelihood that the

149

sentence would be carried out, but Mountnorris lost his office of vice treasurer and had an application to farm more customs turned down in favour of the deputy. Next, Wentworth quarrelled with the lord chancellor, Lord Loftus, suspended him from office and ordered him to hand over the Great Seal. When Loftus obstinately refused, he found himself imprisoned in Dublin castle.

But the great ones of Ireland had many English connections, and got their revenge. In 1639 Charles, realizing the seriousness of the threat from Scotland, called Wentworth to England to help him. The mighty deputy had no friends in either country and when, created earl of Strafford, he was impeached in the English parliament – an early victim in the struggle between parliament and the king – he found Cork, Loftus, Mountnorris and many other familiar faces from Ireland ranged against him. Charles had assured Strafford his life and fortune would be safe, but when a mob demonstrated against him the frightened king, to whom Strafford had been a most faithful servant, consigned him to death. He was executed on 12th May 1641.

The Irish broke into rebellion. For years they had been smarting under the loss of their lands, the banning of their religion, the suppression of their language and culture, and their exclusion from government office. During the summer of 1641, plans were made, taking advantage of Charles' growing difficulties with the English parliament; in October Dublin castle was to be taken, and immediately afterwards the dispossessed gentry of Ulster, having lost almost all their estates to the planters, were to lead a rising. The plot to take the castle was betrayed, but the Ulster Irish rose just the same; the pent-up fury of years was released on the planters, mainly the English but soon the Scots as well. Huge bonfires lit up the night – so that the bandits, the wood-kerns and the wretched, exploited peasantry could gather to attack and burn the planters' homesteads, plunder their goods, cut the throats of some of them, make prisoners of others and drive the rest, half-naked, into the bogs and fields to find their way, if they could, to the shelter of the towns. Though many of the towns, too, had fallen to the Irish: Dungannon, Charlemont, Mountjoy and Newry were taken in the first couple of days,

Dundalk and Strabane a few weeks later. Horror stories swept through England and Scotland; the Irish were said to be intent on the murder of the whole Protestant population, and though the leaders of the rebellion never condoned its cruelties and excesses, up to 10,000 people were said to have been massacred.

The government was taken completely by surprise. Wentworth's army had been quietly disbanded during his impeachment and the two lords justices, who were rather feebly running the country, had to call upon the Protestant earl of Ormond to lead a defence. Ormond immediately set about raising troops from among the refugees streaming into Dublin, but was timidly forbidden to lead them out against the rebels until reinforcements came from England. And they did not come quickly. The English House of Commons was reluctant to send any troops to Ireland who might end up fighting for the king, and it was December before a paltry 1,100 English soldiers arrived in Dublin. Scotland still had many thousands of Covenanters under arms and was eager to send 10,000 of them into Ireland, but this time the English House of Lords, which was royalist in sympathy, demurred, and it was April 1642 before 2,500 Scots landed at Carrickfergus and began to recover large areas of Antrim and Down, and Ulster's captured towns.

The leaders of the rebellion had given it out that they had the support of the Old English, fellow Catholics who, like the Irish, smarted at being 'the only subjects in Europe not allowed to serve their prince'. But the Old English were, by tradition, loyal; their ties had always been to the English court and nobility and not, as was the case among the Irish, with France and Spain. They would not budge – until they found their tenants rising even within the Pale, bands of armed rebels ranging through their lands, their Protestant English neighbours being driven from their homes, and the tide of rebellion sweeping through Leinster and into Munster. Then in August the government, taking the common Protestant view that all Catholics, even Old English Catholics, were traitors, summoned a parliament of Protestants only. The Old English found themselves cut off, lost in a sea of disorder, without even a voice to be heard; and in October they set up their own rival assembly, which came to be known as the Confederation of Kilkenny. They declared their support for a Catholic Irish church, freedom of conscience, government by Catholic officials, the restitution of lands confiscated on grounds of religion, the independence of the Irish parliament from England and the repeal of Poynings' law. At the same time they declared their support for the king; as Catholics, they feared the Puritan English parliament far more than Charles' milder form of Protestantism.

Charles, now engaged in a civil war with the English parliament, instructed Ormond, the new deputy, to seek a truce with the Confederates. If the war in Ireland were over, perhaps the royalist Ormond would bring his Irish army to England to fight the English parliament on Charles' behalf? The Irish war was at a stalemate; unpaid government troops were foraging for food in the countryside, the Scots held Ulster and Owen Roe O'Neill, the leading Irish commander, had fallen back into Connacht. In September 1643 Ormond signed a truce with the Confederates, and ten days later the English parliamentarians entered into a Solemn League and Covenant with the Scots against the king. In the spring of 1644 the Confederates and the Irish Protestants both sent delegations to Charles with irreconcilable demands, the Confederates seeking freedom for the Catholic church and the Irish parliament, and the Protestants wanting the enforcement of the recusancy laws and their own political supremacy reestablished. Charles contrived to keep up the hopes of both parties for the next two years, while the War of the Three Kingdoms, as it was called in Ireland, dragged on, the Confederates losing their cohesion as the old distrust between Irish and Old English reappeared.

In 1644 and 1645 Charles was badly defeated by the English parliamentarians; he had to have another army at any price. He sent an emissary to grant the Confederates anything they wanted in return for 10,000 men and secret terms were made. But when the bargain was accidentally disclosed a few months later, Charles was so deeply discredited amongst the English that such support as he still had fell away. In March 1646, Ormond managed to negotiate another treaty with the Confederates, which removed various Catholic disabilities and became known as the 'Ormond peace'. But there was a fiery and unrealistic papal nuncio in the country, Giovanni Battista Rinuccini, and he threatened to excommunicate anyone who accepted any terms which did less than confirm the supreme authority of Rome! The

threat was too much for the ordinary Irishman to withstand, and
Ormond could not make his 'peace' stick. In June, O'Neill routed
an over-confident force of English and Scots at Benburb, on the
river Blackwater, and left 3,000 of them dead on the field. But
then, instead of marching on Dublin, O'Neill led his men off to
Kilkenny, where Rinuccini had taken over the supreme council
of the Confederates.

Charles had virtually lost the war. When Colonel Michael Jones
arrived in Dublin with 8,000 parliamentarian soldiers, or
Roundheads, Ormond surrendered the city to him and left the
country. All Ireland was a kaleidoscope, a shifting sand. Rinuccini hung about in Galway until the Confederates asked him
to leave, O'Neill campaigned fruitlessly in Munster and then
withdrew to the north, and the Ulster Scots turned royalist,
Ormond reappeared in Cork and organized some royalist resistance, but in August 1649, seven months after Charles had been
tried and executed, he was surprised with his army at Rathmines,
on the southern outskirts of Dublin, and forced to flee. A fortnight later 3,000 English cavalry, nicknamed Ironsides, came into
the city under the command of Oliver Cromwell.

Cromwell was a gentleman farmer from eastern England who
had emerged, in his forties and quite without military training,
as the most brilliant general of the English civil war. He had a
forceful personality and strong Puritan convictions. Like almost
everyone else in England, he had believed every word, and
every exaggeration, contained in the horror stories of Protestant
massacre which had circulated ever since the 1641 rising, and
never considered the grievances which had led the Irish to rebel.
Ireland before the rebellion had been a blissful Arcadia, he liked
to think, which only the barbarous and bloodthirsty Irish had
spoiled. Like other Englishmen before him, even the poet
Spenser, he believed the only solution to the perennial problems
of Ireland was to extirpate the Irish, to root them out and destroy
them, as the Israelites had extirpated the idolatrous inhabitants
of Canaan.

Ormond had withdrawn into Ulster after his check at
Rathmines and deputed Sir Arthur Aston, with a little over 2,000
men, to hold Cromwell as long as possible at Drogheda; Aston

stood no chance in the open field against Cromwell's army of 8,000 well-trained foot soldiers and 4,000 horse, all told, but Drogheda, built on heights at the mouth of the river Boyne and strongly walled, was an excellent defensive position. Aston expected to hold it until his food supplies ran out. But Cromwell was well prepared for siege warfare; he set up a battery of heavy guns to the south of the town and then, on 10th September, summoned Aston to surrender. 'If you refuse', he commented, 'you will have no cause to blame me.'

The rules of war in the seventeenth century were clear. Both Cromwell and Aston, who was a professional soldier, knew that a besieged commander who refused a call to surrender risked the lives of everyone fighting on his side. He could surrender, and expect quarter, at any time until the walls were breached, but once that had happened, he could expect no quarter. Aston refused Cromwell's call to surrender. In a letter to Ormond, he said his men 'were unanimous in their resolution to perish rather than deliver up the place'.

Cromwell replaced his white flag of truce with a red one and opened fire on the city walls, which began to crumble and give way. The defenders put up a very stiff resistance and it was some time before the breaches in the wall were big enough for 7,000 or 8,000 of Cromwell's men to pour through them into the town. They put the defenders to the sword and then streamed through the streets, mercilessly killing about a thousand of the townspeople. Many may have been technical combatants: who, in such a situation, would not arm himself with a piece of metal or a stick? Others were certainly defenceless. One group which had climbed into a church steeple refused a call to surrender – they may have been too frightened to surrender – and found their refuge on fire. Their attackers had made a pile of the wooden pews beneath them and set it alight. 'God damn me, God confound me,' one of the wretched victims was heard to cry, 'I burn, I burn.'

But Cromwell felt no pity; to him the war was holy. When he wrote to the English parliament he described the carnage as 'a righteous judgement of God upon these barbarous wretches, who have imbrued their hands in so much innocent blood.' It did not occur to him that some might think the bloodied hands his own; nor did he realize that the people of Drogheda were mostly Old English, and not the 'barbarous' Irish who had slaughtered Protestants in Ulster. In his naive response to the legends of 1641, he had provided the material for similar legends, which would fester in the hearts and minds of people in Ireland for centuries to come.

The rules of war governing sieges were intended to save lives; by giving the besieged an incentive to surrender, useless resistance was reduced. Cromwell believed the sack of Drogheda would prevent 'the effusion of blood' in the future, and in that he was correct. When he moved to Dundalk and Trim, the garrisons were so terrified they obeyed his call to surrender immediately and when, with the north more or less secured, he turned south, the castle at Enniscorthy was his without a blow being struck. At Wexford, however, the Confederate governor prevaricated when called upon to surrender, hoping for reinforcements, and an 'unexpected Providence' came to the aid of the English forces in the person of a young Captain Stafford, who betrayed the castle which stood next to the city wall. The English set up their scaling ladders, swarmed over the fortifications and stormed the town, running amok among the surprised and defenceless townspeople and killing more than 2,000 of them, for the loss of only twenty men. Wexford had had its chance.

When garrisons surrendered in time, Cromwell was merciful. The terms he offered were generous and he kept his word; his religion would allow him to do no less. From Wexford he moved on to New Ross, bypassed Waterford and spent the winter at Youghal which, with Cork and Kinsale, came over to him. In the spring Kilkenny surrendered and then, at Clonmel, he suffered his most serious setback; Hugh O'Neill, a nephew of Owen Roe, had reinforced the fortifications and when the English assaulted the walls, singing hymns as usual, they were repulsed and about 2,000 of them killed. O'Neill and his men slipped away during the night, with the walls still unbreached, leaving the mayor to surrender pacifically on terms to a furious Cromwell!

Soon afterwards Cromwell sailed from Ireland, leaving his son-in-law, Henry Ireton, to mop up what resistance was left. The Confederacy was breaking up; there were still 30,000 armed men on the Irish side, almost as many as the English had brought into Ireland, but they were leaderless. Owen Roe O'Neill had died in November 1649, and Ormond left Ireland in December

1650 to join the new king, Charles II. Limerick surrendered to Ireton in October 1651, and Galway in May 1652. More than ten years of rebellion were over.

But was it rebellion? In the first instance, when the Ulster Irish rose against the government and the planters, it certainly was. But when the Confederacy swore allegiance to the king, and the king acknowledged their allegiance, the state of rebellion was, *ipso facto*, ended. The king's difficulties with the English parliament had nothing to do with the Old English or the Irish; they had their own Irish parliament and could not, even if they had wanted to, have taken the English parliamentary side. Ireland suffered the supreme misfortune for a subsidiary state of supporting a losing king, being defeated by the rebels who had overthrown him and then being treated as rebels themselves.

The English intended the Irish to pay for the suppression of their rebellion – and to pay for it in the only way they could, with their land. In 1642, soon after the rebellion had broken out, the English parliament had passed an Adventurers' Act which declared the lands of the leading rebels forfeit and offered them for sale to English subscribers, the adventurers. With a curious blindness, the English were planning to perpetuate the wrong which had led to the rebellion in the first place. In 1652, with Ireland quiet once more, the act was put into effect.

Ireland had suffered terribly during the years of war. A third of the country's Catholics had been killed, and the population had fallen back to its medieval level of half a million. The government planned to fill the emptiness with a massive new plantation, covering two-thirds of the country; the counties of Dublin, Cork, Kildare and Carlow were to be reserved to itself as a kind of piggy bank, or nest egg, out of which all its debts could be paid, whether incurred in England or Ireland, and its servants rewarded, and another ten counties were to be shared amongst the adventurers and the officers and men of Cromwell's army, who were to receive Irish land in lieu of arrears of pay. Those Irish and Old English who stood in the way of this massive resettlement were to be transplanted to forfeited lands in Connacht. Ireland was to be divided, as it had been in the Middle Ages, into English and Irish areas, but this time the English

156

Pale was to cover most of the country, and no more than an impoverished wilderness, rather like a South African homeland, left to the Irish.

The Cromwellian Act of Settlement, passed by the English parliament in 1652, categorized the people of Ireland according to the 'constant good affection' they had, or had not, maintained towards the parliamentarians and deprived them of their land accordingly. Ormond, Clanricarde and 102 others were expressly excluded from any kind of pardon, along with all who had taken part in the original rising. Those who had fought for the Confederate army were to lose two-thirds of their estates, landowners sympathetic to the Confederacy one-third and others, less 'diligent', one-fifth. All three categories were to suffer enforced transplantation to Connacht, where they would receive fresh lands of equal value to what remained to them of the old. Only the poorest, those with goods worth less than £10, were to receive a free pardon – not through clemency, but because the new owners needed somebody left to tend their livestock and till the soil. Towns which had held out against the parliamentarians, such as Waterford and Galway, were to be planted with New English and their burgesses moved at least two miles outside the walls.

The transplantation was carried out with amazing speed. An English geographer, Sir William Petty, surveyed and mapped almost the whole of Ireland in thirteen months and the Irish and Old English gentry and aristocracy were ordered, on pain of death, to be across the river Shannon by 1st May 1654. Naturally they prevaricated, hoping against hope for some change of heart in the English, and the date was put back twice, to December 1654, and then to March 1655. By then 44,000 people had been turned out of their homes and farms in the fertile east and south to made the long trek, with their families, followers, cattle, pigs, sheep, chickens and such goods as they could take with them to Connacht. They travelled through the wet and cold of winter, some half-starving because they had not been able to reap the harvest before setting out, and others knowing they would reach their new lands too late for sowing.

Yet, for all the ruthlessness of the transplantation to Connacht and efficiency of the Puritan administrators who, in the name of religion, carried it out, the Cromwellian settlement failed. One of its objects was to fill Ireland with so many Protestants that the Catholics would be swamped and eventually, lacking the leadership of their gentry and priests, converted. But the difficulties were the same as they had been in previous plantations. Many private soldiers could not afford to take land in lieu of cash and sold up immediately to their officers, who soon had far more land than the government intended. English labourers, artisans and tenant farmers showed their usual reluctance to come to Ireland; the New World was far more attractive to them than a damp papist island beset by trouble – and tales were already reaching England of the tories, men from the disbanded Irish armies who preferred to stay in their home areas and live by brigandage, rather than join a foreign army or make the long trek to Connacht.

For a brief while, Ireland was united to England as never before. An English Protestant gentry wielded total power over landless Catholic Irish peasants. Catholic priests were banned and hunted – an iniquitous Cromwellian law offered £5 reward to anyone bringing in the head of a wolf or a Catholic bishop – while the Protestant church reorganized itself with fresh vigour. Trading restrictions were removed, greatly to the benefit of Irish commerce, and the Irish parliament was merged into the English. Then in 1658 Cromwell died and the Commonwealth he had created fell to pieces. In May 1660 Charles II was brought back from exile and proclaimed king. Ireland's royalists had been too crushed to play a part in his restoration, but nevertheless hoped for some redress of their wrongs.

And Charles, pleasure-loving, tolerant and a Catholic sympathizer, gave them what he could. In 1666 one-third of the lands granted to the adventurers and Cromwell's soldiers were returned and Catholics freed from persecution, retaining their right to vote though not to sit in the revived parliament. The Presbyterians were helped with a *regium donum*, or royal grant, of £600 a year paid from 1672. But Charles made it clear that, while his justice, as he said, was for every man, his favour must be given to his Protestant[4] subjects, and the Protestant position maintained. But the New English Protestants soon found out what it meant to live in the second kingdom. In 1666 Cromwellian free trade gave way before the jealousy of English farmers and an Irish Cattle Act was passed which cut back Irish livestock exports – the only sizeable Irish export left after twenty-five years of war and disruption – until the price of a beef animal in Ireland fell from 40s to 12s. And in 1663 and 1670 British navigation acts decreed that all Irish goods destined for America must be carried in English ships. Ireland was not to share in the prosperity generated by the British empire.

Towards the end of his reign, Charles began preparing the ground for the accession of his Catholic brother James; in Ireland Richard Talbot, a leading Catholic, was given the task of replacing Protestants by Catholics in the army, the administration and the judicature. When Charles died early in 1685 and his brother became James II, Ireland's Catholics were ready for change and jubilant. They felt their time had come.

But the English had had difficulty putting up with James as heir to the throne, and he was not to last long as king. He was honest, a trifle slow-witted and far too tolerant for his times; he could not believe in the strength of English anti-Catholic feeling. When he tried to force a 'Catholic design' upon England, leading Englishmen wrote secretly to his Protestant son-in-law, the Dutch prince William of Orange, inviting him to invade the country and take the crown. In November 1688, William sailed up the English Channel with 15,000 men, landed in Devon and waited for the English to come to him. If they had not done so, he would have sailed away again, but there was a rising in the north in his favour and the Protestants in James' army deserted him. Early in 1689, William and his wife, James' daughter Mary, were proclaimed joint sovereigns in England, Scotland and Ireland, while James escaped to France.

James intended to make his stand in Ireland, and in March he landed in Cork, bringing with him French officers, money and supplies. Richard Talbot, who had been raised to the peerage as earl of Tyrconnell on James' accession, was now the deputy, and James proceeded to Dublin, where Tyrconnell provided him with troops. Then he led his army to the city of Londonderry.

Londonderry had shown its Protestant colours as early as September 1688, when the apprentices, the working lads of the city, had closed the gates against the Catholic earl of Antrim and his men; later, when Tyrconnell had most unwisely withdrawn whole regiments from the north, the Protestant gentry had raised levies in support of William. Tyrconnell had defeated them in a confused engagement known as the 'break of Dromore', where-upon those who could not get a sea passage away from the country had crowded as refugees into the garrison town of Enni-skillen, in Fermanagh, and into Londonderry. James, beneath the city walls, called repeatedly upon the citizens to surrender, promising them a free pardon for their rebellion; although the governor was ready to make terms, the feeling in the city was overwhelmingly in favour of resistance. The governor was over-thrown and James' terms rejected. The city prepared for a siege.

The besiegers had no chance of taking the city by assault. James' troops were untried and ill-equipped; they had no spades and shovels for mining the city walls, and no guns heavy enough to breach them. They could only wait until the defenders were starved into submission. Refugees had swelled the population to 30,000 and food supplies soon began to run out; people were dying of starvation and the garrison was too weak to fight. The governor had been replaced by two Protestant stalwarts, Major Henry Baker and a country clergyman, George Walker, who refused to make terms. Then in the middle of June, six weeks after the siege had begun, an English fleet arrived in Lough Foyle to relieve the city. But James' troops had blocked the river Foyle, before it reached the city, with a massive wooden boom, which streched right across it. The English ships cast anchor and for six weeks simply sat there, within sight of the city, tantalizingly idle; and then on 28th July, when the people of the city had been reduced to eating cats and dogs, three ships filled with provisions forced the boom and, after fifteen weeks, the siege was over. On the same day, Protestant troops from Enniskillen defeated an Irish force at Newtownbutler, on the upper reaches of Lough Erne.

James had lost in the north, and his Irish parliament, which sat between May and July, while Londonderry was being besieged, deprived him of whatever political influence he had left. He had been careful never to threaten his Protestant subjects with any alteration of the Cromwellian plantations or Charles II's land settlement of 1666, but the Old English who dominated the parliament had no such inhibitions. Gleefully they removed all penal clauses against Catholics and threatened to confiscate the property of all Protestant landowners. This Patriot Parliament, as it was called, was far more concerned with righting its members wrongs than the cause of its Catholic king.

William of Orange had accepted the English invitation to take the throne because Protestant Holland was at war with Catholic France and James was reputed to support the French king, Louis XIV; William thought James might lead England into the war on the French side. In the event, James did not go to Louis' aid, but Louis did come to his. James was not short of men, though they were untrained and armed mostly with scythes and staves, and when, in the spring of 1690, Louis offered him 6,000 French troops in exchange for his raw Irish recruits, James accepted them gratefully. James was growing tired of the Irish and only too glad to ship five Irish regiments off to France.

Ten thousand of William's troops, under a continental commander, Marshal Schomberg, had wintered in Ireland; in the spring, they were reinforced with English, Danish and Dutch troops. Then on 14th June William landed at Carrickfergus, and both kings knew that the decisive battle was upon them: decisive not only for themselves but for the future of Catholic Ireland. William reviewed his army of 36,000 men in Co. Down on 22nd June. Then he moved south towards Dublin, which was the immediate prize, and reached Dundalk. James decided to make his stand upon the river Boyne. He was only slightly outnumbered, he had had all winter to train his Irishmen, and he picked his ground well; he stationed his troops within the curve of the river, about three miles from Drogheda and close to a good road to Dublin, which was about twenty-five miles away. He doubted

17.   The battle of the Boyne (courtesy of the National Library of Ireland)

if he would win, and the road would help his retreat. And William, for his part, hoped James would retreat successfully; he wanted to avoid the embarrassment of making a prisoner of his father-in-law!

The day of the battle, 1st July 1690, was sunny and bright. William bombarded James' position with his superior artillery and then the veteran Dutch guards crossed the river in a frontal attack, followed by Englishmen, Danes, French Huguenots and Ulster Protestants. James' Irish infantry could not hold them, though his cavalry under Tyrconnell (now a duke) charged with reckless valour again and again. The French had been positioned too far away to be of much help; they only lost six men in the whole battle, but they checked William's men sufficiently to give James the chance of a fairly orderly retreat. Dublin was evacuated, and Tyrconnell ordered the French and Irish forces to Limerick, while James slipped quietly back to France.

The war dragged on for another year. The Irish and Old English were fighting for themselves, their lives and their liberties, rather than the departed James and his cause. In the summer of 1691 Athlone, in Westmeath, fell to William's general, Ginkel. Then James' French commander, the marquis de St Ruth, fought a pitched battle at Aughrim, near Ballinasloe, to block Ginkel's advance on Galway, but was killed at the critical moment so that the Irish, disheartened, fled into Limerick. Patrick Sarsfield, a dashing cavalry commander whom James had made earl of Lucan, defended Limerick courageously but, with William's troops round the town and an English fleet in the estuary of the Shannon, prolonged resistance was useless; it could only weaken the Irish negotiating position. Sarsfield procured the best terms he could and surrendered.

The Treaty of Limerick, which Sarsfield negotiated, provided first and foremost for religious toleration for all Ireland's Catholics, the same religious tolerance they had enjoyed in Charles II's reign, secondly, protection for James' officers and men submitting to William, along with the civilian population of Limerick and elsewhere which had held out against him and, thirdly, the opportunity for Irish Catholic soldiers to be shipped abroad, so they could fight in the armies of France, Spain and

18.   Patrick Sarsfield, earl of Lucan (courtesy of the Library of the Franciscan
       Friary, Merchants' Quay, Dublin)

Austria. The century that had begun with the Flight of the Earls
ended with the Flight of the Wild Geese, as it was called – when,
led by Sarsfield, the greater part of the Catholic gentry, and their
followers, departed into exile. Some nursed a romantic notion
that they would, one day, return to fight for king James and

others sought more realistically for adventure and fulfillment in foreign lands. The Irish brigades formed from the Wild Geese became famous in the continental wars of the eighteenth century.

The estates of some 270 Catholic landowners, some of them rebels and others absentees, were forfeited. It was the final blow in a century of confiscation. In 1603, when the Tyrone wars ended, considerable areas of Munster had belonged to Protestants, such as the Butler family and the parvenu earl of Cork. Twenty-five years later, when Ulster had been planted with Scots and English, a quarter of all the land of Ireland was in Protestant hands. Wentworth ruthlessly carried plantation into Connacht, and the Protestant proportion rose to 40 per cent. Then the Cromwellian settlements took root, and Protestants came to own threequarters of the Irish land. In 1692, after James' defeat, Catholics had only one-seventh of the land, which they had once owned, left. Unable to follow the vagaries of the English, when they executed one king and drove out another, the Irish found themselves, for their loyalty, dispossessed – and reduced, in many instances, to the level of dependent tenants and labourers.

CHAPTER 8

THE PROTESTANT ASCENDANCY

The Treaty of Limerick was quite unacceptable to Ireland's Protestants. The Catholic enthusiasm of the Patriot Parliament had terrified them; they had seen their farms and estates, which, in their view, had been carved out of an empty wilderness, about to be lost. Armed bands of Catholic tories and rapparees, a new kind of bandit, roamed the countryside; pirates attacked the ships which carried Protestant goods abroad. There was lawlessness everywhere. Protestants felt there was only one safe place to be, and that was on top.

From 1691 onwards, even before the Treaty of Limerick had been sent to William, an act of the English parliament was applied to Ireland which required members of both houses of parliament to take an Oath of Allegiance and make declarations against the mass and the pope, which no conscientious Catholic could do; the first principle of the Treaty of Limerick, which granted Catholics the same toleration under William as they had had under Charles II, was being denied. The Irish parliament summoned in 1692 was Protestant and determined to remain Protestant; Catholics were to be subjugated and kept out of the way. The lord lieutenant, who had to placate parliament in order to raise funds, promised that Catholics would not be allowed to join the army. In 1695 another parliament made it illegal for Catholics to keep schools, become school teachers or private tutors, send their children abroad to be educated, as many of the Catholic gentry were used to doing, or become the guardian of a child; as Catholics were already barred from obtaining degrees at Trinity College, Dublin, their education was effectively truncated. Catholics were hindered from buying confiscated land; when about a million acres were put on the market, Catholics were not allowed to buy, or lease, more than two acres each. Catholics were forbidden to wear swords, a normal part of a gentleman's dress in those days, to own a sporting gun, or a horse worth more than £5; if a Protestant admired a Catholic's horse, he could take it from him, there and then on payment of that sum.[1] Then in 1698 Catholics, with a few exceptions, were excluded from the practice of the law; not only was a career denied to young, ambitious men, but Catholics as a whole were deprived of legal representation from amongst their own people.

The Privy Council in England hesitated when confronted with some of the virulently anti-Catholic legislation sent over from Ireland. William himself had hoped to be magnanimous in victory. Ireland's Catholics were not rebels; they had been fighting for their lawful king. It was not their fault that the English, less loyal than they, had pulled the rug from under James' feet and preferred a different prince. But after the Flight of the Wild Geese, Irish brigades were fighting for France and Spain. And France was England's enemy; the Wild Geese were fighting English armies. Out of patriotism, fear and kinship, the English were bound to support Ireland's Protestants.

In 1704 the Irish parliament passed an act 'to prevent the further growth of popery' which was the most severe of all the Penal Laws which discriminated against Catholics. Known as the Gavelkind Act,[2] it stated that Catholics should only inherit land from each other, never from Protestants, and on the death of a Catholic landowner, his property must be equally divided amongst his sons, causing the family to decline in wealth and status, unless the eldest son conformed to the established Protestant Church. In a rule which was bound to cause family dissension, the son could take over the estate within his father's lifetime, if he turned Protestant, and reduce his father to the status of his life-tenant. Other laws prevented Catholics from giving mortgages or acquiring land on a lease of more than thirty-one years, and fixed their rents at two-thirds of the value of the crops grown or livestock reared on it. If a Catholic improved the output of his holding through his skill and hard work, his rent would go up; and if he tried to avoid the increase by hiding his improved output from his landlord, the first Protestant who found him out could take his land from him. Similarly, if a Catholic bought land from a Protestant in secret, any Protestant who caught him out could evict him. A Catholic could not acquire property by marriage with a Protestant, but a Catholic wife who turned Protestant would be rewarded with part of her husband's estate. A Protestant woman who married a Catholic was deprived of her property. Later on, marriages between Protestants and Catholics were declared null and void, and priests who performed such marriages could be hung.

Catholics were grossly hampered in business too. They were more heavily taxed than Protestants, restricted in their choice of premises to work in and limited in the number of their employees, so that their businesses were prevented from growing. They could not vote in parliamentary or local elections, or enter the government service in any capacity, however humble. They had no place in the judicial system; a Catholic plaintiff had to be represented by a Protestant lawyer, to come before a Protestant judge and a Protestant jury. The law employed and protected Protestants; it punished Catholics. In a very famous statement the Lord Chancellor, John Bowes, and the Chief Justice, Christopher Robinson, declared 'that the law does not suppose any such person to exist as an Irish Roman Catholic.'

Naturally, many Catholics belonging to the landed and merchant classes turned Protestant; they were not all prepared to be martyred for their religion any more than people are now. 'Tis sad for me', wrote a Catholic father, 'to cleave to Calvin or perverse Luther but the weeping of my children, the spoiling them of flocks and lands, brought streaming floods from my eyes.' Such men were often hypocritical Protestants, timeservers who attended what Protestant services the law required and went on hearing mass privately, in their own homes. Their children might still go abroad for a Catholic education – nominal Protestants could not be prevented from sending their children abroad – but they were more likely to attend Protestant schools at home. Within a generation or two, much of the Catholic heritage was forgotten.

The people of Ireland were, once again, divided into two nations.

The Protestants, nearly all English or Scots but including a few Irish families, comprised no more than a quarter of a population which had increased, by the beginning of the century, to almost two million; yet they owned nearly all the land, ran most of the businesses, filled the government and judicial posts, and provided both officers and men for the army and the navy. Their manners, customs and speech were English. Below them, unconnected with them by any ties of history, culture, or common interest, speaking the Irish of their forefathers and not the English of their conquerors, were the country's Catholics, a depressed, subjugated people, without rights, who lived more poorly than any other peasantry in Europe and felt for their masters little but hatred.

In 1583 the bishop of Meath had bequeathed his best cooking pot to the people of Dunboyne, and they had queued up to use it. In England, and in most other countries, the common people would have scorned such a benefaction; they had had adequate cooking pots for centuries. But the poor cottiers of Ireland, who formed the broad base of Irish society, had nothing. A century after the bishop's death, they were still living with their animals in tiny, thatched cabins, with the smoke pouring out of the open doorways as there were seldom chimneys, and sleeping on straw. Hungry and emaciated, with swarms of skinny children, their main concern was growing enough food – and they paid exorbitant rents for little plots of land where they could grow corn or oats, a few vegetables and, increasingly, potatoes. A family of six could live off an acre planted, year after year, with potatoes.

These little plots of land provided the cottiers with the only security they had. But it was a poor kind of security. There was a class of people in the Irish countryside, described by Arthur Young, an English traveller, as 'your fellows with round hats, edged with gold, who hunt in the morning, get drunk in the evening and fight the next morning', who made their living out of exploiting the cottiers. They were the middlemen, Protestants who discovered they could make huge profits out of renting large tracts of land from major landlords, generally absentees, and then sub-letting them in tiny parcels to the Catholic poor. Landlords with no responsibilities, and no interest in the land beyond the rents they could extract from their tenants, these middlemen were the worst element in the countryside. They traded on the poor cottiers' desperate need for land, and the cottiers and small farmers had no protection against them; their rents could be raised whenever the middleman wanted, and they could be ruthlessly evicted and their cabins burned if they did not pay.

Cottiers tried to supplement their income by doing casual work on the larger farms, but around 1715 a great deal of land was turned over from arable use to pasture, which required less labour. So they took to begging. When they had planted their crops in the spring and cut the turf for the next winter's fires, they wandered off, to spend the summer migrating from place to place, very much as their forefathers had done when they drove their cattle to upland summer pastures a thousand years earlier. Even employed people would spend the summer begging; wages were so low that servants left their jobs and farm hands quit the farms to join the seasonal migration. Thousands of poor Irish would simply wander along the roads and paths, barefoot, ragged, feckless and idle, living in the open and begging for their food, less often from more prosperous wayfarers and the houses of the great than from other poor cottiers like themselves. Most communities expected to support some beggars, generally about ten in the winter and thirty or forty between planting and harvest time.

When cottiers had handed over two-thirds of their produce as rent, they still had to pay the government hearth tax of 2s or 3s a year and their religious dues. The first of these dues, very much resented, was the tithe paid to the Protestant clergy of the Established Church, who lived in comfortable parsonages up and down the country and attended to the spiritual needs of the upper classes. They seldom visited the hovels of the poor. Secondly, the cottiers supported their own parish priests. Protestants did not want to stamp out Catholicism; they had far too much to gain from the subjugation of the Catholic population, whom they referred to as 'Catholic enemies' and exploited as a conquered race, to wish them to turn Protestant, and they believed that religion, any religion, spread 'civility' and reduced the crime rate. In 1703 Catholic parish priests were asked to register with the government and over a thousand did so, including a number of bishops and friars masquerading as parish priests in order to carry on their work.

Catholic priests had been holding their services in old barns, in gentlemen's houses and in the open, setting up altars on 'mass-rocks' and under trees. After they were registered they were allowed recognized church buildings, where their congregations could gather quite openly. Simple houses were put up for the priests, and soon became landmarks. Parishioners paid for their priest in grain and vegetables, milk, livestock sent to market, cloth they had woven – whatever they had, besides the usual fees for marriages, funerals and baptisms. And the priest, in return, acted as their leader. He was generally a farmer's son, so he understood rural problems, with a superior education at a Catholic seminary abroad which enabled him to arbitrate in disputes, arrange for some kind of village schooling, negotiate on behalf of his flock with the outside world and organize relief during times of famine. After 1720, the presence of Catholic priests was tacitly accepted by the ruling Protestants, and in 1727 the Protestant primate, archbishop Boulter, reckoned that there were 3000 Catholic priests in the country as against a mere 800 Protestant clergy – a telling testimony to the superior zeal of the outlawed Catholic church.

Ireland's third religious group, the Presbyterians, was also caught by the Penal Laws. The Protestants of the Ascendancy, as it came to be called, belonged to the Established Church of Ireland, but the Presbyterians were dissenters. The English Test Act of 1673 already prevented them from playing any part in politics and local government; they had no votes and could not belong to city corporations. After the passage of the Penal Laws, the position of their ministers became, in some respects, worse than that of Catholic priests. They were recognized by the Crown; the annual *regium donum*, instituted by Charles II, was still paid to them, but they could be heavily fined for celebrating the Lord's Supper, marriages they performed could be declared invalid and the children born of them bastards, and burial by Presbyterian rites was frequently forbidden. Catholic priests suffered less humiliation; though often persecuted, as Presbyterian ministers were not, they were nevertheless acknowledged to be priests and allowed to fulfill their priestly functions.

The Protestant Ascendancy saw the Presbyterians as a threat. The Catholics seemed poor and dispirited, the wretched remnant of a defeated nation, whereas the Presbyterians were tough, energetic and self-assured: hard-headed, practical Scots who had come to Ireland because of the opportunities they saw in the country for acquiring cheap farms and opening up businesses. Presbyterians built their meeting houses and attended services quite openly, sent their missionaries out among the Catholics, and set up their own church hierarchy under the Protestant bishops' noses; one exasperated archbishop described how four or five thousand Presbyterians would congregate for an open-air service, generally the illegal Lord's Supper, and no government authority dared molest them.

Presbyterians were thick on the ground, too. Most of those who made the short sea crossing from Scotland were peasant farmers, but there were many traders, artisans and craftsmen as well. The numbers of Catholics and Presbyterians in the Ulster countryside were about equal, but the large new towns were peopled almost entirely by Presbyterians. A rising mercantile class of Presbyterians dominated the provisions trade in London-derry and the linen industry in the growing town of Belfast; drapers, who finished and sold linen cloth, shopkeepers, carriers, leatherworkers, shoemakers and tailors – all were Presbyterian.

The most conspicious members of the Protestant Ascendancy were the landlords, who lived off their rents, hunting, breeding horses, attending race meetings, which were becoming very popular, and dispensing lavish hospitality. It cost them practically nothing; food came off the estate, drink, which flowed very freely, was either the local whiskey or cheap wine smuggled from the continent, and servants were rarely paid money wages. In the 1720s, the new landlords were already rich enough to build themselves fine country houses, after the manner of the English aristocracy, with parks and gardens round them and a wall to keep out the poverty of the Irish.

Country towns aquired a new elegance; the gentry built fine Georgian houses in them, and assembly rooms for balls and concerts. Killarney became a fashionable watering place. But the centre of Anglo-Irish social life remained Dublin. The first duke of Ormond, lord lieutenant in Charles II's time, had been determined the city should have the magnificence due to the seat of government, and, following his lead, the nobility had built town houses round College Green, and the ancient common, St Stephen's Green, had been laid out as a residential square. Ormond's Georgian successors had a colonnaded parliament house built, as well as a new facade for Trinity College and splendid state rooms in Dublin castle. Especially during parliamentary sessions, Dublin was extremely gay, with routs and balls and all the paraphernalia of eighteenth century fashionable life.

But this imitation of English life was, all too often, not enough. Most landlords preferred to live in England, and used the proceeds of their Irish estates simply to cut a dash abroad. Ireland's wealth was constantly being drained away. Nowadays ex-colonial territories make stringent laws to prevent their foreign settler populations taking their money out of the country. Colonial Ireland had no such protection. In the seventeenth century, the English government had occasionally rewarded its servants with a pension on the Irish establishment, and in the eighteenth century the practice was greatly extended; both George I and George II used the Irish pension list to provide for their mistresses, bastards and German relations. Pensions and sinecures on Ireland were worth about £100,000 a year, and rents going abroad to absentee landlords built up, in the second half of the century, to a staggering £700,000 a year. As the total annual revenue was little more than £1 million about 1770, Ireland was losing the amazing proportion of four-fifths of her income.

Ireland's Protestant landlords, or the Anglo-Irish, as they came to be called, were certainly on top; but very early in the century they realized that, in the wider context of Great Britain, they were no more than the middle tier in a sandwich.

In earlier times, the Irish parliament had dealt through the lord lieutenant with the king and his English Privy Council. During the seventeenth century there had been a shift in power in England from the monarch to the English parliament; it had not affected Ireland greatly after the Restoration as Charles II and James II had both contrived to rule as far as possible without parliaments, but after the curiously named Glorious Revolution which made William king, the English parliament, instead of the monarch, chose the prime minister and he was, of course, responsible to those who had put him in power. The Protestant Ascendancy found that the English parliament, responsible only to the English people, was standing between their own Irish parliament and the monarch.

England had already shown her jealousy of Ireland with the Irish Cattle Act and the Navigation Acts; in 1696 the English forbade the direct import of goods from America into Ireland, decreeing that they had to enter and leave a British port on the way, incurring British handling charges and paying customs duty to the British Treasury. By the time such goods reached Ireland, they were prohibitively expensive. Next, England attacked the Irish woollen industry which, although it was tiny in comparison with the English one, aroused the jealousy of English manufacturers, who saw themselves being undercut in continental markets. In 1699 the English parliament legislated to prevent the export of woollen goods from Ireland to any country except England – and the English industry was, of course, protected by high customs duties. By way of compensation the budding linen industry was encouraged to grow. But Ireland's Protestant middle class of merchants and manufacturers had learned their lesson; any Irish enterprise which competed with English trade or manufacture would be stifled at birth. Ireland must always be poorer than England.

The demise of the Irish woollen industry at the hands of the English parliament provoked a member of the Irish House of Commons, William Molyneux, into publishing a pamphlet entitled *The Case of Ireland's being Bound by Acts of Parliament in England, Stated*, in which he argued that 'if the English parliament may bind Ireland, it must also be allowed that the people of Ireland ought to have their representatives in the parliament of England.' That, however, the English parliament would not allow; it regarded itself as an imperial, not a national, parliament, with a right to legislate directly for its colonies, such as Ireland, and to supervise all administrative matters. Then in a famous lawsuit about an inheritance, Sherlock vs. Annesley, the judicial authority of the Irish House of Lords was overthrown. One disputant appealed against a decision of the Irish House of Lords to the English Lords, and the Irish judgment was overturned. The Irish were furious; but in 1719 the English parliament ratified the decision in a Declaratory Act 'for the better securing of the dependancy of the kingdom of Ireland on the Crown of Great Britain', declaring it had authority to make laws 'of sufficient force and validity to bind the kingdom and people of Ireland.' And the Irish parliament could do nothing about it.

The Protestants who made up Ireland's parliament felt they could not survive amidst a sea of Catholic 'enemies' unless they were staunchly loyal to England, and they were quite prepared to do the viceroy's bidding so long as he did not ask them to ease the laws against Catholics and Presbyterians. The English viceroy was sent to Ireland to carry out English policies to achieve English aims. Holding splendid court in Dublin castle, he dispensed patronage and favours to a Protestant oligarchy which, in return, 'managed' parliament as he wished. In Ireland, as in England, there were many ancient constituencies with hardly any electors. Nowadays constituency boundaries are re-drawn every few years to take account of the movement of population, but in the eighteenth century many of them were medieval. Some cities which had grown up recently, such as Londonderry, were scarcely represented at all, while towns which had disappeared centuries before still returned members to the House of Commons. These pocket boroughs were controlled by the local magnate, who nominated the candidate who would best serve his interests. The House of Commons had 300 members, of whom 178 held seats in the possession of about 30 rich men. Parliamentary sessions were the occasion of a gay social whirl, with much jockeying for position behind the scenes, rather than tough discussion of the country's needs.

Behind the beautiful town houses of Georgian Dublin and the fine, colonnaded public buildings were narrow medieval streets of rotting, malodorous tenements inhabited by Dublin's poor. The worst of these districts, known as the Liberties, was where the weavers lived, who had been thrown out of work when the English parliament destroyed the Irish woollen industry. It lay between St Patrick's Protestant cathedral and the rambling Deanery House, and every day the dean made his way through the filthy lanes on foot, distributing coins to the beggars and noting, with passionate concern, the wretchedness of the people. The dean of St Patrick's was Jonathan Swift.

Though he was born in Ireland of Anglo-Irish parents, and spent nearly seven years as a student at Trinity College, Dublin, Swift detested Ireland; he abhorred the hopelessness of the place, and the uselessness of effort. As soon as he could, he escaped to England, where his political satires on behalf of the English Tory party made him famous. He hoped to be rewarded with a comfortable English bishopric and was deeply disappointed when, in 1713, he was given the Dublin deanery.

For seven years he lived obscurely, and then in 1720 the misery of the weavers prompted him to write an anonymous pamphlet entitled *A Proposal for the Universal Use of Irish Manufacture* which contained the resounding injunction to the Irish to 'burn everything from England except her coal.' He was telling the Irish people to improve their prospects by buying Irish. To us, such a policy is unexceptionable; all countries urge their citizens to buy the home product. But eighteenth century Ireland was a market for England, and the Irish government prosecuted the printer, as they did not know who the author was, for sedition. Juries could often be intimidated into doing what a judge wanted them to do, but not on this occasion. Nine times the jury was sent out to reach a verdict of guilty, and nine times they refused. Whereupon the prosecution was quietly dropped.

Three years later Swift took up the cudgels once more. For some time, Ireland had been short of small coins. The Irish had asked repeatedly for their own mint, but since Charles II's time coins for Ireland had been minted in England, and in 1720 George I granted a patent to mint £108,000 worth of copper halfpennies and farthings to his German ex-mistress, the duchess of Kendal, and the duchess sold the patent for £10,000 to an English iron-master, William Wood, who reckoned he would make a profit of at least £25,000 on the deal. When the Irish heard of it, they were extremely angry, and Swift, impersonating a draper, ridiculed Wood's mountains of ha'pence in the first of four famous tracts, the *Drapier's Letters*. Then the report of a Committee of Inquiry set up in London was leaked and reprinted in Dublin. A second equally virulent *Drapier's Letter* appeared and then a third. Wood's effigy was carried through the streets of Dublin and the new ha'pence kept back from circulation. The lord lieutenant was recalled, his successor, Lord Carteret, hastened to Dublin – and Swift issued the fourth *Drapier's Letter*.

It was not really ha'pence the Irish were fighting about, but freedom. 'By the laws of God, of nature, of nations, and your own country, you are and ought to be as free a people' Swift told the Irish, 'as your brethren in England.' Carteret decided to prosecute the author but, though everyone knew the drapier was Swift, it could not be proved, and again the unfortunate printer took the brunt of the attack. Then Swift wrote an open letter to the jury and they threw the case out. Quite unconstitutionally, a second jury was empanelled – and they not only rejected the case for the prosecution but Wood's ha'pence as well, declaring those who tried to force the ha'pence upon Ireland were 'enemies of His Majesty and the welfare of this kingdom'.

Afterwards, Swift was silent for a while. He had taught the Irish the invaluable lesson that they could defeat England by constitutional means. Then between 1727 and 1730, Ireland endured three years of famine; the bodies of people who had starved to death lay unburied outside their hovels, and Swift wrote the most grotesquely ironic of all his tracts. In *A Modest Proposal for Preventing the Children of Poor People in Ireland from Being a Burden to their Parents or the Country*, he ingeniously advises that 'one-fourth part of the infants under two years old be forthwith fattened' as 'dainty bits for landlords, who, as they have already devoured most of the parents, seem to have best right to eat up the children.' He was so deeply shocked by the exploitation of the common Irish, which seemed to him next to cannibalism, that he wanted in turn to shock his complacent, well-fed, and especially English, readers.

Yet Swift was no liberal, or democrat. The poor loved him, as they loved no-one else, but he saw them as ignorant savages with an absurdly superstitious religion. He believed in the Protestant Ascendancy, though not in its cruelties, and in the right of Protestants to lead a free Ireland. He was the first of a new breed of Anglo-Irish Protestant nationalists.

After Swift had spoken, some Protestants began taking their responsibilities more seriously. In 1731 wealthy Protestant clergy and landowners founded the Dublin Society for the improvement of agriculture, which set up a model farm, published instructive pamphlets and offered prizes for good husbandry. Parliament supported the society with grants, to be spent not only on encouraging improved agriculture but manufacture and fisheries as well. Improving landlords became a new feature in the countryside. Some set up small industries on their estates, others reclaimed waste land to provide holdings for landless labourers, and many more tried to teach good husbandry by example. Then in 1733 special Charter schools were set up for the children of the poor. They had a strong Protestant bias, which prevented them from becoming popular, but were, nevertheless, a sign of good intent.

Protestant hostility towards Catholics was gradually declining. The eighteenth century was the Age of Reason, when people valued cool rationality above everything and abhorred what they called 'enthusiasm' and we would term fanaticism. Excessive religious zeal came into that category. Though Protestants still considered many Catholic beliefs and practices absurd, they were far more ready than they had been in the past to tolerate them, and to give a helping hand to their Catholic neighbours. When Irish Catholics showed no interest at all in supporting James II's descendants, who led rebellions in Scotland in 1715 and 1745, the Protestants were gratefully prepared to allow the Penal Laws, though they were not repealed, to fall into abeyance.

The Penal Laws had never been fully enforced; there was not, and never could be, the machinery to enforce all of them, all the time. But they had done their work. They had enslaved the bulk of the Catholic Irish for the enrichment of their Protestant superiors, and they had also, less intentionally, encouraged in the Irish the characteristics of slaves: idleness, mendacity, a protective foolishness, and a light, smiling gaiety that masked a sense of wrong. The Penal Laws had also eroded what respect the Irish had ever had for the law. 'The law does not suppose any such person to exist as an Irish Roman Catholic.' The Catholic Irish, including their leaders, the priests, turned away from a system of law which punished but did not protect them. They ignored and forgot about it and, developing a characteristic which has lasted to this day, found their own remedies for injustice in the formation of secret societies.

Tories and rapparees still haunted the bogs and mountains, especially in the south and west. Between 1711 and 1713 a group, known as the Houghers, had terrorized the whole province of

Connacht, 'houghing', or ham-stringing, cattle and driving sheep over cliffs into ravines; their grievance was the wholesale conversion of arable land into pasture, which threw many small tenant farmers off their holdings. Then, in 1759, after a long period of comparative tranquillity, Britain lifted the restrictions on the import of Irish cattle and yet more land was put down to pasture; in Tipperary whole villages were swept away and the common land enclosed for grazing. A new society of militant peasants was formed, the Whiteboys, so called because they met at night, with faces blackened and white smocks over their clothes, so they could be recognized as a body but not individually. The Whiteboys pulled down fences, maimed livestock and punished small farmers who were over-subservient to the landlords. Before long Whiteboys were carrying on their activities through most of Munster, Leinster and Connacht. Only Ulster was free of them – until, in 1763, the peasants of Armagh and Londonderry, styling themselves Hearts of Oak, or Oakboys, and wearing sprigs of oak in their hats, attacked landlords for putting too much pressure on them to work on the roads. In 1770 the earl of Donegal demanded unjustly high fines, or premiums, from his tenants in Antrim for the renewal of their leases. Those who could not pay were evicted and replaced, and Hearts of Steel, or Steelboys, attacked the property and cattle of the new tenants.

The Whiteboys, Hearts of Oak, Hearts of Steel and other organizations which followed them were not patriot or freedom movements. Irish peasants still dreamed of king James, but their societies were mainly concerned with such local tyrannies as the harshness of a landlord, the rapacity of tithe-proctors, who were collecting for a clergy the people considered alien and heretical, and less often, Catholic priests who charged exhorbitant fees. Sometimes they attacked their oppressors directly. In Co. Cork landowners and their resident agents had to keep their windows shuttered and their doors barricaded against the Whiteboys, who roamed the countryside in armed bands of five to 500 men. More often, though, the secret societies attacked the weaker peasants, who paid the exorbitant tithe or the higher rent. Those cottiers who, through the pressure of their needs, or their own frailty, could not stand up to tyrannical superiors, were caught in a cruel dilemma; if they refused the extra rent, or the renewal premium, they lost their holding and their livelihood. If they paid it, the society took its revenge.

All the societies carried out secret oathing ceremonies, often forcing their oaths upon unwilling recruits. Their leaders were shadowy figures who went under pseudonyms, such as Captain Eaves, or Captain Starlight, one pseudonym sometimes covering several men. The local people had no way of knowing who were members and who were not, or where the gangs might strike next. But they knew their methods. The old warning to children, 'Watch out, or the fairies will get you,' goes back to those times. 'Fairies' was the country name for society members, and what the fairies did was to hamstring cattle, pull down houses, burn ricks and barns, fire shots into houses, deliver threatening letters and apply torture to those who fell foul of them, branding them, cutting off bits of their ears, and 'wool-carding', or drawing the steel comb used on wool through the victim's flesh.

Irish peasants had been impoverished, degraded, exploited and brutalized. When they made war upon their superiors in the only way they could, by combining into what amounted to primitive trade unions, it was inevitable that the cruelty of their methods would match the cruelties that had been practised upon them.

In the towns, things were looking up. Britain was still afraid of Irish competition; even the linen industry, which had been fostered to compensate Ireland for the loss of the woollen industry, was hampered when the British parliament, pressed by Scottish linen weavers, excluded Irish coloured linens from the British market; and when Ireland started her own brewing, Britain forbade the importation of hops, which do not grow well in Ireland, from any country except herself and, at the same time, increased the duty on them. The price of Irish beer was pushed up, the native industry declined and the beer drunk in Ireland mostly came from England. A budding glass industry was similarly hampered; in 1746 Britain forbade the export of Irish glass to any country whatsoever.

Nevertheless a growing Catholic middle class was finding new opportunities for itself; all those educated young Catholics prevented by the Penal Laws from making careers in the law or public service were putting their skill and energy into business ventures. They built up the provisions trade, started in the seventeenth century, by exporting corn, oats, meat and fish to the continent and provisioning ships for the Atlantic crossing. Warships of both French and English navies were provisioned in the beautiful harbour of Cork. The Navigation Acts which had restricted trade with America and the West Indies were eased and when, in 1759, the English allowed Irish cattle into Britain, the trade in beef, butter, tallow and hides took a leap forward. Some Catholic merchants became exceedingly rich, far richer in terms of money and goods, though not, of course, in land, than their Protestant overlords in the Irish parliament.

The Protestant middle class that also developed was largely a Presbyterian one, derived from the Presbyterian peasants who had settled in Down and Antrim. Ulster peasants were never as wretched as Irish peasants elsewhere; all foreign travellers remarked upon that. It was worth their while to work hard and improve their holdings because they enjoyed what was known as the Ulster custom, which was the right to sell their tenancies. And many of them had a second string to their bow; the linen yarn spun in the cabins of Connacht was sent to Ulster to be woven. Nearly every farmhouse had a loom in the living room, where the farmer's family made cloth, to be bleached and finished by the linen drapers of Belfast.

The Anglo-Irish gentry and aristocracy, the Protestant oligarchy which ran the country, was becoming more and more unhappy about the powerlessness of the Irish parliament. Swift had voiced the feelings of all Irish Protestants when he declared Ireland to be a sister kingdom to England, England's equal under the Crown and in no way subject to the English parliament. Why, if he was a free man in England, should he become a slave, he had asked, after a six-hour sea crossing? Protestant members of parliament remembered that. Ever since the 1720s, parliament had contained a group called the Patriots which demanded constitutional rights for Ireland and resisted English encroachments.

The Irish parliament of the eighteenth century was controlled by a few rich and powerful undertakers who, in return for money, high office and sinecures, undertook to push government business through both houses. They were of necessity Castle men, that is, supporters of the viceroy, but increasingly often they found themselves taking the Patriot side, and fighting for the rights and independence of parliament. In 1751, largely due to the trading success of the new middle classes, the Irish government found itself in credit. Parliament decided the surplus should be used to reduce the national debt, and sent a bill to that effect to the British Privy Council, only to have it returned with an additional clause saying that the king, George II, had already given his consent to this use of the money. It was a way of claiming that the Irish surplus belonged, not to Ireland, but to Britain, and another time the British could spend it themselves, if they wished. In 1753 there was another surplus, and once again the British Privy Council added a clause to the Irish bill indicating that the money really belonged to Britain. This time the Irish parliament fought the bill. One of the undertakers, Henry Boyle, rallied the Patriots to his side and, after a considerable struggle, defeated the bill. Boyle was toasted all over the country, and in the capital people went wild with delight; aristocratic hostesses gave parties, poets wrote odes and the mob lit bonfires.

Boyle had shown the Irish people, as Swift had done, that they could get their way; public opinion could prevail. When the next general election came along, in 1760, the people, especially the new Protestant middle classes in the towns, determined to make their views known. Hardly any of them had votes and they did not demand them; they simply lobbied the candidates so publicly and so vociferously that they had to take notice, and the Patriot group returned to parliament with a programme, based on popular demand, which included a reduction in the huge number of people on the Irish pension list, an Act of Habeas Corpus to ensure prisoners were brought to trial instead of being detained indefinitely, and security of tenure for judges, to enable them to reach impartial verdicts. The Patriot leader responsible for putting this programme before parliament was a rich young lawyer called Henry Flood; an amateur actor and a student of the Greek and Roman orators, he was a brilliant speaker, the first of a line of orators which was to give the Irish parliament the reputation of being the most eloquent assembly in Europe.

Oratory swayed people, but in the battle for the control of the Irish parliament, it was machination that got things done. In 1767 a new viceroy, Lord Townshend, let it be known that he supported some of the Patriot demands, and sent the necessary bills to England. Before they came back, however, he asked parliament to increase the Irish standing army from 12,000 to 15,000 men. The Irish resented having to raise and pay such numbers when Britain, with far greater resources, was only prepared to raise 28,000, but the British government was afraid of making itself unpopular at home and preferred, as usual, to shift the burden to Ireland. Then the Augmentation of the Army bill was put forward. Once again the undertakers saw it was rejected; they probably thought Townshend would offer them the usual inducements, offices, pensions and so on, to push such an unpopular measure through. But they had mistaken their man. Townshend was a bluff and convivial soldier, much liked in Dublin society, but he was out to break them.

In 1768, after a general election, Townshend put the Augmentation of the Army bill before the House of Commons, and once again the undertakers saw it was rejected. Then they had a government money bill thrown out because the house had not initiated it, and immediately brought in an identical money bill which passed through both houses, as well as the Augmentation of the Army bill. The Irish parliament had made its point: it was not prepared to be a rubber stamp. But Townshend would not tolerate such independence; he prorogued parliament, deprived the chief undertakers of their lucrative posts and gave them, instead, to those who had supported the government. When parliament reassembled in 1771, the government was in control and the power of the undertakers broken.

Townshend's popularity vanished and he left Ireland in 1772. It became the chief secretary's task to manage parliament and the next holder of the office, Sir John Blaquiere, was so successful that all opposition ebbed away. In 1775 even Flood, for fifteen years the leader of the Patriots, accepted a government post. A man of firmer character would have maintained his independence and three months later, to Flood's chagrin, just such a man came into the House of Commons and took over the Patriot leadership. He was by far the greatest of the Irish parliamentarians, Henry Grattan.

Grattan had much in common with Flood. He was a lawyer, a student of ancient as well as modern orators, and a brilliant speaker. Flood, being tall and good-looking, had a better presence than Grattan, who was a slight, unprepossessing figure with a thin, sharp voice and graceless gestures. And Flood could probably lead the House through the twists and turns of a complicated argument better than Grattan. But Grattan had imagination – and he had warmth. He reached out to people in a simple, direct way – and swept his hearers along on the tide of his passionate enthusiasm.

Flood believed, like most Protestants, in the supreme value of the Ascendancy. He was prepared to give Catholics relief from the Penal Laws, freedom to worship as they chose and economic concessions, but he was adamant that they should not have political power. Grattan was more generous, and declared that 'the Irish Protestant could never be free till the Irish Catholic had ceased to be a slave'; he saw that Ireland would never be free of control by the British parliament so long as there was a division into two nations, the Protestant and the Catholic. And Catholics had been quiescent for decades. They seemed to have forgotten their confiscated lands and their dreams of rescue by a foreign power so completely that Protestants were reassured. There were Catholic clergy all over the country, bishops, monks and friars as well as parish priests; handsome Catholic churches had gone up and were openly attended. In 1759, when Britain had been fighting the Seven Years' War against the Catholic powers, France and Austria, Irish Catholics had sent their loyal addresses to the lord lieutenant and when, the following year, a French force captured Carrickfergus, in Ulster, the Catholics never stirred. From 1768 onwards Catholics offered prayers in their churches for the British king. To most of Ireland's Protestants, Catholics had ceased to be 'enemies' and become compatriots.

Over the years, the Penal Laws had been eased. In 1772 a measure known as the Bogland Act was passed, which allowed Catholics to take leases of up to sixty-one years, instead of the thirty-one allowed under the Penal Laws, on unprofitable land, so that they could reclaim and develop it. In 1778 the greater part of the Anti-Popery Act of 1704 was repealed; Catholics were

HENRY GRATTAN Esqr

19. Henry Grattan (courtesy of the National Library of Ireland)

allowed 999-year leases, a Protestant son ceased to be able to dispossess his Catholic father and Catholic landowners no longer had to divide their land equally among their sons. Catholics were also allowed to become schoolmasters, provided they only taught Catholic children. But in 1782 a bill to legalize marriages between Catholics and Protestants was defeated.

The Irish parliament considered the position of Presbyterians too; it was inappropriate to disburden Catholics without doing the same for dissenting Protestants, and a clause abolishing the sacramental test was put into the Catholic Relief Bill of 1778, the measure which cancelled the greater part of the Anti-Popery Act. But the British Privy Council struck the clause out.

Ever since 1718, when the first cheap leases granted after the battle of the Boyne had fallen in, Presbyterians had been emigrating to the West Indies, where hundreds of plantation owners were from Ireland, and to North America. They were pioneers and the sons of pioneers, and when their legal disabilities chafed too sorely, or the demands of their landlords grew too great - whenever the harvest failed, or the linen industry took a plunge – they packed their bags and moved on. Before long, thousands of Presbyterians had friends and relatives in America; tales of American religious freedom and limitless opportunity kept on coming back to them; they knew what America stood for. And that disturbed the British government, for in 1778 sympathy with America was almost treason. Three years earlier, American colonists had clashed with British troops at Lexington, Massachusetts and the American revolution had begun.

Irishmen – Protestant and Catholic, as well as Presbyterian – understood only too well why the Americans had rebelled. Had Irishmen not suffered, like the Americans, from British commercial jealousy and restrictive practices? When American demonstrators, calling themselves the Sons of Liberty, emptied 342 chests of tea into the waters of Boston harbour in protest at a Brtish tea monopoly, a chord was struck in every Irish breast; and the American rallying cry of 'No taxation without representation' was an echo of a statement made by William Molyneux, much earlier in the century, that 'to tax me without consent is little better, if at all, than downright robbing me.'

The Irish could see both sides; when, in parliament, government supporters referred to the Americans as rebels, the Patriot opposition fought hard to have the references withdrawn. At the same time, both Protestants and Catholics displayed a warm, emotional loyalty to Britain in her hour of need. And the British, who certainly did not want another America on their doorstep, responded with concessions: new fishing rights, an easing of the Navigation Acts, fresh relief acts for Catholics and, in 1780, the removal of the sacramental test for Presbyterians.

The most important of these concessions was an act allowing the Irish to raise a Protestant militia. France, Spain and Holland had come into the war on the American side, there was a serious danger of invasion, and yet nearly all the troops in Ireland had been withdrawn for foreign service. The government could do nothing to defend the country. Pirates and privateers swarmed round the lengthy Irish coast, sometimes capturing Irish ships within sight of the ports, and in April 1778 a well-known American privateer, Paul Jones, sailed into Belfast Lough, seized a Royal Naval vessel and made off with it! The people of Belfast appealed to the lord lieutenant for help, only to be told that there was none available, except half a troop of cavalry without horses and half a troop of invalids! They must protect themselves.

Belfast had formed its own troop of volunteers in 1777, and there were others in Wexford and King's County. Now these small groups expanded, more or less spontaneously, into a militia that covered the whole of Ireland. Ulster Presbyterians, who were afraid not so much of stray American pirates as the papist French, recruited vigorously; Presbyterian ministers often accepted military rank and dressed up in colourful uniforms. Elsewhere the larger landowners had already formed their tenants into armed companies to combat the Whiteboys, and it was easy to transform these bands into a militia. There was tremendous enthusiasm everywhere; everybody who was anybody was given a military rank; every old soldier found himself drilling squads of recruits; and subscriptions were raised to buy muskets, brightly coloured uniforms and even a few cannon. By the summer of 1779 Ireland had over 40,000 men under arms, and a year later nearly 80,000. A lively new hopefulness spread through the country, even affecting Catholics, who, although still ignominiously prevented from defending their country, supported the militia, or Irish Volunteers as they were called, with generous subscriptions.

Irishmen had never been so united. The Volunteers could protect them, not only from Britain's enemies, but from Britain herself. Ireland felt a new surge toward independence, a new resolve to be free. At last Irishmen took Swift's advice, given half a century earlier, and bought only Irish. All the bright scarlet, orange, green and blue uniforms were made in Ireland of Irish cloth, and society women led a fashion for Irish materials. When parliament met in October 1779, Grattan immediately moved a resolution 'that it would be inexpedient to grant new taxes' and, with unprecedented boldness, the House of Commons voted money for six months only. 'England has sown her laws in dragons' teeth,' one Patriot member observed, 'and they have sprung up armed men.'

Grattan moved on to make a daring demand for free trade. He had overwhelming support in the country, government place-men in parliament moved to his side and, for the first time in Irish politics, the opposition in the British parliament, led by the Liberal orator Charles James Fox and the Irishman Edmund Burke, supported him. Britain was too weak to resist. Restrictions on the woollen industry were lifted, Ireland was allowed to export glass and import hops, to trade freely with any country in the world except the British colonies, and in their case to charge the same duties as the British did. It was a tremendous victory; the people of Ireland were overjoyed; but Grattan and the Patriots did not rest there. The British could renew trading restrictions whenever they wished, unless Ireland won full parliamentary independence.

In February 1782 Grattan arranged a convention of some 250 delegates from the Volunteers, who met in the parish church at Dungannon. Flood, who had at last given up his government post, Lord Charlemont, the Ulster peer who commanded the Volunteers, and numbers of other leading Protestants adopted, almost unanimously, resolutions asserting the necessity of legislative independence, declaring Poynings' law to be unconstitutional and a grievance and demanding parliamentary control of the regular army. A final resolution, prepared by Grattan without the approval of either Flood or Charlemont, expressed the view, extremely modern for the 1780s, 'that we hold the right of private judgement, in matters of religion, to be equally sacred in others as in ourselves.' The convention concluded with the revolutionary words which, again, have the ring of Grattan about them: 'We know our duty to our sovereign, and are loyal. We know our duty to ourselves, and are resolved to be free.'

A week later, Grattan moved a Declaration of Independence in the House of Commons. The government managed to stall it for a while – and then everything happened very quickly. The Tory government fell in Britain and the Liberals took over. On 16 April Grattan, who was in poor health, rose from his sick bed and came to a tense and excited house, the public galleries packed with the leading figures of Dublin society, and moved the Declaration of Independence once more. Accompanied by his peculiar lurching gestures, he made the most triumphant speech ever to be heard in the Irish parliament. 'I am now to address a free people,' he declared. 'Ireland is now a nation; in that new character I hail her and, bowing to her august presence, I say, *Esto perpetua.*' In May the British parliament led by Fox repealed the Declaratory Act of 1719 and amended Poynings' law. The Irish parliament had regained its ancient position as the sole legislator for Ireland and the Irish House of Lords was, once again, Ireland's supreme court. The passage of bills via the Irish privy council to the English privy council was scrapped. From henceforth, all Irish bills were to be sent direct, for approval or veto, to the king.

The triumph of the Patriots was complete. A grateful parliament voted £100,000 to Grattan and he accepted £50,000; MPs had no salaries in those days, he was not a rich man, and the money meant he could devote himself full-time to politics, instead of having to earn his living at the bar. Next, parliament voted to provide 20,000 sailors, or £100,000, for the British navy. Britain was weak and tired; most of the American colonies had gone but the war still continued, and Ireland wanted to show her friendship and to share, in Grattan's words, not only in the freedom of her sister kingdom, but her fate.

CHAPTER 9

UNION

Between 1782 and 1800, the period of what became known as Grattan's parliament, Ireland enjoyed an unprecedented prosperity. Although the native Irish people had suffered appalling injustices and deprivations, the country had been stable, without war or rebellion, for the longest period in history since the Viking invasion; as a result the population had risen from less than two million in 1700 to four million and was to go on rising. A land which had been hampered by its emptiness now had people to exploit its resources. Trading restrictions were lifted, Catholic businessmen were at last able to invest at home, instead of sending their money to France and Spain, and the Irish economy was ready to boom.

In 1706 Ireland's total exports had been worth £50,000. By 1783 they had risen to almost £3 million, and by 1796 they were over £5 million. Linen exports had increased from a mere half million yards in 1706 to sixteen million yards in 1783 and then almost tripled to forty-seven million yards by 1796. The woollen industry never did well in export markets but benefited from an expanding home market, and a cotton industry, begun in the 1770s, was so well supported by parliament with bounties and a protective tariff that by the 1790s its exports rivalled those of linen. Irish glass revived so rapidly in the 1780s that it supplied almost the whole of the home market, and an increase in Irish brewing led to a decline in the import of beer from England.

There was greater prosperity on the farms, too. The harvests were bad from 1782–4, but parliament regulated the situation with a system of state bounties, similar to modern agricultural subsidies, which encouraged export to foreign markets except in times of shortage at home. For the first time, Ireland became a great corn-growing country. Rents went up but so did profits, and there was far more work for labourers. It was a common sight to see bands of men from the west, tramping along the country roads to work on the harvest in the midlands and the east. The provisions trade flourished and cattle exports went up. The Anglo-Irish improved their houses and built new ones, industrialists dug a network of canals and Dublin, already embellished with wide streets and fine squares, acquired the stately Custom House, the Royal Irish Academy and the strikingly domed Four Courts. It became one of the most elegant capital cities in Europe.

But Grattan's parliament, independent of Britain though it was, did not truly represent the people of Ireland. It consisted of a handful of rich Protestants, floating a raft for the 'Protestant nation' amidst a sea of disenfranchised Catholics and Presbyterians. It was an irresponsible parliament, without control over the executive which carried out its decisions. Sometimes it was little more than a brilliantly oratorical debating chamber; at other times it was merely an opposition to His Majesty's Government. For the king, on the advice of his British ministers, could veto any Irish legislation, and the executive in Ireland was still headed by the lord lieutenant, always an Englishman and responsible to the British home secretary. The lord lieutenant still appointed and dismissed Irish government ministers, and his chief secretary went on managing parliament in the old, corrupt way, bribing powerful men with titles, pensions and places. Large numbers of peerages were created and the expenditure on pensions rose annually. Ireland was still being run in the interests of England.

The Patriots called for reform. In 1783 Flood even went so far as to appear in the Commons in Volunteer uniform, hot-foot from a Volunteer convention, with a plan for reform in his pocket. But the heyday of the Volunteers was over; they had been formed to threaten a British government, not a free Irish parliament, and Flood's bill was thrown out. But neither he, Charlemont nor other leading Patriots were prepared to strengthen the hand of parliament against the government by giving political power to Catholics. They could not forget that earlier Patriot parliament of

James II's reign, when Catholics had made ready to reclaim their ancient estates. Catholics were dangerous. Only Grattan was wiser; he knew his parliament must broaden its power base. 'I should be ashamed of giving freedom to but 600,000 of my fellow countrymen,' he said, 'when I could extend it to two million more.' Sadly, the Patriots were not persuaded.

Then in 1789 the French Revolution toppled the monarchy and the feudal aristocracy of France. For almost the first time in history, it was power to the people, and the people proclaimed, as a major principle of their revolution, that every kind of religious discrimination should be abolished. The French tithe system was swept away and church property confiscated. Ireland's Catholics were shocked by this treatment of the Catholic Church in France, but the Presbyterians, who had always had leanings towards republicanism, took up the French ideas avidly. In 1790, when one of the few remaining corps of Volunteers met in Belfast, resolutions were passed advocating the abolition of tithes, at least those paid by Catholics and Presbyterians to conformist Protestant clergy, and urging Presbyterians to support the enfranchisement of Catholics and parliamentary reform. Then in 1791 the theme was taken a stage further; a pamphlet appeared, entitled *An Argument on Behalf of the Catholics of Ireland*, which attacked the parliamentary constitution of 1782 and advocated a union of Catholics and Presbyterians to force political reform.

The author was Theobald Wolfe Tone, a young Protestant lawyer descended from one of Cromwell's soldiers, whose father, a Dublin coach-builder, had given him a good education at Trinity College and then at the Inns of Court in London. But Wolfe Tone had found the law tedious in comparison with politics. In his first pamphlet of note, written when Britain was about to declare war on Spain, he declared an independent Ireland need not join in the war and was delighted when, hanging around the Dublin bookshops on the day of publication, he heard bishops express their fury! He was prepared to go much further than Grattan in the cause of Irish freedom; he acknowledged no loyalty to the king, who never visited Ireland anyway, and believed (though prudence sometimes prevented him from saying so) that Ireland should separate herself entirely from Britain.

Tone knew he could count on Catholic support for the *Argu-*

ment because he was well known to members of the Catholic Committee, a hitherto genteel and inoffensive body which had recently shed some of its staider elements. He was less sure of his support among Presbysterians, and gratified when he received an immediate invitation to Belfast.

The major towns of Ulster contained many political clubs, formed when the local Irish Volunteer detachments had broken up; middle-class Protestants, including Presbyterians, had found the Volunteers gave them a chance of political expression, and the political clubs performed a similar function, bringing patriots together so they could exchange ideas and form pressure groups to lobby members of parliament. In Belfast these clubs were already being taken over by a secret committee, headed by a Presbyterian woollen draper with very radical leanings named Samuel Neilson. Neilson and his secret committee entertained Tone to dinner, and round the table they hammered out the basis of a new reforming organization which would adopt, as its first principle, the union of Catholics, Protestants and Presbyterians. It was to be known as the Society of United Irishmen.

To most people, Wolfe Tone's idea of a patriotic union between members of different branches of the Christian faith seems entirely reasonable; their common love of Christ ought to be stronger than differences of form and doctrine. Tone soon found, however, that the reality was otherwise. Some 90 per cent of Belfast's Presbyterians were decidedly anti-Catholic. They still retained the old Protestant fear that one day Catholics would take back all that had been wrested from them.

In the countryside, this fear had some substance. Over much of Ireland there was a hunger for land. With the rise in population, farms had become even smaller as they were divided and sub-divided among the members of a family. In Ulster, however, so many Presbyterian farmers had emigrated to America that there was land and to spare. Catholics from the south and west flooded in to take it and, in their desperation, outbid the local Presbyterians in the matter of rent, just as they had done over a century earlier. Presbyterian peasant farmers joined societies such as the Hearts of Oak and forced landlords to agree to fixed rents; through solidarity and a show of force, they put landlords where they wanted them. They were not going to allow Catholic newcomers to queer their pitch.

About 1785 a new Presbyterian peasant organization, the Peep o'Day Boys, had begun attacking Catholics who outbid Presbyterians in rent. At dawn, the peep o'day, they would appear at Catholic homesteads and either burn the house down or terrorize the occupants by threats, physical abuse or firing through their windows. When they had no specific target, the Peep o'Day Boys would congregate in country towns and villages, hold military-style parades with colours flying, bands playing and shots being fired, and then smash the windows of Catholic houses and churches, beat up any Catholics unfortunate enough to be around and create a general atmosphere of aggression and terror, designed to drive Catholics away from the area. Naturally the Catholics formed a rival society, appropriately called the Defenders, and held similar military-style parades. It was the beginning of a bitter sectarian warfare that, in Ulster, has never ceased.

From the start, the Peep o'Day Boys controlled Armagh. Then in 1791 and 1792 there was a great deal of fighting in the surrounding counties of Tyrone, Down, Louth, Meath, Cavan and Monaghan. Large bodies of men, mostly armed with pikes and staves, scythes and pitchforks, but sometimes also with firearms, fought pitched battles in broad daylight. The Protestant landlords, who were, for the most part, the magistrates, tried to maintain order with the local militia and, occasionally, regular troops, but large areas were in the control of one society or the other for months at a time. The Defenders spread into parts of the country which were entirely Catholic, where there was no threat from members of any other religion, and took over the role of the Whiteboys as a secret, militant organization dedicated to the redress of grievances, such as the payment of tithes and excessive rents.

In the north, they were still mainly a sectarian movement, concerned with protecting Catholics. The Peep o'Day Boys had become seriously alarmed when, in 1793, Catholics were given the franchise on the same terms as Protestants, and sectarian feuding had increased in ferocity. Then in September 1795 a large party of Defenders, acting on the principle that the best method of defence is sometimes attack, went for a smaller group of Peep o'Day Boys on a patch of ground near the city of Armagh known as the Diamond. In spite of their inferior numbers, the Peep o'Day Boys beat their attackers off, and the bodies of twenty to thirty Defenders were left dead on the field. That same evening, jubilant in their victory, the Peep o'Day Boys re-formed themselves into the Orange Society, the colour orange being a symbol of the victory of William of Orange over James II more than a century earlier.

The Orangemen attacked Ulster Catholics with merciless brutality. They assaulted them, turned them out of their homes, or 'papered' them, pinning notices to their doors telling them to go 'To hell – or Connacht', that is, go to Connacht or die. Poor Catholic weavers had their looms broken, and labourers' houses were burned down; sometimes as many as a dozen houses would be burned in one place in a night. At the end of 1795 the governor of Armagh wrote: 'No night passes that houses are not destroyed, and scarce a week that some dreadful murders are not committed. Nothing can exceed the animosity between Protestant and Catholic at this moment in this country.'

Against such a background, it is not surprising that the United Irishmen could not, at first, make much headway. Then the ideas of the French Revolution gradually pulled the different religions together. The Protestant Ascendancy was, on the whole, in favour of the *ancien regime*; its members were, to use the terms of the Revolution, 'aristocrats'. But the young men of the new middle classes, whether Protestant, Presbyterian or Catholic, were looking for a political alignment that was fresh, idealistic, nationalist, untainted with the corruption endemic in high places and far more radical than any group in Grattan's parliament. Their sympathy went to the 'democrats', the revolutionaries, who had declared the Republic. If Ireland became a Republic, the last link with Britain would be gone.

For some time William Pitt, the British prime minister, had been worried about the belligerence of revolutionary France, which had declared war on Austria and then Prussia in 1792. Pitt certainly did not want Catholic Ireland, which, until recently, had had so many military, commercial and religious ties with France, to catch the fever of revolution, and perhaps provide a back door for the invasion of Britain. The Castle, that powerful group which surrounded the lord lieutenant, was frightened into a reactionary and repressive stance, and a Catholic Relief Bill put before parliament in 1792 was largely (though not entirely) withdrawn. Pitt was bolder; he had relieved British Catholics of their penal restrictions in 1791 and he was convinced that Irish Catholics should be conciliated; the Catholic Church looked with horror on the new French Republic and most members of the Irish brigades, which had served the French monarchy, were transferring their loyalty to George III. If Catholics were given relief, they would be less likely to ally themselves with Wolfe Tone and other Protestant radicals.

In 1793, when war broke out between Britain and France, another Catholic Relief Act was passed, with the support of two-thirds of a parliament dominated by Patriots. It enabled Catholics to bear arms, vote, sit on juries, take degrees at Trinity College, Dublin, and hold commissions in the army below the rank of general. But Catholics still could not hold government office or sit in parliament. 'If the Catholics deserved what has been granted,' Wolfe Tone commented wryly, 'they deserve what has been withheld; if they did not deserve what has been withheld, what has been granted should have been refused.' But the House of Commons, less logical than Tone, rejected a motion admitting Catholics to parliament by 163 votes to 69.

Grattan, consistent and highminded, was deeply regretful that Catholics were not to take their seats in parliament. The Catholics themselves joyfully dissolved their own lobbying body, the Catholic Committee, as if all their dreams had come true, and gratefully presented Wolfe Tone, who had been their secretary, with £1,500 and a gold medal, but Grattan immediately began preparing a new Catholic Relief bill of his own to enable the Catholic upper classes to stand for parliament. It is a measure of the extent to which his prestige had fallen since 1782, and how far Tone and the radicals had advanced, that when the bill was introduced in 1795, it was heavily defeated. Pitt and the British government would not support it because of their fear of Tone and the United Irishmen, and Grattan's so-called 'independent' parliament still could not pass any measure Britain did not want.

The government compensated Catholics for their disappointment by the foundation of a college at Maynooth, where the earls of Kildare had had their seat, for the training of Catholic priests. For more than two centuries, priests had been trained in seminaries in France, but since the Revolution the Catholic bishops had been far less inclined to send novitiates to that godless country, and the last thing Pitt wanted was a Catholic priesthood indoctrinated with revolutionary ideas.

The French were very interested, not to say intrigued, by the United Irishmen, and in 1793 they sent a secret agent into Ireland, an Anglican clergyman of Irish descent called William Jackson. Jackson, however, was ill-chosen, having no undercover skills whatever, and before long his mission had turned into farce. He found himself accompanied everywhere by an old friend from London, a solicitor called Cockayne. But Cockayne was not visiting Dublin's clubs and taverns with Jackson merely for old time's sake; he had been planted by the British as a counter-agent. Cockayne, though, turned out to be no more competent than Jackson. When Jackson was arrested and brought to trial a year later, in 1794, Cockayne's evidence was pathetically inadequate; he had 'partly' overheard treasonable conversations and 'partly' understood them. Yet he remembered enough to compromise Wolfe Tone and others very seriously before the trial came to a macabre conclusion, Jackson dying in the dock from a self-administered poison.

It came out during the trial that Tone had told Jackson, knowing he was a French emissary, that an invasion from France would be welcomed in Ireland. Such a statement, made in wartime, was clearly treasonable. Nevertheless Tone managed to make a bargain with the government whereby he could avoid prosecution by exiling himself to America, and when Jackson's trial ended he went to Belfast to take ship for Philadelphia. When he was in Belfast he was in touch with Neilson. The United Irishmen had been proscribed when Jackson was arrested, but Neilson told him that a new, secret organization of United Irishmen was being set up throughout the country, with district and county committees, an elaborate elected hierarchy and a secret leadership. Neilson asked Tone to tell the French minister in Philadelphia that the new underground organization intended to combine with the Defenders in the cause of revolution.

During the last two years, the crude, loosely organized but massive Defender movement had spread through the whole of Ireland, animated, not so much by sectarian feeling, as the poverty that went with being Catholic. If the rich would alleviate the sufferings of the poor, the government was told more than once, they would hear no more of risings or Defenders. But the rich were greedy and the government shortsighted, and everywhere the Defenders rounded up the peasantry, administered unlawful oaths and intimidated those who resisted, burning the turf they needed as fuel and rooting up the potatoes they fed on. In some districts the Defenders fixed the rent a cottier should pay and the labourer should get, and threatened with death any peasant who accepted worse terms.

There were no police in the countryside, no effective authority, and bands of several hundreds, even thousands, of Defenders raided the houses of the gentry for arms, horses and saddlery. When some landlords fought them, using local militia, as many as a hundred Defenders might be left dead on the field and even larger numbers captured. Yet there were always thousands more. And among them, French revolutionary sentiments were taking root. Defenders were swearing to 'dethrone all kings and plant the tree of liberty on our Irish land', 'to be loyal to brother Defenders and the French' and 'to pull down the British laws'. They were ripe for the picking by the better educated, more experienced and mostly middle-class United Irishmen.

When Wolfe Tone arrived in Philadelphia, he put a plan for France's intervention in Ireland to the French minister there. He was depressed by what he felt was a lukewarm reception, and even made plans to forget all about Ireland and her troubles[1], until he received a letter describing the progress being made by the reorganized United Irishmen. On 1 January, 1796, he sailed for France.

The French minister in Philadelphia had given him a letter of introduction and armed with that, besides a great deal of charm, ability and perseverance, he contrived to reach members of the Directoire, which ruled the country, and persuade them that an invasion of Ireland could be successful. French troops would be met by Irish revolutionaries, he told them with irresistible optimism, the British driven out and a republic set up. Britain was the only country in Europe which had not fallen to French arms, and if France could take over a friendly Ireland, the French persuaded themselves, the conquest of Britain would surely follow. In the summer the brilliant young General Hoche, whose reputation rivalled that of Bonaparte, was put at the head of an expedition to Ireland. Hoche and Tone, who had French military rank himself by now, went to Brest to assemble an invasion force. On 16 December, 'in delicious weather, with the sun as warm and bright as May', to use Tone's words, all was ready. Nearly 14,000 French troops, 'as gay as if they were going to a ball', to quote Tone once more, embarked in thirteen ships and, during the night, set sail.

But the French had sacked their experienced naval officers during the Revolution, and the seamanship of their replacements was not up to sailing men o'war in winter gales. One ship foundered on a rock outside Brest. The next day a violent storm blew up, another ship was lost and the flagship, carrying Hoche, was separated from the rest of the fleet; it was three weeks before it turned up again in a French port. The storm was followed by fog and more ships were dispersed, but on 21 December all but eight or nine ships had reassembled and were sailing, slowly and majestically, into the broad waters, sheltered by towering mountains on either side, of Bantry bay. Sailing *too* slowly. The wind was against them; they made almost no headway; and in the evening they cast anchor only just inside the bay.

During the night, a strong wind got up and twenty ships were blown into the Atlantic. The previous evening, a messenger had galloped for all he was worth over snow-covered roads from Bantry to Cork, carrying the dread news to the government. But the gale prevented the French ships from landing their troops on a headland or sailing further into the bay. On Christmas Day the weather was even worse, the French were still nowhere near a landing and their admiral ordered them to make for the safety of the open sea. Some ships weighed anchor immediately and followed him back to Brest; others delayed because of fog. A few were still in the bay on 31 December. When one of them sent out boats, the local contingent of the Galway militia, some 400 men, bravely lined up on the beach. But the Frenchmen soon returned to their ship and three days later the whole of the French fleet had left for home.

Tone, who was with the ships in Bantry bay, commented in his diary that England had had her greatest escape since the defeat of the Spanish Armada.

The government was badly frightened by the news from Bantry. Had the French invaded, they would have met no more than 8,000 troops, many of them militia, on their way to Cork. The Catholics, the government supposed, would rise . . . . It would have been impossible to hold a rebellious Ireland against a sizeable force from the nation which, at that time, had won military glory all over Europe.

But the Catholics did not rise. For ten days the French fleet lay in Irish waters, and the Munster peasantry remained loyal. 'Their goodwill, zeal and activity exceeds all description,' the commanding British general wrote to George III. Catholics were traditionally monarchist, their church leaders upheld authority, and many Catholic peasants, ignorant and illiterate as they were, suspected the French of having been invited over by Orangemen to drive them off their holdings.

The government knew the respite was only temporary; the French would try to invade again. Much earlier in the year, the Castle had pushed a merciless Insurrection Act through parliament, which allowed magistrates to hang anyone who administered an unlawful oath, such as the oaths of the Defenders, Orangemen and United Irishmen, and to transport for life anyone who swore such an oath. Then Habeas Corpus had been suspended.

The French failure was felt most keenly in Ulster, where the United Irishmen were attracting those young, educated, middle-class Irishmen of all three religions who were without patrons, representation in Grattan's parliament and, all too often, the vote. Britain, and the British connection, had given them nothing. They could not be grateful – and neither could they be be loyal. 'Disloyalty was often a fashion, a sentiment, and almost an amusement,' wrote W. E. H. Lecky, the great historian of eighteenth-century Ireland. It had always been a British idea that Irishmen should be loyal to Britain. The patriotic attachment of the United Irishmen was to Ireland, and Ireland alone. And the name of the game they were to play for Ireland was sedition.

In the beginning of 1797 Ulster was in a condition of anarchy. The United Irish leadership found that, in the Defenders, it had taken on a monolith it could not control. Defenders took readily to the 'wearing of the green', a green ribbon, or piece of clothing, which betokened membership of the United Irishmen, and under its cover indulged in all manner of cruelties, private vendettas, lawlessness and crime. Bands of Defenders, several hundred strong, swept the cells of United Irishmen along with them when they terrorized Co. Monaghan, and Co. Tyrone was more or less taken over by them. In the daytime, parades were held quite openly, and at night bonfires flared on the hilltops, lighting the way for marauding parties of Defenders in search of arms or, simply, plunder. Law was set aside, and the countryside controlled and terrorized by various Defender bands.

In March the government ordered General Lake, who commanded such government troops as there were in Ulster, to pacify and disarm the province. He adopted a policy of pardon for all those who surrendered their arms by a given date, and extreme toughness towards those who did not. The first military raid seems to have come as a surprise to the people, and in a fortnight more than 5,400 guns, 600 bayonets and 350 pistols were seized in peasants' cabins. During the following weeks many sworn United Irishmen surrendered some of their arms, took an insincere oath of allegiance, and hid the rest of their arms carefully away. The regular troops were supplemented by Catholic militia and a Protestant yeomanry commanded by the local gentry. They were, all of them, totally lacking in military discipline or restraint, and when small parties were detailed to make a night search of a large number of cabins, scattered over a wide area, shocking atrocities occurred. Cabins were burned down almost as a matter of routine, and their occupants cut about and sometimes killed, even when no weapons were found.

Suspects were flogged and tortured by half-hanging[2] and then sent off in droves to serve in the British army.

Grattan decided to take a stand. For three years, he had been trying without success to persuade the government to redress the grievances of the peasants. As a final effort he reintroduced his bill to enable the Catholic gentry to stand for parliament. But once again the reactionary and repressive government saw that the bill was thrown out and Grattan, after this second failure, withdrew from the House of Commons.

Wolfe Tone was soon back in France from Bantry bay in company with General Hoche. In April the British navy was paralysed by mutinies at its bases in the Channel, caused largely by disaffected Irishmen pressed into its service. On the much-quoted principle that England's difficulty is Ireland's opportunity, Tone and Hoche agreed that a small expedition to Ireland should be got together immediately. The Dutch had an army and a fleet at their port of the Texel, waiting for employment, and it was decided they should make the invasion as soon as possible, and Tone should sail with them. Hoche would follow with a French fleet from Brest.

It was July before the Dutch fleet was ready. The British difficulties were long since over – indeed, British ships were beginning to gather outside the Texel and hem the Dutch in. Tone fretted on the Dutch admiral's flagship while the winds chopped and changed and the British fleet beyond the harbour built up. Then in September General Hoche, the only Frenchman entirely committed to the Irish cause, died suddenly; and in October, when the Dutch fleet at last left port, it was annihilated by the British in the battle of Camperdown.

Tone had left the Dutch fleet several weeks earlier, and in December he had an audience with Napoleon. But while Napoleon was impressed with Tone, he needed a rich enemy to defeat and plunder, rather than sympathizers to liberate, so that he could finance his vastly expensive armies. He doubted, anyway, whether the French fleet could carry troops safely to Ireland, or even across the English Channel; French forces were victorious on land, but the British were supreme at sea. Nevertheless, early in 1798 Napoleon made a whirlwind tour of the Channel ports and ordered flat-bottomed invasion barges. But British sea power continued formidable and in May he embarked his troops for Egypt.

Ireland had reached a state of vast, cataclysmic disorder. There was no clear-cut war between Irishmen and Englishmen, or Scots – of the regular troops in the country, less than a quarter were British – but a massive disturbance, involving those termed loyal Irish, that is, Irish men and women who supported the government, and the so-called disloyal Irish, most of whom had taken the oaths of the United Irishmen. In Ulster, loyal Irishmen were mostly Protestant, or Presbyterian Orangemen, or Anglo-Irish gentry, or their tenants; disloyal Irishmen numbered Protestants and Presbyterians among their leaders, but were otherwise mostly terrified Catholics. In the rest of Ireland, both sides were largely Catholic.

The United Irishmen were organized as a hierarchy with a National Directory, named after the French Directoire, drawn from four provincial committees. In March 1798 the government, tipped off by an informer, arrested the whole of the Leinster provincial committee, which included sixteen members of the National Directory, most of whom were at a meeting at the house of one of their members, a Dublin woollen merchant named Oliver Bond. It was a very severe blow; the Society of United Irishmen was, in effect, decapitated.

Its chief military organization was, unlike the rest of its leaders, a nobleman, Lord Edward Fitzgerald, the brother of the duke of Leinster. He was forewarned and escaped when Bond's house was raided, only to be betrayed by a second informer a few weeks later, when he was staying at the house of a Dublin feather merchant. He was lying on his bed when the police entered, but rose and fought furiously, mortally wounding a police officer with his dagger. He was shot himself in the shoulder and died in prison six weeks later. He was not particularly clever, but young, handsome, aristocratic and brave; he had the qualities Irishmen looked for in a leader. When he died a hero's death,

202

the United Irishmen were suffused, for a brief moment, with a romantic glow.

At the end of March the government proclaimed martial law in most of Leinster and – shades of coign and livery – billeted soldiers on the people without payment, while they searched for arms. They despoiled the peasantry of their food and goods, and abandoned all restraint in their attempts to rout out the local leadership, the colonels, captains and sergeants of the United Irishmen, adding to the native cruelties of half-hanging, pitch-capping[3] and house burning the common military torture, learned from British and Continental armies, of excessive flog-ging. Men were stripped to the waist, tied to a wooden triangle and flogged with the cat-o'nine-tails until they named a United Irishman. He would be fetched and the same procedure gone through again. No-one was safe. Whole villages were terrorized, the innocent being tied to the triangles alongside the guilty. The country people would kneel in the streets weeping, their hats off, while the floggings went on.

The United Irishmen had to rise. They had waited for the French so long that their leaders had been arrested; if they waited any longer their organization would break up. They fixed on 23 May as the day they would attack Dublin and paralyse the government, but for their members in the capital it was already too late; they had no leaders left. The risings came, instead, in Kildare, Wicklow, Co. Carlow, Offaly and Laois and Meath. United Irishmen turned on government troops, the militia, and especially Protestant loyalists; prominent Catholic loyalists were generally left alone. Towns and villages were swept alternately by government troops and rebels, the government forces, being slightly more soldierly, generally contriving to massacre rebels and mildly dissident peasants in their hundreds. The peasants were for the most part so terrified of the troops that they readily surrendered what arms they had.

The most formidable outbreak was to come in the south. Wexford had always been a quiet county; Protestant houses were not raided for arms, as they were elsewhere, and the number of regular troops and militia garrisoned there was small. But the government received information that Wexford was a probable

20. Captain Swayne pitchcapping the people of Prosperous
(courtesy of the National Library of Ireland)

landing point for a French invasion and sent the North Cork militia (who were supposed to have invented pitch-capping) into the country to search for arms. The people were given fourteen days to surrender any arms they had, but the soldiers could not wait to start their floggings and torture. The Catholic peasantry, in danger whatever they did, decided to make a fight of it, and about 14,000 of them, some carrying the green flag of the United Irishmen and others the white flag of the Defenders, roamed through town and countryside, with no clear objective but to face government forces bravely whenever they came upon them. A Catholic curate, Father John Murphy, became their leader. Dreadful atrocities were committed. An unknown number[4] of Protestants were slaughtered in a windmill on Vinegar Hill, a rebel stronghold outside Enniscorthy, and another 200 people, mostly Protestant, burned to death in a barn at a place called Scullabogue. Wild rumours had been spreading through the countryside that Protestant Orangemen meant to murder all Catholics, and the severity of the government forces, firmly on the Orange side, had persuaded the populace that the rumours were all too true. When the rebels broke into the city of Wexford itself, about 100 Protestants were shot, or killed by pike thrusts on Wexford bridge and thrown into the river Slaney below.

No-one had been prepared for such events in Wexford. The major outbreak had been expected in the north, where the United Irishmen had their origins. But they had been so damaged by General Lake's campaign in 1797 and the loss of their leaders in March 1798, both Catholics and Protestants were so horrified by tales of massacre in the south, and Presbyterians so disenchanted with the French revolutionaries because of their hostile attitude towards Americans,[5] that when Ulstermen fought at all, they did it along the old sectarian lines. Such attempt as there was at co-ordinated rebellion soon fizzled out.

There remained the mopping up. The government forces, ill-trained and poorly led, behaved with careless cruelty. When they retook Enniscorthy, which had fallen for a while to the Wexford rebels, they cheerfully set fire to a makeshift rebel hospital with the patients still inside. In the town of Antrim, which the northern United Irishmen attacked, the dead and wounded were left in the streets for two days before the garrison cleared them away in carts and buried them, dead and alive together. Elsewhere the militia shot and hanged people indiscriminately, without trial or questions asked, neither knowing nor caring who was a rebel and who was not. Houses were set on fire almost as a matter of course; one soldier alone fired fourteen in a morning. In some areas every house was burned, though the rains of winter would soon be coming on. People were desperate for a way out of their dreadful situation. General Lake offered what he called 'the deluded masses' a chance to surrender, provided they brought in their arms and betrayed their leaders. Otherwise, he said, he would destroy 'every town, cottage and farmhouse' found empty and slaughter without trial every person having arms.

Pitt, in England, sent out the marquis Cornwallis to be both lord lieutenant and commander-in-chief; Cornwallis was the only British general to have emerged from the American War of Independence with his reputation not merely unscathed but enhanced. He overrode Lake: troops were certainly not to be let loose on the countryside and there was to be no punishment without trial. On the one hand, fugitive rebels were streaming into camps in Kildare and the Wicklow mountains; they had to fight on or be hanged. And on the other the Castle, the Irish establishment, was talking glibly of exterminating all Catholics. Cornwallis took the sensible and liberal course of granting a general amnesty and forced the necessary bill through parliament, so that on 17 July 1798 the country had the respite it needed. About 50,000 people had been killed in little more than a year, most of them in cold blood. But the rebellion was over.

Then – the French came! Wolfe Tone had not seen the calamaties that had overtaken the United Irishmen, nor the distress of the mass of the people. He had refused to believe that the Irish were not united at all, and the great revolt against Britain had degenerated into bloody sectarian warfare, but persistently assured the French, with his usual attractive optimism, that the Irish would rise as one man when the French 'liberators' reached their shores. So the French prepared three invasion fleets, each to carry troops, arms and ammunition to the beleaguered Irish. Some light ships were to sail from the Channel ports, heavier vessels from Rochefort, on the Atlantic coast, and the largest fleet, with 3,000 troops, from Brest.

On 22 August three warships flying the British flag sailed into

Killala bay in Co. Mayo. A British army officer who was fishing in the bay sailed across to offer them some of his catch. When he arrived on board, he was taken prisoner, for the ships, though flying the British flag, were from Rochefort and had a thousand French troops on board. When the Protestant bishop of Killala was entertaining guests that evening, he was interrupted by a terrified messenger who told him there were French soldiers outside the town. The local yeomanry made a brief stand against them in the streets, but in no time the French leader, General Humbert, was in the bishop's house.

The next day Humbert hoisted a green flag, bearing the words 'Erin go brach', or 'Ireland for ever', and called upon Irishmen to rise and be free. But Connacht had taken no part in the rebellion and the people there, though hardly loyal to Britain, did not aspire to independence. The peasants greeted the French rapturously enough, and were only too pleased to be given hand-some blue uniforms, muskets and shot, but had no wish to be turned into soldiers. Many disappeared with their uniforms and muskets, sold them for whiskey, and then came back for more.

Humbert moved south and within a week had routed Lake's much larger force in an engagement remembered as the Races of Castlebar, that is, races to get away from the French at the first cannon shot. Then Humbert set up a nominal Irish republic with a young local Catholic Irish gentleman as president, and headed for Co. Leitrim, where he had news of a rising. Cornwallis was approaching with 20,000 men and the French desperately needed Irish help. But when the Irish saw how few the Frenchmen were, they went home; they would not risk the vengeance of the loyalist army after a French defeat, and a few days later Humbert had to surrender. He and his men were taken to Dublin, gaily singing the *Marseillaise*, and then, after a banquet in honour of their officers, shipped home to France.

The second French expedition consisted of one fast ship with a cargo of arms and 280 men aboard, under the command of one of the original United Irishmen in Dublin, James Napper Tandy. The ship had left Dunkirk on 4 September, four days before Humbert's surrender, and anchored in the harbour of Rutland, on the north-west tip of Co. Donegal, on 16 September. The French took over the post office and distributed leaflets calling upon Irishmen to rise – until the postmaster, who turned out to be an old friend of Napper Tandy's, told them of the failure of the rebellion and Humbert's surrender. Tandy was appalled; in Paris he had been saying that 30,000 Irishmen would rebel at his nod. He had supper with his old friend, drank himself into a stupor and had to be carried back to his ship, which sailed for France the next morning.

The third and last of the French expeditions was the largest, with ten ships and 2,800 men on board. Wolfe Tone was in the flagship, appropriately called *Hoche*. The fleet sailed from Brest into the Atlantic and round to the northern coast of Donegal where, early in the morning of 12 October, after twenty-three days' sailing, it was sighted by a British naval squadron far more heavily equipped than the French ships with guns. The French urged Tone to escape in a fast schooner they had with them, but naturally he refused and commanded a battery in the ensuing battle, the first he had ever been in. *Hoche* had lost her topmast in rough weather, and surrendered after four hours' fighting, while the other French ships sailed for France. Six of them were captured later.

Tone made no attempt to hide his identity from the British and was, of course, made a prisoner. Though he wore the uniform of a French general, he was put in irons for the journey to Dublin. He was charged with treason and, as the outcome of the trial was inevitable, he did not put up a defence, simply saying that he had done his duty and no doubt the courts would do theirs. 'From my earliest youth', he told the court, 'I have regarded the connection between Ireland and Great Britain as the curse of the Irish nation, and felt convinced that, while it lasted, this country could never be free nor happy.' All he asked was to be shot, out of respect for the uniform he wore, instead of being hanged.

Nevertheless, after his trial ended he had to listen to the gallows being erected outside his window. He was to be executed on the Monday, and on Sunday evening he was told that his request for a soldier's death had been refused. When his gaoler came to wake him about four o'clock the next morning, he found him with his throat cut yet still alive; he had tried to kill himself with a penknife and hacked through his windpipe. Some loyalists thought he should have his wound sewn up and then be hanged, but his friends raised a valid query about the legality of his trial: he had come before a court martial, although he was not a member of any of the Irish armed forces and Ireland was not under martial law. He lingered for a week in agony, and then heard a surgeon say that if he were to move or speak, it would be fatal to him. 'I can yet find word to thank you, sir,' he is said to have whispered. 'It is the most welcome news you could give me.' And he died immediately. He was thirty-five.

Wolfe Tone was brave, honourable, highly intelligent and very likeable. But he was not realistic. He had a lighthearted optimism with which he misled his French allies, his followers and even himself. If things had turned out as he thought they would . . . . If a larger French force had landed sooner . . . . If the Irish had risen in support of the French . . . . But Tone, fired with enthusiasm, mistook the facts. He made the disastrous error of encouraging the Irish to rebel unsuccessfully, and the result for Ireland was not the separation from Britain he craved, but union.

When the rebellion was no more than a fortnight old, William Pitt, the British prime minister, had decided the only way of dealing with Ireland was to bring her into an indissoluble union with Britain. The dangers of the situation, if neglected, were appalling. Britain was fighting for her life against a most powerful enemy; to have a dissident Ireland on her flank, likely to welcome French invaders, was more than the larger country could cope with. Nowadays, when the population of Britain is fifty million and that of the whole of Ireland not more than five million, we do not always understand why Ireland was such a problem to Britain, but during the French revolutionary wars the relative populations of Britain and Ireland were quite different. Ireland had as large a population as she has now, but the population of Britain was only eleven million, little more than double that of Ireland. Britain had to have Ireland on her side.

Then there was the chronic state of disorder, the dreadful discontent of Ireland. The Irish government, in Pitt's view, had failed; and so had that loyal. eloquent, but corrupt body, the Irish parliament. Government from Westminster might be more effective, leading to the redress of grievances, a weakening of the Protestant Ascendancy and full Catholic emancipation.

In the early days of the century, the English in Ireland had suggested a union, and Britain had turned them down. Much

later, Britain had made tentative approaches to Ireland and, likewise, been turned down. Up to the time of the rebellion, none
among 'the Protestant nation', and certainly no Catholics or
Presbyterians, wanted to risk the individuality and cohesiveness
of Ireland which, in spite of the deepest divisions, was emerging.
Union with Britain could turn Ireland into a backwater, her
energy drained off to another country, and her political leaders
no more than a minority in a foreign parliament, where her
problems would be forgotten. But after the rebellion people were
afraid. No-one in Ireland had been able to look after himself, and
when Pitt's men put the case for union, they were listened to.
The Protestants did not want to lose their privileges but, on the
other hand, a union could prevent them from being swamped,
eventually, by emancipated Catholics. And Catholics, too, began
to see advantages in union. The nationalism of the peasants
remained dormant; they did not seem to care who ruled them,
the English, the French, or anyone else, so long as their grievances were attended to, but the Catholic church in Ireland, and
the small Catholic upper class, realized that union could be a
means of breaking the Protestant monopoly of power.

Other groups had very real fears of union. The merchants and
traders, who had benefited so greatly under Grattan's parliament, hesitated to trust a British government; they remembered
only too well how British jealousy had hampered the wool trade,
the glass industry, brewing, the export of livestock and all
attempts to develop Irish shipping. On the other hand, union
might enable them to join freely in the commerce of the British
empire. Lawyers saw union as bringing the separate Irish
judiciary to an end, just as, in the case of Sherlock v. Annesley,
the English House of Lords had taken over from the Irish Lords
as the supreme court for Ireland. The Presbyterians, represented
by the Orange Order, made it clear that, in any clash between
their interests and the union, they would put their interests first.
And Dublin – one of the liveliest capitals in Europe? When the
government left and parliament was shut down, the aristocracy
and gentry would give up their town houses, dismiss their
servants, abandon the coachbuilders, tailors, stonemasons and
plasterers who depended on their custom, and move away.
Dublin would dwindle into a dull provincial city.

When Cornwallis took over in June 1798 he brought with him

as his chief secretary Lord Castlereagh, later to become a famous British foreign secretary. When the amnesty had been declared and the worst of the crisis was over, they began their negotiations. Catholics were told rather vaguely that union would bring them state funding for their clergy, an end to the payment of tithes to Protestant clergy and full emancipation, that is, seats in parliament. The Catholic bishops met at Maynooth in January 1799, accepted the offer of state provision and agreed, in return, that the government should be able to verify the loyalty of Irish bishops and clergy.

The Protestant Ascendancy unashamedly put itself up for sale. Leading Protestants traded their power and privileges for money, places, or improved peerages as if they were dealing in cattle in a cattle market. Political power was regarded as property and pocket boroughs valued at £15,000 each; £1,260,000 was paid out to their owners and charged to the Irish exchequer. Sixteen borough owners were given English peerages, twenty-eight new Irish peerages were created and twenty Irish peers were promoted.

Yet parliament fought tooth and nail against the union that would destroy it. Protestant magnates sold their pocket boroughs, but not their votes. When union was first mooted in parliament in January 1799, it was furiously debated twice, the opposition losing the first debate by a single vote and winning the second by 111 votes to 106. Castlereagh had to promise not to bring up the subject of union again 'so long as it appeared repugnant to the sense of the parliament and the country'. But Pitt was determined; he refused to allow a general election on the issue of union and let it be known that it would be reintroduced in session after session of parliament until it was accepted.

Castlereagh set himself to buy votes as well as boroughs. Office-holders who would not toe the government line were dismissed, and it was made generally known that no-one had any chance of government office in the future unless he supported union. Opponents of union were bribed to stay away from parliament and others, strangely enough, gave up their seats to supporters of union rather than vote for it themselves. The opposition, as well as the government, bought votes; one member of parliament sold his vote to the government and then accepted another £4,000 from the opposition to vote for them!

Cornwallis, who was less detached than Castlereagh, hated himself for engaging in such dirty work. 'How I long,' he wrote, 'to kick those whom my public duty obliges me to court!'

When parliament met again on 15 January 1800 members debated the union, with extreme heat, all night and into the next morning. About 7a.m. Grattan entered the House of Commons. Since his withdrawal from parliament three years earlier, he had been ill and listless. Then, on the very day parliament met, his friends bought him a seat in Wicklow and rushed his election through. He appeared in the house wearing his old Volunteer uniform, hardly able to walk but supported by a friend on each side of him, with his head hanging and his face deathly pale. At first his voice could hardly be heard, but as he went on the old fire came back to him. For two hours he upheld the right of Ireland to dignity, sovereignty and its own legislature – in a word, to liberty – and denounced the union. To no avail. Castlereagh had done his work too well, and at ten o'clock that morning the union was carried by 138 votes to 96.

For some months the opposition fought on, organizing petitions and trying to arouse public opinion. But the people had deserted them. There were 50,000 British troops in the country and Ireland was cowed. By 28 March the terms of union had been accepted by both houses. The bill of union was drawn up and, despite the passionate eloquence of the opposition, passed its first and second readings. Before the debate on the third reading was over, the bulk of the opposition left the House of Commons in a body. They could not bear to wait for the miserable end.

The Irish parliament was corrupt and ineffectual; it had never represented much more than the English interest in Ireland, and during its last years it was the tool of the Protestant Ascendancy. If Grattan had succeeded in bringing in Catholics, it might have lasted longer. Yet for 500 years it had been the legislative body of Ireland, a focus for Irish political life and a counterpoise to the rule of justiciars, lord lieutenants and viceroys from England. When parliament had been dissolved for the last time, the fine eighteenth-century Parliament House was sold to the Bank of Ireland with the secret stipulation that the chambers where the two houses had met should be altered until they were unrecognizable, to lay all ghosts. The Commons chamber became the banking hall, but the Lords, by some oversight, has remained unchanged to this day – a monument to the Protestant Ascendancy with tapestries commemorating William's victory at the Boyne and the siege of Londonderry.

The union had hardly touched the people of Britain; they were more concerned about the war with France. Pitt gave a masterly dissertation on the value of the union to a lackadaisical House of Commons, and was met with but one dissentient voice. It belonged to Richard Brinsley Sheridan, remembered nowadays mainly as a playwright, who said the English were more ignorant of the affairs of Ireland than of any other country in the world. He was an Irishman; he knew. In the upper house, the poet Lord Byron said it was 'the union of a shark with its prey'. But no-one was very interested and on 1 August 1800, the Act of Union received the royal assent.

In September Castlereagh outlined the terms of the union, which was to come into force on 1 January 1801. Ireland was to have 100 seats in the British House of Commons, twenty-eight peers and four bishops in the Lords. The Church of Ireland was to be amalgamated with the Church of England. Ireland was still to have a viceroy and the Irish laws and judiciary, contrary to the lawyers' fears, were to remain unchanged. Trade was to be free between Ireland and Britain, Ireland was to share British privileges in trade with the Empire, and the bounty on Irish linen was to remain. As far as taxation went, Ireland was to contribute to the expenses of the new United Kingdom in the proportion of 2:15 for twenty years, and then the ratio was to be reviewed. During that time, Ireland would have her own exchequer and her own national debt. So far so good; the terms were generous. But Irish members of parliament were to take the oath of allegiance, which would exclude Catholics, although Irish Catholics would retain the right to vote granted them in the Catholic Relief Act of 1793.

Pitt had intended to make Catholic emancipation part of the treaty of union. He was well aware that differences in the treatment of Catholics and Protestants were a great part of the trouble in Ireland. But he had had so much opposition from Protestants that he had abandoned all thought of Catholic emancipation for the time being, simply to push the union through. Yet the vague promises to Ireland's Catholics had been made in good faith. Pitt had every intention of introducing a Catholic emancipation bill as soon as the union was in being, and early in 1801 he proposed to George III that Catholics should be admitted to parliament and state provision made for the Catholic clergy. But Farmer George, never the brightest of British kings, was convinced that the royal assent to a Catholic emancipation bill would constitute a breach of his coronation oath to uphold the Protestant church. George was elderly and none too well; we know now that he suffered from the physical disease of porphyria, which induces delirium, but his contemporaries, including Pitt, thought his mind was disordered. Pitt could have pressed George harder; he might even have persuaded parliament to amend the coronation oath. But he was so afraid that any argument or contradiction would push the king over the brink into madness, leaving Britain, in the midst of a terrible war, to the tender mercies of the frivolous, spendthrift prince of Wales, that he promised never to raise the question of Catholic emancipation again, so long as the king should live. Pitt was cold and austere, but not unprincipled; he could only drop Catholic emancipation if he resigned, and resign he did, followed by Cornwallis and Castlereagh. The Irish Catholics were flabbergasted; they felt they had been duped. No specific promises had been made to them, but they had most certainly been led to understand that emancipation would follow union, and their support had been secured on that understanding. And now the author of the union, the man behind the understanding, had quit: he would not even fight for them.

The union had been genuinely intended to benefit Ireland as well as Britain, but nothing in the Irish situation changed. Religious differences still ran like a gaping wound through the country, Irish peasants were still the poorest in Europe, and the same waves of crime and disorder swept through the countryside as half a century earlier. During the next twenty years, the government passed frequent coercion acts, martial law was almost permanent and Habeas Corpus was suspended as often as not. The British garrison of 25,000 men, kept in Ireland in case of a French invasion, was used to keep order. From the Middle Ages until the seventeenth century, the English government of Ireland had been a military one; at the beginning of the nineteenth century, military government seemed to be back.

In 1803 there was a flicker of rebellion; for a brief moment, the United Irishmen lived again. A young Protestant student, Robert Emmet, whose elder brother had been among the leaders of the United Irishmen in 1798, met an American armaments specialist in Paris and became so enthusiastic about a kind of primitive land mine, a wooden box filled with explosives and shrapnel the American showed him, that, on his return to Dublin in 1802, he made plans for a rising, using the land mine, for the following summer. For months United Irishmen made arms in various hideouts in Dublin, to be used in attacks on the castle and other key points. In July of 1803 a proclamation headed *The Provisional Government to the People of Ireland* was rushed off the presses and distributed, while Emmet, in the green uniform with gold epaulettes of a United Irish general, waited for his supporters. He expected 2,000 of them, but only eighty turned up. And the organization which was to support them proved haphazard, to say the least; the fuses for hand grenades were lost, the man who was to have made fuses for the land mines had forgotten to do it, the scaling ladders for the attack on Dublin castle were not ready, and the horses pulling the coaches, which were to take the rebels to the castle, had mysteriously bolted!

Without much hope, Emmet drew his sword and led his handful of followers out among the Saturday evening crowds. Arms were handed out and before long an uncontrollable mob, waving pikes and blunderbusses, was rampaging through the streets. It found itself surrounding a coach carrying the Lord Chief Justice, not an unpopular man, and piked him to death. Emmet was appalled when he heard of it later that night. His own band of followers dwindled until there were only about twenty left and, to avoid more bloodshed, he called the whole thing off. But the mob went on rioting all night.

Emmet was caught about a month later, tried and condemned to be hanged. He spoke from the dock with such feeling about Irish liberty that many of his friends who were there, and even the judge, were deeply moved. Then he asked to be buried in an unmarked grave, concluding: 'When my country takes her place among the nations of the earth, then and not till then let my epitaph be written.' In later years he became a folk-hero to the people of Ireland, a figure of romantic, youthful protest, like the Czech student martyr Jan Palach in our own day. Following in the footsteps of Wolfe Tone, he became part of the myth that was, eventually, to free Ireland.

After Emmet's execution, Ireland went politically dead. Dublin stagnated; the viceroy had moved to the suburban Phoenix Park, there was no 'season' any more, noblemen sold their town houses and trade declined. The French wars imposed a heavy burden; the requirement that Ireland should pay 2:15 of the cost had seemed reasonable enough, but in practice it meant that during the next fifteen years Irish government expenditure tripled, whereas the British expenditure only increased by 50 per cent. Irish taxes were increased by 52 per cent after the union, but the Exchequer still had to borrow, and the loans had to be serviced. By 1817 the Irish national debt had gone up by a staggering 250 per cent. Then the British and Irish exchequers were amalgamated, so that Britain could take over some of Ireland's debt.

Protestants remained in the ascendant and became ardent supporters of the union when they saw it for what it was, a strengthening of the British connection. The Presbyterians found the market for linen improved and they, too, became avid unionists. The *regium donum* was greatly increased and paid, not as a single lump sum, but to individual Presbyterian ministers as a reward for their loyalty. But the Catholics, the great mass of the people, remained sadly disappointed. Their churches and chapels had been repaired at government expense after the rebellion of 1798 but, beyond that, there was no help. Catholics still maintained their priests themselves, as well as paying the hated tithes to the Protestant clergy. The government and the law remained alien to them, and Protestant members of parliament sitting over the water at Westminster were totally remote.

Yet Catholics were not forgotten. Grattan waited sadly until 1805, then obtained an English seat (Malton, in Yorkshire) in the House of Commons and took up the case of Catholic emancipation once more. Pitt died in 1806, worn out at the early age of forty-eight; George III remained inflexibly opposed to emancipation and the prince of Wales, who became regent in 1811, maintained the same position. Most Britons did not see what Irish Catholics had to complain of; British Catholics still had no votes and were excluded from all government service, except at the lowest levels. Britons did not realize that, whereas in Britain Catholics were a small minority, in Ireland they were the bulk of the population.

Grattan's approach was conciliatory. In his various proposals he included a government right to veto the appointment of any Catholic bishop whose loyalty was questionable, a term the Catholic bishops had accepted at Maynooth in 1799. But Catholic opinion in Ireland was hardening; the old aristocratic Catholic leadership, with its mealy-mouthed addresses of loyalty, was being thrust aside by the far more vigorous and radical lawyers and merchants of the middle class, who denounced the veto as a betrayal of Irish interests.

Prominent among those middle-class Catholics was Daniel O'Connell, the bold, down-to-earth and extremely dextrous lawyer who was to take over Grattan's mantle as the supreme Irish patriot, become the champion of the Catholics, especially the poor, and earn the title of Liberator of the nation.

The O'Connells were Old Irish, a well-to-do landowning family in Kerry, which had kept its Catholic religion and contrived to increase its estates during the penal period, with the help of a Protestant kinsman. Like other such families, they had developed ties with Catholic countries abroad; one of Daniel's uncles became a general in the French army, and another was chamberlain at the Austrian court for sixty years. A third uncle, Old Hunting Cap, remained behind in Kerry and maintained the family fortunes by smuggling; privateers, loaded with French silks and wines, anchored regularly off Cahirciveen, on the O'Connell stretch of the wild Kerry coast. Daniel himself was fostered, following the old custom, with a herdsman and then sent to France to be educated. From there he went to London to study law and in May 1798 was called to the Irish bar.

He could not have come to Dublin at a more devastating time. The rebellion went off, like so many firecrackers, all around him, and he was appalled by it. In London he had picked up liberal, even radical, views; he shared Wolfe Tone's ideal of a united Ireland, with people of every religion playing their part, and he admired the independence of Grattan's parliament. But when he saw the horror of armed rebellion, and the cruelty of its suppression, he decided the first tenet of his political creed must be – loyalty. Rebellion was not only horrific: it was impractical. It did not work. And he himself would always operate on the right side of treason.

For several years, he built up his practice at the bar. Since the union, the courts had replaced parliament as the scene of oratory and debate, and O'Connell, prodigiously energetic, witty, skilful and even unscrupulous, was soon well known. His fame brought him the opportunity to lead the Catholic radicals in their continuing campaign for emancipation which, for many years, he did quietly enough, merely forwarding petitions to the Westminster parliament, where Grattan was gradually educating the opinion of British MPs.

In 1819 Grattan introduced a Catholic emancipation bill into the British House of Commons for the third time. The earlier bills had both been defeated fairly substantially, but this bill was only lost by two votes. In 1820 Grattan died, and in the following year his successors put up two more bills, which were passed in the Commons and defeated in the Lords. In Ireland, people were bitterly disappointed, and O'Connell decided the time had come for the Catholic movement to be more aggressive.

In May 1823 he formed a new Catholic Association, which would put members into parliament who, though necessarily Protestant, would fight for Catholic emancipation. At first, the Association seemed just another middle-class political group and aroused little interest, but then in 1824 O'Connell broadened the membership. Those who could not afford the annual membership fee of one guinea were invited to join as associate members for a shilling a year, or a penny a month – and the situation was transformed. The parish priests, who were automatically members, enrolled their parishioners and, week after week, collected their subscriptions. The 'penny a month' soon became known as the Catholic Rent and brought in about £1,000 a week from a quarter of a million poor Catholic families. For the first time the Catholic peasantry was being organized for political ends.

The early nineteenth century was not a democratic age; in neither Britain nor Ireland were the common people permitted to speak for themselves. A tenant's vote was part of his landlord's property. When the Catholic Association began organizing the peasantry into a disciplined body, with the funds and the leadership to get what it wanted, the government was extremely alarmed. It seemed as if the Whiteboys, the Defenders and other secret societies were banding together: as if the forces of violence which had, within living memory, broken into rebellion with such appalling ferocity, were about to break out again. In March 1825 the Catholic Association was banned. O'Connell, who had boasted earlier that he could drive a coach and four through any legal restriction placed on it, set the Association up again four months later with the innocuous aims of pursuing 'public and private charity', promoting 'public peace and tranquility as well as private harmony between all classes' and 'all purposes not prohibited by law'. But the fact that the Catholic Association was palpably not treasonable, and could not be dealt with as if it were, left the government helpless.

The Catholic Relief Act of 1793 had given the vote to all Catholics who were forty shilling freeholders[6] and that meant in theory that everyone, except the very poorest, could express his political will, for almost any piece of property, even a couple of chairs, could count as a forty shilling freehold. But there was no secret ballot, and in practice tenants voted as their landlords directed them to do. It was a 'disgrace to our constitution and our country', Wolfe Tone had said, to see 'that wretched tribe of forty shilling freeholders . . . driven to their octennial[7] market by their landlords'. Since the formation of the Catholic Association, however, priests had occasionally prevailed upon their parishioners to defy their landlords at the polls.

In 1826, when a general election was to be held, O'Connell still thought the peasants would be led to the polls by their landlords like so many sheep, but in Westmeath, Co. Dublin, Roscommon and Monaghan the priests, not the landlords, directed the people how to vote, and gave their support to emancipationist candidates. In Louth the emancipationist defeated a candidate whose family had controlled the country for half a century and in Co. Waterford, where Lord George Beresford, a member of the most powerful landed family in Ireland, had sat for twenty years, an emancipationist was put up too. Ten days before polling day, O'Connell swung the weight of the Catholic Association behind him; members paraded through the town *en masse*, wearing 'the green' as the symbol of nationhood, green handkerchiefs, green sashes, green ribbons and green cockades. The Association patrolled the town and maintained perfect order; elections were usually the occasion of drunkenness and rioting, but this time drunks were ducked in the river and there was no riotous behavior whatsoever. Lord George castigated his opponent for his 'ungentlemanly' behaviour and withdrew his candidature. The Catholic Association had put its man in.

In March 1828 the duke of Wellington became prime minister and Sir Robert Peel, the leading opponent of Catholic claims, home secretary. The Catholic Association immediately resolved to oppose all government candidates, whether they were emancipationists or not, and held some 2000 protest meetings simultaneously in parishes all over Ireland, a brilliant piece of organization by the priests. Then in June, William Vesey Fitzgerald, one of two members for Clare, had to fight a by-election for his seat; he had become president of the Board of Trade, and the rule was that any member appointed to the government had to go back to his constituency for re-election.[8] Vesey Fitzgerald was an emancipationist, a kind and popular landlord, an experienced politician and the son of a Patriot in Grattan's parliament. But he supported the wrong government and O'Connell himself decided to stand against him.

There was nothing in the law to prevent a Catholic from being elected to parliament, and it was obviously the next step for the Catholic Association to put a Catholic candidate up. When, as was inevitable, the new Catholic member refused to take the oaths of allegiance and supremacy in the House of Commons, the government would be seriously challenged; the might of the million or so forty shilling freeholders would have to be taken into account.

O'Connell stood as a Man of the People. Nothing could have been better calculated to frighten the government. In the general opinion, only the gentry and those above them were fitted to select governments because they owned property – real property, not paltry forty shilling freeholds – and the desire to safeguard their property rendered them stable, reponsible and unlikely to rock the boat. O'Connell was quite well off – he had inherited an estate in Kerry and earned a high income at the bar – but as a Man of the People, uncrowned king of the forty shilling freeholders, he seemed to be what the government most dreaded, a demagogue, a rabble rouser, the leader of a popular revolution.

When the election came, the atmosphere was tense with excitement, alive with optimism. Once again, officials of the Catholic Association made sure that the crowds of forty shilling freeholders, decked in 'the green', behaved impeccably, marching to the polls in long, orderly columns. They were divided into squads like soldiers but, to show there was nothing warlike about them, each squad was led by an official known as a pacificator.

The government was far more frightened of pacific than of fighting Irishmen; it could not send its troops against them. When O'Connell was victorious, winning the seat by 2,057 votes to 982, the government found the extent of his support unnerving. They dared not refuse the Irish masses what they had voted for, and early in 1829 a Catholic Emancipation Act was passed, which enabled Catholics to be judges, admirals and generals, as well as members of parliament, the only position still withheld from them being those of lord lieutenant or viceroy, lord chancellor (in either England or Ireland) and regent. At the same time the government made sure the Irish peasantry would never again be able to force its hand by putting a second act through parliament which raised the minimum freehold for the franchise to £10, immediately reducing the Irish Catholic electorate from 1,160,000 to 86,000. Whereupon the Catholic Association, having achieved its object, disbanded itself.

O'Connell arrived in Westminster to take his seat after the Catholic Emancipation Act had received the royal assent, but the government had meanly refused to make the act retrospective, so that he had to go all the way back to Clare to be re-elected. When he reached Ennis, the county town, he was met by 40,000 people and, after a triumphal entry, re-elected unopposed.

As soon as he had taken his seat in the House of Commons, O'Connell began campaigning for the repeal of the union. At first he had no success whatever; no British MPs had any interest in the subject and only thirty-nine Irish members were in favour of repeal. But the arguments put forward on both sides when he first moved the repeal of the union were to remain in force for the rest of the century.

O'Connell wanted Ireland's position to be the same as it had been during Grattan's parliament, when Ireland had been a sister kingdom to Britain, loyal to the same monarch but with her own independent legislature. This time, though, the Irish parliament was to be reformed and truly representative of the predominantly Catholic Irish people. The government contended that Ireland and Britain were already equal, Irishmen and Britons having equal rights in each other's countries, and claimed, quite correctly, that industry in the north had developed so greatly since the union that the population of Belfast had tripled. But British ignorance of the problems of the agricultural south and west remained total. O'Connell struggled on, fighting one coercion act after another and supporting a Tithe Act, passed in 1838, which incorporated the tithe into the rent and made the landlord, not the parson or the tithe proctor, responsible for its collection, rendering the injustice of the system less apparent. Then in 1841 the Liberals, with whom O'Connell had allied himself, were swept from office, and he took his campaign for repeal out of parliament.

An ineffectual Repeal Association already founded in Dublin was remodelled on the lines of the Catholic Association and the 'penny a month' reintroduced as the Repeal Rent. For a while, it could not get started. Then the Catholic bishops and priests declared for it and brought the peasantry and the Catholic middle classes with them, the Protestants remaining firmly unionist. O'Connell began addressing weekly meetings of the Repeal Association, describing repeal vaguely and emotively as the panacea for all ills.

The Repeal Association lacked the broad power base among the peasants of the old Catholic Association, but it included among its members a group of talented and idealistic young men from the middle classes, both Catholic and Protestant, who, in 1812, founded a newspaper, *The Nation*, which soon became the organ of the association. *The Nation* covered O'Connell's meetings, reported his speeches and rapidly gained a readership of more than a quarter of a million – far more than that of any other newspaper in the country.

In 1843 O'Connell carried his campaign forward with a series

21. A monster meeting (courtesy of the National Library of Ireland)

of huge public demonstrations in the open air, 'monster meetings' as they were called in the London *Times*, which habitually opposed him. Vast numbers turned up, half a million people packed the streets, and even climbed on the rooftops for a mass meeting in the city of Cork; hundreds of thousands heard O'Connell speak at Roscrea in Co. Limerick, at Donnybrook, outside Dublin, at Ennis and at Wexford, and three quarters of a million converged on the Hill of Tara. These huge crowds were just as well disciplined, orderly and peaceful as the members of the Catholic Association had been; nevertheless they resembled an army, albeit an army without arms. They were organized into squads and columns, and at one meeting a troop of horsemen appeared in cavalry formation. O'Connell maintained his belief in a pacific movement and fostered in the huge crowds a warm, emotional loyalty to the young queen Victoria, but his oratory did not lack warlike metaphors, which *The Nation* duly recorded.

The monster meetings often began with an open air mass, conducted from the low hill, or promontory, where O'Connell, the clergy and the local Catholic gentry stood. Then O'Connell, the Liberator, made his address. He was a tall, powerful man with an excellent voice. 'You'd hear it a mile off,' one of his listeners said, 'as if it was coming through honey.' And he was an extremely experienced agitator. He whipped up the crowds by asking if there was a man who would not die for Ireland, and immediately answered on their behalf that 'there was not a man amongst them would not brunt the battle's blaze and glory in achieving victory for Ireland.' *The Nation*, in reporting his meetings, used metaphors reminiscent of the United Irishmen and 1798.

The government was alarmed. Although O'Connell had little following in the House of Commons, at home in Ireland he was the powerful head of a huge national movement. There had been some sympathy at Westminster for the cause of Catholic emancipation, which had been on the cards for thirty years before it was granted. But there was little support, even among Irish members, for an end to the union. Sir Robert Peel, the prime minister, even said that civil war would be preferable to repeal, as that would lead to the 'dismemberment of the Empire'.

The Nation announced another monster meeting for 5 October 1843, at Clontarf, the scene of Brian Boru's great victory, and in a leading article headed 'The Coming Struggle' described it hectically as a 'Muster and March of the Repeal Volunteers!!!' and called for cavalry. The government took action. British troops were made ready and on 4 October, only twenty-four hours before the meeting was to take place, the authorities banned it. O'Connell could have ignored the ban: huge crowds would have assembled to hear him and the troops might not have been able to contain them. He could have instructed the crowds to come armed, and successfully resisted the British contingent. But O'Connell was law-abiding; he had always protested his absolute loyalty to the Crown and non-violence was part of his creed. It was a difficult thing to turn back half a million people, many of whom had already left home, in a big, wild country with poor communications, but O'Connell did it. With the agreement and support of the journalists of *The Nation*, he contrived to call the monster meeting off.

But the government was not content. Five days later O'Connell and seven others, including Charles Gavan Duffy, the editor of *The Nation*, were arrested. O'Connell refused to travel to Dublin's Kilmainham jail in a hackney cab, but insisted on walking with his captor through the streets, so everyone could see that the Liberator, the chosen leader of Ireland, had been picked up like a common housebreaker. With the others, he was charged with conspiring to alter the constitution by force – he, who had run his associations openly, peacefully and loyally, was being tainted with treason!

The lengthy state trial at the Four Courts ended in February 1844, with a conviction from the wholly Protestant jury. O'Connell was granted bail for three months before sentence would be passed and, as a convicted traitor and bailee, went off to England to hold public meetings in Birmingham, Manchester, Liverpool and London! A huge dinner was held for him in the Opera House, Covent Garden, which had the auditorium and stage boarded right across for the occasion. Then a sentence of a year's imprisonment was passed. With his fellow prisoners, O'Connell was comfortably ensconced in the prison governor's and deputy governor's houses at Richmond prison in Dublin; they had streams of visitors, food was brought in from outside, and their dinner parties sometimes had twenty-four guests! But the injustice of the sentence, however easy its terms, sent a wave of sympathy through Ireland, and the Repeal Rent rose to more than £2,500 a week. Then quite suddenly, in September, the House of Lords quashed the conviction on the ground that the prosecution had illegally manipulated the jury lists. A triumphal procession of 200,000 people escorted O'Connell to his Dublin home, while all over Ireland bands played, bonfires were lit and houses were decked with laurel.

It was a hero's return, but the ageing O'Connell had had his fingers burned. His campaign for repeal by peaceful means had failed and the bluff of the monster meetings had been called. He turned to federalism: the plea of moderate Irishmen for an Irish parliament for home affairs, with foreign and imperial matters directed from Westminster. A half measure seemed better than no measure. But the young men of *The Nation*, Young Ireland as they had come to be called, were not to be deflected.

In July 1846 the Repeal Association debated its future policy. 'I do not disclaim the use of arms as immoral,' Thomas Meagher, a Young Irelander from Waterford, declared, 'nor do I believe (it is the truth to say) the God of Heaven withholds his sanction from the use of arms . . . . Be it for defence, or be it for the assertion of a nation's liberty. I look upon the sword as a sacred weapon'. Then he used a metaphor which, though confused, made his feelings plain. 'If (the sword) has sometimes reddened the shroud of the oppressor,' he said, 'it has at other times blossomed into flowers to deck the freeman's brow.' A peaceful expression of the people's will had been spurned; inevitably Irishmen would one day turn again to violence to achieve their legitimate ends.

CHAPTER 10

THE GREAT FAMINE

The movement for repeal of the union was dealt a shattering blow in the mid-1840s when Ireland was devastated by the Great Famine. This was a succession of four years' failure of the potato crop. The famine ravaged Ireland from 1845 to 1848. That is a miniscule part of the 8,000 or so years of Ireland's history which are treated in this book. Yet it was probably the most cataclysmic event in that long period, and its effects are still with the Irish in Ireland and with people of Irish descent in many parts of the world, particularly in the United States. Some of the changes it wrought in the economy, in society and in politics were immediate, some took longer to emerge, some are still emerging. And, true to the tendency of the Irish to decorate – and on occasion to obscure – their history with myths and legends, the famine and its aftermath are cloaked in their own peculiar brand of mythology. Yet many of the facts are inescapable, for they are documented in reports and statistical material, while the full horror of the famine itself as it was experienced in every corner of the island is more than amply testified in contemporary reports, letters and interviews[1] and – most distressingly of all – in the horrendous decline in population through death and emigration in that four years. A key part of the mythology, sustained to this day, is the damning indictment of the British government's role, that it created the potato famine and then watched the Irish die.

No one seriously disputes the gravity of the impact of the famine upon Ireland in general or upon the potato-dependent millions in particular. It cannot have been entirely unexpected and much could and should have been done to avert its worst effects. The potato had been the staple diet of a continuously growing proportion of the Irish people for well over a century (and by the 1840s it had become the sole diet for three million out of a total population of about 8,000,000). The diet, particularly when it was combined with buttermilk, was highly nutritional, and in the view of some authorities it made a contribution to Ireland's relatively low infant mortality rate in the eighteenth and earlier nineteenth century which, in turn, was a key factor in Ireland's rapid population rise between the 1760s and the 1840s (1767=2½m; 1781=c.4m; 1800=5m; 1821=6¾m; 1841=8¼m). A potato crop grown on one acre of land was enough to feed a family of five or six for the best part of a year. It was easy to plant and easy to harvest: all you needed was a spade. But there were disadvantages. The potato could not be stored for long, and a crop might not stretch over the whole period from one harvest to the next. From June to August every year, many potato dependents went short and had to find other food such as meal or go out and beg. Dependence on potatoes discouraged the small farmer and the cottier from cultivating alternative food for their own sustenance, or as a hedge against a possible failure of the crop – and there were many failures in one region or another in the century between the 1740s and the 1840s, particularly in the last years, but until 1845 there was never a national failure. If a small farmer did grow cereals, it was usually to pay rent for the land he worked, or as on some small farms, to sell them for cash. In some parts of the west, many small farmers had actually forgotten how to grind corn into flour, and some had even forgotten how to plough or to sow.

Rural poverty in Ireland was the biggest social problem in a land blighted by other deep-seated difficulties and injustices, and it was part and parcel of the rapid population rise. It was also in large measure the result of grossly irresponsible attitudes of landowners who insisted on extracting as much rent from their lands as they could, which they spent recklessly outside of Ireland instead of investing it at home. As the laws operated, if a tenant-farmer wanted to improve his holding and its yields, he would generally have to cough up the bulk of the better profits in increased rent to his landlord. This did not encourage him to be responsible, and many tenant-farmers turned to sub-dividing and further sub-dividing the land so that they, in turn, could earn rents from the increasing number of people wanting smaller and smaller plots of land as potato gardens. There was never enough land for all, even when cottiers and labourers moved on to the mountain sides to grow potatoes in hitherto rough and uncultivated land. Sub-division spread, fathers broke up small plots into smaller ones for their increasingly more numerous sons, and the average holding became smaller and smaller. By the 1840s less than 7 per cent of holdings in Ireland were of thirty or more acres (in Connacht, 64 per cent were less than five acres).

A few landowners were seriously worried about the dependence on the potato and the fragmentation of estates, and even tried to educate cottiers and labourers in new farming methods and in growing alternative crops for food. Agricultural societies were formed for this purpose (see p. 176) but they achieved little. The situation was highly perilous: the potato crop might fail at any time, leading to widespread distress. As it was, in the years following the end of the war against France (1815), a slump in agricultural prices, coupled with the continued rise in population and a virtual collapse of Irish industry (except in Ulster), produced 'gigantic' unemployment and rampant poverty. Even Dublin appeared a half-dead city. Begging was common: travellers to Ireland often commented upon clusters of mendicants crowding round their coaches. Some of the travellers had much harsher comments. De Beaumont from France thought the Irish poor were in worse misery than the negro in his chains, and Kohl from Germany believed no kind of life anywhere else in Europe could be considered pitiable after a visit to Ireland. The duke of Wellington, an Anglo-Irish landlord in addition to his other roles, said there never was a country in which poverty existed to the extent it existed in Ireland, and he had spent years abroad in many of the world's poorest parts, including Portugal, Spain and the Indian sub-continent. The Devon Commission (named after its chairman, the earl of Devon), set up in 1843 to investigate the Irish land system, sent its members to visit all parts of Ireland in 1843 and 1844, and in its report it admitted that 'It would be impossible adequately to describe the privations which they (that is, the Irish labourer and his family) habitually and silently endure . . . in many districts their only food is the potato, their only beverage water . . . their cabins are seldom a protection against the weather . . . a bed or a blanket is a rare luxury . . . and nearly in all their pig and manure constitute their only property . . .' It would not be right to omit the fact that in all their misery, the Irish demonstrated time and again to visitors, commissioners, journalists and so forth a seemingly inexhaustible reserve of gaiety and lightheartedness that were duly noted, but it must be wondered, too, how much of this was a cover.

Distress could be partially though never totally relieved on a regional basis by a number of expedients such as grants, relief from landowners themselves (generally available only after hard pressure from the authorities, who were at the same time reluctant to interfere with landowners' universally recognized inalienable rights of property), encouragement to emigrate, public works programmes, charity, and in the last period before the Great Famine (and of course during it), the workhouse. But a national failure was quite a different matter, and when in the autumn of 1845 the potato crop failed in about half of Ireland, the disaster caught the country unprepared.

The summer of 1845 was particularly wet in July, but a good potato crop was nonetheless expected. One paper, the *Freeman's Journal*, actually stated that 'the potato crop was never before so large and at the same time so abundant.' That was towards the end of July. At about the same time, however, disturbing news from the south of England reached the government in London: potato crops (especially in the Isle of Wight) were being decimated by 'a blight of unusual character', which appeared to have come in from western Europe where crops in several countries were also being destroyed. The blight had arrived there from North America where in 1842 it had got into the potato crops along the Atlantic coast and ruined them. We know now that the blight was a fungus hitherto not identified, *phyophthora infestans*. Scientists of the time thought the disease hitting the potato was in the tuber itself. By September 1845, the fungus had reached Wexford, and it spread rapidly, though some of the crop had already been lifted and was free from it. Among the grimmest features of the blight was the manner in which it did its work. A crop was dug out of the ground, seemingly wholesome: within a day or two, however, the tubers turned into a foul-smelling, putrefying mess. This happened without warning, in big fields and small gardens alike, in barns, shops, kitchens of houses great and small. In front of his eyes, a labourer's or a cottier's entire stock of food for the coming year would disintegrate.

Despite some of the crop having been lifted, starvation and consequent disease affected almost every part of the country, even though the crop failure itself was confined to little over a half of Ireland. Starving labourers and cottiers and their families fled from their neighbourhoods in search of food, but thousands were sick with contagious illnesses and spread the germs to hitherto unaffected districts, particularly the towns. Much, much worse was to follow; the crop of 1846 failed completely; the 1847 crop was blighted widely though not as completely as 1846, yet the effects were perhaps worse because thousands of people had eaten their seed potatoes (free of blight) and only a fraction of the necessary planting had been done; and in 1848, for the fourth successive year the crop failed, this time completely. As if that were not enough, the winter of 1846/7 was the longest and the coldest in living memory.

The misery for millions of potato-dependent people and for others was compounded by a number of factors that even singly would have been overwhelming: government attitudes to the provision of relief; the spread of typhus, relapsing fever, bacillic dysentery and famine dropsy; evictions from land and from mean one-room hovels by heartless landlords; the sight of cart-loads of grain and other crops being taken along the roads to ports for shipment to England and other markets while they starved. The full horror of those years is poignantly described with a welter of incontrovertible evidence in Williams and Edwards, *The Great Famine*, and Cecil Woodham-Smith, *The Great Hunger*. Perhaps we can illustrate a miniscule fraction of the horror in one short account by a magistrate from Cork visiting Skibbereen in December 1846.

I entered some of the hovels . . . and the scenes that presented themselves were such as no tongue or pen can convey the slightest idea of. In the first, six famished and ghastly skeletons, to all appearance dead, were huddled in a corner on some filthy straw, their sole covering what seemed a ragged horse-cloth, and their wretched legs hanging about, naked above the knees. I approached in horror, and found by a low moaning they were

231

22. Searching for potatoes (*Illustrated London News*, 22 December 1849)

alive, they were in fever – four children, a woman and what had once been a man . . .

In 1849, when the worst of the famine was over, one more murderous blow was struck against Ireland, an epidemic of cholera that hit many of the largest towns, including Dublin and Belfast. By 1850 the population of Ireland, which in 1845 had stood at about 8½ million, had been reduced to 6¼ million, that is, slashed by one-quarter. A million people had died from starvation and disease, another million had fled from their native land on overcrowded ships to seek refuge in Britain, Europe or North America (chiefly the last). The great bulk of this two million people were part of the 'gigantic' unemployment problem that was 'solved' by the famine – as one of the British officials of the time, Charles Trevelyan, permanent secretary to the Treasury, so succinctly put it: in his view the famine reflected the wishes of an all-wise Providence.

What did the government in Britain do to help relieve the distress created by the famine?

The famine struck Ireland at a time when Britain was racked by political argument over the Corn Laws. These had been introduced during the long war with France to put heavy duties on corn imported into England, to keep foreign corn out and to maintain high prices for home grown crops. But they caused tremendous suffering among the poorer classes in Britain who had to pay artificially high prices for bread and other foods. They also damaged trading generally. Agitation to repeal the laws began to gather momentum in the 1830s, but it was resisted stubbornly by the government and by the landlord classes. The potato blight of 1845 and the hardship it created in Ireland convinced the prime minister, Sir Robert Peel, that the Corn Laws must be repealed so that grain could be released at prices which the Irish peasantry could afford. Peel's earlier career in Ireland and his attitudes fortunately did not affect his essential humanity, and in making the moves necessary to get the laws repealed he risked – and was willing to risk – his position at the head of the administration. He stands out as one of the very few Englishmen who showed something other than callous indifference to the plight of the victims of the famine.

When the first reports of the famine reached the government

in London, Peel responded fast. While initiating the moves for repeal, he ordered the purchase of £100,000 worth of Indian corn and meal on the United States market to hand out to the starving Irish, doing so without first consulting his colleagues. The corn began to be distributed in the New Year of 1846. Peel also initiated public works programmes where the poor could earn money, and in the first season some 150,000 people obtained jobs. It has been said that his measures helped to the extent that no one died in the first season as a result of the famine, although thousands endured extreme hardship and deprivation. It is certainly pleasing to be able to record that in his lifetime Peel received the credit for his promptness and energy. There is some irony in that in the summer of 1846, before the second 'visitation' of the fungus, he was defeated in parliament and resigned office as a result of the repeal, and that his administration was followed by a Whig government under Lord John Russell, which took a quite different course when in the autumn the second failure struck the Irish potato crop.

Among the principal men in the government involved in the new administration's programme was Charles Wood, chancellor of the Exchequer, and he had as permanent secretary to the Treasury the civil servant Charles Trevelyan (who, we have noted, acknowledged the intervention of Providence in the solution of the Irish high population problem, p. 233). Both were devotees of the concept of dissociating the government from helping the Irish in their tribulations and determined that Ireland herself should stand the cost of bringing succour to her less fortunate millions in the famine crisis. Between them these two did more than any others to create the miseries that followed the change of administration at Westminster after Peel was defeated. Whether this was a series of deliberate acts which to-day we might classify as genocidal, or whether more simply they were the manifestation of breathtaking meanness and callousness from officials too rigidly tied to the prevailing ideas of *laissez faire* economics must still be open to debate. Certainly, Trevelyan said, and wrote, time and again that the Irish were exaggerating their miseries, that they must do more for themselves, and he intervened frequently to nullify on-the-spot remedies being applied by sympathetic officials in Ireland, and constantly complained about expenditure and alleged extravagance.

Very briefly, the Whig policy applied in 1846 and again in 1847 was that there should be no buying of food for the Irish starving by the government; this was to be provided by private enterprise, which of course meant that it would be sold to those who could raise the money. Government aid was to be strictly limited to generating public works to provide employment, but even this was to be largely funded by property owners in the areas of distress. But these works did not – could not – relieve distress because there were only enough jobs for about one-tenth of the number of people looking for them, and when the government finally saw that the schemes would not work, it took a year or more to make meaningful adjustments. By that time, several hundred thousand poverty-stricken people had succumbed to fever or disease and died or joined the emigration queues that were fast becoming a new feature of Irish reaction to the Famine.

The government tried other schemes, such as a network of soup kitchens. These did afford relief of a temporary nature to over two million people. Then the government decided to transfer the whole problem of Ireland's poor to the Irish landlords through special poor law legislation, which served only to encourage the landlords to evict as many poorer tenants as they could. The government also expanded the workhouse scheme, though not at the same time the size or the number of workhouse buildings, so that by 1848 nearly a million people were in workhouses that normally were capable of accommodating a total of 250,000. All these and other schemes took time, and were administered by – for the most part – honourable but bureaucratic people who stuck rigidly to the rule book, and so numerous victims suffered far more than they need have done because of delays, inefficiencies, mistakes and injustices. What probably caused more resentment and despair than anything was the sight of cartloads of grain and other food products being shipped over to England or elsewhere from healthy Irish fields while Irishmen, Irishwomen and Irish children starved and slid into slow and premature death because the potato had failed.

In telling the story of the Great Famine, hovever briefly, we should not overlook the splendid voluntary relief work done by generous organizations and individuals (the latter, sadly, all too rare among the rich landowner class in Ireland). Among these were the Society of Friends, or Quakers, who did so much with their own soup kitchens, the British Relief Association sponsored by well-wishers in Britain who were anxious to put funds where the government would not, and by several agencies in the United States and Canada, in particular the New York Irish Relief Committee which alone sent nearly £¼m. Chief among the individual families who dug deep into their pockets and provided food and work were the Guinness brewing family at Stillorgan Park, Co. Dublin, and the earls of Courtown, who set examples to their fellow landlords that were not followed.

The 1846 failure added another dimension to the famine, a panic to get out of the country altogether, and thousands of cottiers and labourers gathered their families and such possessions as they had (generally no more than the ragged clothes they stood in) and made the journey to harbours and docks to buy or beg passages on ships bound for Britain, or Canada and the United States. Greedy and unscrupulous middlemen – and to their shame, some ships' captains and owners, too – took their money and put to sea in old and decrepit ships carrying two, three or four times the numbers of passengers considered safe for voyaging across the Atlantic, ships in which more than one-fifth of the starving and debilitated emigrants

23. Irish emigrants leaving home – the priest's blessing (*Illustrated London News*, 10 May 1851)

perished before they even saw the New World. Coffin ships they were aptly called. Nearly a million people emigrated to Britain and North America between 1846 and 1849.

What did the famine leave in its wake? Paradoxically, it led to considerable improvements in agricultural economy, which had started to emerge even when the potato failures were at their peak. The great majority of the victims had been potato-dependents in the rural areas. Their disappearance in such appalling numbers drastically reduced the number of smallholdings and led to a sharp increase in bigger holdings, largely the kind of small family unit that grew crops (cereals as well as potatoes) and also pastured livestock, with the emphasis shifting from crop growing to livestock farming over the years that immediately followed. Before the famine less than 20 per cent of all agricultural holdings were more than fifteen acres in size: by 1851, the figure had risen to over 50 per cent. The proportion of larger holdings (over thirty acres) rose from about 7 per cent to over 26 per cent in the same period. The demand for Irish agricultural produce was high and in the 1850s the yields were particularly good, leading one commentator to consider that Ireland's agriculture was one of the most economically advanced in the world.[2] The fundamental problems between landlords and tenants, however, remained unsolved.

Politically, the effects of the famine were bad for Ireland. There was the deepest anger and resentment against England and its callous response to the distress. As we have seen, the campaign for repeal of the union had been dealt a death blow by the potato failures. In his last months, Daniel O'Connell could only think and talk of the terrible times: 'more awful than you have any notion of', 'a nation is starving', 'Ireland is in your hands . . . if you do not save her, she cannot save herself . . . a quarter of her population will perish unless you come to her relief . . .' This last extract was in the very last speech he made to the House of Commons a few weeks before he died in 1847. How right he proved!

In 1848, before the outbreak of the last of the four fungus attacks, fired by the story of revolutions against existing governments in many parts of Europe, the Young Irelanders made a desperate and foolhardy bid to emulate their European 'brothers' and declared for an Irish Republic. Led by Thomas Meagher,

John Mitchel (son of an Ulster Presbyterian minister) and William Smith O'Brien, a Protestant MP and member of one of the few ancient Irish aristocratic familes still owning land in Ireland, and claiming direct descent from the great Brian Boru himself, they began to drill in the streets, to publish daring, radical articles demanding independence, and to hold meetings to declare solidarity with the Chartists of England who were demonstrating at the same time. The authorities arrested the leaders and charged them with sedition. Mitchel was found guilty and sentenced to transportation, while Meagher and O'Brien were acquitted, and immediately returned to their activities. But the movement was badly organized and badly supported (not surprisingly, when millions were totally preoccupied with starvation and illness). The ranks of the Young Irelanders were infiltrated by government agents and in July 1848 the 'revolt' collapsed in an inglorious scuffle in a widow's back garden cabbage patch at Ballingarry. O'Brien, Meagher and others surrendered, and mercifully were not put to death but transported to join Mitchel in Australia. No sooner had they been despatched than the last of the four potato crop failures struck.

One consequence of the famine was the steady continuation of emigration that had accelerated enormously during the famine years. This more than anything produced the reduction of Ireland's population down to just over four million in the early years of the present century. The bulk of the emigrants settled in the United States where extensive 'colonies' of discontented Irish people hating England grew up, that hatred continuing in succeeding generations of Americans of Irish descent. Another result was a deep widening of alienation between the north-east region of Ulster, largely Protestant, part-industrialized, on the whole better off economically and less affected by the famine because it had been much less dependent on the potato, and the remainder of Ireland.

CHAPTER 11

THE STRUGGLE

FOR

HOME RULE

Ireland lay shocked and hopeless after the Great Famine; she was, wrote Gavan Duffy in *The Nation*, like a corpse on the dissecting table. There was no leadership any more, no great movement, no cause, no political clubs, no heroism and no ideas.

But a country cannot die – and everyone, British as well as Irish, knew what the sickness was. The Irish land system produced poverty instead of riches, hunger instead of food, enmity instead of cooperation and clearly needed to be changed. Tenants had to be enabled to improve their farms without risking an increase in rent or eviction. But it was easier said than done. Almost every member of the British parliament came of a landed family and, while British landlords had little sympathy for their Irish counterparts, whom they thought selfish and irresponsible, they were afraid that any change in the law in favour of Irish tenants would soon cross the water and affect what they considered their own 'just rights of property'; several bills to improve the lot of Irish tenants were drawn up, but all defeated.

Another solution was to sweep out the inefficient and shiftless Irish landlords and replace them with highly skilled British gentleman farmers, who would instruct and encourage their tenantry, and so improve the Irish estates. Encumbered Estates Acts were passed in 1848 and 1849 to make the sale of estates encumbered with mortgages, entails and family settlements easier, and before long many hundreds of Irish landlords, almost bankrupted by the famine, had put their estates on the market. Land became very cheap, but the 300 or so buyers who did move in from Britain were not the good, improving landlords the government had hoped to attract, but speculators, who promptly put the rents up, so they could get the best return possible for their money, and evicted those who could not pay.

Tenants took matters into their own hands. Encouraged by their priests, they began forming tenant protection societies. In Ulster, where the price a tenant could obtain under the Ulster custom for his right of occupancy had fallen very low because of the reduced population, although rents remained as high as ever, Presbyterian ministers helped in the formation of an Ulster Tenant Right Association, which joined with similar associations in the south to form the Tenant Right League. The League commanded many thousands of tenants' votes, and of the Irish members returned to parliament in the general election of 1852, 40 were elected on the tenant right ticket. Within a few months, though, many of them had broken their election pledges to the League. Its members lost heart and eventually it was disbanded. All idea of land reform was shelved.

Then a fresh political impetus came from abroad. Following Smith O'Brien's abortive rising in 1848, thousands more Irishmen had followed the million or so Famine emigrants to America, continental Europe and even Britain herself. The most radical had gone to Paris, where they could study the methods of revolution, and among them were James Stephens, a railway engineer from Kilkenny, who had been an aide-de-camp to Smith O'Brien, and his friend John O'Mahoney, who came of an ancient landowning family with a tradition of rebellion. Both his father and his uncle had been 'out' in 1798.

In 1854 O'Mahoney left Paris for New York, where a quarter of the population was Irish, so he could raise men, money and supplies for a new Irish revolt, and in 1856 Stephens went to Ireland. For the next two years he walked all over the south and the west, an odd figure in his dandified Parisian clothes, searching among shopkeepers, artisans and peasant farmers for past members of political clubs, traces of tenant right societies and remnants of Young Ireland – any dying embers of political fervour that he might fan into a blaze. At first he found nothing, and no sense of nationality. Men of Connacht, for instance, seemed to regard Leinstermen as foreigners, almost as strange as the English or the French. But there was plenty of discontent:

wages were low and landlords as rapacious as ever: and Stephens contrived to harness this discontent in a new patriot movement organized, on the French Revolutionary model, in a number of cells, each unknown to the others to maintain secrecy. O'Mahoney, who had a deep love of the Gaelic past, named the movement after the Fianna, the warriors who had followed the Gaelic legendary hero, Fionn Mac Cumhaill as the Fenian Brotherhood, or the Fenians.

The Fenians were the very opposite of the open, peaceful and constitutional organizations of the 1820s and 1830s, with their aim of orderly and limited change; they wanted separation and revolution, the immediate and total overthrow of British power in Ireland. And they saw no other way of achieving it except by force. They harked back to Wolfe Tone and Robert Emmet; they wished to take the literary violence of Young Ireland and make it real.

Recruits came in slowly at first. Though the Irish people looked favourably on Fenianism, they would not commit themselves. The Catholic Church habitually refused to condone sedition, condemned all secret societies and excommunicated those who joined them. So in 1861 Stephens started a newspaper, *The Irish People*, which was considerably more extreme than *The Nation*, and took other opportunities for advertising the Fenian cause. When Terence Bellew McManus, a Young Irelander who had taken part in the Rising in 1848, died in California, his body was brought all the way to Dublin for burial. Stephens drummed up crowds of between 20,000 and 30,000 people to line the streets and policed them with Fenian horsemen, wearing a uniform of black scarves and armlets. It was among the earliest of those huge funerals, staged to encourage popular support for an underground cause, which have become such a feature of Irish life.

In the same year, 1861, the American Civil War broke out. The Fenians gave up all idea of an immediate rising, but placed their hopes on the experience of warfare that a brigade of American Irish, some 3000-strong, was acquiring. When the war ended in April 1865, these American Irish veterans began filtering back into the home country. And there Stephens had done his work well. He was vain, boastful and opinionated, but a brilliant organizer, and he had brought 200,000 people into the Fenian organization in Ireland. Many were not much more than sympathizers, but 40,000 were armed, after a fashion, and another 12,000 were trained soldiers, serving in the British garrison; Fenianism had infiltrated the British army so thoroughly that one-third of the troops serving in Ireland were sworn Fenians. Yet, when the rising came, the Fenians meant to avoid pitched battles and to fight, not as regular troops, but in the traditional Irish way as guerrillas. Groups of Fenians were to destroy rail and telegraph links, attack police barracks and harass government forces until a Fenian army arrived from America.

In one major respect, however, the Fenians were to break new ground. Since the Famine so many thousands of Irishmen had emigrated that the initial attack need not be made in the mother country. When the Fenian leaders gathered in January 1867 they set up their headquarters in London, not Dublin, and made plans for an initial raid on the English town of Chester. The plan was a daring one. Fenians were to take over the British army barracks and arms store in Chester castle, seize the trains between Chester and the Welsh port of Holyhead as well as the Irish packetboat, and rush the captured arms to Ireland, where the rising would have already begun.

During the morning of 11 February, about a thousand Irishmen travelled by train from Crewe, Manchester, Warrington and other northern English towns, and gathered around Chester station. Then at the eleventh hour John McCafferty, who was in charge of the attack on the barracks, discovered that the plan had been betrayed to the British by an informer. He managed to call off the attack and postpone the rising in Ireland. But the postponement was not to be for long. The Fenians had waited several years for action and, although they knew their chance of success had gone, they were determined, in a desperate, foolhardy way, to carry on with the rising whatever happened. They may have intended to make a grand, heroic, hopeless gesture in the legendary manner, but they ended up with a damp squib.

On 4 March the leadership in London delivered a proclamation to *The Times* which described in the fiery, desperately sincere tones of Young Ireland what the Irish cause was. 'We appealed in vain to the reason and sense of justice of the dominant powers,' the Fenians declared. 'Having no honourable alternative left we appeal to force as our last resource . . . . It is better to die in the struggle for freedom than to continue an existence of utter serfdom . . . . All men are born with equal rights.' They ended by proclaiming an Irish republic. Then the various leaders went to their posts for the rising the next day. But the informer who had betrayed the Chester raid was still with them. He took their plans to the British and in the evening the Fenian commander in Ireland was arrested on Limerick station.

Nevertheless the next night the Fenian, or Irish Republican, army was on the march. Two police barracks outside the Dublin area were taken, and columns of Fenians made their way to various rallying points, which were lit by rockets, but when they marched against the police at central points in the towns and villages, they proved half-hearted. In the little town of Tallacht, fourteen armed police dispersed many hundreds of rebels. In Co. Cork, the Fenians were more successful. They captured a coastguard station and a police barracks, and sabotaged railway lines, derailing the Dublin express. Outside Tipperary they tore up railway lines and telegraph poles. But in Drogheda a thousand Fenians were routed by less than forty police, and in Limerick fifteen police at Kilmallock barracks held off a Fenian attack for three hours until they were relieved.

The rising was badly led, the Fenian leaders endlessly complaining, backbiting and getting drunk in London. They had not prepared, armed or inspired their men. Yet they remained incurably optimistic, inviting the Americans, even after the rising had fallen flat on its face, to 'fit out your privateers' with help from Ireland, just as Wolfe Tone had urged the French to do in 1798. And the Americans, like the French, responded; they loaded a privateer with 5,000 rifles, 1½ million rounds of ammunition and three mounted cannon. In late May the vessel slipped into Sligo bay, but on hearing it would receive no help from the people of Sligo, slipped out again and sailed on southwards. Still the Americans could not find anyone willing to take their cargo of arms and in June, when provisions began to run low, they sailed away again, back to New York.

The Irish Republic, proclaimed at the time of the rising, had elected as its chief executive an American Irishman, Colonel Thomas J. Kelly. On 11 September he was arrested in Manchester with another Fenian, Captain Deasey. A week later a group of about thirty Fenians ambushed a closed prison cart taking them from the police court and released them. Unfortunately in the fracas a police sergeant was killed. Four Fenians were tried and condemned to death for his murder; in English law, not only the man who shot the police sergeant was guilty of murder, but others connected with the attack as well. In the dock, the condemned men spoke, with a kind of poetic heroism, about the wrongs of Ireland. 'I will die proudly and triumphantly', said one, 'in defence of an oppressed and enslaved people.' 'Look to Ireland,' said another. 'Look at what is called the majesty of the law on one side and the long, deep misery of a noble people on the other. Which are the young men of Ireland to respect: the law that murders or banishes their people, or the means to restrict relentless tyranny?' Then all the defendants cried out in a loud voice: 'God save Ireland.' It was this spirit, this devotion of the men who are remembered as the Manchester Martyrs, which won the people of Ireland to the Fenian cause.

In December there was another rescue attempt. The Fenian organizer of armament supplies had been arrested after the rising in March and sent to Clerkenwell prison in London. A group of Fenians, trying to get him out, blew up part of the prison wall, demolishing several houses and damaging many more. The explosion failed to rescue the Fenian prisoner but killed twelve Londoners and seriously wounded thirty more. The British were outraged – and frightened too. They saw the Irishmen in their midst as a menace, a danger that had to be contained. Special constables were recruited in England's towns and cities to combat the Fenian threat; there were more than 5,000 of them in London alone. For a long time the Irish had hated the British: for a spell, the British hated the Irish. But at the same time the wiser among the people of Britain became aware, as they have never been before, of the problems of Ireland. And the Irish found that they had, most unexpectedly, a powerful British champion.

A few days after the Clerkenwell explosion the leader of the British Liberal party told a public meeting that Irish violence was the result of Irish grievances, and it was Britain's duty to remove those grievances. The speaker was William Ewart Gladstone, a devout Christian who saw his mission in life as serving God in the highest manner possible, and that, he believed, was through politics. He started his parliamentary career in the 1830s with the usual British misconceptions about Ireland; he resigned from the government when Peel repealed the Corn Laws and in 1853, as chancellor of the Exchequer, he made swingeing increases in Irish taxation. Until then, Britain had been generous to her poorer neighbour in the matter of taxation but Gladstone, like other Britons, was afraid that Ireland, if treated lightly, might become dependent upon Britain. He wanted Ireland to stand on her own feet.

Yet for many years he had regarded Ireland as wronged. In 1845 he had spent some time travelling in Europe and European statesmen, particularly the French foreign minister, Francois Guizot, had given him their view that the condition of Ireland was a blot on the honour of Britain. 'Ireland, Ireland!' Gladstone had written in torment to his wife, 'that cloud in the west, the coming storm, the minister of God's retribution upon a cruel and inveterate and but half-atoned injustice!' He was haunted by Ireland, and after the Clerkenwell explosion he felt the plight of the Irish must be put before the British people. There was to be a general election the following year, and he decided the Liberal party should fight it on an Irish issue. His speech after the explosion had been the opening salvo in the election campaign.[1]

At one time Gladstone had wanted to be a clergyman rather than a politician, and it is not surprising that the issue he chose to fight the election on was the disestablishment of the Protestant Church of Ireland. Brought up a conforming Protestant, an Evangelical, he nevertheless had a broad sympathy with the Nonconformists who bulked large in the Liberal party, and could carry them with him in his view that the establishment of a Protestant church in a predominantly Catholic country, with all the endowments and revenues that establishment brings with it, was an injustice. Non-conforming Liberals could appreciate how bitterly the established Protestant church was resented by the Irish people as a constant reminder of the Protestant Ascendancy.

A census taken in Ireland in 1861 had shown just how small the Protestant minority was. Out of a population of 5¾ millions, Catholics accounted for 4½ millions and members of the established Protestant church a mere 700,000. Over half of them lived in Ulster, in Leinster they comprised 11 per cent of the population, in Munster 5 per cent and in Connacht 4 per cent. When Gladstone put those figures before the British people and

245

described Catholic grievances, the Liberals were returned with a sizeable majority. Gladstone was chopping wood, a favourite pastime, when he was given the election result. 'My mission is to pacify Ireland', he told his informant. And for the remaining thirty years of his life, he bent his very considerable moral and intellectual energies to the task of reform in Ireland.

In 1869 Gladstone's bill for the disestablishment of the Church of Ireland was passed. All the church's vast properties, its lands, buildings (except churches in use) and tithes were confiscated by the state; one half was set aside to provide annuities for the clergy, schoolmasters and various ecclesiastical officials, and the other to be administered for the benefit of the people of Ireland – for the relief of poverty, encouragement of agriculture and fisheries, and endowment of higher education. At the same time the annual grant to the Catholic priests' college at Maynooth and the *regium donum* paid to the Presbyterian ministers were commuted to lump sums; no Church in Ireland was to be endowed in any way by the state.

Much Church land had, of course, to be sold. Instead of making simple, straightforward transactions with the landlord class, the traditional way of handling such a situation, Gladstone slipped clauses into the act which gave the Church's tenants the chance to buy their holdings with the help of mortgages given at a fixed interest rate of 4 per cent, and over the next ten years over 6,000 tenants out of 8,400 took advantage of the offer and bought their holdings. Nowadays, when many western countries are rapidly becoming property-owning democracies, Gladstone's approach seems normal enough, but in the nineteenth century it was revolutionary.

The clauses in the Irish Church Act governing land tenure discreetly paved the way for a comprehensive Irish Land Act, piloted through parliament in 1870, which gave the Ulster custom the force of law and tenants not covered by the custom the right to compensation for improvements. In the past the landlord was always presumed to have made any possible improvement and the onus of proving otherwise placed on the tenant. Under the new act the positions were reversed. The tenant was presumed to have made the improvement (which, in Ireland, was much more likely) and the burden of proving the contrary was placed on the landlord. If evicted, a tenant was entitled not only to compensation for improvements but also – and this was a new idea – for disturbance, provided his lease was for less than thirty-one years and his rent had been paid up to date. The principles involved were far-reaching. Landlords regarded their relationship with their tenants as a personal one, which the state should not interfere with, but Gladstone had recognized that tenants needed protection and, more importantly, that the cultivator of the land had an equal interest in it with the landlord collecting rents from it. Yet the act failed; the safeguards Gladstone had put in the bill were taken out by the Lords and Irish tenants found their position virtually unaltered. Competition for land was still so fierce that a prospective tenant was often prepared to buy his way into a tenancy, spending money which could have been used for improvements, and occasionally to compensate a landlord for the cost of evicting a sitting tenant. Evictions without compensation were still easy enough. If a landlord raised the rent beyond what the tenant could pay, but not so much that a court would deem the increase exorbitant, he could evict the tenant without compensation when, inevitably, he fell into arrears.

Disappointed Irishmen turned, once again, to the idea of having their own parliament, not, as the Fenians had advocated, after a complete separation from Britain, but as part of a federal arrangement. Irish MPs would still sit at Westminster, where foreign and imperial matters would be handled, but an Irish parliament would be responsible for domestic affairs, including the land laws. When Gladstone had disestablished the Church of Ireland, he had tampered with the Act of Union, which linked the Protestant Churches of England and Ireland. Irishmen had been much encouraged by that; it showed the union was not, after all, sacrosanct.

In 1870 a prominent Irish lawyer and MP, Isaac Butt, drew together a group of nationalist Irishmen, some of them Protestants dismayed by disestablishment, some Catholic Liberals and others Fenians, and formed them into a Home Government Association. Three years later he superseded it with the Home Rule League. Rather like O'Connell's Catholic and Repeal Associations, the Home Rule League had very low subscription rates, a member paying £1 a year and an associate member as little as a shilling, and very soon it became a genuinely national organization. In the following year, 1874, it put up its own candidates in a general election, fifty-nine of whom were elected, a large enough number to make quite an impact in the House of Commons, provided they all acted in concert. Most, however, took the line that party discipline threatened their integrity, and Butt was not the man to coerce them. He had money troubles, so he spent a great deal of time away from London working at the Irish bar, and he held the naive belief that the best way of gaining points from the British was by being nice. Consequently the Irish Home Rule party failed completely to pierce the indifference of the new Conservative government – until J. C. Biggar, a Belfast pork butcher, newly elected to parliament, came to the fore. Tough, ugly, hunchbacked and shrewd, Biggar developed a technique of obstruction in the Commons which infuriated his British opponents; he would hold the floor for hours, interspersing a speech with extracts from the newspapers, or passages from acts of parliament, until the government programme of business was thoroughly snarled up.

But Biggar was too plebeian to become party leader. The Irish gentry who comprised most of the parliamentary Home Rule party would not follow a tradesman with a rasping Belfast accent. They wanted a leader with presence and an impeccable background as well as dynamism. And before long they found him. In April 1875 a new member was returned for Meath in a by-election – an Anglo-Irishman, a Protestant with an English education, tall and handsome with an air of cool self-confidence besides great force and determination. He was Charles Stewart Parnell.

A Parnell had moved from Cheshire to an estate in the Wicklow mountains during the seventeenth century; in the eighteenth century, his descendants had come to identify themselves wholly with Ireland and 'the Protestant nation'. They had opposed the Act of Union and supported Catholic emancipation. Parnell's mother was an American whose father had fought as an admiral against the British in 1812. She was virulently anti-British and her son adopted her attitudes. Yet he had some English characteristics himself. Though intense and passionate, with the burning eyes of a fanatic, he had an English pride and reserve; at the beginning of his political career he was so nervous and inarticu-

24.   Charles Stewart Parnell, (courtesy of the National Gallery of Ireland)

late that his backers despaired. He had to push himself to become a fluent and forceful speaker.

Parnell first took notice of politics when the Fenians rose in 1867; he was only twenty-one at the time and had no thought of joining them but, imbued with his family's tradition of nationalism, he felt a fervent sympathy for their aims. He saw

249

the Home Rule party as an alternative to Fenianism; more practical, less extreme, open instead of secret, using constitutional methods rather than physical force. But the intensity of Fenianism always struck a chord in him.

In the House of Commons, Parnell joined Biggar in the obstruction of parliamentary business. He had no respect for parliament, and in those days the smooth running of the Commons depended on a certain respect, even affection, from its members. The two major parties, the Liberals and the Conservatives, both had to form governments and take the responsibility of power, and it was an unwritten rule that the opposition would not impede a government bill, even a bad bill, if the result would be serious disorder, or revolution. It followed, as a second unwritten rule, that parliamentary business must not be unduly disrupted. The Irish Home Rule party, though, had no intention of taking part in any British government; its members were not afraid of revolution and believed that public disorder could have advantages. It was a third force in the Commons which had everything to gain from disrupting and obstructing the other parties, and its skill and ingenuity was put into developing obstructionist tactics.

Parnell and Biggar disrupted government business by endlessly proposing innumerable amendments to bills, making interminable speeches and calling for unnecessary divisions. In 1877 desperate government ministers sought Butt's help, and Butt was foolish enough to give it. He delivered a public rebuke to Parnell, saying with great indignation that he disapproved entirely of the conduct of the honourable member for Meath. It was the end of him; he had committed the cardinal sin of rebuking an Irishman in a foreign assembly, and afterwards his leadership of the Home Rulers was merely formal. He declined in both health and influence, and in 1879 he died.

Parnell's force and energy were winning him new adherents. The Fenians decided to make a New Departure, as they called it, by supporting a constitutional nationalist movement, provided it pressed for land reform with protection for tenants and, ultimately, peasant ownership. Militant extremists, financed from America, and the non-violent, almost respectable Home Rulers were finding a common ground in the struggle of the wretched peasantry against their landlords.

By the late 1870s the peasants were, once again, desperate. For some years after the Famine agriculture had prospered, exports to Britain fetched good prices and, although rents were still high, Irish farmers had been making headway. Then both Britian and Ireland had begun to suffer in the face of American competition. American grain and beef flooded into Britain, causing a depression among the farmers there, who could no longer find adequate markets, and forcing down British imports from Ireland. Irish rents did not, however, follow prices downwards. Thousands of tenant farmers fell into arrears and found that the Land Act of 1870 afforded them no protection against eviction. Then in 1877 the potato crop failed; only one million tons was produced instead of the usual four millions. The people of Connacht in particular, who were still almost entirely dependent on the potato, found themselves starving. In 1878 the potato failed again. Peasants who were already in debt to the banks, or, if they were not substantial enough to deal with banks, the village gombeen men, or moneylenders, found they could not pay their debts or the rent. The number of evictions rose sharply; whereas 400 families had been evicted in 1877, over a thousand were turned out of their homes and farms in 1878 and again in 1879, and over 2,000 in 1880. Taking an average of six people to a family, in that year 12,000 people were rendered destitute.

25.   An eviction scene (courtesy of the National Library of Ireland)

26. Powerscourt House, an Ascendancy mansion (courtesy of the National Library of Ireland)

In 1879 an Irishman personally scarred by eviction arrived in Mayo from America. He was Michael Davitt, a 31-year-old Fenian who had never forgotten how his own family had been thrown out onto the hillside in that same county in 1852, when he had been an impressionable child of five. The family had emigrated to England, Michael had begun work as a child labourer in a Lancashire cotton mill, and when he was eleven lost an arm in an industrial accident. He grew up with a deep and almost obsessional sympathy for the poor, almost inevitably joined a revolutionary group, the Irish Republican Brotherhood, and in 1870 was sentenced to fifteen years' hard labour for possessing arms. As he could not wield a pick or a shovel in the stone quarries, because of his lost arm, he was harnessed to a cart, as if he were a horse, for his day's work. He was released in 1877, after seven years of such labour, and went to America, where he contacted the Fenians before returning to his native Mayo.

Irish peasants had reacted to the rise in the number of evictions with a sharp increase in agrarian outrages, from the maiming of sheep and cattle to the burning of farm buildings and attempts on the lives of landlords and their agents. A period of extreme disorder, which became known as the Land War, had begun.

Davitt harnessed the discontent he found in Mayo by forming the peasants into a Land League, which would protect its members from rack-renting and eviction and, in the long term, press for peasant ownership. Then in June he asked Parnell to address the new Land League at Westport.

Since the days of O'Connell, all politicians had known how powerful a peasant organization could be. Parnell came to Westport, at the request of the unknown Davitt, and told the assembled peasants they must stand up to their landlords. Then in October he agreed to become president of the Land League, partly to check the extremism of Davitt, who had thoughts of nationalizing the land, and partly so that he could use the power of the Land League in the cause of Home Rule.

In March 1880 the Conservative government fell. It had passed two Irish Education Acts, one encouraging secondary education with government grants and the other establishing a royal university which awarded degrees to students from all other colleges and universities in Ireland, including a Catholic university set up in Dublin in 1854. Otherwise the Conservatives had given no thought to Ireland; they had no Irish policy.

Gladstone returned to power at the head of a jubilant Liberal party. He was still deeply concerned with the moral issue of British misrule in Ireland and aware that another Irish land act was necessary, but he intended to proceed with caution and thoroughness. The Conservatives had set up a commission to inquire into the workings of his 1870 Land Act, and he wanted to consider its findings before presenting another bill. But Parnell had enjoyed a personal triumph in the general election and brought sixty-one Home Rulers with him to the House of Commons, doubling the size of the parliamentary Home Rule party. He would not wait and one of his supporters brought in a private member's bill to protect tenants from eviction for non-payment of rent due to crop failure. Gladstone showed his sympathy by incorporating the gist of the bill into a government measure, a considerable triumph for Parnell's party, but, though the bill passed through the Commons, the House of Lords, that bastion of the landlord interest, threw it relentlessly out.

There was an inevitable reaction in Ireland. As landlords went on evicting their starving tenants, the membership of the Land League went up until it numbered thousands. Money poured in from America and the League, ignoring the state judiciary, set up its own courts to deal with disputes according to its own rules. In September Parnell told a gathering of peasant farmers at Ennis, in Co. Clare, how they could get their way. 'When a man takes a farm from which another has been evicted,' he said, 'you must show him on the roadside when you meet him, you must show him in the streets of the town, you must show him at the shop counter, you must show him in the fair and at the market-place, and even in the house of worship, by leaving him severely alone, by putting him into a sort of moral Coventry, by isolating him from the rest of his kind as if he were a leper of old, you must show him your detestation of the crime he has committed.' A few days later the tactic was applied, not against a land-grabbing tenant farmer as Parnell had envisaged, but Captain Charles Boycott, an evicting land agent in Mayo. No local men would help Captain Boycott harvest his crops, so he brought fifty Orangemen from Ulster to do the work, and the British army provided 7,000 troops, one-sixth of the garrison in Ireland, to protect them! When Boycott visited Dublin, he was refused admission by the city hoteliers. His nerve failed him, and he left Ireland altogether for a while.

The Land League was not a violent organization, as the Whiteboys and the Defenders had been. Davitt, a gentle soul, would not willingly countenance violence, and Parnell was no revolutionary. But the members of the Land League included extreme and desperate men, and their agitation often led to violent outrages. Ireland was becoming ungovernable and Gladstone agreed, with the greatest reluctance, to put forward two coercion bills, one suspending Habeas Corpus yet again and the other giving the authorities the power of arbitrary arrest: anyone could be arrested and held indefinitely without trial, public meetings could be prohibited, newspapers seized and the right to trial by jury suspended.

Parnell and his supporters fought the bill with dogged anger, employing every kind of obstruction; the debate on the Queen's speech at the opening of parliament was prolonged for eleven nights and a single debate spun out, through the stamina and belligerence of the Irish members, to forty-one hours. The coercion acts were passed, nevertheless, in February 1881. They were the price exacted by parliament for land reform. Yet the controversy surrounding them brought the appalling condition of Irish peasants to the attention of the British public. In December 1880 General Gordon, remembered now for his stand in Khartoum in 1885, wrote a letter published in *The Times* in which he described the state of the people in most parts of Ireland as worse than that of the Indians or the Chinese. 'I believe that these people are made as we are,' he declared, 'that they are patient beyond belief, loyal, at the same time broken-spirited and desperate, living on the verge of starvation in places in which we would not keep our cattle.' The British people were not hard-hearted, and they warmed to the Irish peasants' cause.

In April 1881 Gladstone introduced a land bill which went very much farther than his Land Act of 1870. He conceded the demand of the Land League for what were popularly known as the three Fs: Fair rents, Fixity of tenure so long as the rent was paid and, as a perpetuation of the Ulster custom, the tenant's Freedom to sell his right of occupancy. Land tribunals were set up to fix judicial rents, which would remain unchanged for fifteen years, and tenants who wanted to buy their holdings were offered long-term government loans. The law had successfully intruded upon the contract of landlord and tenant, the power of the landlords was broken and peasant ownership seen in the distance. The Land Act of 1881 was very far-reaching indeed.

The Irish were not grateful. The House of Lords had shown, only a year earlier, that it would not countenance security of tenure for tenants in arrears with their rent, whatever the circumstances, and in order to push his bill through, Gladstone had had to leave out provision for hardship cases. Yet there were 130,000 tenants in Ireland, mostly in the west, who were in arrears and starving, because the potato crop had failed again. The atmosphere was already embittered by the coercion acts, and except in Ulster, where the British connection was so greatly valued, the new Land Act was greeted with hostility.

The government needed Parnell's support to make the act a success. But Parnell was performing a circus act, balancing the extremists in Ireland against the right-wing constitutionalists and, at the same time, juggling with the aspirations and uncertainties of the peasants: a satisfied peasantry could lose interest in his real aim of Home Rule. He made highly provocative speeches, hurt Gladstone by describing him as a 'masquerading knight-errant', and advised tenant farmers to put test cases to the land tribunals, set up under the Act, and not to pay a penny in rent until the cases had been heard. The chief secretary, W. E. Forster, concluded that Parnell was trying to wreck the Act and reacted with undue precipitation. In October he arbitrarily arrested Parnell, as he had the power to do under the coercion acts, and clapped him into Kilmainham jail!

Nothing could have suited Parnell better. His prestige in Ireland and America soared, and within a few days the Land League had organized a strike against rents. Forster suppressed the Land League (which, Parnell wrote, was 'breaking fast' anyway) and a wave of violent disorder swept the country. Parnell had remarked dryly that in his absence Captain Moonlight, that is, the secret societies, would take over, and he became seriously afraid that extremists would bring the country to a state of anarchy. Negotiations were tentatively opened between Parnell and Gladstone in November, culminating the following spring in what came to be known as the Kilmainham Treaty, whereby Parnell agreed to use his influence to calm the country (though he had been imprisoned as an agitator!) and secure the acceptance of the Land Act in return for an amendment to the Act giving protection to tenants suffering hardship, a relaxation of the coercion acts and his own release. On 2 May, after six months' imprisonment, he left Kilmainham and the next day crossed to England. He made a brief appearance in the House of Commons and then, on 6 May, brought Davitt back to London from Portland, on the south coast, where he had served a similar term of imprisonment under the coercion acts. On the same day Lord Frederick Cavendish arrived in Dublin to take up the post of chief secretary, which Forster had left. During the evening Lord Frederick was walking in the Phoenix Park, just outside the vice-regal lodge, with his under secretary, T. H. Burke, when both men were set upon and stabbed to death.

Parnell was so shocked that he wrote immediately to Gladstone offering to resign his seat: an offer Gladstone declined. Then, with Davitt and others, he worked on a manifesto, addressed to the Irish people, denouncing the murders in the strongest terms. The following day he repeated his condemnation in the House of Commons. The murders had been committed by a group of extremists who belonged to a secret society, composed mostly of members of the Irish Republican Brotherhood, called the Invincibles. Parnell was deeply afraid that the murders would destroy the Kilmainham Treaty but, paradoxically, they helped him make the final break with extremism that he wanted. When the government brought in another coercion act, to satisfy British public opinion, Parnell opposed it vigorously, becoming once more the champion of Irish rights while, at the same time, cooperating with the government over the Land Act. Henceforth he was to be free to pursue his objective of Home Rule.

In October 1882 the suppressed Land League was superseded by the Irish National League, a nation-wide organization for collecting funds and putting up candidates for a Home Rule party. The party machinery worked extremely well; when the next general election was held in 1885, Parnell and the Home Rule party won every seat in Ireland outside eastern Ulster except Trinity College, Dublin. Eighty-five members from Ireland were Home Rulers and another returned in England, an Irishman representing a Liverpool constituency. They formed a highly disciplined parliamentary party, with each member committed to sit, act and vote *en bloc*, or resign his seat.

Gladstone had committed himself to what was vaguely termed 'justice for Ireland' as part of the Kilmainham Treaty, and had never made any secret of his support for Home Rule. But he was not yet ready to devise a Home Rule bill, and a few months before the election Parnell had withdrawn his support from the Liberal government, which was promptly voted out of office. A minority Conservative government carried on for a few months while arrangements were made for a general election, and rewarded Parnell for his decisive help in ousting the Liberals by giving the Irish a new Land Act, making it easier for tenants to buy their holdings and landlords to sell. Parnell, in return, advised Irishmen living in England to vote Conservative when the general election came.

The Liberals may have lost twenty seats as a result. In any event, their majority over the Conservatives was eighty-six - exactly the number of seats Parnell commanded! The Irish leader had, very adroitly, put Home Rulers into the position which all third parties in the House of Commons hope to attain: he held the balance. He could keep either party out of office, or, if he combined with the Liberals, he could put the Liberal party in.

Gladstone believed fervently that all peoples capable of self-government should have it; he had championed self-government in Italy, the Balkans and other European countries dominated by a powerful neighbour and he could not, with any consistency, hold back self-government from Ireland. Parnell, it is true, twisted his arm – but it was Gladstone's own conscience, his deep moral sense, that drove him forward. In January 1886 he formed a government, with the support of the Irish Home Rule party, and prepared his first Home Rule bill providing for the government of Ireland by an executive in Dublin responsible to an Irish parliament, under the over-all authority of the imperial parliament at Westminster. But he could not win acceptance for it; too many Britons still thought of the Irish as enemies, a violent and untrustworthy people who, in a war, would stab Britain in the back. Leading members of the Cabinet resigned, the Liberal party split, one section becoming Liberal Unionists, and in June the bill was defeated. In July Gladstone took the issue to the country in a general election. Parnell kept his eighty-five Home Rule members from Ireland intact but lost his Liverpool adherent, the Protestants of Ulster remained firmly Unionist and in Britain the Liberals were overwhelmingly defeated.

The Irish remained full of hope. Parnell had, as Gladstone put it, 'set the Home Rule argument on its legs', and his prestige in Ireland and America could not have been higher. Before long he had the sympathy and admiration of the British too. There was a bad harvest in much of Ireland in 1886, many tenants found they could not even pay the judicial rents fixed under the 1881 Act, and Parnell's Irish National League organized what was called the Plan of Campaign, which ingeniously proposed that hard-hit tenants should offer their landlords lower rents and, if the landlords refused them, pay no rent at all, but put the money into a fund for those who were evicted. When the new Conservative government tried to destroy the Plan of Campaign through the coercion acts, its high-handed arrests and imprisonments, of priests among others, were reported and bitterly criticized in England. British members of parliament went to Ireland and watched evictions: and when they described what they had seen Parnell, as the champion of the Irish poor, became the hero of the hour. Then in 1887 *The Times* opened a vicious campaign against him, accusing him of inciting the Irish to crime and, in particular, condoning the Phoenix Park murders. The government set up an inquiry which went on for the best part of two years until, in February 1889, a Dublin journalist broke down in the witness box and confessed to forging the letter on which the accusation was based. When Parnell appeared in the House of Commons shortly afterwards, the entire opposition rose to its feet and gave him a standing ovation. He was on the crest of a wave.

Then the wave broke. In 1880 Parnell had met Mrs Katherine O'Shea, the English wife of Captain William O'Shea, an Irish Home Rule member of parliament. They had begun a passionate love affair and in 1882 Mrs O'Shea had given Parnell their first child, a girl who died a few weeks later. In 1883 and 1884 two more daughters had been born to the couple. O'Shea, an impecunious, somewhat raffish character who had his own affairs on the side, was a complaisant husband so long as complaisance could help his career, and Parnell did all he could to further the captain's ambitions. But in 1886 O'Shea resigned his parliamentary seat and his antipathy to Parnell revealed itself.

Mrs O'Shea had an exceedingly rich aunt, Mrs Ben Wood, who provided for her and her children and made an allowance to O'Shea. Mrs Wood had made a will in her niece's favour, but if any breath of scandal had reached her ears, she would have changed it. In 1886, when O'Shea left parliament, Mrs Wood was ninety-three, and the gallant captain no doubt believed she would soon die. He could not attack Parnell while she lived. But Mrs Wood did not die until 1889 and it was the end of that year, on Christmas eve, that O'Shea started divorce proceedings.

In Victorian England divorces were so rare they were given a great deal of attention. They were heard at great length in open court and fully reported in the newspapers. The puritanical Nonconformists who made up the bulk of the British Liberal party were so shocked by Parnell's adultery over so long a period with the wife of a colleague[1] that Gladstone was in danger of losing their support for Home Rule. So he gave the Irish Home Rule party an ultimatum. Parnell's continued leadership was, he said, likely to render his own leadership of the Liberal party 'almost a nullity'; the Irish party must choose between Parnell as its leader and Liberal support for Home Rule.

'Resign – marry – return' was the laconic advice sent to Parnell in a telegram from South Africa by Cecil Rhodes. But Parnell was determined to hold onto the leadership. The Irish Home Rule party debated Gladstone's ultimatum for several days in a committee room in the House of Commons and then voted by 45 to 29 against Parnell, but he would not accept the decision. He allowed the tightly disciplined, highly effective Home Rule party, which he himself had moulded, to destroy itself by splitting.

He married Mrs O'Shea in June 1891 and set up house with her in Brighton. From there he carried on a frenetic campaign in Ireland, making the crossing from Holyhead every week to travel the country, address meetings and try to drum up support. But the Catholic bishops were against him, as Victorian Britain had been, and his standing in Ireland slumped; his nominees were defeated at three by-elections, and when he appeared at North Kilkenny, in support of one of them, he had mud flung in his face. Yet he struggled on, a gaunt, proud figure, until his health gave way. He suffered from a rheumatism so severe it damaged one arm. In September he spoke in the pouring rain in Co. Galway, bareheaded and with his arm in a sling, and then sat about in sodden clothes before leaving for Dublin. A few days later he arrived home in Brighton, collapsed and died. He was worn out at the age of forty-five.

The fall of Parnell was a heavy blow to Gladstone – the heaviest, he said, he had ever received. For five years he had been battling for Irish Home Rule, 'laboriously rolling uphill the stone of Sisyphus', as he put it. When he lost Parnell's dynamic support, the Irish Home Rule party split, the stone broke away and rolled back to the bottom of the hill. Gladstone, the Grand Old Man of British politics, was eighty-one: too old to roll it uphill again.

Nevertheless he did introduce a second Home Rule bill in February 1893. He fought for it throughout the spring and summer, and forced it through the House of Commons in September. But he knew, as did everyone else, that the Lords would reject it: as indeed they did, by an overwhelming 419 votes to 41. Very reluctantly, Gladstone accepted defeat; he neither resigned nor went to the country, but quietly allowed the bill to drop. The next year, when he was eighty-five, he retired from the leadership.

Gladstone failed to give Ireland Home Rule, but he taught the British people, most of whom had known nothing whatsoever about Ireland, that Irish problems, the misery and misgovernment of Ireland, were for them to deal with. For upwards of twenty years he made Irish difficulties the leading concern of a major British party, and used the votes of ordinary British people, most generously given, to bring about a transformation in the lives of Irish peasant farmers which continued to unfold many years after he had gone.

In 1895 the Conservatives and Liberal Unionists joined forces in a government that was to last for the next ten years. Home Rule still aroused passionate feelings in Ireland, as much among that quarter of the population which abhorred it as the majority which was in favour. Ireland still had about a million Protestants, half of them Presbyterians living in Ulster and the rest still forming an ascendancy, or ruling class.

The Orange League remained the focus of Protestant unionism, but in 1867 the more aristocratic Ulster Defence Association had been formed as well. To Protestants, Home Rule meant Rome Rule, and that they would resist with fanaticism. In 1886, after a visit to the thriving industrial city of Belfast, a leading Conservative, Lord Randolph Churchill, wrote in a letter words which are still remembered: 'Ulster will fight, and Ulster will be right.' Then in 1892, when Gladstone was about to bring in the second Home Rule bill, the duke of Abercorn, who had large estates in Ulster, stated with aristocratic simplicity: 'We will not have Home Rule.'

The Conservative government took up Gladstone's great cause of land reform; they intended, in a famous phrase, to 'kill Home Rule by kindness'. When Ireland had become a land of independent smallholders, the theory went, the contented peasantry would become stable, law-abiding, and probably conservative in their politics, in so far as they were interested in politics at all. Home Rule would be forgotten. The Conservative chief secretary,

Arthur Balfour, pushed on with the sale of land and procured large sums of government money for the peasants to buy it with. Then in 1903 the last of the land acts was passed, making it extremely beneficial to landlords to sell their estates and for tenants to buy them. Wyndham's Act, as it was called after George Wyndham, chief secretary at the time, in succession to Balfour, cut through the red tape which had sometimes discouraged tenants from buying, and gave landlords generous bonuses if they sold out completely. In the next ten years Irish landlordism, that compound of selfishness, exploitation and neglect, was ended.

It seemed to outsiders that Irishmen need not be Irish any more; they owned their land, they were becoming richer, they shared in imperial trade and they had equal rights with Britons in both Britain and Ireland. In the Middle Ages the English language and customs had been impressed upon the Irish in an attempt to render them English; in the latter half of the nineteenth century it happened again. Only English was to be used in Irish schools, English and not Irish history was to be taught and, throughout the country, English games were to be played.

But it is both the curse and the blessing of the Irish that they do not forget. The restless craving for nationality was not to be put down. With political life almost dead, Irishmen revived their ancient culture. In 1884 Michael Cusack, an Irish civil servant, founded the Gaelic Athletic Association, which organized local competitions in Gaelic football and hurling, an Irish game played with curved sticks and a ball, rather like hockey, and forbade its members to take part in such English sports as tennis, polo, croquet and cricket. And in 1893 a Gaelic League was formed, to encourage the use of the Irish language and preserve the literature which, over 1500 years, had been composed in that language.

The first president of the Gaelic League was Douglas Hyde, an Anglo-Irishman born and brought up in Sligo, where the country people still spoke Irish. He heard Irish poetry recited, saw the manuscripts which the peasants still treasured, and wrote poems in Irish himself. He attacked the absurdity of teaching schoolchildren to read and write in English, when the language they spoke was Irish; children went into school intelligent and bright-eyed, he wrote, with a vocabulary of some 3,000 Irish words, and came out of it dulled into stupidity and with a vocabulary of some 600 English words, which they misused.

Hyde and the Gaelic League also intended to promote a modern Anglo-Irish literature, written in English on Irish themes, particularly the myths and poetry of Ireland's past. Hyde was friend and mentor to a young poet, who came from an artistic Anglo-Irish family in Dublin; he was William Butler Yeats. Yeats was already publishing poems in English based on Irish folk tales, and during the next few years he became the chief progenitor of what came to be called the Irish Literary Renaissance. Yeats did not speak Irish himself and knew far less about Irish peasants than Hyde, but he was deeply attracted by their imaginative ability to see all around them what he called a 'dim kingdom' of ghosts and fairies, sorcerers, enchantresses and god-like heroes. A romantic and a visionary, he was moved by the beauty of this ancient, magical Ireland, and called it his land of heart's desire.

In Co. Galway there lived a middle-aged widow who shared the literary ideals of Hyde and Yeats. She was Augusta, Lady Gregory, and from 1896 onwards her home, Coole Park, became the meeting place of a brilliant literary coterie. Yeats and Lady Gregory founded an Irish Literary Theatre, which was to present Irish themes, often from folklore, in new plays written in English. In 1904 it moved into the Abbey Theatre, Dublin.

But the venture was not well received. For years the Irish had been hurt and shamed by Ascendancy portrayals of Irishmen as simpletons, the butt of endless jokes, and they wanted the new literature to give an idealized, propagandist view of Ireland, similar to that put out by *The Nation* in the 1840s. Dublin audiences felt that Yeats, though an idealist, did not always get his ideals right. Yeats' play, *The Countess Cathleen*, was about an Irishwoman who sold her soul to demons during a famine so that the people should have food. Catholics in the audience could not bear the idea of an Irishwoman selling her soul under any circumstances and criticized Yeats and Lady Gregory for being both Protestant and Anglo-Irish. Yeats' next play, *Cathleen ni Houlihan*, was nationalist in a more direct way and aroused intense emotion. The sad and beautiful woman who symbolizes Ireland appealed to audiences to remember the heroes of the past, Sarsfield, Emmet and Wolfe Tone, and spoke of those who might die for Ireland in the future. Then a new dramatist, John Millington Synge, joined the Irish Literary Theatre. Yeats had portrayed the Irish peasant as a romantic innocent; Synge's view was more realistic. His peasants spoke a beautiful language, an adaptation into English of their native tongue, but they were human and sometimes amoral - and that gave offence. Synge's first play, *The Shadow of the Glen*, was about a peasant woman with a much older husband, who ran away with a 'travelling man', or tramp. Audiences protested that Irishwomen were the most virtuous in the world and literature should ignore those few who fell by the wayside. Then in 1907 the Abbey Theatre put on Synge's play *The Playboy of the Western World*, which showed Irish peasants hospitably entertaining a lad who said he had murdered his father, and there was tumult in the audience. From the second night onwards there were disturbances in the auditorium and even rioting in the streets outside. On the last night of the week's run, 500 police were stationed in and around the theatre!

Twenty years later the plays of Sean O'Casey, a genius from the Dublin slums, caused the same shock and dismay. O'Casey's plays were anti-hero, anti-war – and when his satiric *The Shadow of a Gunman* was put on in 1925, the audience could not take the grim humour, or the realism, and they rioted. And in the following year, when in *The Plough and the Stars* Synge showed slum-dwellers as the victims of a nationalism the audience regarded as heroic – vegetables, shoes and chairs were hurled at the stage!

But Yeats, as the doyen of Anglo-Irish literature, believed passionately that the artist with his vision, and not the propagandist, must have his way. The Irish Literary Renaissance burst the bonds which tried to contain it, and the plays of Synge and O'Casey, besides Yeats' own poetry, spread to Europe and America. And so, eventually, did the work of another great writer on the Ireland of the period, the novelist James Joyce. Joyce, like Synge and O'Casey, despised folksy myth – 'history as her is harped' – and wrote about Dublin and Dubliners with his own musical, humorous and streaming, endlessly streaming realism. His fictional autobiography *The Portrait of the Artist as a Young Man* appeared in serial form in 1914–15, and his mammoth novel

Ulysses, about a single day (June 16, 1904) in the life of its Dublin hero, in 1922. Joyce's books were banned in England and burned in New York; Jung, the great psychologist, said he was schizophrenic, mad. Yet he has been acknowledged for many years now as a great innovative master. And Joyce, along with Yeats, Synge and O'Casey, produced for the first time an Irish literature, written in a beautiful, poetic and Irish-flavoured English, that helped Irishmen, the most literary of peoples, to feel and remain Irish.

CHAPTER 12

BLOOD
SACRIFICE

Yet the Irish passion for politics, the fierce political nationalism which had inspired the uprisings of 1798, 1848 and 1867, was by no means dead. While Yeats believed it was the task of Ireland to uplift her voice for spirituality, ideality and simplicity, a columnist called Cuagan, the dove, writing in a new newspaper, *The United Irishman*, declared that the work of Ireland was to uplift herself. Cuagan was the penname of Arthur Griffith, and *The United Irishman* a nationalist newspaper founded by him in 1897. A printer by training, the Catholic descendant of a Protestant farming family in Ulster, the young Griffith soon made a name for himself as a brilliant, scathing journalist in the tradition of Young Ireland and *The Nation*.

Griffith was not very dovelike; he was tough, rugged, courageous and single-minded. He focused the whole of his attention on separation from Britain – a total separation which, in his view, could only be achieved when Ireland had disentangled herself economically, as well as politically, from the sister nation. He had no time for military risings, which had always failed, and none for constitutional solutions. The policy he put forward was a new one: non-cooperation. In 1902 he called on Irish MPs to withdraw from Westminster and set up their own parliament in Ireland, to be called the Council of Three Hundred. If its decrees were carried out by county councils and other local bodies, British rule would soon become impossible and then, Griffith believed, the British would peacefully withdraw.

In 1907 Griffith put his ideas at the core of a new movement called Sinn Fein, which in English means Ourselves, or, as it is often put more emphatically, Ourselves Alone. The aim of Sinn Fein was stated very broadly as the re-establishment of the independence of Ireland, an objective so deliberately vague that all nationalists, from the most tentative Home Ruler to an extreme separatist, could subscribe to it. Griffith was hard-headed, practical – and he gave Sinn Fein some very practical objectives, such as tariff protection for Irish industry, the establishment of Irish merchant shipping lines and Irish control of the civil service. He also urged the Irish not to buy goods which yielded a tax to the British exchequer and, above all, not to join the British army. But this humdrum programme did not catch the imagination of the Irish people; only 150 Sinn Fein clubs were formed and they had very few members. The Irish Republican Brotherhood seemed a more dynamic organization to most nationalists. And then, in 1909, Home Rule became once again an active issue.

The Irish parliamentary party had remained divided for nine years after Parnell's downfall in 1890. Then the centenary of the rising of 1798 was celebrated, and in the following year the Boers in South Africa began a war of independence against the British. The two events shamed the Irish MPs into a reunion, and in 1900 they elected as their leader John Redmond, an astute politician and a good orator, able to make his presence felt in parliament. Like Parnell, Redmond was a country gentleman from Co. Wicklow, but, unlike Parnell, he could not dislike the English; he admired Britain as a great imperial power and was convinced the Irish cause would be best served by constitutional action within parliament.

In January 1906 the British Liberal party won a landslide victory against the Conservatives. British Liberals had become considerably less interested in Home Rule since Gladstone's departure, and they did not need the support of the Irish parliamentary party. Nevertheless Sir Henry Campbell-Bannerman, their leader, offered the Irish 'a little, modest, shy, humble effort' at Home Rule in the form of an Irish Council, which Redmond promptly rejected. After another general election in 1910, however, the position was very different. The Liberals defeated the Conservatives by a mere two votes, producing the hung parliament that the Irish party had exploited so successfully in the past. Redmond did the obvious thing; he gave the Liberals his support on condition they brought in a third Home Rule bill. Herbert Henry Asquith, the new Liberal leader, accepted – but he, like everyone else, knew that first he had to break the power of the House of Lords, which would undoubtedly use its veto against a third Home Rule bill, just as it had against the earlier Home Rule bills and Gladstone's land bills. Asquith was not only concerned with the impediment the House of Lords represented to reform in Ireland, but in Britain as well; the Lords could stop any legislation they chose, setting aside the recommendations of the elected Commons, which represented the will of the people. The constitution had to be amended and brought up to date. Another general election produced a deadheat between the Liberals and Conservatives, who had 273 votes each. Redmond and the Irish party put Asquith and his Liberals into office, just as Parnell had put Gladstone into power, and Asquith threatened the Lords with a massive creation of Liberal peers if they refused to amend their right of veto. They had no choice but to give in and were granted, instead of the veto, the right to delay legislation for up to two years. It meant that any legislation passed by the House of Commons for three years running would automatically become law.

To the Irish nationalists of Dublin, the south and the west, the way ahead seemed clear. Redmond and the Irish party had the whip hand in the House of Commons, Asquith would have to bring in a Home Rule bill and in three years' time Ireland would be free. But Irishmen were by no means all nationalists. The Protestant businessmen of Ulster, and a sprinkling of middle-class Protestants throughout Ireland, set a supreme value on the British connection. While nationalists talked of tariffs to protect the Irish economy, Irish industrialists, those who owned Dublin's breweries and the mills, shipyards and distilleries of Belfast, were convinced that, if they were shut out of the British free trade area, with its access to raw materials and markets, their prosperity would disappear. Lower down the social scale, Protestant farmers, agricultural labourers and workers in industry felt beleaguered; they competed fiercely with Catholics in the cities, especially Belfast and Londonderry, and in the countryside, where, numerically, they only just held their own. The Orange Order, 'a barrier to revolution and an obstacle to compromise', was generally led by a Unionist MP. After the defeat of Gladstone's first Home Rule bill in 1886, there was sporadic fighting between Catholics and Protestants; by the end of the summer, thirty-two people had been killed, 442 arrested and 337 policemen injured. In 1893, when the second Home Rule bill was on its way through the House of Commons, Unionists threatened to resist by force.

Then in 1910, when the third Home Rule bill was about to be introduced, the Unionists found themselves a most formidable leader. He was Sir Edward Carson, a brilliant lawyer from – not Belfast, but Dublin; a southern Unionist convinced that any break in the connection with Britain would be a disaster. Maintenance of the Union was, he said, 'the guiding star of my political life'. Born in 1854, he had been educated at Trinity College and then in 1877 begun a meteoric career; in 1892 he became Irish solicitor-general and was elected MP for Dublin University, and then in the following year he transferred his law practice to London, where he was soon famous for his cross-examinations. It was his exposures that led to the downfall of Oscar Wilde.

Carson was a Protestant, as befitted his Anglo-Irish background, but by no means anti-Catholic; he never shared the Ulster Orangemen's antipathy towards Catholics, but seized upon it, and the fear that lay behind it, as factors he could manipulate. If Ulster would fight – then, Carson believed, Home Rule would become impossible for the rest of Ireland. And he began playing an extremely dangerous double game.

The groundwork had been done by doughty champions of Ulster's right to be Unionist. James Craig, MP for East Down, the wealthy son of a self-made whiskey millionaire, was prepared, paradoxically enough, to go into armed rebellion to preserve the British connection. 'The morning Home Rule passes,' he told a vast Orange audience, 'we must ourselves become responsible for the government of the Protestant province of Ulster.' And no less a man than the new leader of the Conservative party in Britain, Andrew Bonar Law, was an Ulsterman by descent and by sympathy; though born in Canada, he had all the dour stubbornness of the Ulster Scots and a ruthless determination to keep

Ulster for Protestants. He hoped to use the intransigence of Ulster to destroy Home Rule for the rest of Ireland, as Carson did; and yet, unlike Carson, he was ready from the beginning to bargain for the exclusion of Ulster from Home Rule. He was prepared to accept partition.

The Home Rule bill, when at last it came in 1912, was mild enough; it gave Ireland a separate parliament with control of most of her internal affairs, though not the police or customs and excise, and left defence and foreign affairs in the hands of the British parliament, where some Irish MPs would still sit. The bill was a step in the right direction in Redmond's view, and he accepted it. Carson, on the other hand, saw it as the first move towards total separation and fought against it.

When negotiations are being carried out between an imperial power and a colony, there is generally broad agreement within the imperial power as to what should be done. Over the Home Rule bill, Asquith and Bonar Law were almost as far apart as Redmond and Carson. Asquith had a mild Liberal sympathy for Home Rule, fortified by a sharp twist of the arm from Redmond, while Bonar Law was fighting stubbornly to preserve a corner of Ireland for the Protestant Ascendancy. Conservatives supported Bonar Law when he described the Home Rule bill as part of a 'corrupt parliamentary bargain', Asquith giving Redmond Home Rule in exchange for office, regardless of the rights and interests of Ulster Protestants. Then a Liberal MP tried to break the deadlock by proposing the exclusion of the four counties of Ulster with Protestant majorities – Antrim, Armagh, Londonderry and Down – and Carson, with extreme deviousness, voted for it, because he believed Ireland would founder economically without them and the demand for Home Rule would be dropped.

Meanwhile Carson, Craig, and Bonar Law were addressing huge public meetings in Ulster, playing on the fears and prejudices of Protestants and whipping up Unionist support. Bonar Law called upon Orangemen and Unionists in Londonderry to relive the siege of 1689. 'You are a besieged city,' he said. 'The government have erected a boom against you, a boom to cut you off from the help of the British people. You will burst that boom.' Carson, tall, grim and hatchet-faced, with a flair for the theatrical gesture, promised another vast audience that he would resist 'the most nefarious conspiracy' to bring in Home Rule. And in

September 1912 he staged a massive ritual signing, by tens of thousands of Ulster Unionists, of a Solemn League and Covenant that they would 'use all necessary means to defeat the present conspiracy to set up a Home Rule parliament in Ireland and solemnly and mutually pledge ourselves to refuse to recognize its authority.'

For ten days meetings were held all over Ulster; men paraded with dummy rifles to the music of fife and drum. Then on 28 September, known thereafter as Ulster Day, the shipyards and factories of Belfast were closed, services held in the Protestant churches and an immense procession, bearing aloft a faded yellow silk banner said to have been carried by king William's troops at the battle of the Boyne, made its way through the streets of Belfast to the Town Hall, where Carson put his signature to the Covenant, followed by the rest of the vast concourse. Desks where people could sign covered a third of a mile of corridor. Within a few days, 218,206 men had signed the Covenant and 228,206 women. Many signed in their own blood.

In January 1913 the Ulster Unionists decided to raise an Ulster Volunteer Force, reminiscent of the Volunteers of Grattan's time, consisting of 100,000 men between the ages of seventeen and sixty-five. In June a retired English general from the Indian army, Sir George Richardson, was employed to take command of them. In Ireland it was not illegal for bodies of men to be drilled; in earlier days, landlords had drilled their tenants regularly to provide a defence against Whiteboys and Defenders. But Ulster was recruiting a national army, and that was certainly illegal. Almost without intending it, Carson was setting up a separate state, armed to defend its independence; while professing loyalty to Britain, he was planning a rebellion against British laws. As Winston Churchill, a junior minister in Asquith's cabinet, put it, Carson and the Unionists of Ulster were engaged in a 'treasonable conspiracy', albeit a conspiracy to remain subject to Britain.

In the House of Commons, Carson set the ball rolling for 1913 with a proposal that all nine counties of Ulster should be excluded from Home Rule, and Churchill, still swayed by the Unionist sympathies of his father, Lord Randolph, declared such exclusion 'very different from blocking the path of the whole of the rest of Ireland'. Redmond riposted desperately that 'Irish nationalists could never be consenting parties to the mutilation of the Irish nation'. Nevertheless, by the end of the year he had weakened – he could not believe that the British parliament, which he so much admired, would let Ireland down; and when Asquith, unable to shake the redoubtable Carson, wavered in his support for Home Rule, the Irish nationalist leader accepted, as its price, a temporary measure of exclusion: individual Ulster counties were to be allowed to opt out of Home Rule, first for three years and then for six. Carson, failing to see that no British parliament was likely to 'coerce' Ulster after six years of partition, declared furiously that Ulster would never accept 'a sentence of death with a stay of execution of six years', and stormed off to Belfast, where many people expected he would set up a rival government.

Early in 1914 the government decided there had to be a show-down, and in the third week of March security was tightened up at barracks, arms depots and stores in the north. Troops were ordered to key positions and warships sent to Northern Ireland waters. But many of the British army officers stationed in Ireland were Anglo-Irish and had Unionist sympathies; some of them came from Ulster. When Sir Arthur Paget, the commander in chief in Ireland, was in London receiving his orders, he had raised the question of what he was to do about senior officers with Unionist leanings who would not like to 'coerce' Ulster, and he was told that officers whose homes were in Ulster could make themselves scarce while military action was being taken. Any other officer who refused to serve would be dismissed. Paget went to the Curragh, a wide, grassy plain in Co. Kildare, which was the main British army camp in Ireland, and put it to officers not domiciled in Ulster that they could either serve against Ulster, if required, or be dismissed. General Sir Hubert Gough, who commanded a cavalry brigade, told Paget that he and fifty-nine of his officers would prefer dismissal. The same choice was given to infantry officers and most of them preferred dismissal as well. It was not mutiny; the officers had been given an unprecedented choice. But when General Sir Douglas Haig, the commandant at Aldershot, Britain's major military base, declared that the officers in his command, too, would resign if they were used against Ulster, the British army as a whole showed up as unreliable. It could no longer be counted on to carry out the policy of the elected government without question, as a professional army ought to do.

It was Carson, not Asquith, who had an army behind him. The Ulster Volunteers, already highly motivated, were being moulded into a most efficient fighting force. They had been drilled with dummy guns, but real weapons were on their way. Several thousand rifles, some machine guns and a great deal of ammunition had been brought into Ulster in 1913, before the government banned such imports in December. But they were hardly enough, and in 1914 thousands more guns were smuggled in from Germany, paid for by Irish and English subscriptions. During the night of 24 April, just after the incident at the Curragh, 24,600 rifles and three million rounds of ammunition were landed at Larne, Bangor and Donaghadee. The Ulster Volunteers prevented police and customs officers from interfering, and within twenty-four hours the smuggled weapons had been distributed, with extraordinary efficiency, all over Ulster.

Nationalists in the south had watched the goings-on in the north with incredulous amusement; they were convinced Carson, the Dubliner, was bluffing. Still, not to be outdone, in November 1913 they formed their own defensive body, the Irish Volunteers. The organizing committee included a poet, Patrick Pearse, who ran a nationalist school outside Dublin, and an idealistic Anglo-Irishman who had just retired from the British foreign service, Sir Roger Casement.

The Irish Volunteers were regularly and openly drilled, as the law allowed, but remained an insignificant force until the incident at the Curragh had taken place in April 1914. Then southern nationalists smelled danger, and within a few weeks the numbers of the Volunteers swelled until, at 108,000, they exceeded those of the Ulster Volunteers. But the Irish Volunteers were still unarmed and, as Pearse commented wryly, 'the Orangeman with a rifle is a much less ridiculous figure than the nationalist without a rifle'. If the Irish Volunteers were to match their rivals, more than fine talk was needed.

There was no stockpile of arms in nationalist Ireland. The Irish Republican Brotherhood had received considerable sums of money over the years from Clan na Gael, its counterpart in

America, but it was still too amateurish an organization to have made much use of them, and it fell to a group of Anglo-Irish Liberals and Home Rulers, many of them friends of Casement, to raise money for arms. At the end of May, Erskine Childers, an English sympathizer who had spent much time in Ireland, took the money off to Germany to buy rifles and ammunition. Childers was a British army officer with a knowledge of military equipment, and also an excellent yachtsman, who knew the North Sea coast of Germany well; he had spent much time there collecting material for his novel *The Riddle of the Sands*, which was one of the earliest and most famous of spy stories. And the idea occurred to the London fund-raising committee that arms could be brought into Ireland less obtrusively in private yachts than in other vessels. So 1500 rifles and 45,000 rounds of ammunition were taken in a tug from Hamburg to a point off the Belgian coast, where they were transferred into Childers' yacht *Asgard* and another, smaller, yacht *Kelpie*, which belonged to Conor O'Brien, the grandson of Smith O'Brien, the leader of the 1848 rising. Both yachts were so full below decks that their crews, mostly Anglo-Irish men and women with a taste for adventure, could hardly move around; there were 900 rifles in *Asgard*, as well as boxes of ammunition, and 600 in *Kelpie*. Neither yacht had an engine or a radio, yet they had to arrive at their destinations dead on time: *Kelpie* had to meet another yacht, *Chotah*, off the Welsh coast and transfer her cargo, as O'Brien was too well known a nationalist not to be watched at an Irish port, and *Asgard* had to reach the port of Howth, on the north side of Dublin bay, at the exact time the Irish Volunteers expected her.

For three weekends running, the Irish Volunteers had gone on route marches to various places around Dublin, and when, on the Sunday of the fourth weekend, a thousand Volunteers converged on Howth, the police paid no attention. A number of taxis arrived at the jetty, ostensibly bringing young men and their girlfriends on a Sunday outing. Then *Asgard* slipped into the harbour; she was right on time. It took half an hour to unload the boxes of ammunition and many of the rifles into the taxis; the Volunteers shouldered what rifles were left and carried them off towards Dublin.

The Howth police had, by this time, notified Dublin castle of the arms landing and at Clontarf, on the way into Dublin, the

274

Volunteers were halted by police and a detachment of a hundred men of the King's Own Scottish Borderers, sent out from their Dublin barracks.

Landing arms was illegal, but carrying them was not; in Ulster, the Volunteers paraded their arms quite openly. The police and the Volunteer leaders began to argue – while the main body of the Volunteers slipped away with their guns across the fields. The Borderers were told to load their rifles and a crowd gathered, which jeered and hooted at them and then, after a wait of an hour or so, followed them the three miles into Dublin. The crowd grew larger when it reached the city, and when the column of soldiers turned into Batchelor's Walk, one of the quays along the river Liffey, it was followed by a hail of bottles and stones. A senior officer, who had come to meet the soldiers, ordered the rear of the column to turn and face the crowd. He told five or six men to load, not knowing that the whole detachment had already loaded their rifles at Clontarf, and to be ready to fire. Then he raised his hand for silence, so that he could address the crowd. The soldiers, mistaking his signal, fired; they were tired and angry, fed up with the constant taunting, and probably only too eager to mistake their officer's signal. Three people were killed and thirty-eight wounded, one of whom later died.

Irish hatred of England flared: people felt they had been fired on for demanding Home Rule, and the old sense of oppression and wrong welled up once more. Redmond could no longer make any concessions to the Unionists and the Unionists, under Carson, would make none to him. But Home Rule could not be delayed; the House of Lords had rejected the bill twice and could not reject it again. Then, within a week of Erskine Childers' brilliantly successful gun-running operation and four days after *Chotah* had landed her cargo at Kilcoole in Co. Wicklow, the First World War broke out; Britain joined in an international holocaust which already involved France, Germany, Austria, Belgium, Russia and Serbia. Redmond, determined that the Home Rule bill should become law, war or no war, decided a generous gesture towards Britain was the right and politic one and promised the House of Commons, in emotional terms, that Ireland would support Britain 'in every trial and every danger', also telling Asquith privately that he could not answer for Ireland's loyalty if Home Rule were delayed. On 18 September the Home

Rule bill became law – though it was, at the same time, suspended for twelve months, or until the end of the war. Nationalist Ireland was wild with delight; bonfires were lit, bands played and the Irish Volunteers paraded. It seemed that at last, after so many centuries, Ireland's bitter conflict with England was over.

Redmond fulfilled his promise. He went round Ireland and urged Irishmen to help Britain in a war 'undertaken in defence of the highest principles of religion, morality and right', by joining the British army. He was met with generous enthusiasm, and in little over a year the number of Irishmen serving in the British army had risen from 22,000 to 130,000, including 30,000 reservists; by the end of 1915 81,000 Irishmen, most of them Catholic, had voluntarily thrown in their lot with Britain.

The British were grateful and warmed towards the Irish. But in June 1915 Asquith formed a coalition with the Conservative party. Redmond was offered a job in the government but, as an Irish nationalist, had to refuse it, while Bonar Law joined the Cabinet and Carson became attorney general. The Home Rulers were out in the cold, and people in Ireland began remembering that Carson had described the Home Rule Act as no more than 'a scrap of paper'.

To make matters worse, those thousands of Irishmen who had responded so gallantly to Redmond's appeal and joined the British army to fight the Germans, were finding themselves treated with scant respect. Lord Kitchener, the secretary of state for war, was an Englishman brought up in the west of Ireland and imbued, as a child, with the notion that the Irish were an inferior race, while his officers had already shown themselves to be largely Unionist. Men from the north were looked upon more favourably than those from the south; they were permitted to take the red hand of Ulster as a divisional emblem, whereas a similar division of southern Catholics, raised by Redmond, was refused permission to emblazon the Irish harp on its colours. Similarly, officers from the Ulster Volunteers were given commissions immediately, but those from the Irish Volunteers, including Redmond's son, were not given commissions until they had gone through a course of training. To cap it all, the War Office insisted on describing all Irishmen and Irish units, despite the national status they now had, as British.

The Irish began to feel as if the Home Rule Act, so immediately suspended, might indeed be no more than a 'scrap of paper' – a chimera. Redmond's following and authority in the country began to fall away and, as always when parliamentary action seemed to have failed, the separatists, the extremists and the physical force men came to the fore.

The Provisional Committee which ran the Irish Volunteers had been secretly infiltrated by members of the extremist Irish Republican Brotherhood right from the start; the poet Patrick Pearse had become an IRB member almost as soon as he joined the Volunteers. The IRB had never liked Redmond's recruiting campaign for the British army. They did not believe Ireland should be dragged into foreign wars, and Griffith's organization, Sinn Fein, agreed with them. In September 1914 the secret IRB men resigned from the Provisional Committee and the Irish Volunteers split. The great majority, about 150,000, stayed with Redmond as the National Volunteers and 13,500, mostly Dubliners, followed the anti-British separatists, keeping the name Irish Volunteers, though they were soon popularly known as the Sinn Fein Volunteers. Their leader was Eoin MacNeill, an academic who belonged to the Gaelic League and saw the Ulster Unionists as a body determined to be autonomous, whose example should be followed. 'They have rights who dare maintain them,' he wrote. Nevertheless he had no intention of using his Volunteers unless the government failed to implement the Home Rule Act after the war; he did not know the extent to which the Irish Volunteers, even his own governing committee, had been infiltrated by militant extremists of the IRB.

At the turn of the century, the IRB had been more or less moribund: a group of elderly republicans forbidden, by a clause in the IRB constitution, to take any action unless the majority in Ireland wished it – which they never did. Then in 1901 Denis MacCullough, the eighteen-year-old son of an Ulster Fenian, was almost casually admitted to membership at the side door of a pub, and he brought in another Ulsterman, Bulmer Hobson, who had organized a youth movement, a kind of nationalist Boy Scouts, known as the Fianna. Sean MacDermott from Leitrim was the next notable recruit; a born intriguer and quite ruthless, he was already travelling the country as a full-time organizer for Sinn Fein. Then in 1907 Tom Clarke, a most fanatical revolutionary, was co-opted onto the IRB's governing council. Born in 1857, he was in his twenties when he became involved in a dynamiting campaign in England and was sentenced, in 1883, to penal servitude for life. After fifteen years, he was released and went to America, where he was soon in touch with the Clan na Gael. When he returned to Dublin, he kept a tobacconist's shop and, 'with his large, cheap spectacles, drooping moustache and frail figure', to quote the historian J. S. L. Lyons, 'he looked the small tradesman's part to perfection.' His looks, of course, belied him; they were more or less a disguise. For this meek shopkeeper was the all-important linkman between the IRB and America.

This reanimated IRB had infiltrated MacNeill's council of the Irish Volunteers with three young revolutionaries who, directly in the Irish tradition, were poets. The most flamboyant was Joseph Plunkett, who came of a very well-known Irish Catholic family; delicate in health, he had spent much of his boyhood seeking the sun in Sicily, Malta and Algeria, and grew up deeply attracted to poetry, philosophy and, incongruously, soldiering. In 1910 he had met Thomas MacDonagh, who had already had a play about war with England, *When the Dawn is Come*, produced at the Abbey Theatre. Plunkett and MacDonagh were soon collaborating on more work for the Abbey, as well as the production of a politico-literary magazine. And since 1908 MacDonagh had been helping Patrick Pearse, the third revolutionary on the council, with his nationalist and bilingual school, St Enda's.

Pearse shared Yeats' view that the role of the Gael was to be 'the saviour of idealism in modern intellectual and social life'. He went much farther too. Inscribed over the portals of St Enda's was a saying attributed to Cú Chulaind, the legendary hero of Ulster, who had fought to the death against invaders, which read: 'I care not though I were to live but one day and one night, if only my fame and my deeds live after me.' The words were a motto, an injunction, for, in a deeply romantic way, the three poets were ready to follow in the footsteps of Cú Chulaind. Pearse said with some truth that 'nationhood is not achieved otherwise than in arms', and all three came to the view that there must be an insurrection in Ireland. They knew that in military terms it was bound to fail, but developed a strange, almost mystical view of the inevitable bloodshed. 'Bloodshed is a cleansing and a sanctifying thing'. Pearse wrote, 'and the nation which regards it as the final horror has lost its manhood.' In an uncannily prescient blueprint of what was to follow, they saw sacrifice, a blood sacrifice similar to Wolfe Tone's rebellion of 1798, as a way to revivify Ireland and reach, eventually, success and freedom. They saw such a blood sacrifice in religious terms, as a kind of crucifixion, the shedding of the blood of Christ to redeem mankind. When Pearse looked at his personal situation, he saw victory in death, in *not* surviving, and he brought himself, through a series of moving poems, to a tranquil acceptance of that fate.

There were other groups stirring in Ireland besides self-sacrificing poets. When Redmond's National Volunteers and the IRB-infiltrated Irish Volunteers paraded beside Parnell's grave on 11 October 1914, the twenty-third anniversary of the lost leader's death, they met a third force there, in uniform and bearing arms; and later in the same day, the National Volunteers were embarrassingly confronted by the same small band, flourishing swords and bayonets. It was the Irish Citizen Army.

There were many thousands in Ireland to whom Home Rule, independence, nationhood – whatever people chose to call it - meant very little. They were the working people in the cities, the dockers, the millworkers, the brewery men, the carters, the coalmen, whose waking thoughts were taken up by the fierce struggle for existence. For, since tenant-farmers had begun buying their farms, they had been replaced as the most down-trodden people in Ireland by the urban poor. In 1914 about 63 per cent of the population of Dublin lived in appalling squalor, mostly in decayed Georgian mansions left over from Dublin's heyday in Grattan's time. Almost half the city's working-class families had only one room to live in, and over a third of the rooms let out were occupied by more than six people. As many as ninety people often lived in a single house, without lighting, heating, or a decent water supply. There would be one tap for everybody in the backyard, near two privies, which served not only the occupants of the house but passers-by as well. Human excrement piled up, and was carted away by corporation employees. But those who could not find a room in a tenement house fared even worse; they lived in shelters and had no sanitation at all. It is not surprising that tuberculosis, dysentery and all the other diseases which follow upon very poor living conditions thrived, and Dublin's infant mortality rate was the highest in the United Kingdom.

Nevertheless, those without work in the countryside flocked into the cities; there, they believed, opportunities were to be found. Employers, with so many clamouring for work, exploited the situation by demanding long hours for very low wages. The smaller employers were often, like the slum landlords, ardent Home Rulers because they felt that, with independence, they were unlikely to suffer outside interference. So the poor had to look beyond nationalism for help.

The labour movement hardly existed in Ireland. With so much poverty and unemployment, people were afraid to form trade unions – until a labour leader in the grand, heroic mould came on the scene. He was James Larkin, born of an Irish family which had been driven by poverty to emigrate and settled in Liverpool. As a child, Larkin had earned what shillings he could to eke out the family income and then, when he grew up, worked in the Liverpool docks, became an active socialist and general organizer of the National Union of Dock Labourers. A gigantic, simple man, he had a deep compassion for the poor and a furious hatred of the employers who exploited them.

He came to Belfast in 1907, founded the Irish Transport and General Workers Union and within a few months had the city in turmoil; there were strikes and lockouts involving not only the dockers but carters, coalmen and some of the police. Larkin even persuaded Belfast's Catholics and Protestants to combine against their employers! Then in 1908 he moved on to Dublin, where the plight of the poor was far worse than in industrialized Belfast, and organized three strikes which brought his members higher wages. His union spread to Cork, Limerick, Galway and other port towns, and the membership rose rapidly, from 4,000 in 1911 to 8,000 in 1912 and 10,000 by the middle of 1913.

In 1910 Larkin was joined by another socialist, James Connolly, who had the same boldness, the same large heart, and very much the same background. The Connolly family, like the Larkins, had emigrated from Ireland as a result of poverty, and James had been brought up in Edinburgh, where his father carted manure for the corporation. When he was fourteen, James had joined the British army for seven years, mostly spent in Ireland. Then he became interested in Marxism, obtained the job of paid organizer of a Dublin socialist club and founded the Irish Socialist Republican party. He believed that Irish nationalism would never amount to much unless the welfare of the people were bound up with it.

Larkin's strikes had won substantial pay rises for dockers and agricultural workers. In 1913, with Connolly's support, he demanded more money for Dublin's tramway workers, and when the employer, the United Tramway Company, refused to recognize the union, retaliated by calling a strike on 26 August, during the week of the Dublin Horse Show, which was the most important event of the year for most Irishmen. The strike spread rapidly - but when Larkin tried to prevent an unsympathetic newspaper, *The Independent*, from being distributed, the Employers' Federation, which was some 4,000 strong, locked out all employees who belonged to Larkin's union. By the end of September some 25,000 men were off work and 100,000 people (including the strikers' families) faced a grim winter. Larkin, an imaginative and flamboyant orator, was arrested for using inflammatory language and then released on bail. He tried to address the crowds again, a battle began between police and pickets, two people were killed and several hundreds wounded, including 200 policemen. Then, as if to emphasize the point that the living conditions of the poor were intolerable, two tenement houses collapsed and several more people were killed and injured. The British TUC refused to take sympathetic strike action and Larkin, always impulsive, broke with them. Financial contributions from Britain, which had been considerable, dwindled away and in the New Year of 1914 the wretched strikers, half-dead with hunger and cold, trickled back to work. In October Larkin left Ireland for America, where he remained for the next nine years.

Connolly remained behind. In November 1913 he had gathered together a tiny band of 200 striking men and drilled them, partly to give them some activity and partly to provide a defence force for the strikers against the police. It was a private army, and would have been disbanded as illegal in Britain, but with large

Volunteer forces openly parading in both north and south, it was never even noticed. When the strike was over, it was disbanded until Sean O'Casey, who was still a general labourer and not yet a dramatist, revived it. From that time onwards the Irish Citizen Army, as the little force was called, was dedicated to the Marxist principle that 'the ownership of Ireland, moral and material, is vested as of right in the people of Ireland'.

England's difficulty was, once again, Ireland's opportunity. In August, 1914, the Irish-American Clan na Gael asked the German ambassador in the United States to aid a rising in Ireland. Sir Roger Casement happened to be in America at the time, and it seemed fitting that he should visit Germany on behalf of the Irish extremists; the year before he had written an article declaring that he hoped for an Anglo-German war and a German victory, because he believed it could bring about Ireland's independence.

Clan na Gael funded him and in October he arrived in Germany. His aims were three: to persuade the Germans to declare their sympathy and support for Irish independence, to secure German support, with troops and arms, for a rising, and to raise an Irish brigade to fight against Britain from amongst Irishmen who had been taken prisoner while serving in the British army. He had some success. The Germans declared publicly that, even if their troops were to invade Ireland, they would not come as conquerors; they also agreed to send arms. But the attempt to recruit an Irish brigade failed lamentably. The Germans collected together 2,000 Irishmen from among their prisoners of war, but Casement managed to convince hardly any of them that they would serve the Irish cause by changing sides. They saw Casement as a traitor and despised him accordingly. After several months of effort, he had only persuaded fifty-five men to join him and only ten of them turned out to be genuine nationalists. The rest were rogues and opportunists.

Casement fell into despair. He was a selfless romantic, completely dedicated to the Irish cause, but vague and impractical. The Germans lost interest in him and he himself began to have doubts: perhaps the Irish had no real desire for freedom? During the early months of 1916 he was ill, suffering a mental and physical collapse. Then in March he was told that the extremists in Ireland were moving: within the next few weeks they would rise. He concluded they must have misjudged the outside support they would have and decided to return to Ireland, to give a warning and prevent an insurrection, if he could, and to fight alongside them if he could not.

In Dublin, MacNeill was struggling to hold the extremists back. Redmond's Volunteers, though still nominally a huge force, hardly counted any longer as the more vigorous elements had been creamed off into the British army, and MacNeill felt it was essential that his own Sinn Fein Volunteers, now numbering some 16,000, be preserved, along with the tiny Citizen Army, to secure Home Rule. If a rising were defeated, they would be broken up; and defeated, MacNeill was sure, a rising would be. There were about 6,000 British troops in Ireland, as well as an armed Royal Irish Constabulary of 9,500. The Volunteers drilled, marched about Dublin and made mock attacks on public buildings, but they were only partially armed. They could not win.

But MacNeill was becoming little more than a front man, and his remonstrances were ignored by a secret IRB Military Council within the Volunteer command, consisting of Pearse, MacDonagh, Plunkett, Connolly (who shared their feeling that a rising would be worthwhile, whatever happened, for its moral effect), an almost unknown extremist from Galway named Eamonn Ceannt, Sean MacDermott and Tom Clarke. The Military Council decided in January 1916 that the rising its members had wanted for so long should take place on Easter Sunday, 23 April, and Pearse gave orders for Volunteer manoeuvres to begin on that day.

Though prepared for defeat, the Military Council was aiming for success, and for that the foreign help which Casement had tried to obtain seemed essential. The Germans had refused to send troops, as the seas around Ireland were controlled by the British navy, but they agreed to send a consignment of 20,000 rifles in a German steamship, *Aud*, disguised as a Norwegian trawler. *Aud* was to rendezvous with a German submarine carrying Casement off the Kerry coast on 20 April, the Thursday before Easter, and then land her cargo.

But the Military Council wanted the German arms landed and distributed immediately after the rising, not before it, in case the British authorities discovered them and were alerted. A message was sent to the Germans via America (all communication with Germany followed this circuitous route) instructing *Aud* to delay her arrival until the night of 23 April. The message never reached *Aud*, as she was already at sea and had no radio, but on 18 April the Americans happened to have raided the German embassy in Washington, found the message and cabled its contents to the British in Ireland. The Military Council had made no contingency plans after changing its instructions to *Aud*, and when she arrived off the Kerry coast during the afternoon of 20 April there was no pilot-boat to meet her, as originally arranged; the Irish pilot saw her but, reckoning that she could not land her cargo for another three days, ignored her. *Aud* cruised up and down the coast all through Thursday night and into Friday morning, when she was intercepted by British warships and ordered into Cobh harbour (then called Queenstown) on the coast of Cork. On the Saturday morning, as she steamed towards the port, her captain raised the German flag, put his men into lifeboats and scuttled her, sending her cargo of arms to the bottom.

The German submarine carrying Casement, having failed to rendezvous with *Aud*, put Casement with two companions into a rubber dinghy, to row ashore in Tralee bay. As they went, the dinghy was swamped and Casement half drowned. He recovered lying among the sand dunes along the beach, but a few hours later was picked up by the police and lodged in Tralee gaol, before being sent on to Dublin and then London for the trial for treason which he knew was inevitable.

With the German arms gone, the failure of the rising was certain. MacNeill tried vainly to stop it, and put a notice in a leading Sunday newspaper, *The Irish Independent*, cancelling the Easter Sunday parades. But the Military Council went over his head and summoned all their followers for the Monday. From early morning men, and women too, converged on Liberty Hall, the headquarters on the river Liffey of the Irish Transport and

General Workers Union. The Citizen Army assembled in its full strength, but the Irish Volunteers were thin on the ground. They had not expected a summons after the cancellation of the parades the day before, and only 1,300 of them turned out.

The army that assembled was shabby and ill-armed. Few could afford the full green uniform, and most could do no more to show they were soldiers than sling a bandolier over one shoulder and tie a yellow badge on the left arm. Their weapons were ill-assorted too. More men carried pikes than rifles, and such rifles as there were, were mostly out of date. Some were Italian, but far more were German Mausers smuggled into Ireland by Erskine Childers in *Asgard*. The best had come by various illegal routes from the British army. There were also large numbers of single-barrelled shotguns, such as farmers used.

This motley, variously armed horde was surprisingly well trained and well drilled; it formed columns and wheeled smartly at the command of its officers. Between eleven and twelve o'clock, detachments marched out to occupy strategic sites around the city – the Four Courts, the South Dublin Union and the Mendicity Institution, which were both workhouses, Jacob's biscuit factory, Boland's bakery and St Stephen's Green. At midday a detachment of the Citizen Army fired the first shot outside Dublin castle; it killed the policeman on duty and allowed the insurgents to enter and lob a home-made bomb into the guardroom. It failed to go off, but the six soldiers eating their lunch inside were easily overpowered and tied up. Then the rebels withdrew; they did not realize there were no other soldiers in the castle, only two officers, and Sir Matthew Nathan, who ran the executive in Ireland, was sitting unprotected in his office only twenty-five yards from the captured guardroom. They left, and took over instead various buildings which commanded the castle entrance from outside, and cut it off from the rest of the city.

The rebel headquarters was to be the General Post Office, an elegant, pale stone building with classical columns and statuary in Sackville Street, now known as O'Connell Street, which led to the river Liffey and the O'Connell Bridge. Just before midday the short, bandy-legged figure of Connolly, overall commander of the rebels in Dublin, marched with Plunkett, his throat still bandaged after an operation for glandular tuberculosis, on one side of him and Pearse at the other, leading a column of some 150 men past the Abbey theatre and into the wide, tree-lined thoroughfare. The traffic stopped for him and people strolling past the fashionable shops paused, watching idly a moment. They were used to these parades. Then, at Connolly's command, the men wheeled and charged into the GPO. Staff and customers were ejected,[1] and within minutes the glass was knocked out of the handsome windows and barricades built with books, files, bags of mail – whatever came handy; the building was made ready for riflefire and siege. The curious crowd gathering outside watched while men scrambled over the roof and two flags broke from the flagpoles at its front corners; one an unfamiliar tricolour, orange, white and green, to represent Sinn Fein, and the other green with the Irish harp in gold on it and, underneath, the words *Poblacht na hÉireann* (Irish Republic). Then Patrick Pearse appeared on the lowest step of the GPO's portico and read out the Proclamation of the Irish Republic, as its first president. Afterwards he handed out copies to the crowd and anchored one with stones to the base of a statue in the street, so everyone could read it. Connolly shook him warmly by the hand, but the crowd reacted with a cool, amused indifference.

The Proclamation reminded the Irish people of their dead heroes and declared the right of Ireland to the 'unfettered control of Irish destinies', a right to freedom 'which had been asserted by the Irish people in every generation' and six times, during the previous three hundred years, in arms. Nationalist aims were followed by socialist ones. The new Republic guaranteed religious and civil liberty, with equal rights and opportunities for all its citizens, declared its resolve 'to pursue the happiness and prosperity of the whole nation, cherishing all its children equally' and blamed the divisions of the past on alien government. The signatories to the Proclamation – Tom Clarke, Sean MacDermott, Pearse, Connolly, MacDonagh, Plunkett and Eamonn Ceannt – pledged their lives and the lives of their comrades-in-arms to the cause of Irish freedom and claimed the allegiance of every Irishman and Irish woman, but in fact alienated many with a reference to support from 'gallant allies in Europe', who could only be the Germans. Thousands of Irish families had sons fighting the Germans and links, however tenuous, between the Germans and the newly declared Republic smelled of treachery.

THE PROCLAMATION OF

POBLACHT NA H EIREANN.

THE PROVISIONAL GOVERNMENT

OF THE

IRISH REPUBLIC

TO THE PEOPLE OF IRELAND.

IRISHMEN AND IRISHWOMEN : In the name of God and of the dead generations from which she receives her old tradition of nationhood, Ireland, through us, summons her children to her flag and strikes for her freedom.

Having organised and trained her manhood through her secret revolutionary organisation, the Irish Republican Brotherhood, and through her open military organisations, the Irish Volunteers and the Irish Citizen Army, having patiently perfected her discipline, having resolutely waited for the right moment to reveal itself, she now seizes that moment, and, supported by her exiled children in America and by gallant allies in Europe, but relying in the first on her own strength, she strikes in full confidence of victory.

We declare the right of the people of Ireland to the ownership of Ireland, and to the unfettered control of Irish destinies, to be sovereign and indefeasible. The long usurpation of that right by a foreign people and government has not extinguished the right, nor can it ever be extinguished except by the destruction of the Irish people. In every generation the Irish people have asserted their right to national freedom and sovereignty; six times during the past three hundred years they have asserted it in arms. Standing on that fundamental right and again asserting it in arms in the face of the world, we hereby proclaim the Irish Republic as a Sovereign Independent State, and we pledge our lives and the lives of our comrades-in-arms to the cause of its freedom, of its welfare, and of its exaltation among the nations.

The Irish Republic is entitled to, and hereby claims, the allegiance of every Irishman and Irishwoman. The Republic guarantees religious and civil liberty, equal rights and equal opportunities to all its citizens, and declares its resolve to pursue the happiness and prosperity of the whole nation and of all its parts, cherishing all the children of the nation equally, and oblivious of the differences carefully fostered by an alien government, which have divided a minority from the majority in the past.

Until our arms have brought the opportune moment for the establishment of a permanent National Government, representative of the whole people of Ireland and elected by the suffrages of all her men and women, the Provisional Government, hereby constituted, will administer the civil and military affairs of the Republic in trust for the people.

We place the cause of the Irish Republic under the protection of the Most High God. Whose blessing we invoke upon our arms, and we pray that no one who serves that cause will dishonour it by cowardice, inhumanity, or rapine. In this supreme hour the Irish nation must, by its valour and discipline and by the readiness of its children to sacrifice themselves for the common good, prove itself worthy of the august destiny to which it is called.

Signed on Behalf of the Provisional Government,

THOMAS J. CLARKE.

SEAN Mac DIARMADA,   THOMAS MacDONAGH,

P. H. PEARSE,   EAMONN CEANNT,

JAMES CONNOLLY.   JOSEPH PLUNKETT

27.   Proclamation of the Irish Republic

28. General Post Office, Dublin, after the Rising, 1916 (*Illustrated War News*, 10 May 1916)

The government took little action on that first day; a few government troops found themselves attempting to dislodge the rebels from the South Dublin Union, units from three different barracks tried to get through to the castle, and students were roped in to defend Trinity College, a key central position with a large store of arms which the insurgents had unaccountably failed to invest. Early in the afternoon a troop of Lancers, coming upon the rebels unexpectedly, charged the GPO, only to be repulsed with minor losses. Two dead cavalry horses lay in the roadway for the rest of the week. Inside the GPO, the mood was gay and debonair: tense, excited and hopeful. People laughed easily, some sang, and the leaders bandied ideas about the Republic. Plunkett, who was dying, spoke from a mattress on the floor. The danger was considerable. Whereas there were no soldiers or police to fire bullets outside the headquarters building, the men inside were constantly rushing to the barricaded windows and tripping over guns on their way, so that bullets flew about, ricocheted off walls, ceilings and the marble floor and caused some injuries. Then in the evening the crowds in Sackville Street changed. Those who were merely curious went home and the poor from the tenements, mostly women and children, filled the street.

At dawn the following day troops from other parts of Ireland, including an artillery battery from the Curragh, moved into Dublin, raising the British strength in the city to more than 4,000 men. The army units were deployed in a circle round the city centre, and then the British waited. They had so many imponderables to consider. How many rebels were there? Would the rest of Ireland rise in their support? Were the Irish regiments reliable? Above all, would the Germans invade? On the Wednesday night a division of young lads from the English Midlands, most of whom had only been in the army for three months, sailed from Liverpool to Dun Laoghaire, known then as Kingstown, six miles south of Dublin. The British meant to overwhelm the rebels with an immensely superior force.

The rebels fought with desperate bravery as, during the following days, the British forces slowly moved in. In some areas they had considerable success; a mere seventeen rebel sharpshooters, fighting magnificently from houses overlooking Mount Street Bridge, held up the young English soldiers approaching from Dun Laoghaire for fifteen hours, causing heavy losses. Four

British officers were killed, fourteen wounded, and 214 other ranks killed and wounded. But the outcome was always, as the rebel leaders well knew, inevitable. British artillery smashed into buildings and tumbled walls, dispelling a notion of Connolly's that capitalists would never destroy property but only people, and the net tightened. The rebel tactics had been too pessimistic; men were positioned defensively in large, barricaded buildings and kept there, holed up and static. The seventeen heroes who guarded Mount Street Bridge could have been relieved from a detachment of about 100 men in a railway station nearby, but the order for relief was never given. The men confined in the GPO, and a contingent driven out of St Stephen's Green into the nearby College of Surgeons, grew tired, hungry and desperate, but had little opportunity to help their fellows.

The rebels received no sympathy from the people of Dublin. Dubliners watched the fighting, spread wild rumours, kept on getting in the way and were often accidentally shot. From Easter Monday onwards, the city was at a standstill. There were no trams, no trains, and the shops were running out of food. Dubliners grew angry with the Shinners (or Sinn Feiners) as they called them, for the hardships they were causing, and egged on the British army in its efforts to hunt them down.

There was no great sympathy for the rebels outside Dublin either. In the west, the Volunteers took over the small towns of Athenry and Craughwell, surrounded the police barracks and cut the railway lines to Limerick and Athlone. But when they set off along the coast road to take the city of Galway, British destroyers shelled them from Galway bay; within the city, Redmond's National Volunteers had, in any case, declared for the Crown. In Cork, a thousand Irish Volunteers had been ready to parade on Easter Sunday, before MacNeill countermanded their orders. When they received fresh orders from Pearse, they became so bemused that the British army had seized the city by the time they were ready to move. At Ashbourne, in Meath, the rebels were more successful. They ambushed a party of forty police and fought them for five hours; then the police ran out of ammunition and surrendered. But it was in Wexford, where memories of the rising in 1798 were strongest, that the rebels were most active. They took the town of Enniscorthy without a fight and held it for three days, besieging the police in their barracks; they commandeered arms stores, cut the railway lines, destroyed telegraph links and blocked the roads with felled trees.

By Tuesday night the crowds in Sackville Street, composed of the poorest in Dublin, were surging to and fro in a wild, glorious orgy of looting and window-smashing. The rebels kept them away from the GPO building by stretching a couple of strands of barbed wire slackly across the street and occasionally firing over their heads. It had all begun frivolously enough when a toyshop and confectioner's were raided, and exultant children ran to their mothers with armfuls of sweets and toys. Then hat shops, dress shops, jewellers and, most frequently of all, shoe shops were attacked; many of the Dublin poor still went barefoot. Women who had never owned a decent garment in their lives flaunted fashionable evening dresses, often far too tight for them, fur coats, smart hats and rings on every finger. The street was littered with broken glass, cardboard boxes, bits of window frames, paper and squashed straw hats. Then somebody lit a match, flames leapt up and in no time there was a bonfire. The revellers piled rubbish onto it, danced and sang – as British artillery rumbled from across the Liffey.

The toyshop where the looting had begun was set on fire, along with two shoe shops. British shells crashed into the burning buildings, sending up showers of sparks and creating channels for the flames. By Thursday, the city centre was burning fiercely; there were so many calls on the fire service it could not cope. Buildings collapsed, and the fires were so hot in Sackville Street that a stream of molten glass flowed along the pavement. Inevitably sparks fell onto the GPO.

For most of Friday, the fire was contained in the roof. Ammunition was moved to the cellar and the building was soon awash with water from the fire hoses. The British, who had established positions further up the street, waited – and in the evening, soon after seven o'clock, the flames suddenly blazed up. The rebels abandoned their burning headquarters and threaded their way through holes in the walls into adjoining buildings. Connolly, in great pain from a wound in the foot which was turning gangrenous, was carried out on a stretcher, the last of all. Then the roof and ceilings fell in.

A number of rebels were hit by rifle and machine-gun fire as they ran through the streets. Pearse, Connolly, Plunkett, Clarke and MacDermott spent the night in a corner shop, a grocer's, with sentries posted outside. They knew the end had come. If the leadership had adopted different tactics – if there had been no grand headquarters and every man had fought in the streets or in the hills – the rising might have lasted longer. But that had never been the point. Connolly had known from the start that, in military terms, it could not succeed. He had been asked by a friend, as he left Liberty Hall on Easter Monday, what the chances were, and he had replied with brisk cheerfulness: 'None whatever.'

On Saturday 29 April, Connolly directed the rebels to surrender – there was no further reason for bloodshed. Four hundred men were herded onto a small patch of ground by the city maternity hospital at the head of Sackville Street, and spent a cold and miserable night squatting in the open. In the morning they were marched, still defiant, still singing the patriotic songs of Ireland, to imprisonment in an army barracks. The crowds hooted and jeered at them, calling out to the escorting troops: 'Shoot the traitors! Bayonet the bastards!' As they went through a slum district, the women pelted them with rotten vegetables and emptied their chamber pots over them.

The rebels had held out for six days against odds of twenty to one. During that time, 64 rebels had been killed, while the British army, the Royal Irish Constabulary and the police had lost 134 dead and 381 wounded. Among civilians, at least 220 had been killed and 600 wounded. Dublin was wrecked; in the city centre 179 buildings, occupying 61,000 sq.yds, had been destroyed. One-third of the city's population, amounting to 100,000 people, had to be given public relief.

Then the British made their mistake. A government has to put down rebellion and in wartime especially it must put down rebellion quickly. But the Irish do not respond to severity and when Major General Sir John Maxwell, the British commander-in-chief, decided to teach the Irish a lesson – and to teach it with secret courts martial and hurried executions within the British barracks – Irish public opinion, always mercurial, veered away from him. The prisoners were rebels maybe, but Irishmen; they had fought a clean and courageous fight against tremendous odds, and their compatriots could not but admire them for it. When they vanished into British barracks, the wildest rumours began to circulate, and in the imagination of the Irish the barracks flowed with rivers of blood.

The rumours were fed by silence. For several days, no word as to the fate of the prisoners was sent out. Then, at dead of night, a priest, or a wife or parent, would receive an eerie summons, and the next morning the terse announcement of an execution be made. Pearse, Macdonagh and Tom Clarke were shot in Kilmainham jail on 3 May. The next day, 4 May, Pearse's brother, two Volunteer commanders and Plunkett, wasted almost to death by his illness, were shot; Plunkett had just been married, handcuffed and guarded by soldiers with fixed bayonets, in the prison chapel. There were five more executions during the following week and then on 12 May, MacDermott and Connolly were shot, Connolly so ill from his gangrenous wound that he had to be tied into a chair for his execution.

As, day after day, notices of fresh executions were posted, Dublin's horror grew. When sentence was carried out so grossly on the dying Connolly, the last remnant of Irish sympathy for Britain disappeared. The prisoners had been treated as soldiers and honourably shot instead of being hanged; of ninety rebels condemned to death only fifteen were executed, the sentences on the rest being commuted to various terms of penal servitude. No government in wartime was likely to have done less. But Maxwell arrested thousands of others too, some of them certainly innocent of rebellion. Eoin MacNeill, who had bicycled desperately around Dublin trying to stop the rising, was tried, sentenced to life imprisonment and sent to Dartmoor, and Arthur Griffith, the elderly and non-violent founder of Sinn Fein, was indefinitely interned. Those who had cared nothing about politics assumed an interest now – especially if they found themselves among the two thousand or so sent to England for internment.

Pearse, Clarke, Connolly, Plunkett and the rest began to be seen as heroes and martyrs, as they had known they would be. 'The fools! The fools!' Pearse had said about the British a year earlier at the funeral of a noted Fenian, O'Donovan Rossa, 'they have left us our Fenian dead, and while Ireland holds these graves, Ireland unfree shall never be at peace.' The heroes of the rising were without graves; the British had buried their bodies in quicklime within Kilmainham jail. But they did not need graves. They lived on, without memorials, in the hearts and minds of the Irish people.

CHAPTER 13

THE ROAD
TO
FREEDOM

Dubliners were bitterly hostile, sceptical of all British expressions of good will, when the city remained under martial law, with British troops patrolling the streets, for months after the last of the detainees had sailed for England and Wales. Public meetings were banned, or broken up, without explanation and the speakers held without trial. The city felt it was being punished for its sympathy with brave men. Then Dubliners hit upon the idea of lauding the dead, and the politics they had died for, under the respectable cover of the Catholic Church. Numerous commemorative masses were held, and when the relatives of the dead patriots emerged from them, they found themselves being cheered by vast crowds, which marched in procession and sang nationalist songs.

In June Sir Roger Casement came up for trial at the Old Bailey in London and was found guilty of treason. There were no grounds for a reprieve, but to still agitation for one, the government had pages from his diaries, which showed he was homosexual, circulated among key figures on either side of the Atlantic. On 3rd August he was hanged in Pentonville gaol and, thereafter, joined the roll of Irish martyrs.

The major casualty of the Rising was, as the insurgents had known it would be, Home Rule. Redmond had put Home Rule on the statute book but, because its operation had been delayed by the war, the Irish separatists had not believed in it and his life's work was in tatters. Yet the government was anxious to pacify Ireland by implementing Home Rule without delay; as usual, Britain was ready to give the Irish what they wanted because they had turned to violence. But the problem of Ulster remained; partition was not provided for in the Home Rule Act. A wily Welshman in the Cabinet, David Lloyd George, was given the task of reconciling the opposing parties and he decided to do it, not by bringing the two sides round a table, but by keeping them apart. Redmond was tiring, and he allowed Lloyd George to persuade him that an exclusion of the six counties would be temporary. Carson, on the other hand, was a Cabinet minister and at the height of his powers, who knew exclusion would be permanent; he had a piece of paper in his pocket from Lloyd George which said so. Both sides seemed satisfied until Lord Lansdowne, a peer of the old Protestant Ascendancy, revealed the permanence of exclusion in the House of Lords. Redmond drew back; he had won that Home Rule which O'Connell, Parnell and Gladstone had failed to secure, and it was turning bitter as aloes in his mouth. When Lloyd George renewed his offer a year later, Redmond again refused. Then in March 1918 he died, a sad and disappointed man.

Meanwhile, people in Ireland forgot the parliamentary Home Rule party. They believed, quite mistakenly, that the Rising had been the work of that open, pacifist and hitherto ineffectual body, Sinn Fein; very few had heard of the IRB. When Griffith was released and returned to Ireland, with all the other short-term prisoners, just before Christmas 1916, he found himself the only leader of non-parliamentary nationalists left. He resumed publication of his newspaper, now called *Nationality*, and in its pages appealed for Irish representation at the Peace Conference after the war, fought partition and resisted conscription, which had been introduced in Britain early in 1916 and seemed likely to be extended to Ireland. Thousands of Irishmen had volunteered to serve in the British forces, but Sinn Fein objected to any attempt to compel young Irishmen to fight in Britain's battles.

Early in 1917 Sinn Fein had the opportunity to put into practice one of its basic policies: withdrawal from parliament. The elderly Count Plunkett, father of the executed Joseph Plunkett, defeated

Redmond's candidate in a by-election at North Roscommon and then, on instruction from his Sinn Fein backers, refused to take his seat. In May the Sinn Fein candidate won another by-election and also refused to take his seat, and then in July Eamonn de Valera, a prisoner until the day after his adoption, won a third by-election for Sinn Fein at East Clare and, like the others, refused to take his seat. Tall, dark and saturnine, de Valera had been a cool and tenacious commandant at Boland's bakery during the Rising, and the senior rebel commander to have survived; his death sentence had been commuted to penal servitude, almost certainly due to the intervention of the American ambassador;[1] he had been born on the voyage to America, the child of a Spanish father and an Irish mother, though he had never been an American citizen and had left America at the age of two. As his election manifesto, de Valera took Pearse's Proclamation of the Republic, although he was politic enough to assert that he would accept non-republican government provided it was Irish, and the Irish people wanted it. He had a landslide victory – and every vote cast for him was a vote for the Rising. In October there was a Sinn Fein convention at which Griffith magnanimously stood down and the thousand delegates unanimously voted for the commandant at Boland's bakery as their president. Such was the cachet of being the Rising's senior survivor that he was immediately afterwards elected president of the Irish Volunteers as well.

The British were still arresting extremists. Thomas Ashe, a veteran of the Rising, went on hunger strike in Dublin's Mountjoy prison, was clumsily force-fed and died on 25 September. His was the first political funeral since the Rising, and it turned into a massive demonstration, an expression of grief for all those executed leaders who had had no funerals. In defiance of government regulations, the Volunteers were armed and in uniform when they escorted 30,000 or 40,000 mourners, including Catholic priests and trade unionists, to the graveside at Glasnevin cemetery. There was no oration. Three volleys were fired and the Volunteer commander, a big fellow with the insignia of a vice-commandant, gave a brief valediction in Irish and English. 'Nothing additional remains to be said,' he declared. 'The volley which we have just heard is the only speech which it is proper to make above the grave of a dead Fenian.' The

297

speaker, so forthright and simple, utterly different in manner from the poetic and mystical Pearse, had been an aide de camp to Joseph Plunkett in the GPO, suffered imprisonment afterwards and campaigned for Count Plunkett at North Roscommon. He was Michael Collins.

The Collins family were Catholic tenant farmers in West Cork; Collins' father, aged seventy-five when Michael was born, rented some eighty acres near Clonakilty. In 1906, when he was sixteen, Collins went to London to work as a clerk, first in the Post Office and then in the City. He returned home early in 1916 to avoid conscription which, though Ireland was exempted, applied to Irishmen in Britain.[2] Early in 1917 he became secretary and

29.   Michael Collins (courtesy of the BBC Hulton Picture Library)

accountant to Irish National Aid, which helped the victims of Easter Week and their families. Next he reorganized the IRB, which he joined in London, and the Irish Volunteers, who drilled and practised guerrilla warfare in the hills, using arms run in from England. Collins was exuberant and noisy, with a taste for horseplay, but also businesslike and methodical, with a genius for detail. He was to become the first rebel leader in Irish history to be a brilliant organizer.

In the spring of 1918, the British army on the Somme suffered 300,000 casualties in a month and the government, desperate for more men, took the action dreaded by the nationalists and extended conscription to Ireland. The protests were vigorous; the lord mayor of Dublin described the government action as 'a declaration of war on Ireland'; a one-day strike was staged all over the country, except in the north-east, and the Catholic bishops declared that 'the Irish have a right to resist (conscription) by every means consonant with the law of God,' Most significantly of all, when conscription for Ireland became law, the Irish parliamentary party walked out of the House of Commons. They, too, now accepted the Sinn Fein dictum that self-determination was to be had for the taking, and not for the asking.

If the government had bent with the wind, dropped conscription and appealed for volunteers, it would most likely have got the men it wanted.[3] Instead, it took belated action to halt the revolutionary movement. On 12 May Field Marshal Lord French, who had commanded the British army in France at the beginning of the war, arrived in Dublin as lord lieutenant; Lloyd George, who had become prime minister in 1916, believed a soldier would be better able to maintain order and enforce conscription than a civilian. During the night of 17 May de Valera, Griffith and almost the entire leadership of Sinn Fein, all those thought most likely to organize resistance to conscription, were arrested on the flimsy pretext of a German plot; Irish Americans had never ceased their exchange of messages with the Germans, and a member of Casement's Irish brigade had been picked up in April after landing from a submarine, ostensibly to find out if there was any prospect of another Irish rising. Michael Collins had purposely kept out of the way, but the rest of the leadership, though warned, preferred imprisonment, with its political advantages, to going on the run.

The British do not elect prisoners to parliament; they feel a prisoner must be a bad hat, and do not understand that the

30. Griffith election poster (courtesy of the Imperial War Museum, London)

Irish attitude is different. Griffith was in the middle of an election campaign at the time of his arrest and likely to lose it; most of the voters seemed prepared to settle for what was known as colonial Home Rule and choose the parliamentary party's candidate – until the imprisonment of the Sinn Fein leadership. Then the inevitable reaction put Griffith at the top of the poll.

The government found it had pushed the people into the arms of Sinn Fein, removed the moderate leadership and left the extremists in control. Harry Boland, a Dublin tailor, organized the Sinn Fein clubs which were proliferating everywhere and Collins, in charge of the military wing, made a detailed survey of the Volunteer movement, appointed officers, moved supplies and built up an underground intelligence network which penetrated the prisons, the Post Office and even the detective branch of the police force. While the old, dreary round of coercion went on. Sinn Fein, the Gaelic League and the Volunteers were banned and all public meetings prohibited except with special permission. People were arrested for singing seditious songs, giving their names to the police in Irish and all manner of trivial offences. By the end of the summer, the number of arrests had risen to a thousand.

The Irish everywhere, except in the north, developed a cold, furious hatred for the government. When the war ended in November 1918, the threat of conscription (which had never been enforced) vanished, but the prevailing hatred remained. During the general election which followed the armistice, Sinn Fein, with many of its candidates still in prison,[4] fought on the issue of withdrawal from Westminster, the establishment of an Irish parliament and an appeal to the Peace Conference. Almost a third of the voters, distrusting the militancy of the new Sinn Fein, stayed away from the polls. In the north the Unionists increased their seats from 18 to 26. But in the rest of the country Sinn Fein gained 65 per cent of the votes cast and won an overwhelming victory; the parliamentary Home Rule party was almost wiped out and the number of parliamentary seats belonging to Sinn Fein increased from seven to 73, which, of course, the Sinn Fein members refused to take up.

The Sinn Fein leadership immediately set about forming an Irish

301

parliament, and on 7 January 1919, invitations were sent out to all MPs elected in Ireland to attend the first session of the Dail Eireann, or Assembly of Ireland, to be held in the Mansion House, Dublin, on 21 January. The Unionists[5] and the six members of the old parliamentary party ignored the invitation, so that only Sinn Fein members turned up; and as thirty-four Sinn Fein MPs were in prison and eight more unable to attend for other reasons, there were only twenty-seven members present when the new parliament was inaugurated.

Openly and publicly, with the Irish and British press in attendance, the assembly decided to have an executive president, or prime minister, chosen by itself, and to give him the power to nominate ministers. Then a Declaration of Independence was read out, which reminded its hearers that 'the Irish Republic was proclaimed in Dublin on Easter Monday, 1916, by the Irish Republican Army, acting on behalf of the Irish people', and pledged the Dail and the nation to establish the Irish Republic as a fact by every means possible. Next the members outlined a programme for the creation of a democratic, classless society, and asked the Peace Conference, being held in Paris, to guarantee Irish independence; de Valera, Griffith and Count Plunkett were appointed delegates to the Conference. In a heady two hours, the foundations of a free Irish government had been laid.

The appeal to the Peace Conference failed. The Dail sent an envoy to obtain admission for its delegates, but with no success. Only the Americans could have helped. Irishmen remembered that the American president, Woodrow Wilson, had commented after the Easter Rising that 'every people has the right to choose the sovereignty under which they shall live.' But Wilson had been irritated by the pro-German and virulently anti-British sentiments of Clan na Gael, and when he was approached about Irish representation at the conference, he claimed to have spoken after the Rising 'without the knowledge that nationalities existed which are coming to us today!'

Without the support of the Peace Conference, the key question for the Dail was: What will the British do? In fact, the British did very little. When Lord French had been sent to Ireland, he had been told that, for appearance' sake, the Irish must be allowed – indeed, encouraged – to fire the first shot, and throughout the summer and autumn of 1918 assemblies of armed men had been treated with extraordinary leniency. And when the Dail had its first meeting in Dublin's Mansion House, with the press in attendance, the British government brushed it off as just another idiosyncracy of the Irish scene; a rival, breakaway government had been formed, and the British could do no more than try to laugh it to scorn!

The Irish proved not at all reluctant to fire the first shots Lord French required; they knew they were the opening shots in what must be a civil war of Republicans against Unionists, and even Home Rulers, to drive the British out. On 21 January, the very day that the Dail first met, a group of masked Volunteers in Co. Tipperary shot and killed two policemen at Soloheadbeg; the police were escorting a cartload of gelignite to a nearby quarry and the Volunteers needed it for homemade bombs. They laid an ambush, called out to the policemen to surrender and then, tense and excited, followed the call far too quickly with a hail of bullets.

To the British, the action was a crime, an outrage; they could not regard it as an act of war without recognizing the breakaway Irish Republican government – and that they could not do without most ignominiously abrogating their authority, abandoning their responsibilities and allowing the structure of government in Ireland to collapse. But war is what happens when politics have failed, and politics undoubtedly *had* failed; the Home Rule Act, as the leaders of the Easter Rising had known it would be, was quietly forgotten. The British government and the Irish parliamentary party had undeniably tried to find a compromise which would bring the act into force. But the south would not tolerate even a temporary exclusion of the Protestant counties, the northern Unionists would not accept Home Rule and the British would not, and probably could not, coerce their fellow Protestants. The deadlock could only be broken by war.

The Dail had its second meeting on 1 April and chose Eamonn de Valera, recently sprung from Lincoln gaol,[6] as its president. The following day he nominated Griffith, who had just been released from prison, as minister for home affairs, Collins as finance minister, Count Plunkett as minister for foreign affairs, Cathal Brugha, a tough and heroic fighter who had been badly wounded during Easter Week, as minister for defence and Robert Barton, a landowner educated in England, as minister for agriculture. De Valera had made plans to go to America; he believed it was essential for the new government to win American goodwill. But before he went, he launched a campaign of social ostracism against the police: not the harmless bobbies who patrolled the streets and dealt with petty offenders, but the Royal Irish Constabulary, which was used to enforce coercive laws; they, and not British soldiers, would hold the front line against republican attack.

The Volunteers, who soon became known as the Irish Republican Army, or the IRA, fought in the way Irishmen had always fought against the British, as guerrillas. They laid ambushes, raided police stations (where there were often arms) and made lightning attacks on patrols. The police were handicapped by their uniform, which made them an easy target, whereas the IRA were nearly always in plain clothes. The police never knew which group of youths, standing idly on a street corner, might suddenly turn on them, pulling guns or throwing bombs. Some police stations in the west, which were normally manned by three or four men, were closed down as too vulnerable to attack.

As the year went on, IRA attacks became more frequent and daring; early in September, the IRA shot up a group of soldiers on their way to church in Fermoy, killing one, wounding four more and disarming the rest, before jumping into their cars and driving away. At an inquest on the dead soldier the next day, the jury refused to bring in a verdict of murder and said simply that the soldier 'had been killed by a bullet fired by some person unknown'. The next day, 200 soldiers raided Fermoy, attacking shops and the property of jurymen, and doing £3,000 worth of damage. For the first time, the British had taken reprisals. In December the IRA planned to assassinate Lord French as a propaganda coup; they failed, but in January 1920 their attacks on the RIC, army barracks and country houses, where they might obtain sporting guns, were stepped up. The British made ludicrously high estimates of the numbers of their enemy; French reckoned that the IRA consisted of 100,000 men and his chief secretary 200,000, whereas the true figure was nearer 15,000 and, according to Collins, not more than 3,000 of those were trained and active gunmen. Then on 21 January, the first anniversary of the setting up of the Dail, an IRA group run by Collins and called The Squad killed an assistant commissioner of the Dublin police as he went from his office in the castle to his hotel. The Castle authorities offered £10,000 for evidence leading to the conviction of the killers and a further £10,000 for Collins, dead or alive.

Michael Collins was a militant revolutionary; he believed war was necessary if Ireland was ever to be free. And he knew that revolution cannot be achieved democratically; the majority is always too passive to accept violent upheaval, whatever vague sympathy it may have for revolutionary aims. The Irish people had not voted for war; during the general election of 1918 Sinn Fein had declared repeatedly that there would be no more rebellion. But the secret IRB, with Collins among its leaders, had infiltrated Sinn Fein just as it had penetrated MacNeill's Volunteers in 1916 and, once again, a reluctant Irish people was being forced into the fight. Collins was ruthless; he did not stop the IRA he led punishing those who resisted its aims very cruelly, with shots in the kneecap, the calf, or the thigh, and shots fired at random through the windows of their houses. Girls who went out with policemen or soldiers, even though their boyfriends were Irishmen, had their heads shaved. Ireland had a long history of intimidation and terror; they had been practised by the rapparees and the tories, and then taken up by the Whiteboys, Orangemen, Defenders and all the other secret societies. The IRA knew what methods to use.

Early in 1920 the RIC began running short of men. They had had some resignations as a result of de Valera's campaign of ostracism, and young men had begun to think it anti-Irish and unpatriotic to join. So the British government advertised in Glasgow and Liverpool for recruits, and had a ready response. The Irish liked to think the men who came forward were the sweepings of the gaols, but in fact they were demobbed soldiers who, after risking their lives for their country, could find no work in it and welcomed the chance of doing some quasi-soldiering for ten shillings a day, which was very good pay at the time. The RIC had not enough uniforms for all the men the British sent over, some 1,200 to begin with and nearly 6,000 more later on, so they were rigged out in a mixture of dark green RIC tunics, khaki trousers from the British army, black RIC belts and all manner of strange headgear, including civilian felt hats. The Irish named them after a famous pack of hounds in Co. Limerick, the Black and Tans.

The Black and Tans were never more than a small proportion of the British forces in Ireland, but they were the toughest, the least disciplined, and very soon the most feared. They knew and cared nothing about Ireland; the country was simply a dangerous posting where they might be fired on while drinking in a bar, or shot in the back on a routine patrol. The world war had made them callous; it had also taught them comradeship. When one of their number was shot and appallingly wounded by the expanding bullets which, though banned by international agreement, the IRA sometimes used, the Black and Tans wanted revenge – and, like the British troops who had beaten up Fermoy in the previous September, they took it. They made the civilian population pay for the cruelties of the IRA.

In March 1920, soon after the first Black and Tans had arrived in Ireland, the Lord Mayor of Cork, Thomas MacCurtain, was shot dead in his bedroom by a gang of masked raiders. The British claimed they were IRA, but MacCurtain had recently criticized the RIC very severely for dangerous and unruly behaviour, firing volleys of rifle shots in the streets of the city, and evidence brought at the inquest identified the raiders as police; they were said to have spoken in foreign accents and could have been the first batch of Black and Tans. The jury returned a colourful verdict of murder by Lloyd George, the British government, Lord French and the RIC. A few days later the IRA took an elderly magistrate, who had been given the task of uncovering Sinn Fein funds, out of a Dublin tram and shot him dead by the roadside. The pattern of action by the two sides was set: cold, suave, almost gentlemanly[7] killing by the IRA and wild orgies of revenge and reprisal by the British army and the RIC, particularly the Black and Tans.

The IRA celebrated the anniversary of the Easter Rising with a formidable demonstration of its ability to organize. On Easter Saturday groups of IRA men set fire to 100 income tax offices, destroying their tax records, and that same night burned 182 empty police barracks. Then the incidents built up. Policemen, British officers and soldiers, government officials, landlords, businessmen, and even workmen who did the British bidding,

306

were systematically picked off as spies and traitors. And the reprisals began. Drunken Black and Tans ran amok in Limerick, beating people up and smashing windows. Lorryloads of them tore down village streets, firing their rifles at random as they sang, whooped and yelled. Totally innocent civilians who got in the way were killed. Colonel Smyth, the police commissioner for Munster, told the RIC to shoot first, even if mistakes were made; and the IRA killed him for it a few weeks later in his club in Cork. The IRA attacked coastguard stations, and an RIC sergeant was shot dead as he left church after mass. The Catholic Church, manfully condemning violence on both sides, banned the killer from its services and sacraments. Almost as a joke, the IRA raided the GPO in Dublin, removed military mail and then sent the viceroy's post on to him, stamped 'Censored by the IRA'!

The Black and Tans burned and looted all over the south and the west; town halls, market halls, private houses, shops, pubs and creameries – which gave a living to thousands in the Irish countryside – were destroyed. People took to sleeping in the fields at night, sheltered by hedges and haystacks, as they had not done since the rebellion of 1798; they pushed their belongings along in old prams and handcarts. A senior RIC officer was shot dead in a hotel in Balbriggan, twenty miles north of Dublin; the Black and Tans charged through the village, shot two men unfortunate enough to be about, set fire to nineteen private houses and wrecked thirty more; it was as if a hurricane had gone by. The IRA raided the police barracks at Trim, in Meath, and later, in the small hours, about 200 Black and Tans, aided by Auxiliaries (also recruited in Britain, but from ex-officers) descended on the town, burning, looting and wrecking. The IRA buried a resident magistrate up to his neck in the sand on a beach, so he would drown when the tide came in. When they came back the next day, they found him still alive; they had buried him too far up the beach for the tide to reach him. So they dug him out and reburied him where the tide was sure to get him, and left him watching the water slowly advance.

In September the Black and Tans were posted to Drogheda, and they put up notices warning the townspeople: 'If in the vicinity a policeman is shot, five of the leading Sinn Feiners will be shot . . . . Stop the shooting of the police or we will lay low every house that smells of Sinn Fein.' And the following month, the Anti-Sinn Fein Society in Cork sent round a notice saying, 'If, in future, any member of His Majesty's Forces be murdered, two members of the Sinn Fein Party in the County of Cork will be killed . . . . In the event of a member of His Majesty's Forces being wounded, or an attempt made to wound him, one member of the Sinn Fein party will be killed.' The policy of reprisal was becoming institutionalized.

During the summer, the British government passed a Restoration of Order in Ireland Act, which enabled the army and the RIC to arrest and imprison anyone suspected of having Sinn Fein connections. As almost everyone had such connections, it seemed that the British government had declared war on the whole Irish nation. Lorryloads of Black and Tans, as well as Auxiliaries, raced through the streets at night, rapped thunderously on the doors of houses thought to harbour active Sinn Feiners, and whisked away suspects, who were often held without trial for months. Martial law operated in several counties. And yet there were large areas, particularly in the south and west, where the king's writ no longer ran.

Meanwhile the Dail was successfully setting up its own government as an alternative to the faltering British one. From May 1919 onwards, the Dail had met in secret, its ministers had been on the run and the government offices through which they worked had continually been shifted from place to place to avoid the police. Yet Barton had contrived to set up a land bank, so farmers could carry on with land purchase, Collins had raised a huge Dail Eireann National Loan of £385,000 through door to door collections by Sinn Fein supporters,[8] and W. T. Cosgrave, a forceful Dubliner who had fought in the Rising, had won so many seats for Sinn Fein on the local councils that they had broken with the Local Government Board set up by the British. Sinn Fein was even developing its own judiciary, with a system of courts and circuit judges, supported by a Republican police force, which arrested criminals. The Republican police even arrested three men who had robbed a bank of £20,000; they were sentenced by a Sinn Fein court to be deported (the new judicial system had no means of imprisoning people) and the money recovered.

Ireland was slipping beyond the British grasp – yet the British government still could not give Irish affairs priority. There were more British troops in Mesopotamia and in India than the 50,000 or so with which the RIC garrisoned Ireland, and when Lloyd George searched for a remedy, he could only dredge up Home Rule once again, and propose to the Unionists in the north that the six counties where Protestants predominated – Antrim, Down, Armagh, Londonderry, Tyrone and Fermanagh – be partitioned off. Ireland was to become two states, Northern Ireland and Southern Ireland, each with its own parliament for home affairs, and representatives at Westminster as well, where foreign and imperial affairs, and matters of defence, would be dealt with. A Council of Ireland was to link the two Irish parliaments, and they could be united whenever they wished.

The northern Unionists accepted the British proposals; they would have preferred closer links with Britain but realized that, with Northern Ireland constituted as the British government suggested, they could perpetuate a Protestant ascendancy. As for the people in the south – they seemed not to have heard. They abhorred partition, they had declared their desire for total separation from Britain and a republic, and long since left the concept of federal Home Rule behind. Sinn Fein had withdrawn from Westminster and there was already an Irish parliament. By and large, southern Ireland and Sinn Fein were one.

Ever since the Easter Rising, the Unionists in the north had felt deep anxiety about the republicanism of the south. The IRA staged the same murderous incidents in the north as elsewhere, killing policemen, troops, government officials and anyone else they could label a spy or a traitor. Sinn Fein courts were operating and the Dail claimed, with some justice, to rule. Then on 12 July the ageing but still fiery Carson inflamed a huge Orange audience, which was celebrating the anniversary of the battle of the Boyne, by declaring: 'If there is any attempt to take away one jot or tittle of your rights as British citizens . . . . I will call out the Volunteers.' The fears and belligerence always so close to the surface in Ulster erupted; Unionist dockers refused to work with members of Sinn Fein and then attacked Catholic workers. Policemen and troops stopped the fighting in the dockyards and it spread into the town. Buildings were set on fire and British soldiers had to place themselves between Protestants and Catholics. Eighteen people were killed and 200 wounded in three days of rioting, and almost the whole of the Catholic population put out of work. Riots broke out in Londonderry and elsewhere; Catholic families were driven from their homes, 62 people killed and 200 wounded. The IRA retaliated by leading a boycott of Ulster goods. The divisions widened and partition, which neither side really wanted, drew ever nearer.

The IRA was still an underground, virtually independent force, answerable only to the secret IRB, and not to Sinn Fein or the Dail. Many members of the Dail were, like the generality of the Irish people, dismayed and revolted by the vindictiveness and outrages of the IRA; Sinn Fein still retained a nostalgic yearning for its early pacifism. But as the War of Independence went on the Dail, and even Griffith, began to take a wry interest in IRA successes; for the IRA were the teeth that the new Republic had to have.

The IRA could not win a military victory. Some 3,000 active gunmen could, with almost daily raids and assassinations, render the country ungovernable, but they could not drive 50,000 British soldiers, and an RIC that, with Black and Tans and Auxiliaries, numbered 8,000 more, into the sea. But the IRA could, and did, win the propaganda war. The British greeted the IRA campaign of murder with angry indifference, but when news came through of the Black and Tan reprisals, which the IRA made sure were fully reported, the average British citizen was shocked; it was not his idea of war. Nowadays we are all hardened by news of constant terrorism and reprisal from all over the world, but in the first quarter of the century public sensibility was still tender. War was regulated and honourable; it was fought by national armies, defined by their uniforms, and as far as possible civilians were left out of it. If the IRA operated underground, used terror and dispensed with uniforms, that was their business; they could not be considered real soldiers. But for uniformed British forces to take undisciplined and indiscriminate revenge on a civilian population, dragging innocent people from their beds and shooting them, setting fire to their houses and driving whole families into the fields, outraged the British sense of decency.

The IRA also won sympathy for Ireland with hunger strikes. In 1917, when imprisoned Volunteers went on hunger strike in Irish gaols (a tactic they had picked up from British suffragettes) the authorities had simply let them go and then, when they had had a few good meals, picked them up again. Prison officials had tried force feeding, too, until Thomas Ashe died. Then, in 1919, ninety prisoners detained in Dublin's Mountjoy jail went on hunger strike and, after a week, became ill. Their relatives were summoned to harrowing scenes, a general strike was called, backed by the Catholic Church, and the hunger-striking prisoners were released. But government is not mocked and when, during the summer of 1920, Terence MacSwiney, the republican Lord Mayor of Cork, went on hunger strike immediately after being arrested for carrying the notes of a seditious speech, he was sent to Brixton gaol in London and slowly died there, rivetting the attention of the world for seventy-three days. The British people respected his courage – and began to wonder if, for a man to endure such suffering, there were not something very wrong in Ireland.

Then on 21 November 1920, a day which has gone down in Irish history as Bloody Sunday, the struggle reached new heights of violence. Collins' intelligence service had discovered that certain Englishmen in Dublin were British intelligence agents and he planned their assassination. At about 9 a.m. armed IRA men broke into the houses and hotels where the Englishmen were staying and shot eleven of them, some in front of their wives. In addition, four British officers were wounded, another killed by mistake and two Auxiliaries, who had tried to intervene, shot dead. 'I found out,' Collins explained later, 'that those fellows we put on the spot were going to put a lot of us on the spot, so I got in first.'

But that was not the end of Bloody Sunday. The IRA had had their turn; the Black and Tans must have theirs. In the afternoon they invaded a Dublin sports ground, where a Gaelic football match was being played, and fired indiscriminately on both players and crowd. Twelve people were killed and sixty wounded. Two IRA men imprisoned in Dublin castle were shot, 'while', the British said, 'trying to escape'.

The war entered a new and desperate phase. Flying columns of IRA men, with a core of thirty-five or so highly trained, full-time gunmen, ambushed lorryloads of Auxiliaries in Co. Cork, killing almost all of them. On the night of 10 December, Auxiliaries and Black and Tans took their revenge; they poured into the city of Cork, drinking, looting, wrecking and burning. A large part of the centre of the city was set alight, the fire brigade prevented from reaching the fires and the fire hoses cut. Afterwards, the British government put about a story that the people of Cork had burned down the centre of their city themselves, but the Auxiliaries gave the lie to it with macabre and boastful humour, swaggering about Dublin with burnt corks in their caps.

Yet when 1921 began the IRA was still almost unscathed, and evidence of their dreadful activity discovered almost daily. Corpses were found in the fields or by the roadside with notes attached to them reading: 'Tried by court martial and found guilty – All others beware – IRA', or simply: 'Beware the IRA'. Labourers who had at one time, perhaps years ago, served in the British army were shot, and navvies who obeyed British or RIC orders to dig trenches were shot as well. An elderly woman who warned the RIC of an ambush was shot; a tennis party in Galway was shot up; a British officer in a car with three women was wounded and then, at the command of the IRA, driven by one of his female companions to a lonely spot and killed. Then in May over 100 IRA men broke into Dublin's beautiful Custom House and set it alight; it was virtually the headquarters of British administration in Ireland.

The British government made overtures towards peace. After Bloody Sunday, the authorities had arrested Griffith and Eoin MacNeill, more as a gesture than anything else, and de Valera, still in America raising money for the war, decided to return to Ireland. Early in 1921, tentative three-sided negotiations were opened between him, Sir James Craig, who had succeeded the aged Carson as leader of the Unionist north, and prominent Britons. In May elections were held for the new Northern and Southern parliaments - and then, quite suddenly, the war was over. When the king, George V, opened the Northern parliament he made an emotional appeal to all Irishmen 'to join in making for the land which they love a new era of peace, contentment and goodwill.' His appeal was heard, with overwhelming relief, by Catholics and Protestants all over the country, and after a formal truce, de Valera and Craig went to London to see Lloyd George.

The Dail was rent by division. De Valera claimed not to be a doctrinaire republican; had he not said at the East Clare by-election in 1917 that, if the Irish people wanted to have another form of government, so long as it was an Irish government, he would not put in a word against it? Yet he was ready to turn down any proposal that gave Ireland less than republican status. Others were prepared to compromise. When a delegation consisting of Griffith, Collins, Barton, two lawyers and Erskine Childers went to London in October, it was given no guidelines. Though its members had the power and status of plenipotentiaries, they were expected to report back to the Dail at every stage of the negotiations.

Griffith felt the important thing was to win self-government; the status of Ireland could always be changed from an imperial to a republican one later on. Collins, though he had fought desperately for republican ideals, agreed with him. The IRA was running short of arms and ammunition, and seventy IRA men had been taken prisoner when the Custom House was burned; the IRA could not, in Collins' opinion, carry on fighting for more than three weeks.

The Irish delegation, none of whom had any experience of high-level negotiation, struggled for two months against the Welsh wizard, as Lloyd George was sometimes called, and the best men he could bring forward, Winston Churchill and the eminent lawyer F. E. Smith, Lord Birkenhead. De Valera, prevaricating in the background, floated the idea of an external association between Britain and Ireland instead of an imperial one, and re-wrote the oath of allegiance so that Irishmen would be faithful to the king, not as head of state, but as head of the Commonwealth. The British insisted on maintaining naval bases at Irish ports; the new state was not to have the right to remain neutral in war.

Ulster was the rock on which negotiations were most likely to founder. Lloyd George told delegates that, if Ulster insisted on maintaining partition, he would set up a boundary commission to re-define the border; the commission would almost certainly recommend the return of large areas of the six counties to the south, leaving Northern Ireland so weakened it would no longer be viable as a separate state. Then Lloyd George delivered an ultimatum; either the delegates signed a treaty that very evening, accepting dominion status, similar to that of Canada, in return for a boundary commission, or war would be resumed in three days. The delegates were dog tired; they had travelled continually back and forth between London and Dublin, trying to obtain clear instructions from de Valera, and the unlikelihood of Britain setting up a boundary commission to coerce Ulster simply did not occur to them. Lloyd George met them in the Cabinet room at number 10 Downing Street and waved two letters addressed to Craig: which should he send, he asked, the letter saying agreement had been reached, or the one which said the Irish had refused imperial status? The Irishmen left to consider their decision and later that night, without even telephoning de Valera, four of them, Griffith, Collins, Barton and one of the lawyers, returned and, at 2.10 a.m. on 6 December 1921, signed the Treaty.[9] Without clamour, rejoicing, or even much hope, 700 years of British rule in Ireland was ended.

The delegates were the more flexible members of the Irish government – the hardliners had stayed at home. And when the delegation was back in Dublin, a bitter, wrangling argument began. De Valera, who had claimed earlier not to be a doctrinaire republican, immediately became one – narrow, intensely resentful that the Treaty had been signed without his leave, dogmatic and over-subtle. The Treaty was ratified by one vote in Cabinet and de Valera defeated; then in twelve public sittings and one that was closed, the Dail debated the Treaty. Griffith pointed out that, in the correspondence between de Valera and Lloyd George that had proceeded the negotiations, 'not once was a demand made for the recognition of the Irish Republic.'[10] De Valera countered by attacking the oath of allegiance. Irish ministers would still be His Majesty's ministers, the new Irish army (grown from the IRA) would be His Majesty's army. The king would still rule in Ireland. Then he produced what came to be known as Document No. 2, indistinguishable from the Treaty in most respects but incorporating the idea of external association. Collins pointed out that the Irish government had compromised when it accepted the invitation to negotiate; what the Treaty had won 'was not the ultimate freedom that all nations aspire and develop to, but the freedom to achieve it.' The arguments went on endlessly in an attempt to answer the deeply serious question of what independence really meant. Then on 7 January 1922, a vote was taken: sixty-four for the Treaty and fifty-seven against. De Valera resigned, stood again as president and lost by two votes. Griffith was elected in his stead.

The British government had never officially recognized the Dail and the British authorities had to hand over to a government chosen by the Southern Irish parliament. On 14 January this parliament had its single sitting and its members, all deputies in the Dail except the four Unionists who represented Dublin University, ratified the Treaty and chose Collins as chairman of a caretaker government, while de Valera and his supporters tactfully stayed away. There was some short-lived jubilation, a break in the clouds, when Dublin castle was handed over, the viceroy left and the British army sailed away, accompanied by the Black and Tans and the Auxiliaries.

But the country was fragmenting. Craig wielded authority in the North, Griffith led a pro-Treaty Dail and Collins directed the provisional government, which had the rest of the year to complete the takeover from the British. De Valera and the Republicans had split off and gone into the wilderness. Very dangerously, the IRA was splitting too, into Republican irregulars and a pro-Treaty Free State army; the only point of unity left to the IRA seemed to be its hostility to Ulster, where the Orangemen were organizing pogroms against Catholics and driving them across the border in their thousands. IRA guerrillas were shooting up British troops and Northern police in increasingly frequent border incidents; the incipient civil war between north and south, which had been simmering below the surface ever since 1912, might well have broken out, had not the cracks within the IRA been widening.

The IRA had never come under the control of the civil authority, unless the secret IRB could be called such, and with the politicians so divided, it was growing increasingly independent. Collins issued uniforms to the new Free State army and tried desperately to attract the Irregulars into it; nevertheless fighting broke out and in April the Irregulars took over Dublin's Four Courts, a complex of elegant Georgian buildings on the river Liffey, as their headquarters. De Valera was in no sense the leader of the Irregulars, and in May he and Collins buried their resentments long enough to arrange for the election of a new Dail which, they hoped, would reunite the country under a

315

coalition government; scrupulously they 'rigged' the election with a panel of Sinn Fein candidates, some for and some against the Treaty, in the same ratio as the treaty vote in the Dail! Sinn Fein had never placed true democracy high among its ideals. The Irish people were so weary of strife, however, that they preferred the pro-Treaty faction, and the anti-Treaty group lost seats.

Meanwhile, the Irregulars were passing quite freely in and out of the Four Courts, and the British government called on Collins to drive them out. For weeks he prevaricated; he wanted peace, and certainly not a struggle between different branches of the erstwhile IRA. Then on 22 June Field Marshal Sir Henry Wilson, a leading Unionist, who had been training the police in Northern Ireland, was shot dead by IRA gunmen outside his house in London. No-one knows who ordered his death – it could have been Collins. But the British government assumed the killers were Irregulars and told Collins he must take action against those in the Four Courts if the Treaty was to be preserved. On the morning of 28 June, Collins sent an ultimatum to the men in the Four Courts ordering them to surrender within twenty minutes and, when nothing happened, opened fire with field guns provided by the British. The Four Courts went up in flames, taking thousands of invaluable local records with it, and was abandoned on 30 June. The fighting spread, symbolically enough, to Sackville Street, still unrepaired after the Easter Rising, and the buildings opposite the GPO were burned to the ground. It was eight days before the Irregulars were beaten in the first engagement of a brief but horrendous civil war.

The Republicans were strongest in the wild areas of the south and west, traditionally extreme; they sought to hold a line running from Waterford to Limerick, and to defend what was jokingly called the Munster republic. De Valera, who had joined the Republican army as a private, tried vainly to dissuade them; as a politician out of power, he was not heeded. Collins had a Free State army four times the size of the Republican force, and the British provided him with money and arms. Inevitably the Republicans were pushed back, and in August Free State troops were sent round to Cork by sea. They took the city, and after that the Irregulars could do no more than lay ambushes, burn country houses and fight sporadically in the mountains –

descending from them, now and then, to harrass the civilian population. With 500 people dead, the civil war was fading out.

Then on 12 August, when the Free State troops had taken Cork, the president of the Dail and founder of Sinn Fein, Arthur Griffith, died aged fifty. He had worn himself out with a quarter of a century's intense work for the nationalist cause. Ten days later Michael Collins was dead too – shot in the back of the head. He, and those with him, had been fighting off an ambush near his birthplace, Clonakilty. He had said when he signed the Treaty that it was his death-warrant, and so it had proved.

To many of his compatriots, Collins was the real architect of Ireland's freedom, and some said he was the greatest Irish hero since Brian Boru.

W. T. Cosgrave, minister for local government and a Dublin city councillor of many years' experience, took over the leadership of the provisional government. With the support of a young and energetic lawyer, Kevin O'Higgins, recently elected to the Dail and appointed home secretary, and of General Richard Mulcahy, one of Collins' divisional commanders, who was minister for defence, he decided on measures of extreme severity to crush the Republicans. Republican prisoners were to be treated as rebels, not soldiers, courts martial were set up over much of the country and unauthorized possession of arms was made punishable by death. When Erskine Childers, who had become a fanatical propagandist for the Republic, was trapped by Free State troops, he brandished a pearl-handled revolver given him by Collins, was court-martialled and, in spite of his undoubted services to Ireland, cruelly shot.

The Free State forces had taken about 100 men prisoner when they drove the Irregulars out of the Four Courts. At the end of November Liam Lynch, an IRA commander who had taken the Republican side, issued an order, which the government captured, that all members of the government or the Dail who had voted for the ferocious emergency powers were to be shot; and a few days later two deputies had indeed been shot and a third killed. The government could, with justice, have taken and executed Lynch and his collaborators, but instead they punished the Irregulars taken prisoner months earlier at the Four Courts, who could have had nothing to do with the order; four of their leaders were taken from their cells and shot dead without trial as

317

a reprisal. During the next six months the Free State government executed by firing squad 77 Republicans, more than three times the number executed by the British in the whole two-and-a-half years of the War of Independence and imprisoned between 11,000 and 12,000 people for varying periods, including such figures of undoubted patriotism as Grace Plunkett, who had married Joseph Plunkett before his execution. The Irish Free State, fought for with such heroism, such fanatical and uncompromising idealism, such intense suffering and relentless sacrifice, was born in bitterness and blood.

CHAPTER 14

PARTITION

The Free State government was from the very beginning faced with the most daunting problems. Apart from having to wage war and win it against the republicans, who had a lot of support in their stand against the Treaty, it also had to rebuild a shattered economy to tackle large-scale unemployment, poverty and social distress, and to provide industry, commerce and agriculture with a stable environment in which to flourish. At the same time the government could not afford to lose sight of the principal aim of the 1916 martyrs, as yet unfulfilled – that is, separation altogether from the British empire. Although the first constitution of the Free State, drafted in 1922, had acknowledged Ireland to have dominion status (like Canada) within the empire, with an obligation to recognize the king of Great Britain as sovereign, the Provisional Government led by Cosgrave reconciled these opposite positions in a number of constructive ways.

In the summer of 1923, Cosgrave held the Free State's first general election, leading the pro-Treaty candidates who now belonged to a newly-formed party, which took the name of an older freedom movement, Cumann na nGaedheal. The party won 63 out of 153 seats, not a majority, but with the support of some small groups and some individual independents, enough to form a government. When de Valera and his fellow MPs who opposed the Treaty refused to take their seats, the Irish Labour party (which had won 14) gallantly agreed to form the official opposition so as to give substance to Ireland's enthusiasm for democratic government. The Cumann party governed competently for four years; order was restored largely through the firmness and skill of Kevin O'Higgins, the new minister of justice (sadly murdered in 1927) and General Richard Mulcahy (an old colleague of Michael Collins) who was minister for defence. It was during this first period that the problem of partition again reared its head.

One of the Treaty articles had dealt with the new province of Northern Ireland, Protestant and anxious to remain part of the United Kingdom. How much of Ulster was to become part of Britain was not specified but was to be referred to some future boundary commission. The civil war that raged through the Free State until well into 1923, and its aftermath, pushed the problem to one side, and in so doing allowed the hard core of the north to consolidate an already strong position where in the six northern counties there were majorities of Protestants over Catholics. A boundary commission was set up in 1924, but before its report could be published, the recommendations were leaked to the press. Consequently, the report was not published, and nothing came of the recommendations.* The Free State government had believed that the problem would just go away and that a boundary commission would lean towards the Free State view by reducing the six northern counties to four, thus making a separated Protestant Ulster unworkable in the longer term. This did not happen, and the Free State government had to accept a divided Ireland and also prepare to deal with a likely revival of Republican activity (in the form of IRA terrorism).

Although Cosgrave and his colleagues accepted partition, successive governments in the Free State demanded its end and the absorption of the six counties into an united Ireland. This is still part of the policy of Irish governments today, though they do not of course condone the use of force to obtain it.

In June 1927 Cosgrave went to the country again. This time de Valera, who had re-formed his party (now known as Fianna Fail, or 'warriors of Fa'l – another word for Ireland) won 44 seats to Cumann's 46 (a sharp drop in support for the government). De Valera's MPs took their seats – they had to because of an electoral amendment bill introduced by the government. The Irish Labour party improved its postition to 22 seats. But Cosgrave's majority

---

* They were published in 1969.

was so slim that sooner or later it was bound to fall, and it did so in September the same year. A second election was called and it had a more decisive result. De Valera advanced to 57 seats, but Cosgrave did much better, obtaining 67 seats, and he was able to govern for a second four years. These were years of useful reforms, such as the credit scheme to assist farmers, the encouragement of sugar beet production (a major factory was built and run at Carlow), the Shannon electric scheme – the first national electricity supply scheme in Ireland – and a variety of attempts to keep government spending down, to stimulate industry (employment in industry rose from about 103,000 in 1926 to about 111,000 in 1931) and to improve transport and communications. But the new state could not escape the ravages of the World Depression of the early 1930s. Agricultural prices fell in the period 1930–2, industrial production faltered, orders were lost and unemployment leapt. Some tough austerity measures helped but also increased the government's growing unpopularity and in 1932 the general election produced a major change with the advent of de Valera to power.

In pursuit of its policy to take advantage of the 'freedom to achieve freedom' bequeathed by Michael Collins and Arthur Griffith, the Cosgrave government took a number of steps to assert its independence of the hangover of British rule. It played a leading part in and made important contributions to the long series of meetings and negotiations that were held in the late 1920s among the dominion states of the British empire, that led to the empire becoming the commonwealth, highlighted in the important Statute of Westminster (1931) which recognized 'co-equality between Britain and the dominions and the right of dominion parliaments to repeal or amend Westminster legislation affecting them.' In 1929, the Free State government also decided that henceforth the Free State would put internal disputes to the Court of International Justice when it wished. These progressive moves irritated the government's opponents because they were not radical enough, but when in 1932 de Valera did win power and thus the opportunity to push for that separation from Britain he yearned for, he was to find that the Cosgrave policy had smoothed the way for his ambitions to be achieved.

In the 1932 election, de Valera's Fianna Fail won 72 seats, and with the support of one or two minority groups de Valera was able to form a government and to carry the country through a long period of change. One of his first acts was to push through the Removal of the Oath Act, which abolished the oath of allegiance to the British Crown. Another was to accept the presidency of the Council of the League of Nations, about as clear a statement as he could make that he regarded Ireland as an autonomous independent nation. Four years later, he introduced the External Relations bill, which virtually declared Ireland to be a republic and recognized the sovereign of Great Britain for diplomatic purposes only. In 1937 he introduced a new constitution, which declared Ireland to be a 'sovereign, independent, democratic' state, and this was endorsed in a national plebiscite. The head of the government, or prime minister, was henceforth known as the *taoiseach*. The office of governor-general had already been wound down, and now was replaced by that of president of Ireland. The first holder was Dr Douglas Hyde, the founder of the Gaelic League. This position was intended to be a substitute for a sovereign. And Ireland itself ceased to be called the Free State, becoming instead Eire, 'or in the English language, Ireland'. Eire consisted of the twenty-six counties, but de Valera took the opportunity of reiterating national aspirations for a united Ireland by recognizing in the Constitution the existence of Northern Ireland on a temporary basis only, with phrases such as 'the national territory consists of the whole island of Ireland', and 'pending the reintegration of the national territory . . . the laws . . . shall have the like area and extent of application as the laws of Saorstat Eireann (i.e. the 26 counties) . . . .'

As if to emphasize the drift of his policies, de Valera entered into a major financial conflict with Britain. He held back annual payments to Britain collected by the government from farmers buying out landowners, and broke other financial agreements. Britain responded with tariffs on Irish exports, particularly in agriculture, and this conflict lasted for six years, bringing much hardship to the Irish people who nonetheless stayed solidly behind their leader. In 1938 the conflict came to an end with a final £10 million payment to Britain for the return of the 'Treaty' ports – those ports in Ireland in which the British had retained a naval presence. This was a significant exchange, for when Britain went to war with Nazi Germany in 1939 (the start of the Second World War) the Ireland of de Valera decided to remain strictly neutral: he would not allow either side to have the use of the naval harbours.

Other policies of de Valera's government included measures to strengthen the status of the Catholic Church in Ireland. In 1937 de Valera enshrined the Church's teachings on marriage and the family in the actual constitution itself: the sale of contraceptives was banned, and divorce was not allowed (and it still isn't). Church seemed inextricably linked to state, and indeed since the 1930s the hierarchy of the Church has played a consistently influential – and sometimes decisive – role in national policies and politics. This may perhaps be partly understood in the light of a national historical gratitude for the crucial role that the Catholic faith played in keeping alive the spirit of Ireland through centuries of Protestant Ascendancy oppression. De Valera also strengthened efforts to 'gaelicize' Ireland, begun by Cosgrave, when the study of the Irish language was made compulsory in schools and a sound knowledge of it obligatory for entry into the civil service. Documents and publications were to be in Irish as well as in English (and later on, road signs were posted in both tongues).

De Valera has been criticized for his neutral stance in the Second World War, but it is difficult to see what else he could have done. Lining up with Britain would have negated all he had ever fought for. Within his own ranks and on its extreme edges were elements fully prepared to make a lot of trouble if he were to do so. Britain's quarrel with Nazi Germany had nothing to do with Ireland, they said. Supporting Germany - probably unthinkable for de Valera himself by that time - would have brought down upon him the full force of British wrath. As it was soon to transpire, some members of the UK government, including Britain's wartime prime minister and national saviour, Winston Churchill, were thinking hard about seizing the 'Treaty' ports. There was another point. As John Murphy wrote, in *Ireland in the Twentieth Century* (p.99): 'Neutrality in a world conflict is the ultimate exercise in national sovereignty.' De Valera still found it necessary to underline Ireland's independence from Britain, and indeed was to go on doing so right up to his defeat at the election of 1948. Ireland suffered privations in the war from food shortages, rationing, coal shortages, rail cuts and so forth, and nearly 50,000 Irishmen volunteered to serve with British forces.

By 1948 de Valera had led the government for sixteen years and it was high time for a change. At a general election, Fianna Fail won more seats than any other party but not enough to form a government. An administration was formed from a coalition of de Valera's opponents, to be headed by John Costello as *taoiseach*. His first act was to pilot through a Republic of Ireland bill, which on Easter Monday 1949 created the Republic of Ireland, outside the Commonwealth. Thus was finally demonstrated that compromise 'freedom to achieve freedom' so sensibly negotiated by Collins and Griffith twenty-eight years earlier. The new government also reaffirmed that its authority extended over the whole of Ireland, something that Ulster would not accept then and does not accept today.

John Costello was a lawyer who had been attorney-general for the years 1926–32 in the Cosgrave administration. He was leader of Fine Gael, the party founded in 1933 by the merger of Cumann na nGaedheal with a number of sympathetic but much smaller groups. For three years Costello presided over a team of ministers drawn from several parties (opposed to one another in a number of policies) who were united in only one aim, to keep de Valera out of office. But withal the ministry achieved much. The declaration of the Republic in 1949 was only the final step in separating Ireland completely from Great Britain. The Costello government could and did get on with important measures on several fronts, including government capital investment in a variety of projects. Among these was the Land Rehabilitation project, which set out to generate agriculture on some five million acres of hitherto neglected land, and this was linked to a satisfactory trade agreement with Britain. In industry, a government industrial development organization stimulated a remarkable expansion of industrial production. On the international scene, Ireland had representatives on some of the United Nations agencies, such as the Food and Agricultural Organization (FAO), though the country itself was not admitted to full membership of UNO until 1955. Ireland was also a founder member of the Council of Europe.

The Costello administration fell in 1951 as a result of what is known as the 'mother and child scheme'. The minister of health, Dr Noel Browne, already famous for vigorous efforts to improve the nation's health by tackling the high incidence of tuberculosis, for injecting funds and other help to hospitals, and for generally stimulating public health services, conceived what he believed a reasonable scheme to provide free state maternity care and free medical attention for children (up to sixteen). It seemed a natural extension of the national health scheme introduced by Fianna Fail in 1947. But it stirred up a hornet's nest of opposition among the country's doctors (just as the original proposals for a national health service had done in Britain a year before). Unfortunately, the doctors were supported by the Church, which regarded the scheme as an infringement of the '. . . rights of the family and of the individual and. . . . liable to very great abuse . . .' The Church was incensed at proposals to provide sex education to women, as it saw this as a prelude to the acceptance of contraception and perhaps even abortion. Pressure on Dr Browne grew even from his own colleagues, and he resigned, precipitating a general election in 1951, which was won by de Valera who now came in to govern for a second term. Three years later, a fresh election returned Costello to power, but his Fine Gael ministry was not successful in stemming a deteriorating economic situation that was aggravated by inflation and adverse trade balances, and badly affected by the results of the Suez crisis of 1956. Another election was held in 1957 and de Valera's Fianna Fail was returned to power. Two years later, de Valera himself retired and was appointed president of Ireland. He was succeeded as *taoiseach* by Séan Lemass.

During de Valera's last ministry, the department of finance produced Ireland's first real economic plan, the result of a series of papers and discussions that went back to the late 1940s. The plan was masterminded by T. K. Whitaker, permanent secretary to the department, and was an answer to the period of economic stagnation of the early 1950s, when some 50,000 people were emigrating from Ireland every year. The plan was a bold attempt to set Ireland's economy on an expansionist path on all fronts, with a range of ambitious objectives in sight, including the stemming of the emigration flow, generating employment, raising national living standards, increasing productive capacity and enlarging investment, and expanding agricultural production. The plan was implemented as the First Economic Programme by the incoming *taoiseach*, Lemass, who had had a long career (1932–9, 1940–47) as minister for industry in de Valera's long first ministry and who believed in the need for state intervention in economic activity (among some enterprises, he had initiated Aer Lingus in 1936). From 1958 to about 1964, Ireland certainly enjoyed a sustained growth rate of about 4 per cent per annum, and so the plan can be said to have succeeded. Unemployment was cut by one third; emigration was staunched by nearly a half; capital investment was almost doubled, and national output increased by a quarter. By 1964 Lemass was ready to launch the Second Economic Programme, but this time the steam all but ran out, due partly to ideas running too far ahead of the capacity to translate them into action and partly to adverse effects from abroad, especially Britain whose own economic troubles of the mid–1960s resulted in import levies that hit Ireland hard. Another feature of the Lemass period was an increasing involvement in international affairs, by providing Irish troops for United Nations peace-keeping commitments in a number of theatres of strife, such as central Africa and the Middle East, by exercising Ireland's vote in the UN Assembly on a number of issues such as against the spread of nuclear weapons, for the admission of China to the United Nations, and against some of the more aggressive policies and activities of members of the Communist nations.

Lemass retired in 1966 and was succeeded as *taoiseach* by the Cork lawyer Jack Lynch, who sympathized with the rising tide of minority rights agitation in Northern Ireland. This exploded in the violence in Londonderry and elsewhere in Ulster in the autumn of 1968. Lynch was no more successful than his predecessors or his successors in helping to resolve the growing bitterness between the Catholic minority and the Protestant majority in Ulster, or in curbing the increasing terrorism and violence of the IRA and the INLA who both sought to exploit the bitterness for their own ends. Yet Lynch's ministry was not without achievements. He made changes in the constitution which reduced the special status of the Catholic Church, and these were widely supported by the electorate. He consistently spoke out against the use of force and terrorism in the pursuit of the old ambition of Fianna Fail to bring Northern Ireland into union with the South. And he successfully steered his country (with Fine Gael as well as Fianna Fail support) to an 80+ per cent vote to enter the European Economic Community, of which Ireland became a member on 1 January 1973. It was not to be long before

Ireland began to reap some if not all of the benefits it confidently expected.

The people of Northern Ireland had not welcomed partition in 1920. To Carson it had been, though hardly a surprise, a deep disappointment; he had hoped that, through the manipulation of the north, he would be able to keep the whole of Ireland within the Union. Sir James Craig, however, had been more sanguine. Tough and tenacious, an Ulsterman first and foremost, he cared very little for the fate of Unionists elsewhere; though he wrote to Lloyd George in 1921 that the north had only accepted self-government 'as a supreme sacrifice in the interests of peace', he was well aware of the advantages of partition for northern Unionists. They could create a Protestant state.

The new state was to enjoy limited Home Rule. A governor was appointed to represent the monarch and in 1921 Northern Ireland sent thirteen MPs to take their seats in the imperial parliament at Westminster. In practice, the imperial parliament only debated the affairs of Northern Ireland for about two hours a year! – and yet it retained control of the state's defence, foreign affairs, trading links with Britain and, to a large extent, finance; customs duty and other taxes were passed to the British Treasurey, which made special financial allocations to Northern Ireland. And British law remained paramount, not to be altered or amended by the Northern Irish parliament.

The people of Northern Ireland also voted for their own House of Commons, which consisted of fifty-two members, who, in their turn, elected a cabinet, or executive committee, with a prime minister (inevitably Craig) and five other ministers responsible for finance (in so far as the British Treasury would allow him to be), home affairs, health and social services, education, agriculture and commerce. The House also elected twenty-four members of a Senate, or upper house, whose members included the Lord Mayor of Belfast and the Mayor of Londonderry. But, as most senators were dependent on the lower house for their seats, they seldom ventured to contradict it, and the prime purpose of an upper house, of occasionally compelling a lower house to think again, was not fulfilled.

The Northern Irish parliament inevitably reflected the Protestant and Unionist ascendancy within the country. There had been no protection for the Catholic minority built into the new constitution; the south had never raised the matter of safeguards with Britain, because they expected the northern state to be demolished in three or four years by the boundary commission, and the Unionists established an unshakeable parliamentary majority of three to one. Nevertheless the new government began its rule sensibly enough with an Education Act, passed in 1923, which provided for an integrated and secular system of state education, with no religious teaching during compulsory school hours. Catholic and Protestant children were to grow up together. The Catholic bishops, however, condemned the Act, and the Catholic clergy saw to it that local schools within their control were not secularized, while the Protestants, none too pleased either, called for amending acts. The first, passed in 1925, restored the teaching of the Bible, a Protestant but never a Catholic practice, in state schools, and the second, passed in 1930, allowed the school authorities to select Protestant teachers in preference to Catholics. State schools were then 'safe for Protestant children', in the words of the prime minister, Viscount Craigavon (as Craig had become), and since that time the children of the two religious groupings have been brought up separately, most Protestant children attending the state, or provided, schools and Catholic children the voluntary Catholic schools, not provided by the state but assisted by government subsidy.[1]

Catholics had not helped matters by turning their backs on the new government, and declaring their allegiance lay with the Dail in Dublin. They had been so stunned by partition – so shocked by their sudden abandonment – that they refused to recognize the new state or cooperate with it in any way. They would not take their seats in its parliament, play their part in local government, work in its civil service or join its police, but hoped fervently for its failure and speedy reintegration with the south.

In 1920, when the IRA, in support of the Catholics, had fought all along the border, A, B and C Special Constabularies had been formed in the north to help the RIC. A Specials were full-time, armed, uniformed, paid, trained and sent to trouble spots, B Specials were part-timers, armed but initially without uniforms, who patrolled their own areas, and C Specials formed a reserve for use in emergencies, particularly along the border. All were

Protestants and many were extremists – Orangemen with guns – and too often they regarded their constabulary duties as a licence to attack Catholics without provocation, shooting up innocent passers-by in the streets and hurling hand grenades into Catholic homes. And the Catholics, terrified, turned again and again to the IRA. When a Protestant raider, trying to create terror by night, crept through a dimly lit Catholic street, with blackened face and stockinged feet, anyone who saw him gave a long-drawn-out cry of 'Murder!' Those hearing the cry took it up, and women banged pots and pans and dustbin lids, until IRA youths came hurrying up and the raiders fled.

The IRA and the Specials, whose numbers rose to well over 20,000 within a couple of years, carried on a continual sectarian warfare, with the IRA blowing up shops and factories belonging to Protestant businessmen and the Specials taking reprisals, rather like the Black and Tans. Then in 1922 the new parliament passed a draconian Special Powers Act, which proscribed such paramilitaries as the IRA and the Ulster Volunteer Force, made the illegal possession of arms and explosives punishable by flogging and death, and gave the newly constituted Royal Ulster Constabulary, which replaced the RIC, the right to search without a warrant and detain suspects without trial. By 1924, 2,000 suspects were in detention. The Act, renewed annually until 1928 and at five-yearly intervals thereafter up to 1933, when it was made permanent, became notorious as a means of suppressing opposition to the government by internment.

Unionists, blind to Catholics' very real fears and aware only of their unhelpfulness, regarded them as disloyal: enemies, as they had been the enemies of William of Orange, the Scottish planters before him and even, as the 'wild Irish', the enemies of the people of the Pale. And Unionists began to practise open and widespread discrimination against Catholics. Being in such an overwhelming majority, they had no need to rig parliamentary elections, but in the sphere of local government, there were areas, such as the city of Londondery and Co. Fermanagh, where Catholics were in a majority, and the gerrymandering was unashamed. Only ratepayers and their wives could vote in local elections and plural voting was allowed, placing an emphasis on property which tended to exclude Catholics, because of their poverty, and favour Protestants. But that was not all. In Londonderry Catholics and Protestants were strictly segregated, so that all Catholics allocated corporation houses received them in only one of three wards and, although the city's population was 60 per cent Catholic, the composition of the corporation could always be maintained at twelve Protestants to eight Catholics. Other towns used the same tactics. When council houses were allocated to Catholics, they were always in the same areas, so that a Protestant majority on the council was assured. The Catholic need for council houses was greater than the Protestant, and Catholics received the higher allocation, but as soon as the areas, or voting wards, set aside for Catholics were full, house-building for Catholics stopped.

For many years Unionists were afraid that the Catholic birthrate, being higher than their own, would lead to such an increase in the size of the Catholic population that their supremacy would be challenged. By the 1930s the crude pogroms against the Catholics were over, but Unionists tried, by subtler means, to drive Catholics into emigration. New industries were set up in Protestant areas in preference to Catholic ones, and private employers, who were mostly Protestant, were encouraged to discriminate. In 1933 Sir Basil Brooke, who was minister for agriculture and a future prime minister, declared at an Orange parade that he had not one Catholic in his employment! And on the same occasion J. M. Andrews, the minister for labour and another future prime minister, claimed to have investigated thirty-one porters employed at Stormont, the newly opened parliament building, and found there were thirty Protestants and one Catholic, 'there', he said ominously, 'temporarily'.

Northern Ireland suffered very severely in the Depression of the 1930s. The north was Ireland's industrial area – the only part of Ireland to have taken part in Britain's Industrial Revolution of the late eighteenth and early nineteenth centuries. The population of Belfast rose from 20,000 at the time of the Union to 350,000 in 1901, a century later; shipbuilding and engineering were added to the linen industry to bring the city prosperity. But in the 1930s the World Depression brought widespread unemployment to both communities. There was no labour movement to take up workers' discontent. The government refused to recognize the local Trades Union Congress, and the work force was too cowed by the possibility of unemployment to put up a fight.

330

The monolithic Orange Order, which spread across the boundaries of class to include at least two-thirds of the country's adult Protestant males, provided the sense of solidarity which was lacking. Following the flag with his comrades, wearing the Orange regalia, and watching Catholics scuttle indoors at the sound of the Protestant drum, even the most downtrodden worker felt he was somebody, and safe.

The IRA played a similar role for Catholics. Kept out of Northern Ireland's most prosperous engineering and shipbuilding industries, and faced with a declining linen industry, Catholics were employed largely in the textile industries which were replacing linen manufacture, and the catering and drinks trades, where the major demand was for female skills. As a consequence, male unemployment in such Catholic areas as Londonderry, parts of Belfast and Strabane was twice that of women. Idle youths, lounging all day in the streets, readily moved on from childish stonethrowing at soldiers and policemen to a militant organization which combined a backward-looking idealism, based on the Proclamation of the Republic in 1916, with far-left socialism and repudiation of all three governments - Dublin, Stormont and Westminster – and their courts. They read the fiery IRA newspaper *An Phoblacht (The Republic),* which blamed their plight on 'British imperialism', and discovered a new sense of purpose. They came of a fighting people: they found it exciting to drill in the hills, absorb guerrilla tactics, and handle guns. The Catholic population gave them tacit support – a meal, money, a bed for the night. And wounded IRA men were treated in hospitals north and south of the border without medical or nursing staff giving them away.

When de Valera turned the Free State into a virtual republic in 1932, the political divergence between north and south increased. As the Unionists, feeling beleaguered, intensified discrimination and unemployment went up, the IRA determined, whether Dublin wanted it or not, to 'fight for the Republic', and to do it in England, where Irish lives would not be lost. After a formal declaration of war, made by post to the British prime minister, bombs were exploded in London, the Midlands and the north, at gas and electricity plants as well as GPO letterboxes, public lavatories, telephone boxes, railway cloakrooms, cinemas, post offices, shops, offices and factories. The Dublin government promptly banned the IRA but the British, although rounding up scores of IRA men, displayed their usual tolerance of opposition by allowing some 200 Irishmen to march through London, escorted by British police, with banners demanding the release of IRA prisoners – and that only a day after several explosions! Nevertheless executions and ferocious sentences of imprisonment followed the arrests of bombers and their misguided accomplices, especially after a bombing attack in Coventry, which killed five people and injured fifty-two more.

When war broke out between Britain and Germany in 1939, the gap between north and south in Ireland grew yet wider. While the south preserved its neutrality, Craigavon 'placed the whole of our (Northern Ireland's) resources at the command of the government in Britain'. Conscription was never introduced because it might have offended Nationalist sensibilities, but thousands of Northern Irishmen, both Catholic and Protestant, joined the British services, and Belfast, Londonderry and Larne became British naval bases. They played an important part in the battle of the Atlantic, providing supplies and a refuge for convoys of British naval and merchant ships bringing food and armaments from America to the estuaries of the Mersey and the Clyde. When the United States joined in the war in 1942, Londonderry became an American naval base and large stretches of the country were used as training grounds for American troops.

Northern Irish shipbuilding and engineering came into their own; during the six years of war, 150 ships, 550 tanks and 1,500 bomber aircraft were built. The numbers of workers in the shipyards almost tripled, and in the engineering works they very nearly doubled. The textile industry was busy producing uniforms, though linen manufacture was still down, and agriculture, always the predominant producer, received a tremendous boost; cut off from much of the world, the British market needed all the food it could get, and imported huge quantities of Northern Irish oats, potatoes and cattlefeed.

When the war ended in 1945, Britain thanked Northern Ireland for her help by promising the Northern Irish people all the social welfare benefits, educational grants and subsidies for agriculture and industry which were to be introduced in Britain. Northern Ireland would be taxed at the same rate as Britain, but being a far poorer and more backward country, with a greater incidence of sickness and higher unemployment, Northern Ireland was, most decidedly, the winner in the arrangement.

The Republic, as the south became in 1949, could not possibly offer its citizens the social benefits enjoyed in the north. Even northern Catholics found the view southward less attractive and reconciled themselves to the British connection, and the Northern Irish Labour party declared its belief that 'the best interests of Northern Ireland lie in maintaining the constitutional links with the UK'. But the Labour party commanded few votes. When Catholics, discriminated against and excluded, chafed at their general lack of opportunity, they still turned, in a confused and inconsistent fashion, to the Nationalist party, which favoured reintegration, for help.

Yet reintegration was becoming less and less likely. It had never been debated in any assembly – neither the Dail, nor the British parliament, and most certainly not in Stormont. When the south combined its new republican status with departure from the Commonwealth, the political difficulties of reunification increased immeasurably, but that did not give its politicians pause. And in the same year of 1949 the British reassured the Unionists with a new Northern Ireland Act containing a guarantee that 'in no event will Northern Ireland or any part thereof cease to be part of His Majesty's dominions and of the United Kingdom without the consent of the parliament of Northern Ireland.' Northern Ireland's Catholics, who had never been able to influence their own parliament, felt doubly left out.

In the early 1950s the IRA mounted a new campaign, in pursuance, as ever, of the all-Ireland Republic proclaimed in 1916. Border posts were burned or blown up and policemen, of both north and south, attacked. The campaign failed; Catholics as well as Protestants were shocked at its brutality, and the governments in Dublin and Stormont reacted with equal firmness. Nevertheless between 1956 and 1961 violence flared up in Belfast, with sectarian warfare between the IRA, the Ulster Volunteer Force and a second Unionist paramilitary group, the Ulster Freedom Movement. The Special Powers Act was invoked, about 150 IRA gunmen and IRA supporters detained without trial, and parts of the city turned into no-go areas, where the police dared not venture. In the streets which linked the segregated Catholic and Protestant housing estates, no-one was safe from snipers' bullets:

and people made tunnels through garden walls and even houses, so they could reach shops, schools and doctors' surgeries without being fired upon.

The Unionist government maintained its total insensitivity to Catholic feeling. A new town near the Catholic city of Armagh was called Craigavon, after the first Unionist prime minister, and a new university was established, not in Northern Ireland's second city, Londonderry, where Catholics predominated, but in the nearby Protestant town of Coleraine. Catholics were openly denied jobs – sometimes because they were less qualified than Protestants. Being poorer, Catholics could give less education to their children, who, with fewer opportunities, became poorer still, in a vicious circle. As Unionists had hoped they would, Catholics emigrated. More than half the emigrants from Northern Ireland came from that third of the population which was Catholic.

Then in 1963 the Unionist party, solidly conservative since its inception, began to split. Some more imaginative Unionists felt a need for better relations between Catholics and Protestants, and one of them, Captain Terence O'Neill, became prime minister. Though a Protestant, he was descended from the ancient ruling family of Ó Néill, and he did not share the fear of the Catholic Irish endemic among Unionists of settler descent. He went round Catholic towns and villages, schools and institutions, as no other Unionist leader had done, recognized the trade unions, and even exchanged visits with the *taoiseach* of the Republic, Séan Lemass – an action condemned by many Unionists as almost treason. For this gentle reforming spirit was raising the hackles of hardline Unionists – of Ian Paisley in particular, a huge, thundering, crewe-cut cleric with fundamentalist Presbyterian beliefs and a rabid hatred of what he termed Romanism. Since the 1950s he had been leading an organization called Ulster Protestant Action, which aimed to give preference to Protestant workers over Catholics in the fields of employment and local authority housing. When in 1966 O'Neill had the Ulster Volunteer Force proscribed under the Special Powers Act, it was too much for Paisley; he incited Protestants to oppose a legal demonstration by Catholics and spent three months in gaol for it. And the proscription was too little for Northern Ireland's Catholics. O'Neill had lifted the lid - and their resentments boiled over. Catholics had been better

334

educated since the war; improved schooling and grants for university education had led to the development of a Catholic middle class, which could not be kept down. When in 1968 a Protestant council tried to give a council house to the young, unmarried secretary of a Unionist politician instead of a Catholic family, the Catholic Civil Rights Association, formed a year earlier, organized a protest march in Dungannon and, to everyone's surprise, 2,500 people joined it. A few weeks later, a similar march was organized in Londonderry.

The second Civil Rights march was intended to be peaceful and well conducted, as the first had been. But the Dungannon march had been widely covered by the media, and such leftwing organizations as the IRA felt a march in Londonderry offered an opportunity for publicity too good to miss. They took the march over and clashed violently with the RUC. Sporadic fighting broke out all over the city, the Catholic Bogside area was barricaded and, for the first time in Londonderry, petrol bombs were thrown. The trouble escalated, and for two months there were marches and counter-marches in both Londonderry and Belfast.

31. An Orange march (courtesy of the *Belfast Telegraph*)

O'Neill introduced reforms in local government and the allocation of council houses, though not the reform in the local
government franchise which would have given all Catholics a
vote. Then in January 1969, O'Neill called a general election and
the split in the Unionist party showed itself. For the first time,
Unionists presented conflicting policies to the electors. O'Neill
was returned to power, but his reforms had so alarmed Unionist
extremists, without satisfying the Catholics, that violent clashes
between the two sides grew yet more frequent. He could not
carry his cabinet with him over more extensive reform, and in
April he resigned. His distant cousin, Major J. D. Chichester-
Clark, succeeded him, and proved a bumbling prime minister;
he refused, despite considerable urging from the British, to cancel
the Orange marches in July, and they turned into riots. When
the Protestant Apprentice Boys marched through Londonderry
in August, the Bogside was barricaded again and the RUC kept
out. Rioting spread to Dungannon and Belfast, and before the
month was out, the skeletal British garrison had to be heavily
reinforced.

At first the British army was welcomed by Catholics as their
only line of defence against Unionist fury. The soldiers took up
positions along the edge of the Bogside, without coming in, and
instructed the RUC to keep behind them. But when the 1970
marching season began at Easter, and the British army showed
itself equally willing to use force to restrain Catholic violence
towards Protestants as the other way round, Catholics, deeply
resentful, began stoning and petrol-bombing British troops. In
Catholic areas soldiers were no longer seen as protectors, but
invaders. The IRA sniped at them, inevitably they responded,
civilians got in the way and there were terrible accidents. In the
resultant emotion, centuries of hostility from British governments
and armies were remembered, and IRA recruitment went up.

The IRA are courageous, idealistic and often inept. They shoot
the wrong people and their bombs go off too soon. And they are
cruel. They discipline wavering supporters by kneecapping them
with revolver shots, tarring and feathering, and death. Their
callousness is extraordinary. An IRA hit-man called at the house
of the man he sought, chatted and watched television with his
children, and then, when his victim walked in, shot him dead
in front of them. Another IRA victim was shot at a wedding,

while he held the hand of a three-year-old child. It is the violence of the Whiteboys and the Defenders recurring – the predictable reaction to a gap between government and governed which is too great. The Catholic Church has always condemned violence, and the Dublin government has consistently operated the law against it, but the Catholic community of Northern Ireland, though deploring it, has a sneaking sympathy for its perpetrators. The illegal violence of irregular gunmen seems to them no worse than the institutionalized violence of the forces of law and order.

In 1971, after two years of disturbance, with street fighting involving illegal Unionist organizations as well as the IRA, the Stormont government insisted on reintroducing internment without trial under the Special Powers Act. The British army was used to arrest and interrogate large numbers of Republican suspects, picked out by the RUC from out-of-date and inaccurate files. Some detainees had a terrorist background, but most were merely local politicians with nationalist leanings. The Catholic community was, understandably, outraged – and IRA recruitment and activity increased dramatically. The British decided to take over control of security and the administration of justice, the Stormont government refused such a surrender of authority and, in March 1972, it was suspended. Home Rule in the state of Northern Ireland had failed.

The problem in Ireland since partition has been that of a double minority. In the island as a whole, Protestants are greatly outnumbered; they amount to about 25 per cent. But in the north they compose almost two-thirds of the population. Catholics have considered putting the end of partition to a referendum covering the whole island – which they would win. The northern Protestants, on the other hand, feel the British government should stick to its pledges, made many times, to preserve partition and the Union, so long as the majority in the north vote for it. The two majorities seem, on the face of it, irreconcilable.

Both sides in the north suffer from the fears that come from being an unprotected minority. In the past, Catholic fears were probably the more realistic; since partition, Orangemen have not actually told Catholics to go 'To hell – or Connacht', but they have, through widespread discrimination, driven Catholics into emigration. Since the start of the Civil Rights movement, however, Protestants' power has dwindled – with their government suspended, their police force and paramilitaries subject to British authority and their economic and social dominance gradually being whittled away. Descended from colonists, with a culture and political attachment to Britain that set them apart from the indigenous people, they are in a classic post-colonial situation. As a dominant people, and numerically superior in the north, it was worth their while to try to get rid of the indigenous people, as the Americans did with the Indians, and, like all other peoples in the same situation, that is what they set out to do. But when Stormont was suspended, and the British government imposed Direct Rule, the numbers game went against them. With the Catholics of the south supporting those of the north, Britain trying to be impartial and hosts of Irish-Americans sending aid to the IRA, they are being forced to make some hard decisions. They may come to terms with the native majority, fight a losing battle to preserve the status quo, or find new homes elsewhere.

The south could ease the tensions of northern Protestants very considerably – if its people wished. But the claim of the south to authority in the north, expressed in Articles 2 and 3 of the constitution of 1937, ignores the culture and political attachments of Unionists as completely as the Stormont government ignored the aspirations of northern Catholics. And sometimes the south has behaved as if the north, with its different point of view, hardly counted; Carson had exclaimed in 1921 that 'if the south and the west of Ireland had held out the hand of friendship to the north . . . Ulster would have accepted it'. To many Unionists it has seemed that the south is alien, interested only in harbouring the terrorists who blow up northern shops and policemen.

Yet in 1972 the people of the south did, for their own reasons, take the very constructive step of deleting the article, inserted by de Valera into the constitution, which gave the Catholic Church pre-eminence; looking for a more secular society, 8 per cent voted for the change. In 1979 contraception was made legal, but in 1986 civil divorce was rejected; the move towards a more open society, with room for non-Catholic views, came to a halt.

Meanwhile the IRA progressed from the bombing of shops and

factories, a campaign which proved unpopular because it threw so many people out of work, to attacks on prestige figures, such as the British ambassador in Dublin (killed in July, 1976) and a leading member of the British royal family, earl Mountbatten of Burma (killed in August, 1979). The campaign culminated in October 1984, with an explosion in a hotel in Brighton, where leaders of the British government were staying for a Conservative party conference. There have also been endless attacks on British army patrols. The IRA knows it cannot defeat the British army but, following the old pattern, hopes to make Northern Ireland ungovernable – when, so the IRA believes, the British army would withdraw.

Britain is tired of holding the ring in Northern Ireland. During the fifteen years between 1969 and 1984, 377 British soldiers were killed there, thousands seriously injured, and the annual financial cost to the British taxpayer has equalled the British contribution to the EEC. Yet the Union has no advantages for Britain any longer. Northern Irish MPs may, or may not, take up their seats at Westminster; no government can rely on their votes. Unionists call themselves Loyalists, but the ordinary Briton wonders who they are loyal to? Certainly not the British government, whose laws they flout and whose initiatives they resist every inch of the way. 'Ulster says No.' A lot of British people would like to see the whole pack of troubles float away into the Atlantic.

Yet Britain is to blame for having set up a separate government in Northern Ireland, which that mini-country never asked for, without providing adequate safeguards for the minority. The Unionist leadership should, first and foremost, have promoted unity by taking positive steps to win over the Catholic minority. When, unimaginative and stale, it showed itself more likely to discriminate than unite, Britain should have monitored its progress.

The issue is no longer partition. No-one but the IRA, old-fashioned and unrealistic as it is, really considers the time is ripe for an end to the border. Nor is it the presence of British troops in Northern Ireland; while not ideal as peace-keepers, at least they are non-sectarian. The issue is, as it has been for centuries, the right of different people in the island of Ireland to live in freedom, practise their religion, enjoy their culture, form what foreign ties they wish, and share opportunities.

Since 1972, Britain has been presiding over a radical readjustment in the power balances between the Catholic and Protestant communities - taking initiatives, keeping order, forcing the pace occasionally, and easing transition with social and economic help. A great deal has been done - housing is allocated more fairly now, and local council elections are based on universal suffrage. The demands of the Civil Rights movement of the late 1960s have been met. But the two communities still do not know each other; they are still moved by old stories, fear and prejudice. They march, parade and threaten, organize political funerals and run protection rackets. Unionists back away from Catholics as harbourers of the IRA, and Catholics, secure in their majority in the island as a whole, ignore the Unionist predicament. Looking beyond the border – the people of the southern part of Ireland seem to despise the north for its difficulties, and many northerners are out of sympathy with the Gaelic Republic.

But at least the problems are out in the open; they are being faced. There is no going back to the conditions of the 1930s, '40s and '50s. The IRA will probably continue to be a running sore, but it is not fighting for credible ends. The involvement of Britain and the Irish Republic in the affairs of the north gives protection to both communities, while they make the adjustments and reassessments that will, eventually, bring them peace and prosperity.

NOTES

1 MIGRATIONS AND MONUMENTS: THE FIRST 6000 YEARS

1. Newgrange passage tomb, for long dated to the mid-third millenium BC, was recently redated and is now placed at *c*. 3200 BC. Sited on rising ground overlooking a bend in the River Boyne and occupying over an acre of ground, the tomb mound is covered with grass surrounded by a supporting 10 to 11 foot high wall of granite and quartz (recently restored). The material was originally transported to site from the Wicklow mountains, some 80 miles away. Around the mound, and standing about 13 to 16 yards (12 to 15m) off, is a ring of tall standing stones, spaced widely. Twelve of the original 38 are still standing, four of which are in front of the tomb entrance. This ring was erected several hundred years afterwards by the Beaker people, or perhaps by the Food Vessel people at much the same time.

  The mound consists of many thousands of water-rolled pebbles, from 6 to 10 inches (15 to 25cm) across, fronted at the entrance area by white quartz blocks, and interspersed all round with large round granite boulders that were found in quantity on the site before restoration and which are now inserted in the revetment wall. The revetment wall is surrounded at the bottom by 97 kerbstones, ends touching, about 5ft 6in to 15ft 6in (1.7 to 4.7m) long, lying on their long sides. Many are decorated with intricately carved designs, predominantly circles, spirals, lozenges, circles with rays, many of them having the designs standing out in relief. The best known of the kerbstones are the stone at the entrance; Kerbstone 52, which is

341

diametrically opposite at the other side of the mount; and Kerbstone 67.

In the front part of the passage roof (at the entrance on the south side of the mound), about 8 feet (2½m) back from the passage mouth, is a roof box with a lintel and above it a fanlight over the entry point. This was built with some purpose, demonstrated by the late Prof. Michael O'Kelly, the noted Cork archaeologist, who after several experiments noticed, on the morning of 21 December (the shortest day), at the moment of the rising sun of the winter solstice, that a shaft of light travels up the 20½ yards (19m) of the passage and strikes the floor of the centre chamber, illuminating the whole chamber.

The passage is flanked on the west by 22 orthostats and on the east by 21, about 5 feet (1½m) tall on average. Many are decorated. The chamber itself is unusual. It is roughly circular, or polygonal if you prefer, between 5¼ and 6½m across. At west, north and east, three side chambers open out, giving a Latin cross plan. The chambers have large shaped 'basin' stones, the right-hand chamber having two. 'Basin' stones held the bones, whole or incinerated, or both, of the people buried in the tomb. The cremations took place outside the tomb, perhaps not even on the site. The central chamber is nearly 20 feet (6m) high in the middle, and the vaulting created by overlapping the sloping stones is regarded as the finest of its kind in western Europe. It has stood unaltered and unrepaired for over 5000 years, and it appears never to have leaked. There is not even a hint of dampness in the chamber, even on a visit during a particularly wet period of the year. The whole tomb, with its covering of stones, is thought to have taken over 200,000 tons of stone to build. The mechanics of transporting, cutting and placing this colossal quantity of stone to produce such splendid architecture defy the imagination. Yet it is there in all its glory for anyone to see.

2 CELTS AND CHRISTIANS

1. Free translation by P.S.F.
2. Roman coins were discovered at Newgrange during recent excavations at the passage grave there (1980s).
3. Lloyd Laing, *Celtic Britain*, Granada, 1987, p. 147.
4. Charles Thomas, *Britain and Ireland in Early Christian Times*, p. 66.
5. Eoin McNeill, *Phases of Irish History*, Dublin, 1919, p. 147.
6. Gearóid Mac Niocaill, *Ireland before the Vikings*, Dublin (Gill History of Ireland), 1972.

7. Probably the only authentic accounts of St Patrick are his own *Confession* and his letter written to Coroticus, a British chief.
8. Mac Niocaill, op. cit., p. 26.
9. Françoise Henry, *Irish Art in the Early Christian Period to 800 A.D.* London, 1965, p. 34.

3   THE VIKING CONTRIBUTION

1. Donncha Ó Corráin, *Ireland before the Normans*, Dublin, 1972.

4   THE COMING OF THE NORMANS

1. 'Men from the east', i.e. Vikings, or foreigners.
2. The story of the Norman entry into Ireland is told in *The Song of Dermot and the Earl*, and by Giraldus Cambrensis, a grandson of Nesta and consequently a Geraldine, in *Expugnatio Hibernica*. Numbers tend to be exaggerated in both accounts.
3. The only evidence we have for the existence of this famous bull is the transcript of it made by Giraldus Cambrensis for his book *Expugnatio Hibernica*, finished by 1189, and Giraldus' statement, in the letter of dedication to the second edition of the *Expugnatio*, that the bull was in the archives at Windsor. He had come across a copy of *Laudabiliter* in Waterford.
4. The most obvious surviving example is in the Christian marriage service: 'With this ring I thee wed.' When the bride accepts the ring on her finger, the couple are married.
5. Even though Britain was known as the Isle of Saints and the last king of England but one, Edward the Confessor, was to be canonized in 1161!

5   TWO NATIONS

1. The rest of John de Courcy's life is obscure. He seems to have become reconciled with John, joined his court, and died in 1219.
2. The phrase *merus hibernicus*, 'mere Irish', has commonly been taken as an insult. This is a misunderstanding of the medieval meaning of the word 'mere', which at that time meant 'pure' or 'only'. Later, when Elizabeth I of England was crowned in 1558, she described herself to her people as 'mere English'. She would never have used the phrase in such a context if it had a derogatory meaning.

3. The date of the first recorded meeting of a parliament in Ireland. It was held at Castledermot in Leinster.
4. Although 'degenerate' was not originally any more derogatory than 'mere' – it simply referred to people who lived outside the culture of their race, (*de generis*) – it soon became so.
5. The name was taken from the Pale which surrounded Calais, the last of the English possessions in France. A Pale was an enclosure.
6. 'Alterage' was another word for fostering.
7. Marriages which contravened the Statutes of Kilkenny were often made lawful by act of parliament, as this one was in 1487.

6 TUDOR COLONISTS

1. Shane Ó Néill (*d.* 1565).
2. After fifty years of sporadic warfare, only 300 descendants of the original Irish of Leix had remained. They were forcibly transplanted to smallholdings in Kerry.
3. The acts, which laid the basis for the establishment of the Protestant Church in Ireland, the persecution of Catholics and many of Ireland's later troubles, may have been passed by a trick. The parliamentary vote went against them, there being about thirteen Ayes to twenty Noes – though we have no documentary evidence of the numbers – but the deputy, the earl of Sussex, had been recalled to London and was in a hurry; he may have dissolved parliament and put the acts on the Statute Roll although they had not been passed, or he may have pushed them through later, having told the likely Noes that parliament would not be meeting. Such tactics were not unheard of in dealings with parliaments of the period.
4. A tanist was a chief's successor, elected, or chosen, during the chief's lifetime and treated as his heir. Tanistry was a compromise between the old rules of the *derbfine* and primogeniture.
5. Strictly speaking, Tyrone should now be called Ó Néill as that was the higher title, but we (the authors) have continued to call him Tyrone for the sake of consistency, as he had to return to the English title later on.

7 THE IRISH DISPOSSESSED

1. Archbishop Hurley was executed in 1584 and Richard Creagh, archbishop of Armagh, died in 1585 after eighteen years' imprisonment in the Tower of London.

2. Foreigners were always horrified by the Irish habits of attaching teams of horses to the plough by the tail, which saved harness, plucking wool from their sheep instead of shearing them, which saved shears, and lightly burning corn, so the grain fell easily from the husks, but left no straw for the cattle in winter.
3. Wentworth is sometimes accused of ruining the developing Irish woollen industry in the interests of England. He devised a system of exporting wool on licence, to cut out smuggling. The system was expensive to administer and the licences had to be paid for, yet the English demand remained great enough to absorb all the Irish supply.
4. Although Presbyterians were Protestant, for the sake of simplicity the authors have used the term Protestant (when it refers to people in Ireland) to mean Anglican, or belonging to the Established Church of Ireland, so long as that Church existed. (It was disestablished in 1869.) After that, the term Protestant includes both Anglicans and Presbyterians, unless otherwise stated.

8   THE PROTESTANT ASCENDANCY

1. On one occasion, a Protestant laid claim to two beautiful horses being driven by his Catholic neighbour. Rather than give them up, the Catholic took out his pistol and shot them dead.
2. The term gavelkind, which originated in the English county of Kent, simply meant the equal division of an inheritance.

9   UNION

1. He considered settling down for good on a 80-acre farm near Princeton.
2. The victim was hung until he lost consciousness. Then the rope was slackened and he was revived, often to be half-hung again.
3. Sometimes a linen or paper bag of pitch was clapped on the victim's head and then set alight; much of his scalp would be torn off as he tried frantically to remove the cap. At other times there was no bag – hot pitch and gunpowder were simply smeared onto the victim's head and then set alight.
4. Protestant historians put the number killed at 200 to 300, and Catholic historians at 30.
5. The French Directoire had demanded 'money, a great deal of money' from the Americans in return for not molesting American shipping.

6. A freeholder did not, as today, own freehold property, but a heritable tenancy, which his heirs could claim after his death.
7. General elections were held every eight years.
8. Under the Succession to the Crown Act of 1707. This extraordinary rule, which could delay the formation of an administration by many months, was not modified until the Re-election of Ministers Act was passed in 1919.

10   THE GREAT FAMINE

1. See especially R. Dudley Edwards and T. D. Willams, *The Great Famine*, Dublin, 1956; and Cecil Woodham-Smith, *The Great Hunger*, London, 1962.
2. Joseph Lee, *The Modernization of Irish Society (1848–1918)*, Dublin, 1973, p. 10.

11   THE STRUGGLE FOR HOME RULE

1. Gladstone was not simply being noble. As a practical politician he knew he must have power in order to be effective, and chose to fight the general election of 1868 on the issue of Ireland a) to secure Irish seats for the Liberal party and b) to win the votes of the many thousands of Britons who had felt seriously threatened by the Fenian attacks of 1867.
2. Liberals were especially shocked by what they saw as Parnell's deceitfulness; he had used false names and a great deal of subterfuge during his years as Mrs O'Shea's lover. But his object had not been, as the Liberals supposed, to deceive Captain O'Shea, who knew what was going on anyway, but to evade reporters. If the newspapers had carried scandalous stories about Mrs O'Shea, her aunt would have disinherited her.

12   BLOOD SACRIFICE

1. As a main post office, the GPO in Dublin still opens on Easter Monday.

NOTES

13   THE ROAD TO FREEDOM

1. De Valera's death sentence may have been commuted on the insistence of Redmond, or, as de Valera said himself, simply because the British did not want any more executions, feeling enough was enough.
2. It applied to Irishmen who *had been* in Britain as well. Collins could not entirely escape the possibility of conscription by returning to Ireland, but he greatly increased his chances.
3. In August, when the government did start a recruiting drive 11,000 men volunteered in eleven weeks, in spite of Sinn Fein's intensive campaign to stop them and strong anti-British feeling. If the Irish people had not been alienated by conscription, voluntary recruitment might well have been much greater.
4. Though no evidence had been brought against them - because there was none.
5. Except Sir Robert Woods, who sent a polite refusal.
6. Collins and Boland passed keys in to him inside cakes.
7. The IRA prided themselves on never being drunk on duty. They returned their victims' money and valuables to their families and, when they had given them a chance to write any, posted their last letters to their wives. They modelled their behaviour on that of British officers during the 1914–18 war!
8. And, it must be said, through threatening Unionists, who paid protection money but did not get protection.
9. The official title, which is hardly ever used, was Articles of Agreement for a Treaty between Great Britain and Ireland.
10. If such a demand had been made, Griffith said later, it would have been granted and the negotiations over very quickly.

14   PARTITION

1. The Northern Ireland Education Act, 1972, has provided for integrated education where there is a demand for it. Mostly, though, there is none and 98 per cent of schools remain sectarian.

FURTHER READING

Bagwell, R., *Ireland under the Tudors*, 3 vols, London, 1885–90.

Beckett, J. C., *The Making of Modern Ireland, 1603–1923*, London, 1966.

Connell, K. H., *Irish Peasant Society*, Oxford, 1968.

Coogan, T. P., *The I.R.A.*, Glasgow, 1980.

Corkery, D., *Hidden Ireland*, Dublin, 1925.

Curtis, E., *History of Mediaeval Ireland, 1086–1513*, London, 1938.

Edwards, R. Dudley, *Church and State in Tudor Ireland*, Dublin, 1935.

Edwards, R. Dudley and Williams, T. D, *The Great Famine*, Dublin, 1956.

Flower, R., *The Irish Tradition*, Oxford, 1947.

Foote, P. G. and Wilson, D., *The Viking Achievement*, London, 1970.

Forester, M., *Michael Collins: The Lost Leader*, London, 1971.

Freeman, T. L., *Pre-Famine Ireland*, London, 1957.

Hammond, J. L., *Gladstone and the Irish Nation*, London, 1964.

Hayes-McCoy, G. A., *Irish Battles*, London, 1969.

Henry, F., *Irish Art in the Early Christian Period (to 800 AD)*, London, 1965.

Hyde, D., *Literary History of Ireland*, London, 1899.

Hughes, K., *The Church in Early Irish Society*, Cambridge, 1966.

Kee, R., *The Green Flag*, 3 vols, London, 1972.

Lecky, W. E. H., *Leaders of Public Opinion in Ireland*, 2 vols, London, 1912.

Lecky, W. E. H., *A History of Ireland in the 18th Century*, London, 1892.

Lyons, F. S. L., *Charles Stuart Parnell*, London, 1977.

Lyons, F. S. L., *Ireland since the Famine*, London, 1971.

MacDonagh, O., *Hereditary Bondsman: Daniel O'Connell*, London, 1988.

Martin, F. X. (ed.), *Leaders and Men of the Easter Rising*, London 1967.

Moody, T. W. and Martin, F. X., *The Course of Irish History*, Cork, 1967.

O'Faolain, S., *The Great O'Neill*, London, 1942.

O Riordain, S. P., *Antiquities of the Irish Countryside*, London, revised edn, 1979.

Orpen, G. H., *Ireland under the Normans*, 4 vols, Oxford, 1911–20.

Otway-Ruthven, A. G., *A History of Mediaeval Ireland*, London, 1968.

Pakenham, T., *The Year of Liberty (1798)*, London, 1969.

Powell, T. G. E., *The Celts*, London, 1958.

Swift, J., *The Drapier's Letters*, ed. H. Davis, Oxford, 1935.

Wedgwood, C. V., *Strafford: a Re-evaluation*, London, 1961.

Woodham-Smith, C., *The Great Hunger*, London, 1962.

THE GILL HISTORY OF IRELAND series, eleven volumes, all published by Gill & MacMillan, Dublin:

> Mac Niocaill, G., *Ireland Before the Vikings*, I, 1972.
>
> Ó Corráin, D., *Ireland Before the Normans*, II, 1972.
>
> Dolley, M., *Anglo-Norman Ireland*, III, 1972.
>
> Nicholls, K., *Gaelic and Gaelicized Ireland in the Middle Ages*, IV, 1972.
>
> Watt, J., *The Church in Mediaeval Ireland*, V, 1972.
>
> Lydon, J., *Ireland in the Later Middle Ages*, VI, 1973.
>
> MacCurtain, M., *Tudor and Stuart Ireland*, VII, 1972.
>
> Johnston, E. M., *Ireland in the Eighteenth Century*, VIII, 1974.
>
> Ó Tuathaigh, G., *Ireland Before the Famine, 1798–1848*, IX, 1972.
>
> Lee, J., *The Modernization of Irish Society, 1848–1918*, X, 1973.
>
> Murphy, J. A., *Ireland in the Twentieth Century*, XI, 1973.

THE HELICON HISTORY OF IRELAND series, eight volumes so far published by Helicon Ltd., Dublin:

Frame, R., *Colonial Ireland, 1169–1369*, II, 1981.

Cosgrove, A., *Late Mediaeval Ireland, 1370–1541*, III, 1981.

Canny, N., *From Reformation to Restoration: Ireland, 1534–1660*, IV, 1987.

Corish, P., *The Catholic Community in the 17th and 18th Centuries*, V, 1981.

Dickson, D., *New Foundations: Ireland, 1660–1800*, VI, 1987.

McCartney, D., *The Dawning of Democracy: Ireland, 1800–1870*, VII, 1987.

Fanning, R., *Independent Ireland: The First Fifty Years*, IX, 1984.

Harkness, D., *Northern Ireland since 1920*, X, 1984.

A NEW HISTORY OF IRELAND series, nine volumes (some still in preparation), all published by Oxford University Press, Oxford:

Cosgrove, A., (ed.) *Mediaeval Ireland 1169–1534*, II, 1987.

Moody, T. W., (ed.) *Early Modern Ireland 1534–1691*, III, 1976.

Moody, T. W., (ed.) Eighteenth Century Ireland 1691–1800, IV, 1986.

Moody, T. W., (ed.) *Chronology of Irish History to 1976*, VIII, 1982.

INDEX

Note: All page references in italic indicate an illustration.